Shojo Beat

Absolute Boyfriend

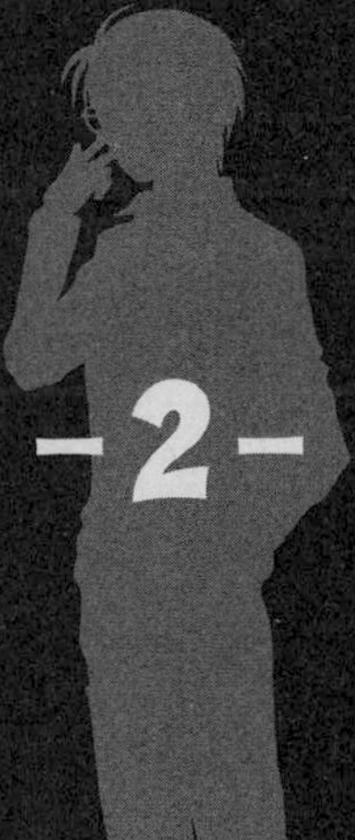

-2-

Story & Art by

Yuu Watase

Absolute Boyfriend

CAST

RIIKO IZAWA

SOSHI ASAMOTO

NIGHT TENJO

GAKU NAMIKIRI

MIKA ITO

SATORI MIYABE

STORY

DEPRESSED ABOUT HER RECENT REJECTION, RIIKO BUYS NIGHT, THE IDEAL BOYFRIEND "FIGURE," FROM GAKU. ALTHOUGH NIGHT LOOKS COMPLETELY HUMAN, HE COMES WITH A $1 MILLION PRICE TAG! IN EXCHANGE FOR A BIG DISCOUNT, RIIKO AGREES TO PROVIDE GAKU'S COMPANY WITH INFORMATION ABOUT THE WORKINGS OF THE FEMALE MIND. NOW, NIGHT HAS STARTED ATTENDING RIIKO'S HIGH SCHOOL TO COLLECT EVEN MORE DATA. HE STANDS OUT RIGHT AWAY AND QUICKLY GAINS A FOLLOWING. EVEN RIIKO'S BEST FRIEND, MIKA, HAS HER EYE ON HIM...

Act 7
School Trip

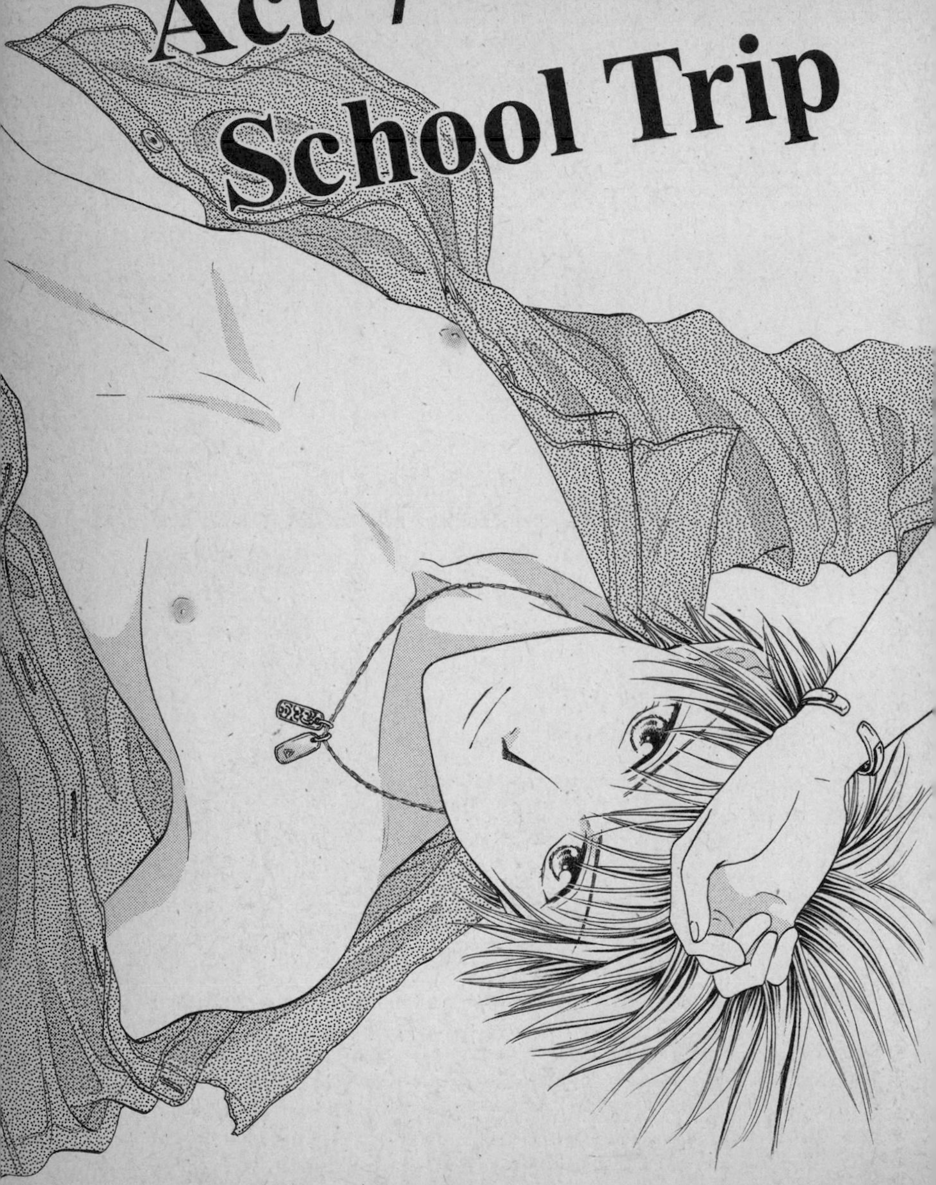

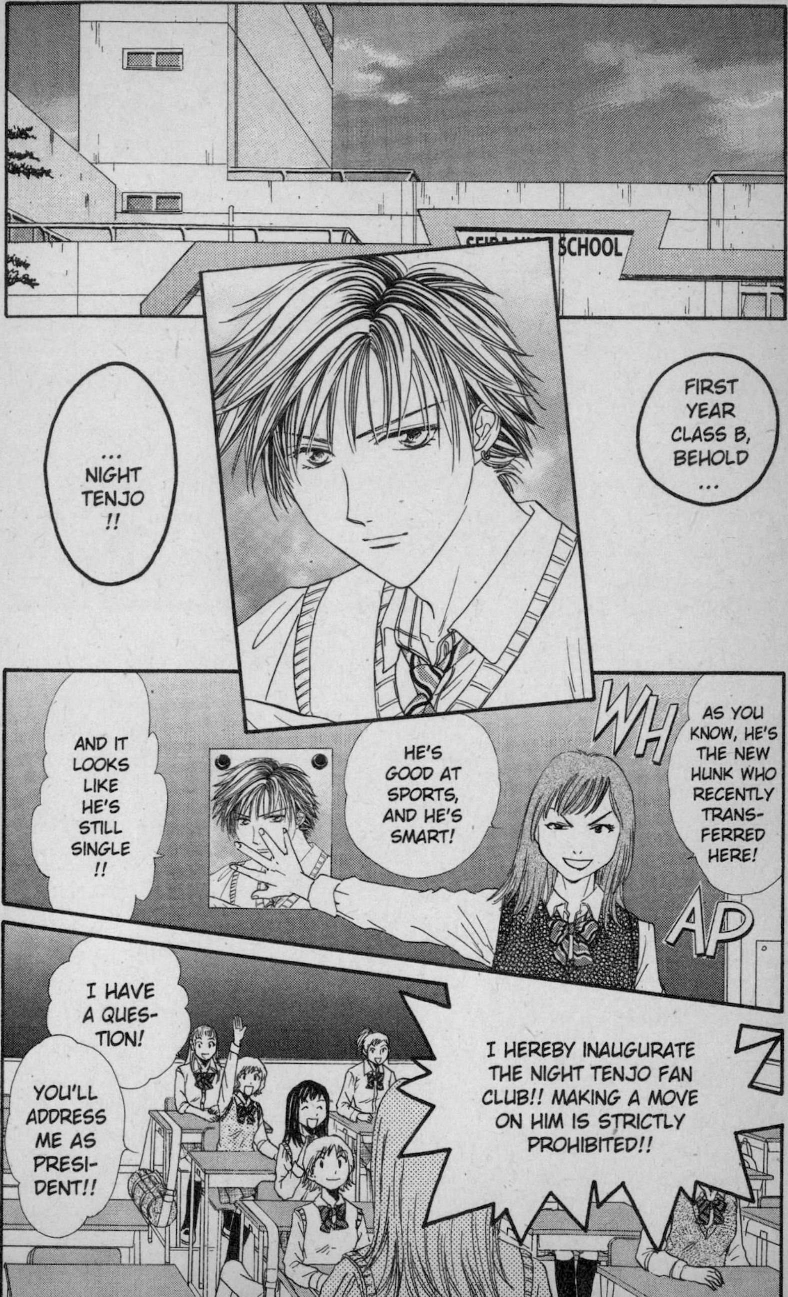
SCHOOL
FIRST YEAR CLASS B, BEHOLD ...
... NIGHT TENJO !!
AS YOU KNOW, HE'S THE NEW HUNK WHO RECENTLY TRANS-FERRED HERE!
WHAP
HE'S GOOD AT SPORTS, AND HE'S SMART!
AND IT LOOKS LIKE HE'S STILL SINGLE !!
I HEREBY INAUGURATE THE NIGHT TENJO FAN CLUB!! MAKING A MOVE ON HIM IS STRICTLY PROHIBITED!!
I HAVE A QUES-TION!
YOU'LL ADDRESS ME AS PRESI-DENT!!

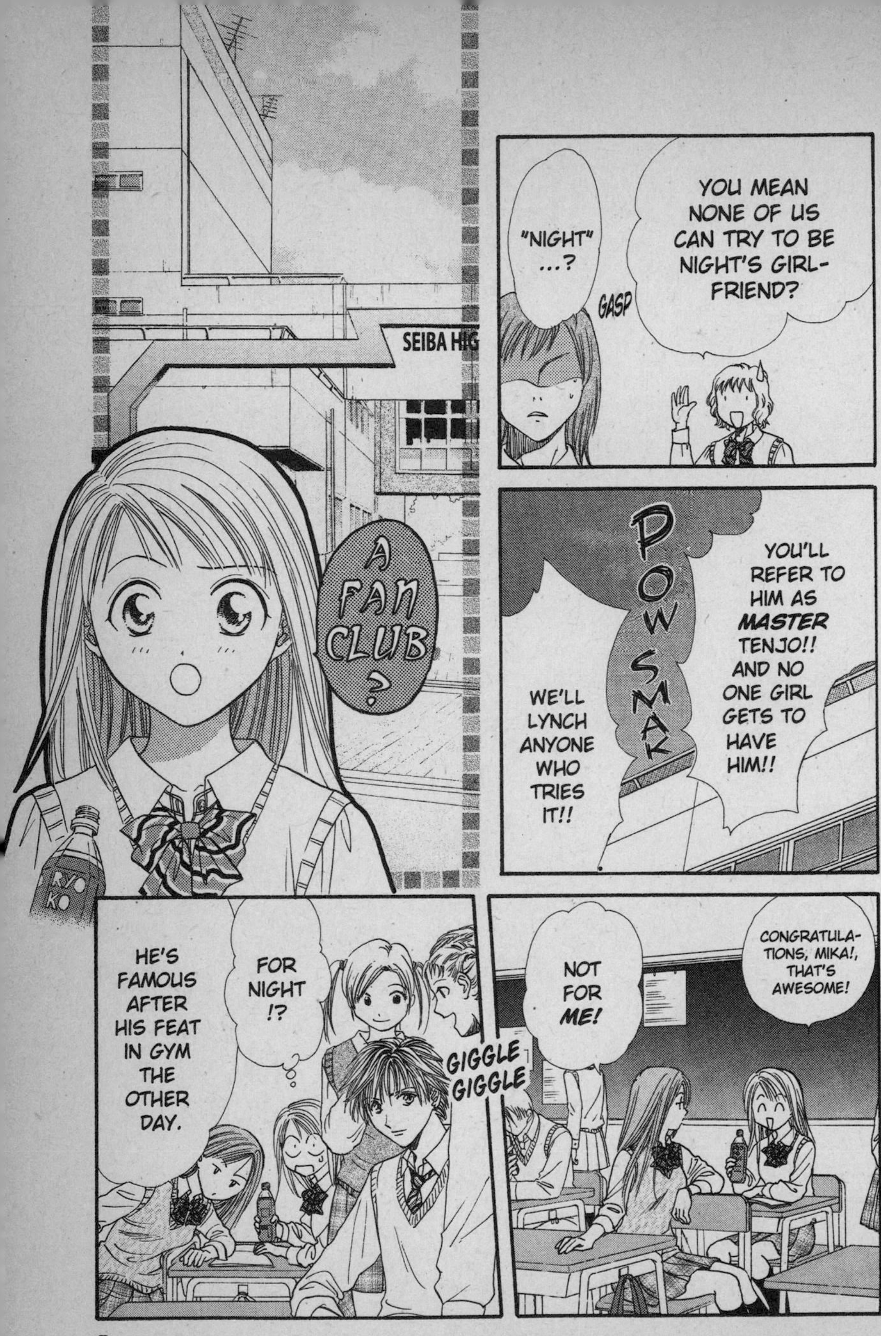
YOU MEAN NONE OF US CAN TRY TO BE NIGHT'S GIRL-FRIEND?
"NIGHT" ...?
GASP
YOU'LL REFER TO HIM AS ***MASTER*** TENJO!! AND NO ONE GIRL GETS TO HAVE HIM!!
POW SMAK
WE'LL LYNCH ANYONE WHO TRIES IT!!
SEIBA HIG
A FAN CLUB?
RYO KO
CONGRATULA-TIONS, MIKA!, THAT'S AWESOME!
NOT FOR ***ME!***
FOR NIGHT !?
GIGGLE GIGGLE
HE'S FAMOUS AFTER HIS FEAT IN GYM THE OTHER DAY.

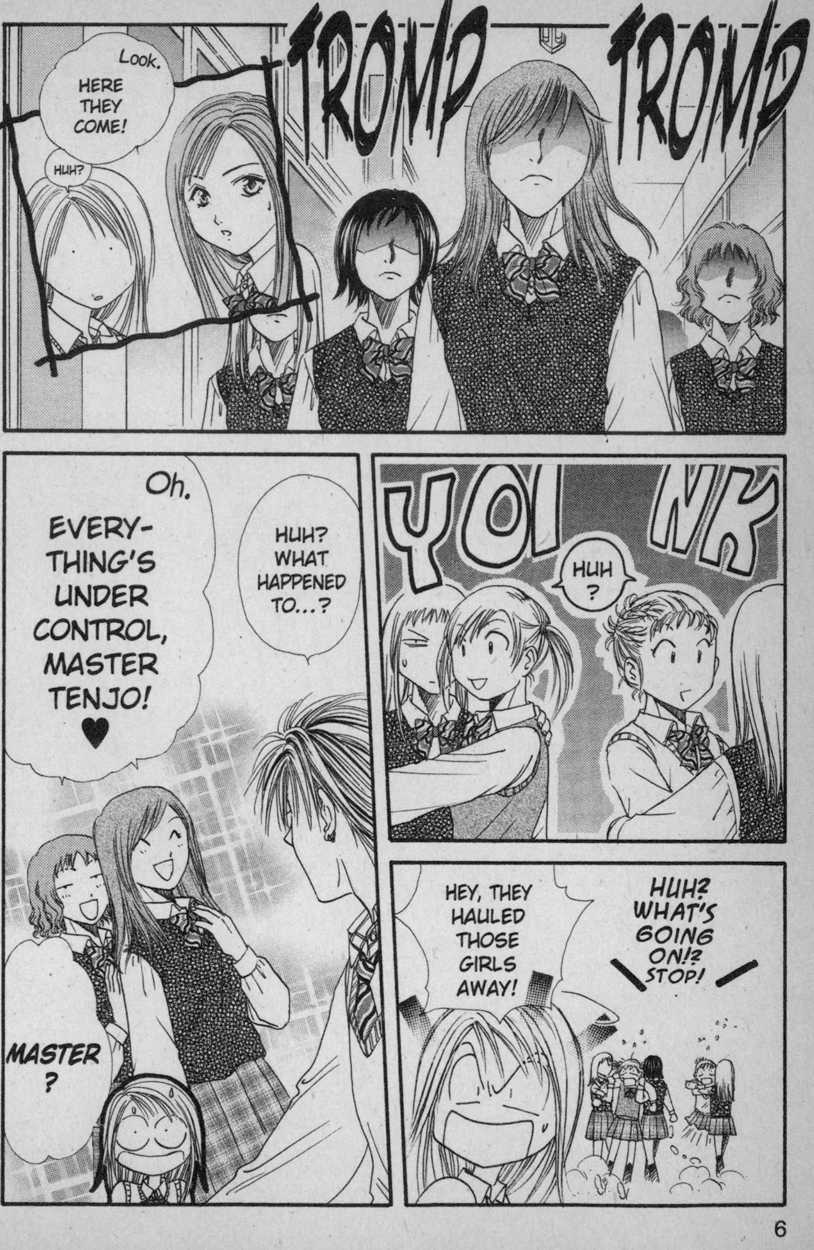
TROMP
TROMP
Look. HERE THEY COME!
HUH?
YOINK
HUH ?
HUH? WHAT'S GOING ON!? STOP!
HEY, THEY HAULED THOSE GIRLS AWAY!
HUH? WHAT HAPPENED TO...?
Oh. EVERY-THING'S UNDER CONTROL, MASTER TENJO! ♥
MASTER ?

Hello! Here's volume 2!

Riiko has it a little tough in this one (smile). My protagonists always end up in unpleasant situations... Actually, every manga is like that! If only nice things happened, it wouldn't be manga! But I'm the one having a tough time. Well, that's par for the course (frown).

Oh, thanks for all your letters. I'm sorry that I can't send replies. My schedule is so full that I can't even take a day off. I guess I should be thankful that I have so much work (smile). But I can't even go to movies or see my friends. There's no way I'll ever find a date!
Because I stay home all the time.
Am I technically a recluse?
I wanna go out!

I can only go out for work-related meetings (smile). But I do get invited to conventions in other countries almost every year, so they're my escape. I had to decline the cons in the U.S. and Shanghai in '03 due to SARS (and the war). But I was able to go to Germany in October. I couldn't go the first year I got invited there because of terrorism, and the second year because I had a scheduling conflict with a con in Spain, but I was finally able to go the third year. It's a beautiful country!! Frankfurt was very urban, but Rothenburg and Heidelberg looked like they were straight out of a fairytale.
I wish I could live there.

Spain was nice, too. I got to talk with the fans during autograph sessions and Q & A panels, and Spain reminds me of Kansai (specifically Osaka). Germany reminds me of the northern part of Japan. I guess the U.S. is more like Tokyo. Differences in national character are so interesting.
I wish I could live in Spain, too!

SO THERE YOU GO.
You can spot 'em by their matching vests.
THERE *WHAT* GOES !?
WOW... A RABID FAN CLUB IN JUST A COUPLE OF DAYS!!
IF THEY FIND OUT THAT NIGHT'S MY BOY-FRIEND...
THEY'LL *TORMENT* YOU, RIIKO!
ACK
WHAT !?
She responded to my internal monologue!
DON'T WORRY. YOU DON'T HAVE TO HIDE IT!

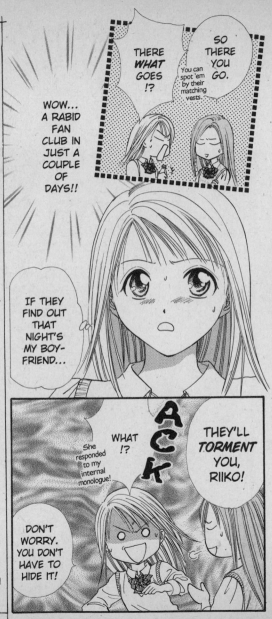

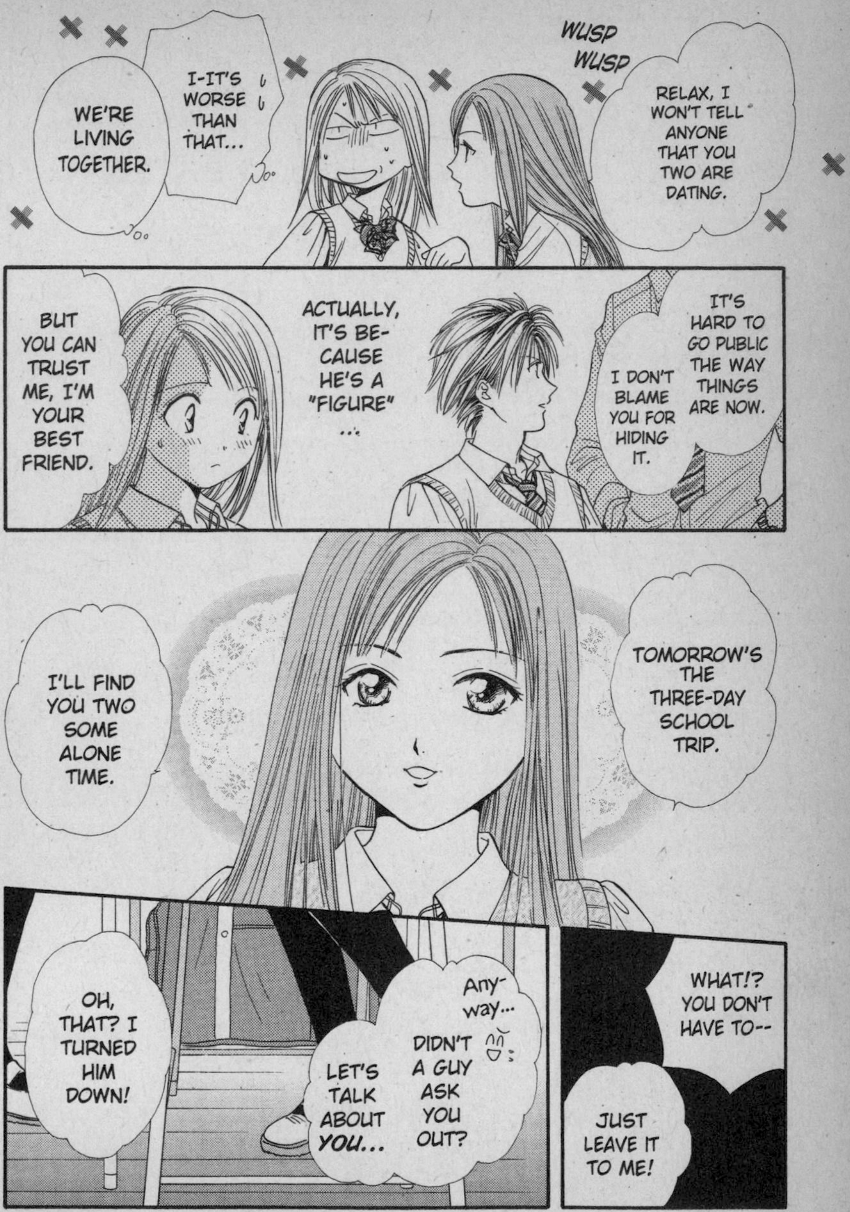
WUSP WUSP
RELAX, I WON'T TELL ANYONE THAT YOU TWO ARE DATING.
I-IT'S WORSE THAN THAT...
WE'RE LIVING TOGETHER.
IT'S HARD TO GO PUBLIC THE WAY THINGS ARE NOW.
I DON'T BLAME YOU FOR HIDING IT.
ACTUALLY, IT'S BE-CAUSE HE'S A "FIGURE"...
BUT YOU CAN TRUST ME, I'M YOUR BEST FRIEND.
TOMORROW'S THE THREE-DAY SCHOOL TRIP.
I'LL FIND YOU TWO SOME ALONE TIME.
WHAT!? YOU DON'T HAVE TO--
JUST LEAVE IT TO ME!
Any-way...
DIDN'T A GUY ASK YOU OUT?
LET'S TALK ABOUT *YOU*...
OH, THAT? I TURNED HIM DOWN!

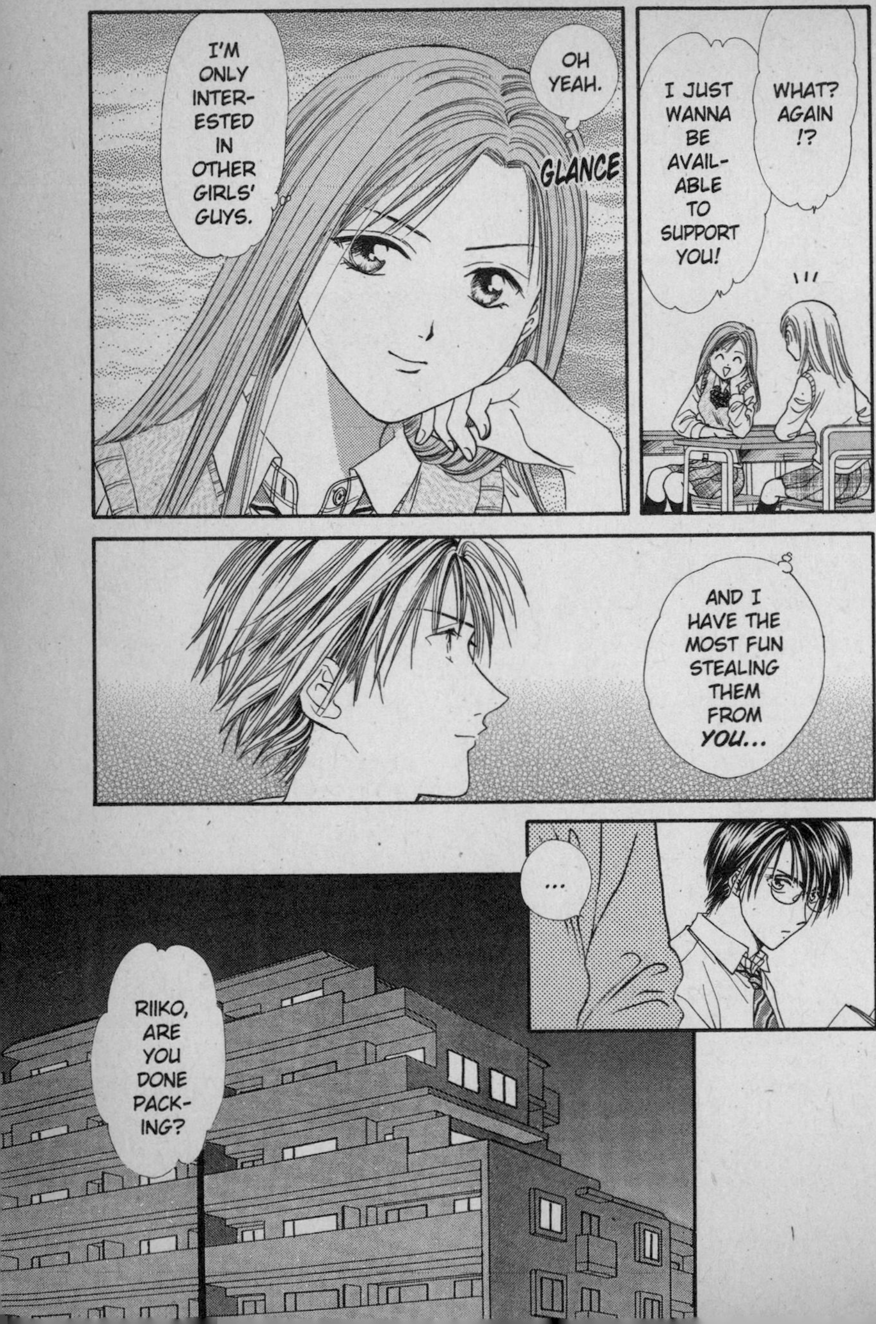
WHAT? AGAIN!?
I JUST WANNA BE AVAILABLE TO SUPPORT YOU!
OH YEAH.
GLANCE
I'M ONLY INTERESTED IN OTHER GIRLS' GUYS.
AND I HAVE THE MOST FUN STEALING THEM FROM *YOU*...
...
RIIKO, ARE YOU DONE PACKING?

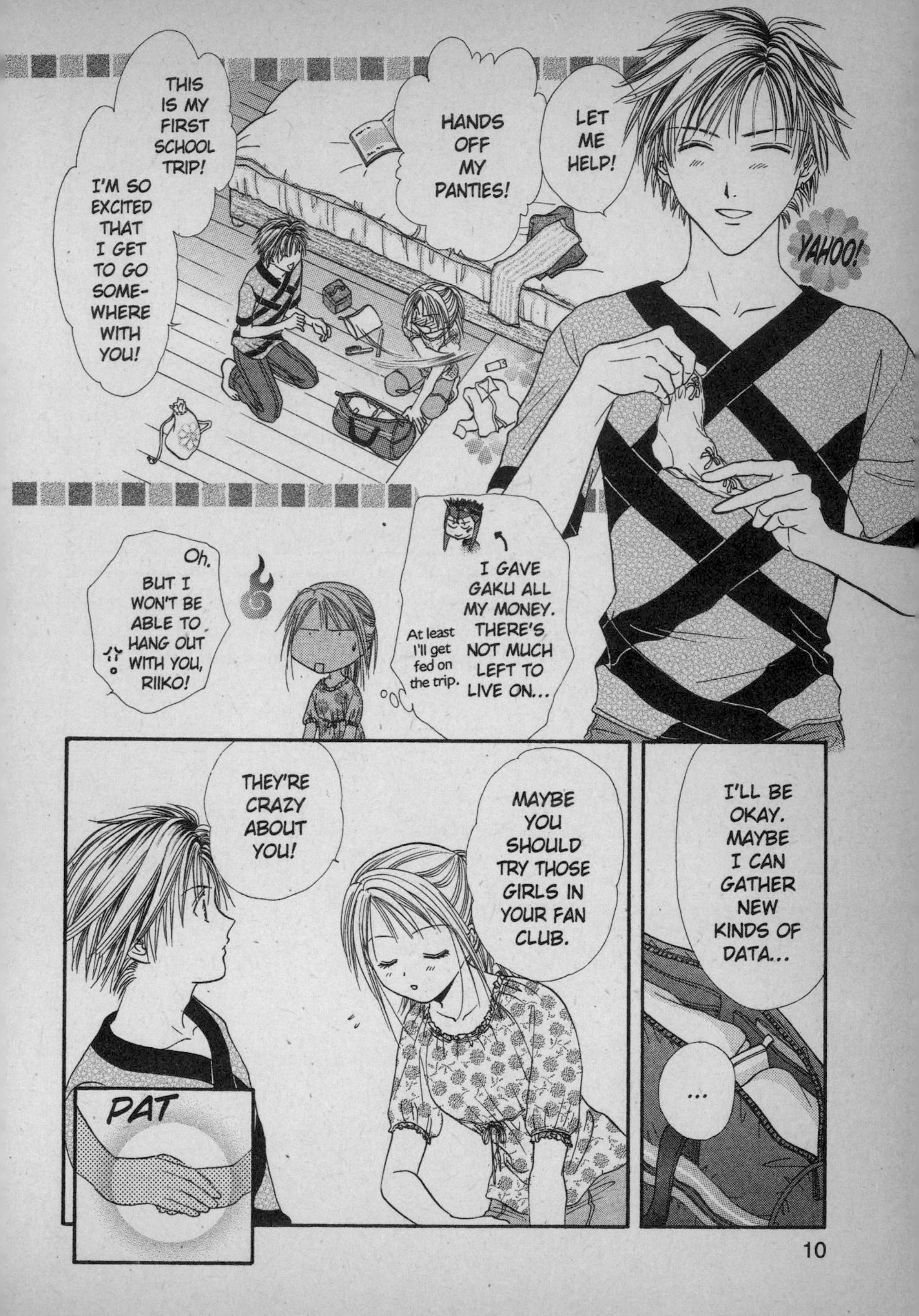
YAHOO!
LET ME HELP!
HANDS OFF MY PANTIES!
THIS IS MY FIRST SCHOOL TRIP!
I'M SO EXCITED THAT I GET TO GO SOMEWHERE WITH YOU!
I GAVE GAKU ALL MY MONEY. THERE'S NOT MUCH LEFT TO LIVE ON...
At least I'll get fed on the trip.
Oh.
BUT I WON'T BE ABLE TO HANG OUT WITH YOU, RIIKO!
I'LL BE OKAY. MAYBE I CAN GATHER NEW KINDS OF DATA...
...
MAYBE YOU SHOULD TRY THOSE GIRLS IN YOUR FAN CLUB.
THEY'RE CRAZY ABOUT YOU!
PAT

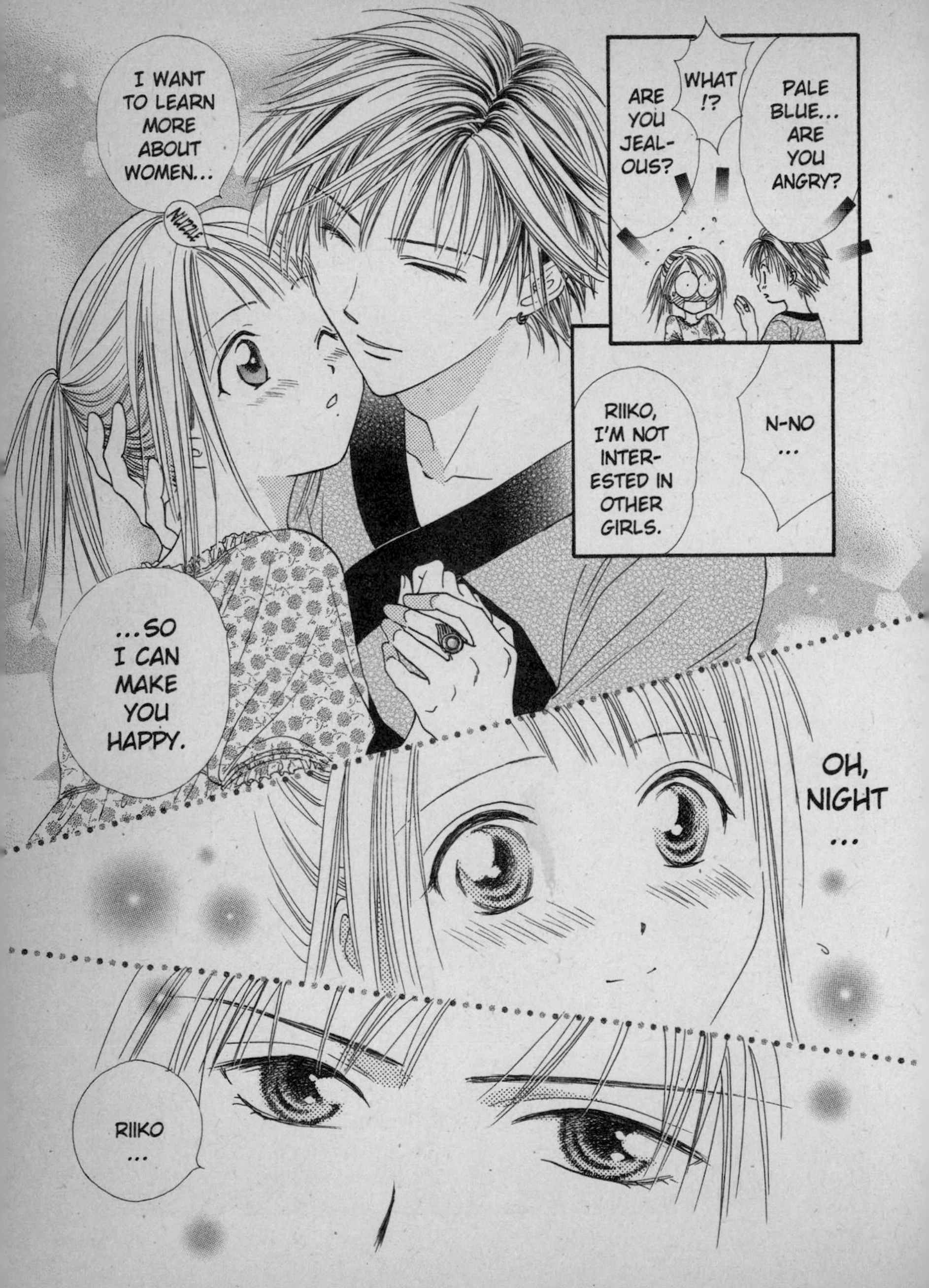
PALE BLUE... ARE YOU ANGRY?
WHAT!?
ARE YOU JEAL-OUS?
N-NO ...
RIIKO, I'M NOT INTER-ESTED IN OTHER GIRLS.
I WANT TO LEARN MORE ABOUT WOMEN...
NUZZLE
...SO I CAN MAKE YOU HAPPY.
OH, NIGHT ...
RIIKO ...

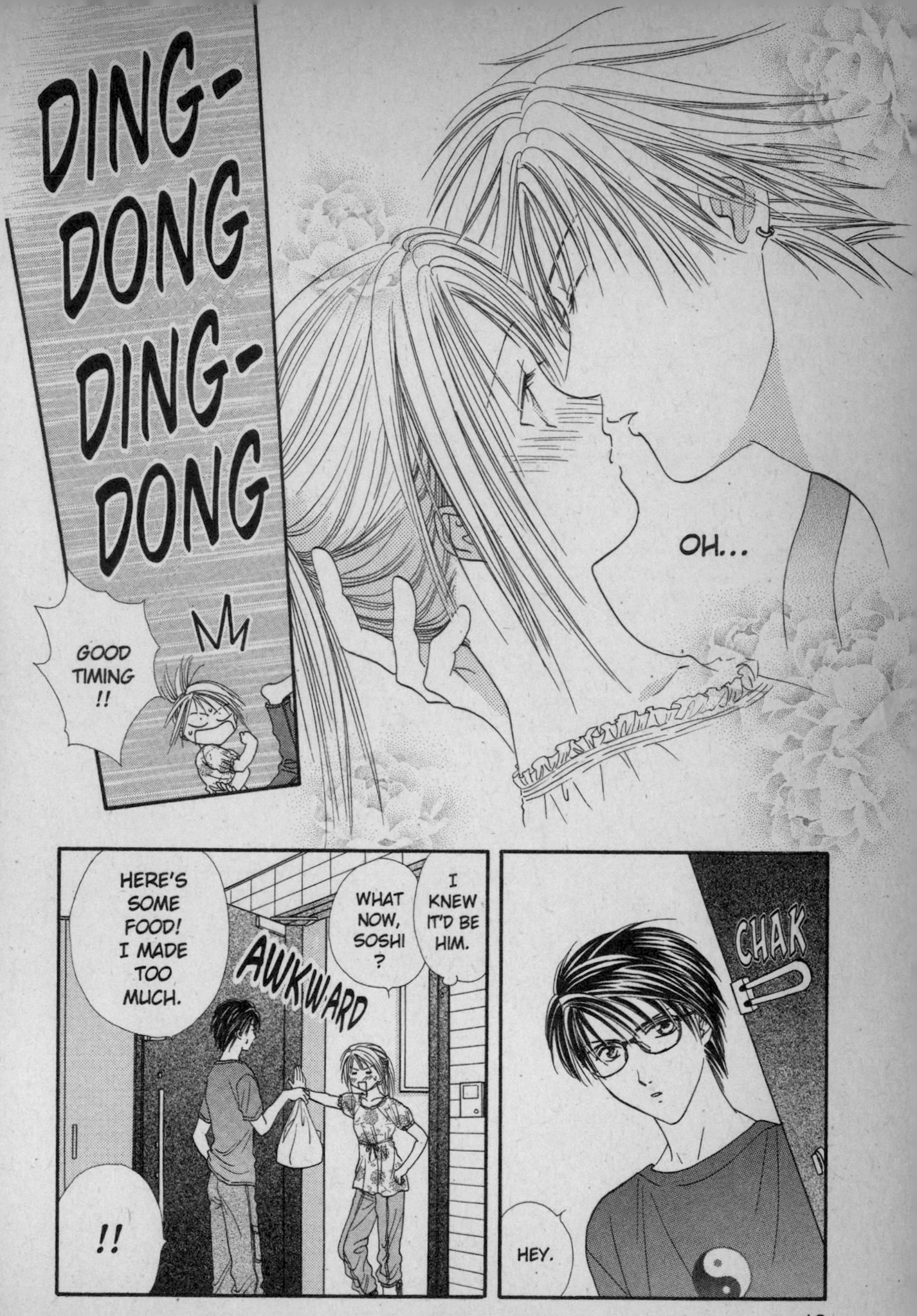
OH...
DING-DONG-DING-DONG
GOOD TIMING !!
CHAK
HEY.
I KNEW IT'D BE HIM.
WHAT NOW, SOSHI ?
HERE'S SOME FOOD! I MADE TOO MUCH.
AWKWARD
!!

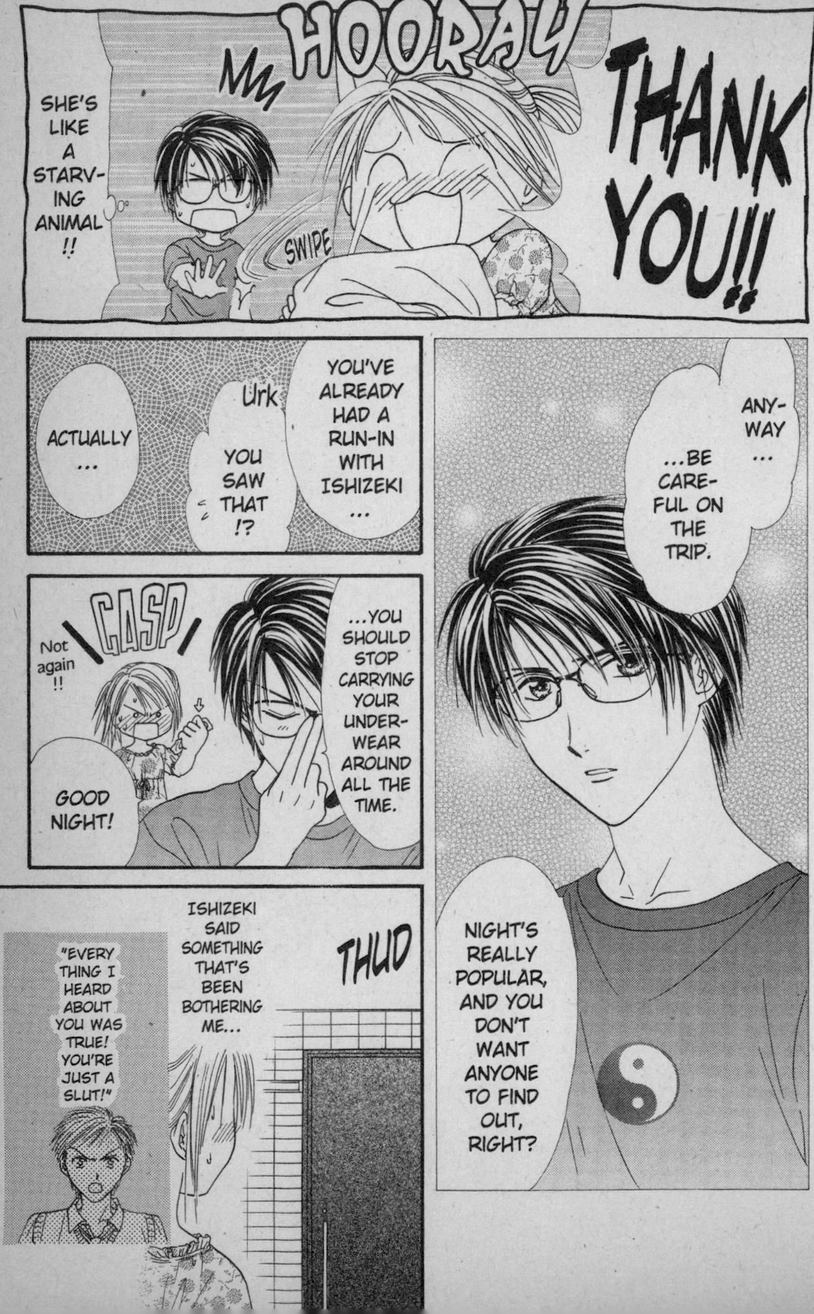
HOORAY
THANK YOU!!
SWIPE
SHE'S LIKE A STARVING ANIMAL!!
ANYWAY...
...BE CAREFUL ON THE TRIP.
NIGHT'S REALLY POPULAR, AND YOU DON'T WANT ANYONE TO FIND OUT, RIGHT?
YOU'VE ALREADY HAD A RUN-IN WITH ISHIZEKI...
Urk
YOU SAW THAT!?
ACTUALLY...
...YOU SHOULD STOP CARRYING YOUR UNDERWEAR AROUND ALL THE TIME.
GASP
Not again!!
GOOD NIGHT!
THUD
ISHIZEKI SAID SOMETHING THAT'S BEEN BOTHERING ME...
"EVERY THING I HEARD ABOUT YOU WAS TRUE! YOU'RE JUST A SLUT!"

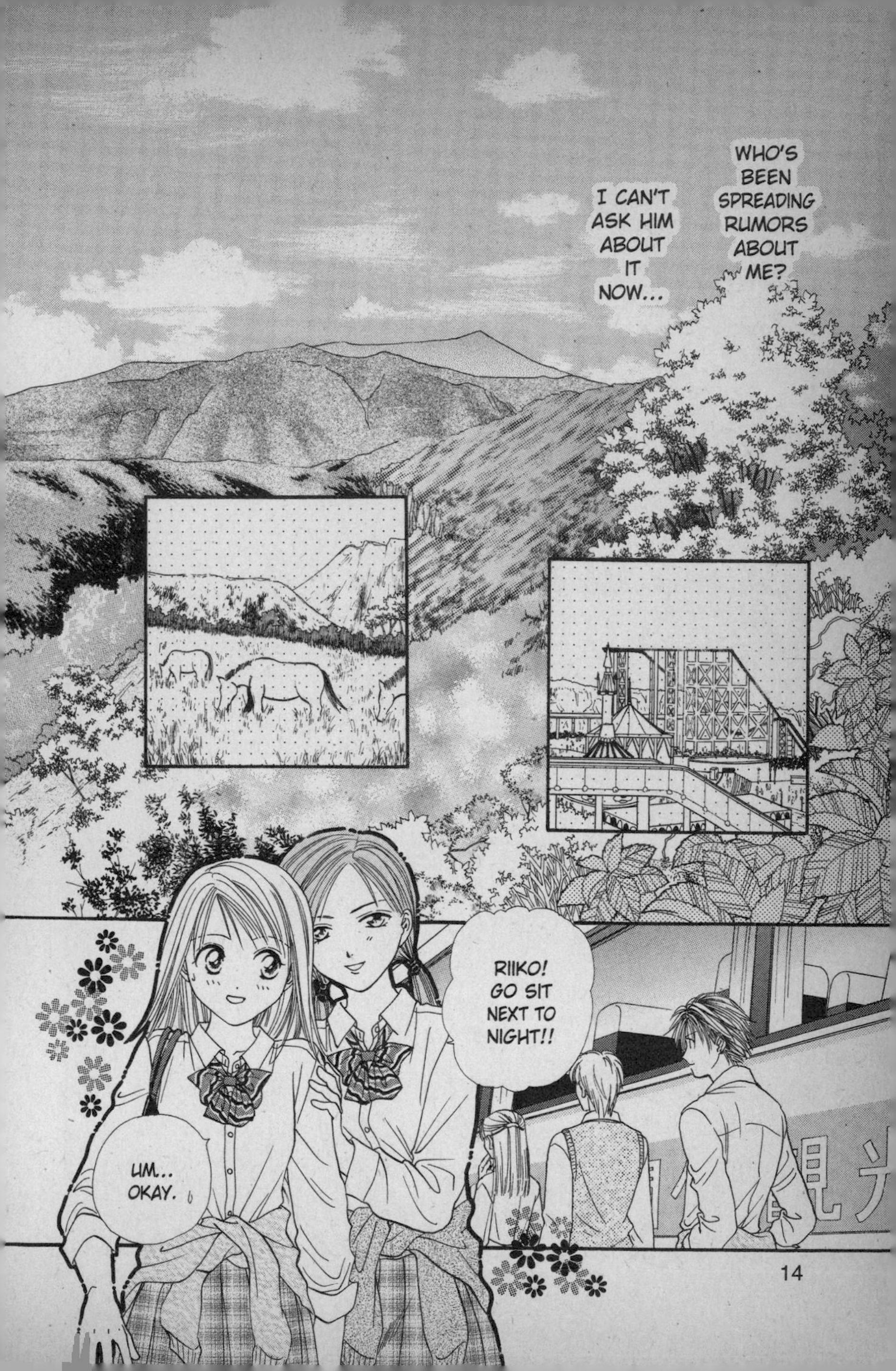
WHO'S BEEN SPREADING RUMORS ABOUT ME?
I CAN'T ASK HIM ABOUT IT NOW...
RIIKO! GO SIT NEXT TO NIGHT!!
UM.. OKAY.

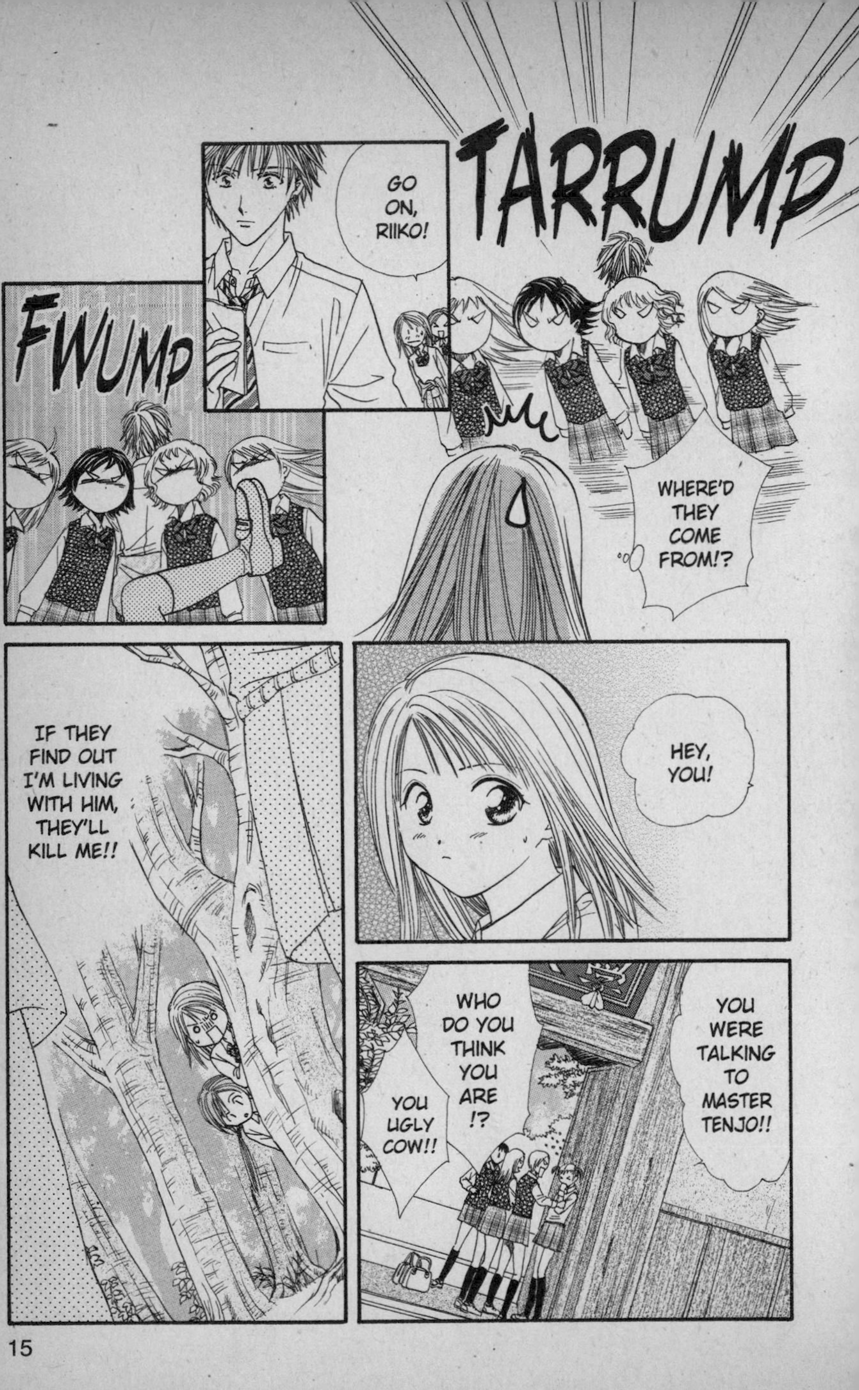
TARRUMP
GO ON, RIIKO!
FWUMP
WHERE'D THEY COME FROM!?
HEY, YOU!
YOU WERE TALKING TO MASTER TENJO!!
WHO DO YOU THINK YOU ARE!?
YOU UGLY COW!!
IF THEY FIND OUT I'M LIVING WITH HIM, THEY'LL KILL ME!!

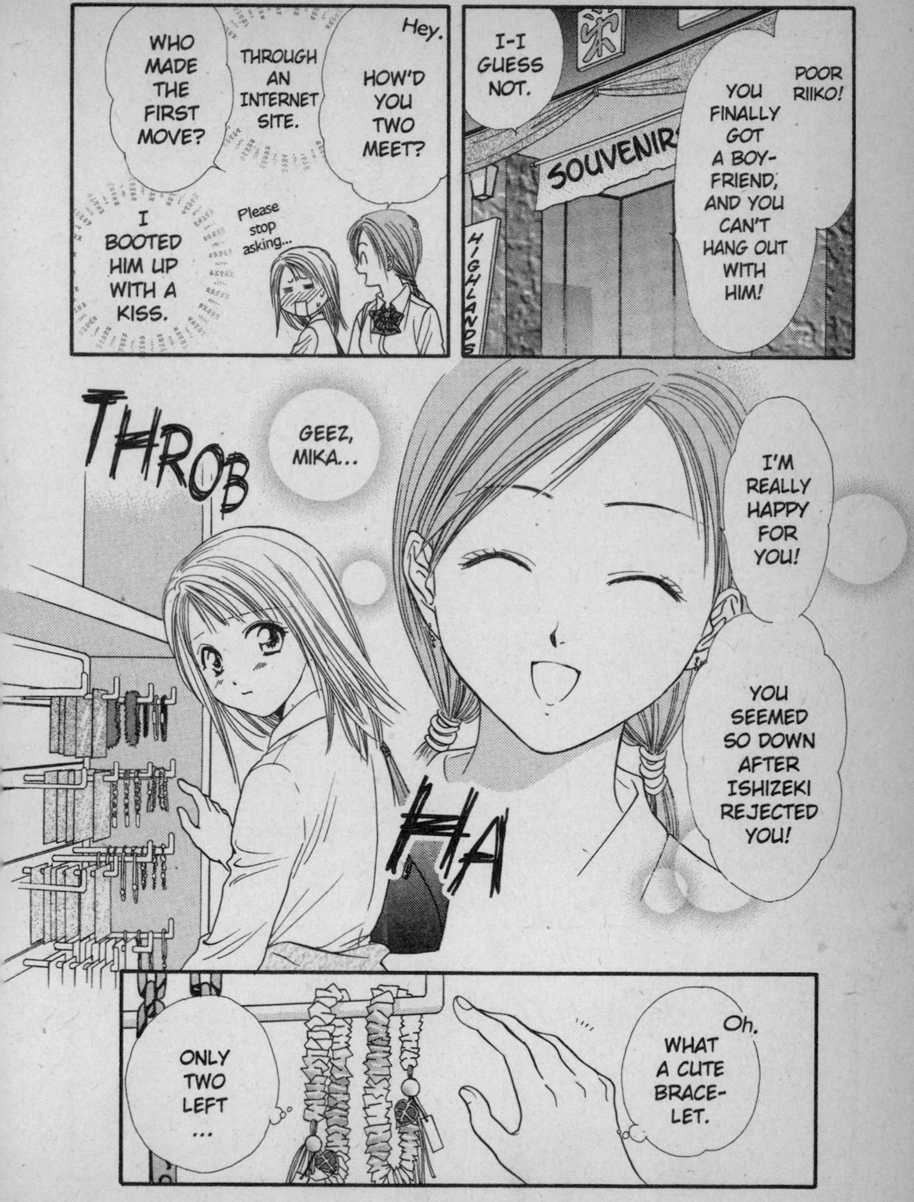
POOR RIIKO!
YOU FINALLY GOT A BOY-FRIEND, AND YOU CAN'T HANG OUT WITH HIM!
SOUVENIR
HIGHLANDS
I-I GUESS NOT.
Hey.
HOW'D YOU TWO MEET?
THROUGH AN INTERNET SITE.
WHO MADE THE FIRST MOVE?
Please stop asking...
I BOOTED HIM UP WITH A KISS.
I'M REALLY HAPPY FOR YOU!
YOU SEEMED SO DOWN AFTER ISHIZEKI REJECTED YOU!
HA
GEEZ, MIKA...
THROB
Oh.
WHAT A CUTE BRACE-LET.
...
ONLY TWO LEFT ...

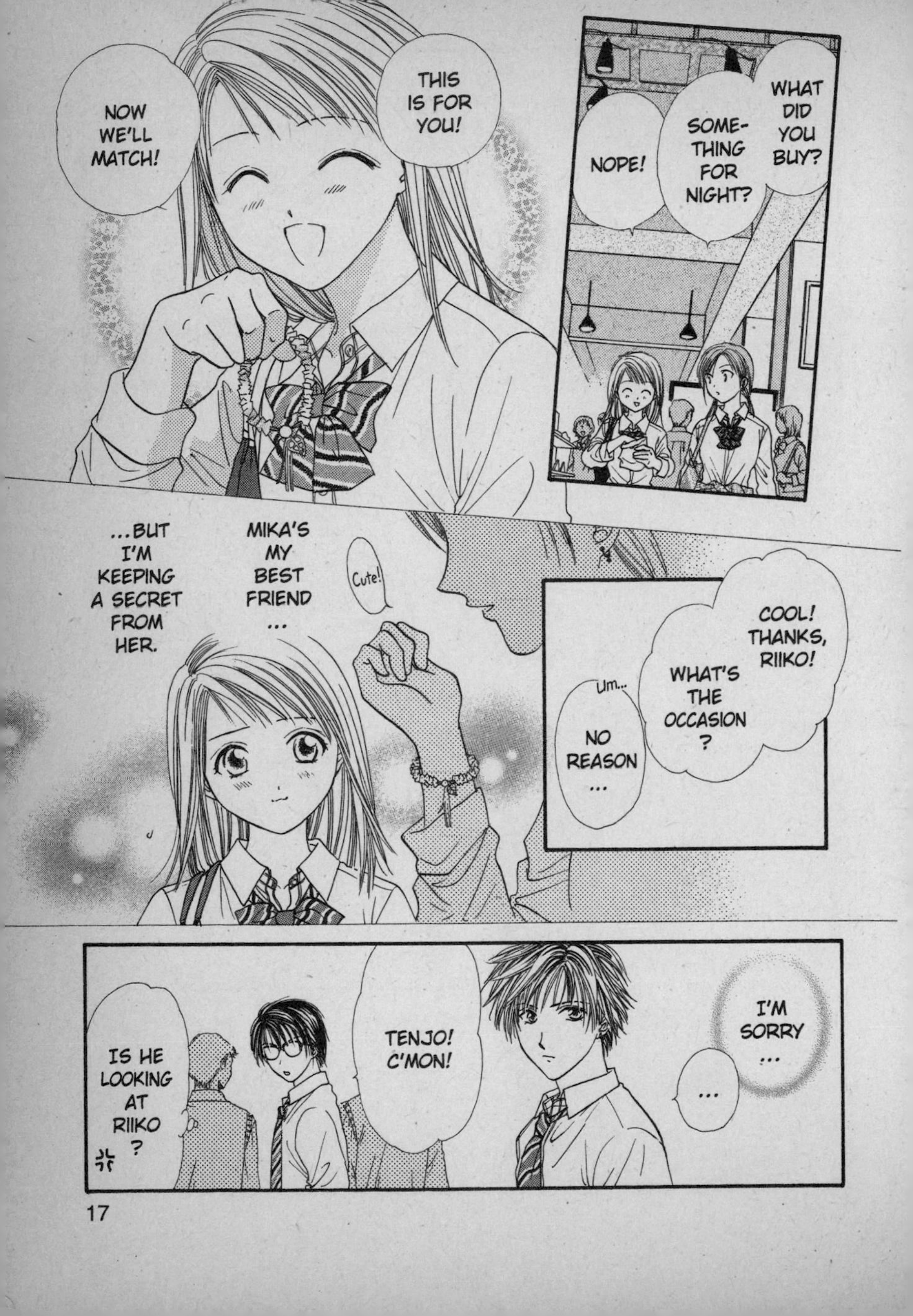
WHAT DID YOU BUY?
SOME-THING FOR NIGHT?
NOPE!
THIS IS FOR YOU!
NOW WE'LL MATCH!
COOL! THANKS, RIIKO!
WHAT'S THE OCCASION?
Um...
NO REASON...
Cute!
MIKA'S MY BEST FRIEND...
...BUT I'M KEEPING A SECRET FROM HER.
I'M SORRY...
...
TENJO! C'MON!
IS HE LOOKING AT RIIKO?

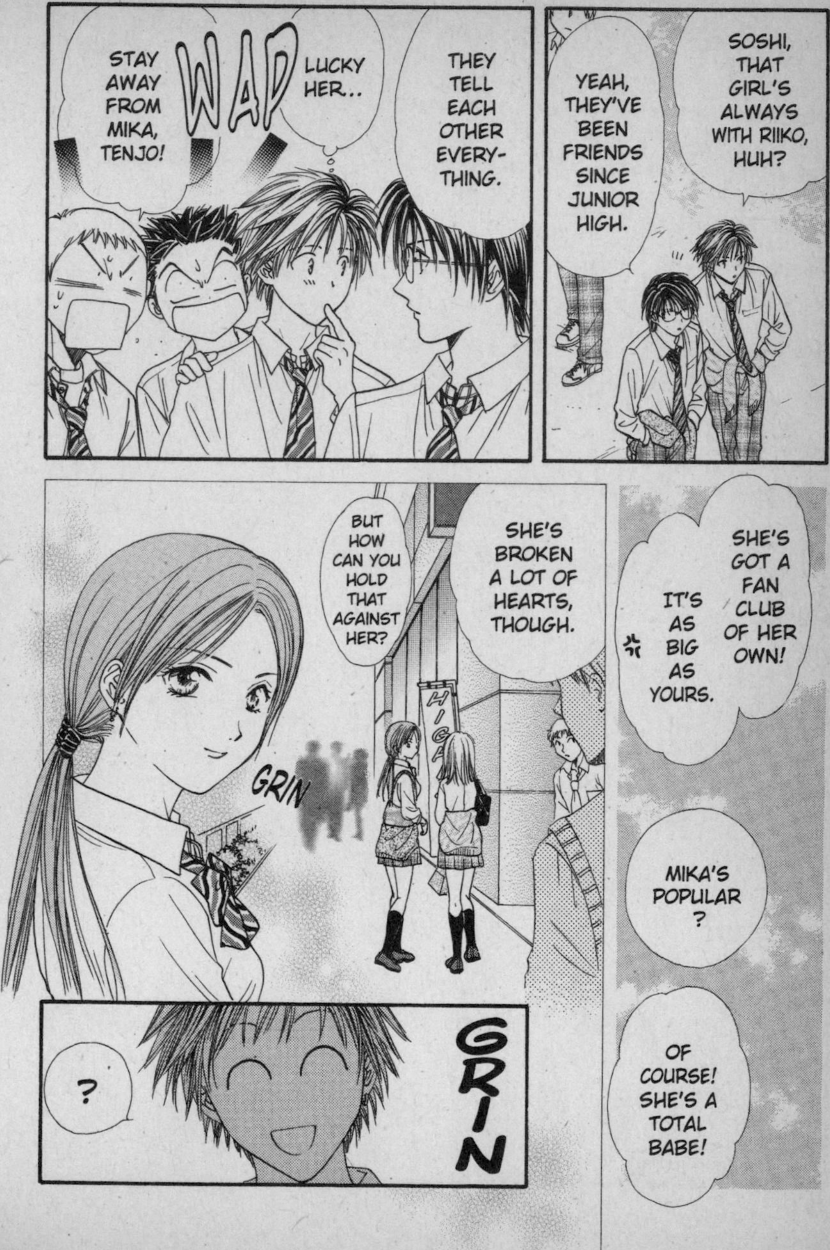
SOSHI, THAT GIRL'S ALWAYS WITH RIIKO, HUH?
YEAH, THEY'VE BEEN FRIENDS SINCE JUNIOR HIGH.
THEY TELL EACH OTHER EVERY-THING.
LUCKY HER..
WAP
STAY AWAY FROM MIKA, TENJO!
SHE'S GOT A FAN CLUB OF HER OWN!
IT'S AS BIG AS YOURS.
MIKA'S POPULAR ?
OF COURSE! SHE'S A TOTAL BABE!
SHE'S BROKEN A LOT OF HEARTS, THOUGH.
BUT HOW CAN YOU HOLD THAT AGAINST HER?
GRIN
GRIN
?

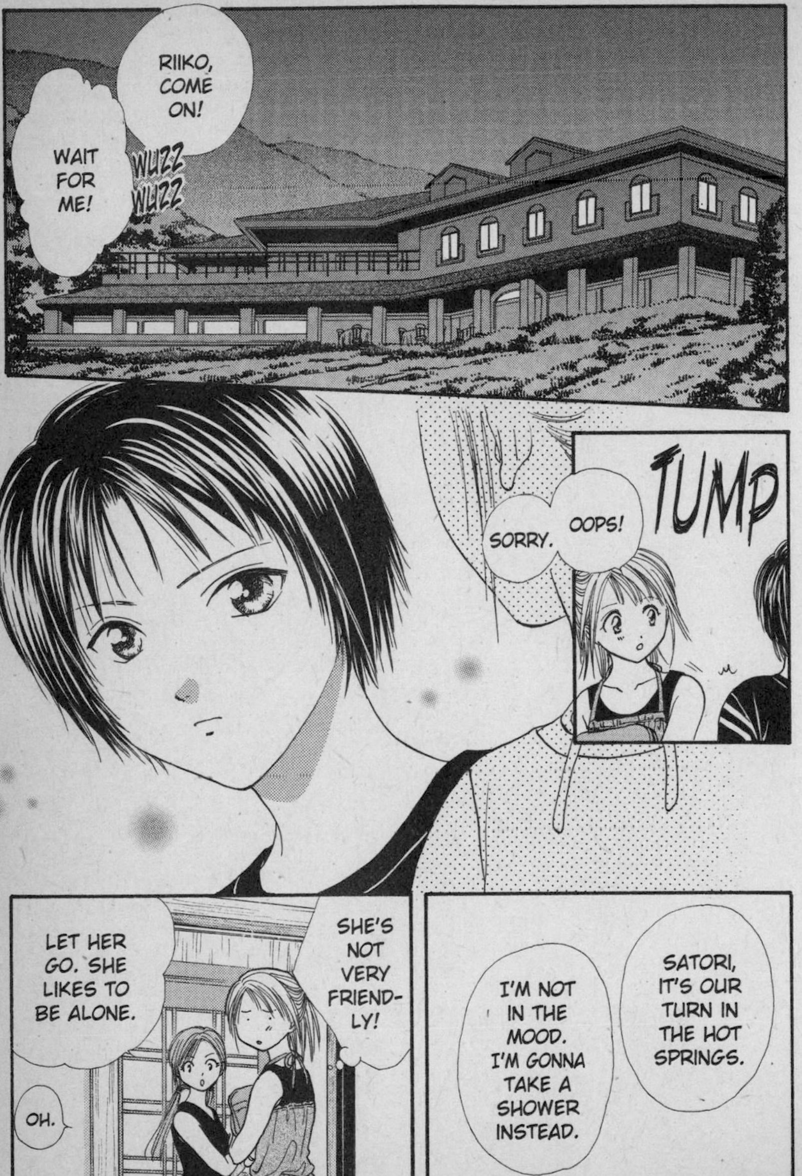
RIIKO, COME ON!
WAIT FOR ME!
WUZZ WUZZ
TUMP
OOPS!
SORRY.
SATORI, IT'S OUR TURN IN THE HOT SPRINGS.
I'M NOT IN THE MOOD. I'M GONNA TAKE A SHOWER INSTEAD.
SHE'S NOT VERY FRIEND-LY!
LET HER GO. SHE LIKES TO BE ALONE.
OH.

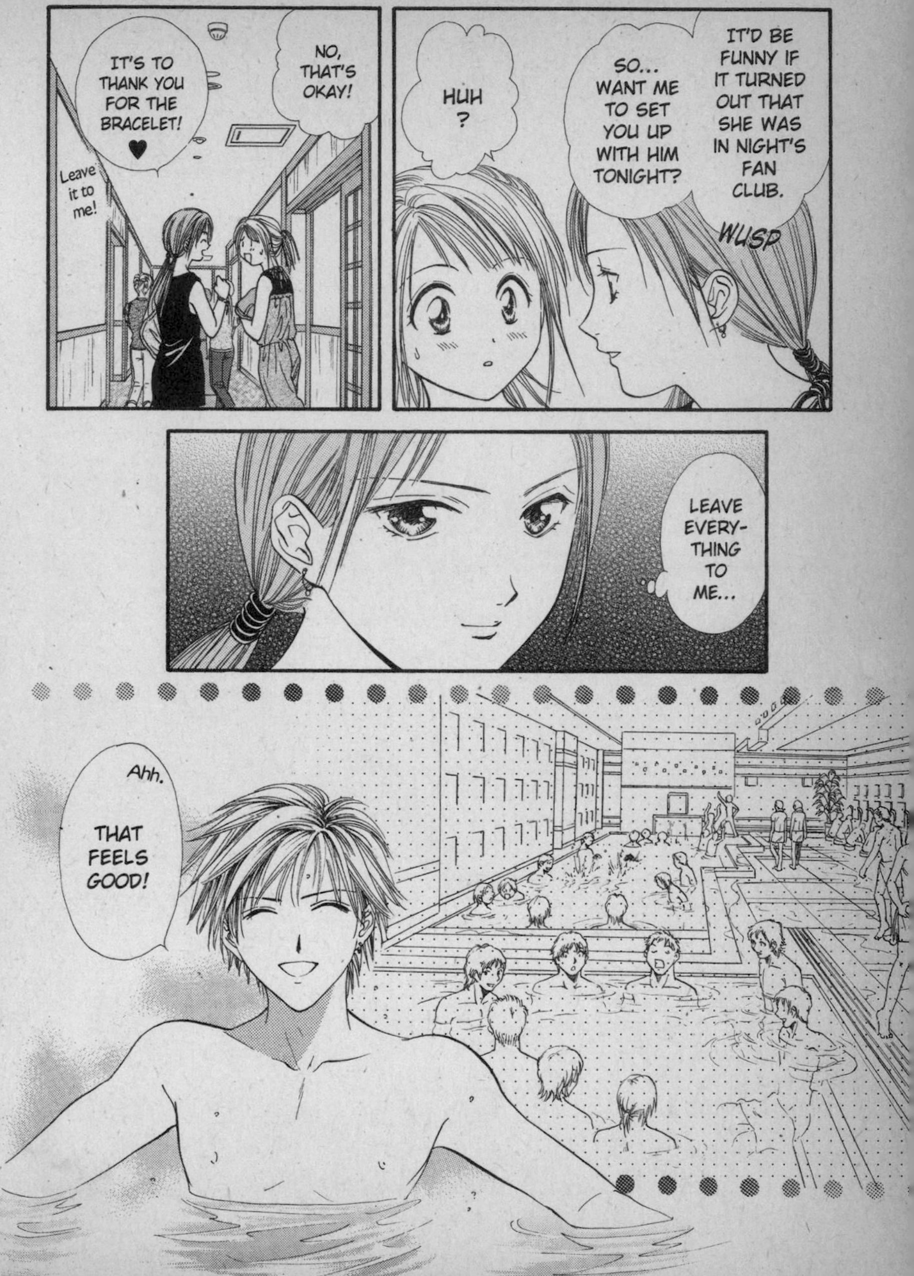
IT'D BE FUNNY IF IT TURNED OUT THAT SHE WAS IN NIGHT'S FAN CLUB.
SO... WANT ME TO SET YOU UP WITH HIM TONIGHT?
HUH?
WUSP
NO, THAT'S OKAY!
IT'S TO THANK YOU FOR THE BRACELET! ♥
Leave it to me!
LEAVE EVERYTHING TO ME...
Ahh.
THAT FEELS GOOD!

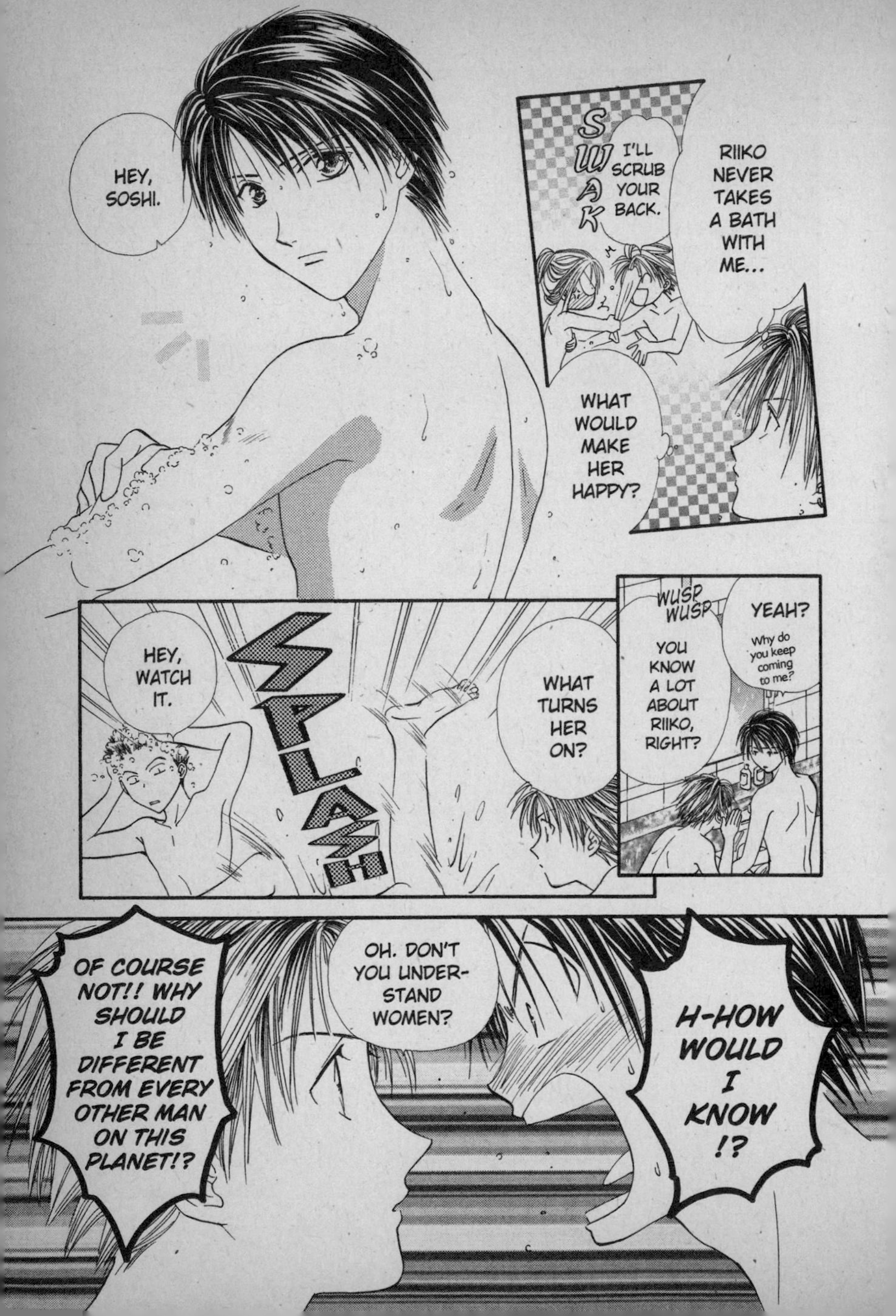

RIIKO NEVER TAKES A BATH WITH ME...
I'LL SCRUB YOUR BACK.
SWAK
WHAT WOULD MAKE HER HAPPY?
HEY, SOSHI.
YEAH?
Why do you keep coming to me?
WUSP WUSP
YOU KNOW A LOT ABOUT RIIKO, RIGHT?
WHAT TURNS HER ON?
SPLASH
HEY, WATCH IT.
H-HOW WOULD I KNOW !?
OH. DON'T YOU UNDER-STAND WOMEN?
OF COURSE NOT!! WHY SHOULD I BE DIFFERENT FROM EVERY OTHER MAN ON THIS PLANET!?

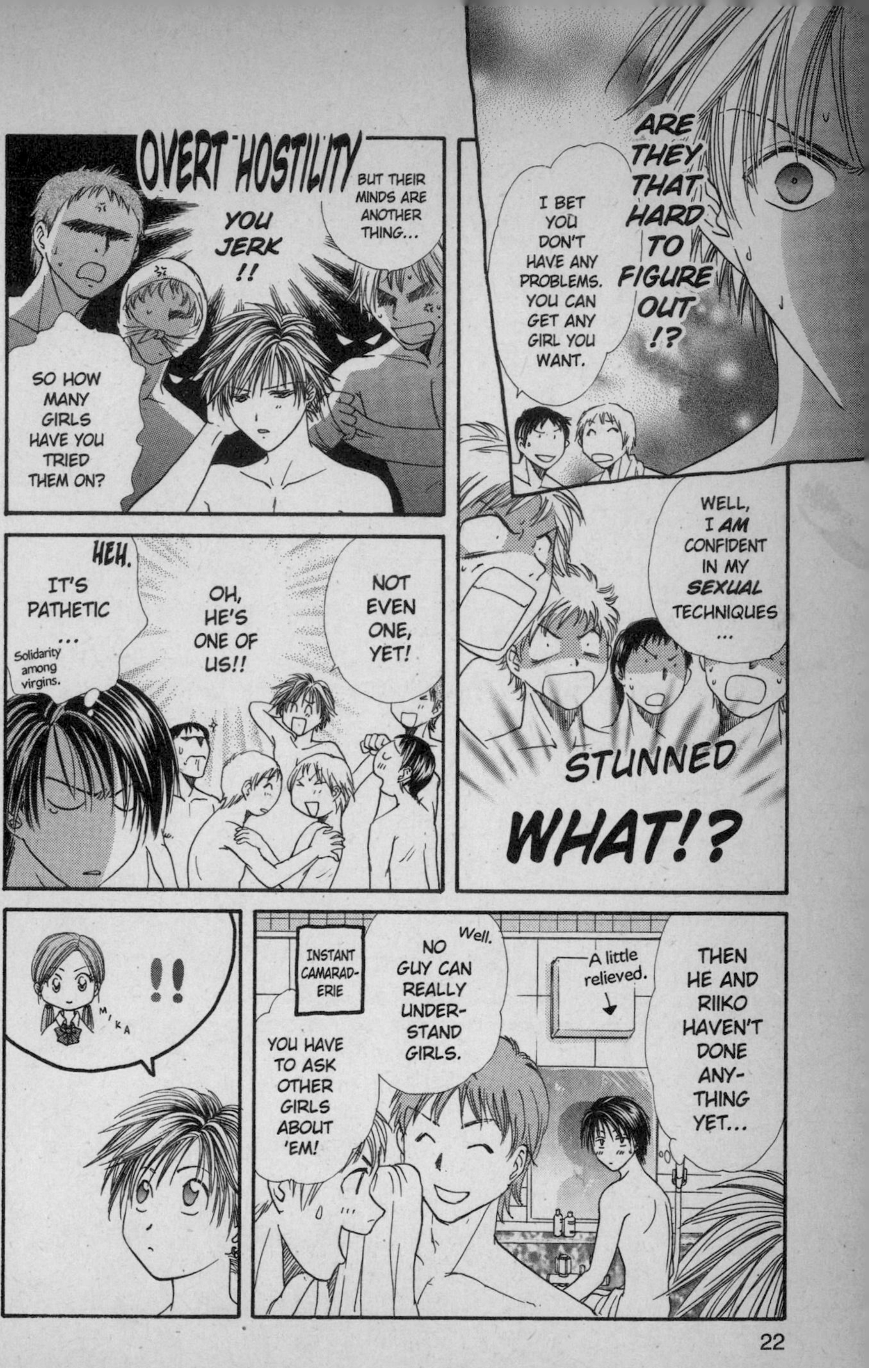
ARE THEY THAT HARD TO FIGURE OUT!?
I BET YOU DON'T HAVE ANY PROBLEMS. YOU CAN GET ANY GIRL YOU WANT.
WELL, I AM CONFIDENT IN MY SEXUAL TECHNIQUES...
STUNNED
WHAT!?
OVERT HOSTILITY
BUT THEIR MINDS ARE ANOTHER THING...
YOU JERK!!
SO HOW MANY GIRLS HAVE YOU TRIED THEM ON?
HEH.
NOT EVEN ONE, YET!
OH, HE'S ONE OF US!!
IT'S PATHETIC...
Solidarity among virgins.
THEN HE AND RIIKO HAVEN'T DONE ANYTHING YET...
A little relieved.
Well.
NO GUY CAN REALLY UNDER-STAND GIRLS.
INSTANT CAMARAD-ERIE
YOU HAVE TO ASK OTHER GIRLS ABOUT 'EM!
!!
MIKA

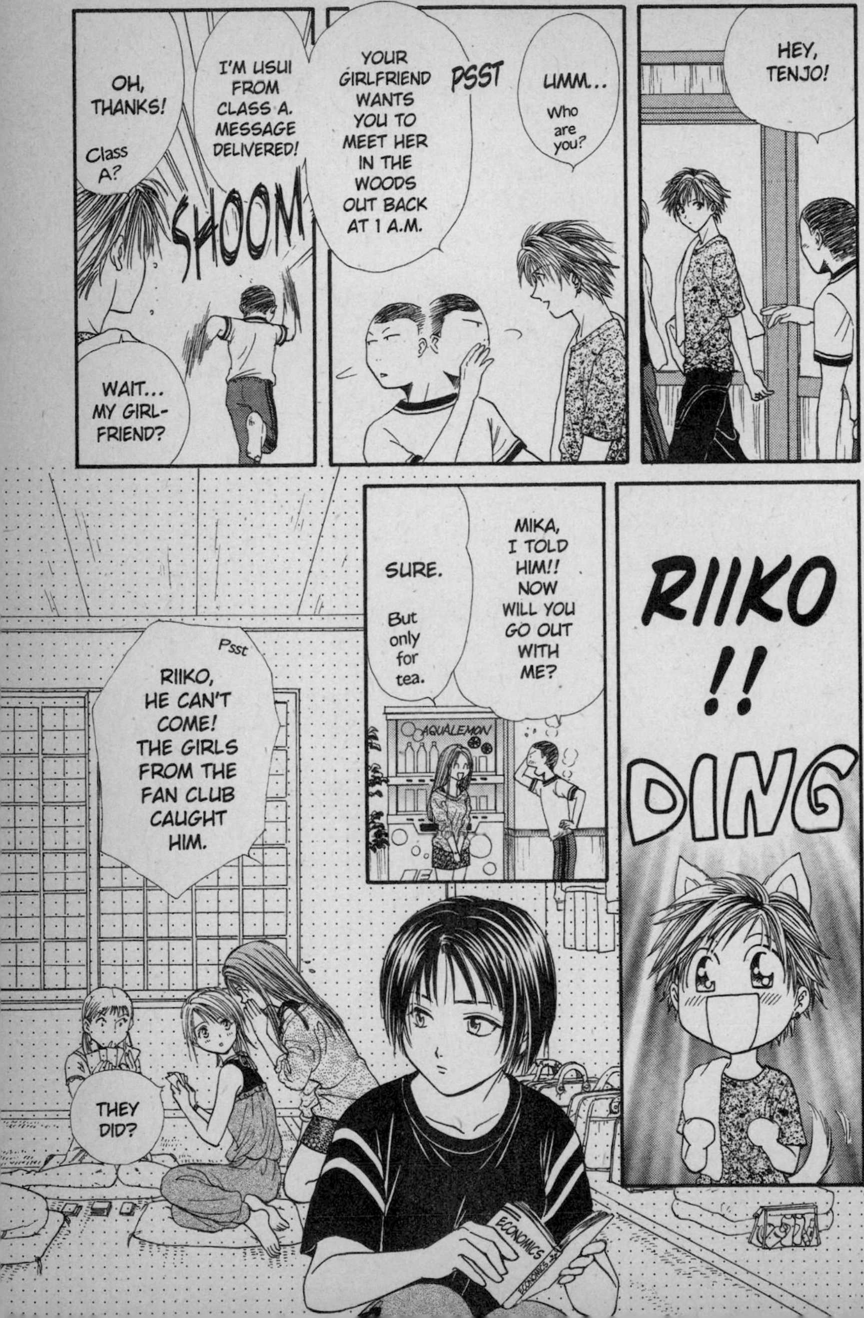
HEY, TENJO!
UMM...
Who are you?
PSST
YOUR GIRLFRIEND WANTS YOU TO MEET HER IN THE WOODS OUT BACK AT 1 A.M.
I'M USUI FROM CLASS A. MESSAGE DELIVERED!
OH, THANKS!
Class A?
SHOOM
WAIT... MY GIRL-FRIEND?
RIIKO!!
DING
MIKA, I TOLD HIM!! NOW WILL YOU GO OUT WITH ME?
SURE.
But only for tea.
AQUALEMON
Psst
RIIKO, HE CAN'T COME! THE GIRLS FROM THE FAN CLUB CAUGHT HIM.
THEY DID?
ECONOMICS

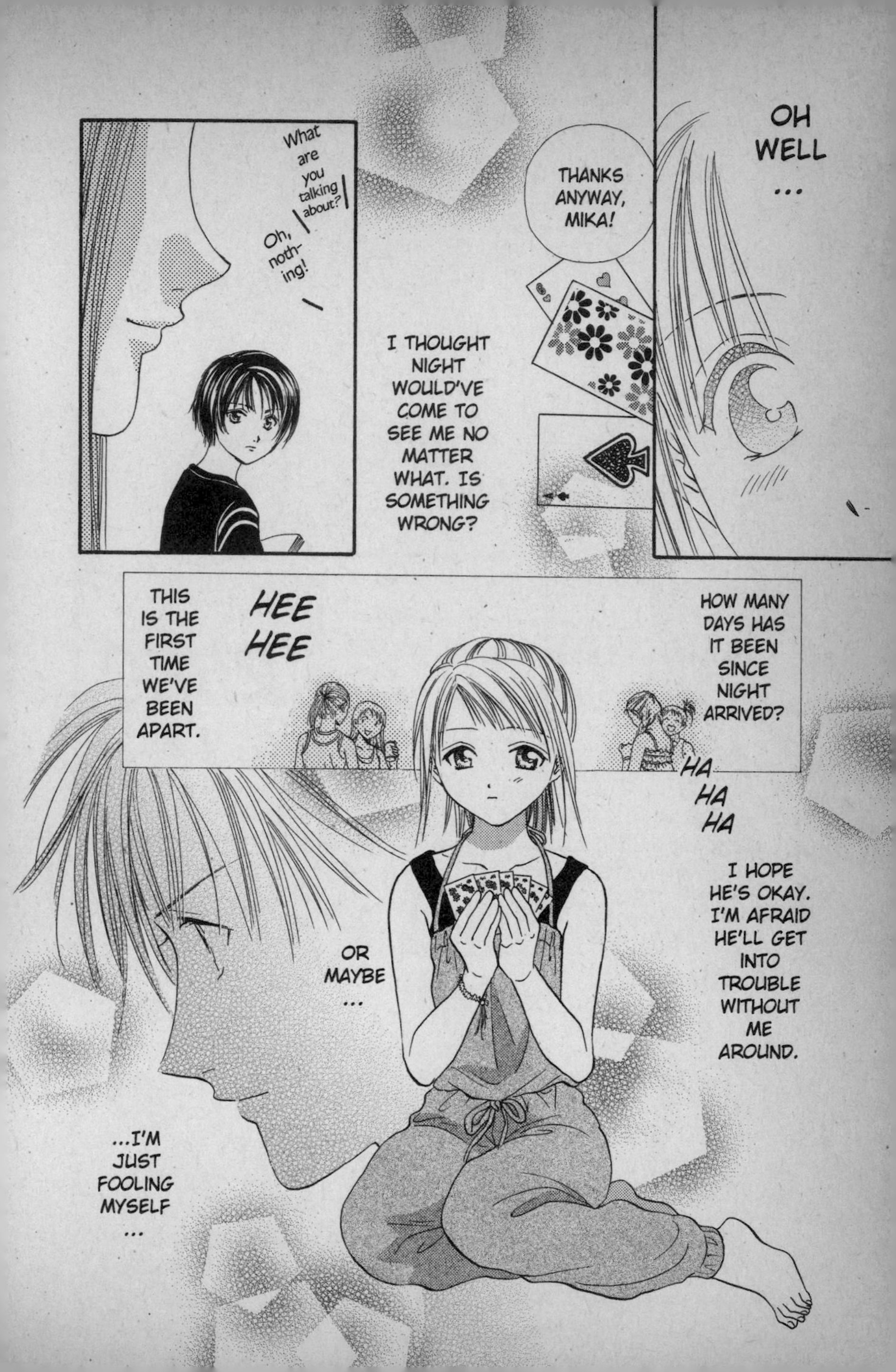
OH WELL ...
THANKS ANYWAY, MIKA!
I THOUGHT NIGHT WOULD'VE COME TO SEE ME NO MATTER WHAT. IS SOMETHING WRONG?
What are you talking about?
Oh, nothing!
HOW MANY DAYS HAS IT BEEN SINCE NIGHT ARRIVED?
HEE HEE
THIS IS THE FIRST TIME WE'VE BEEN APART.
HA HA HA
I HOPE HE'S OKAY. I'M AFRAID HE'LL GET INTO TROUBLE WITHOUT ME AROUND.
OR MAYBE ...
...I'M JUST FOOLING MYSELF ...

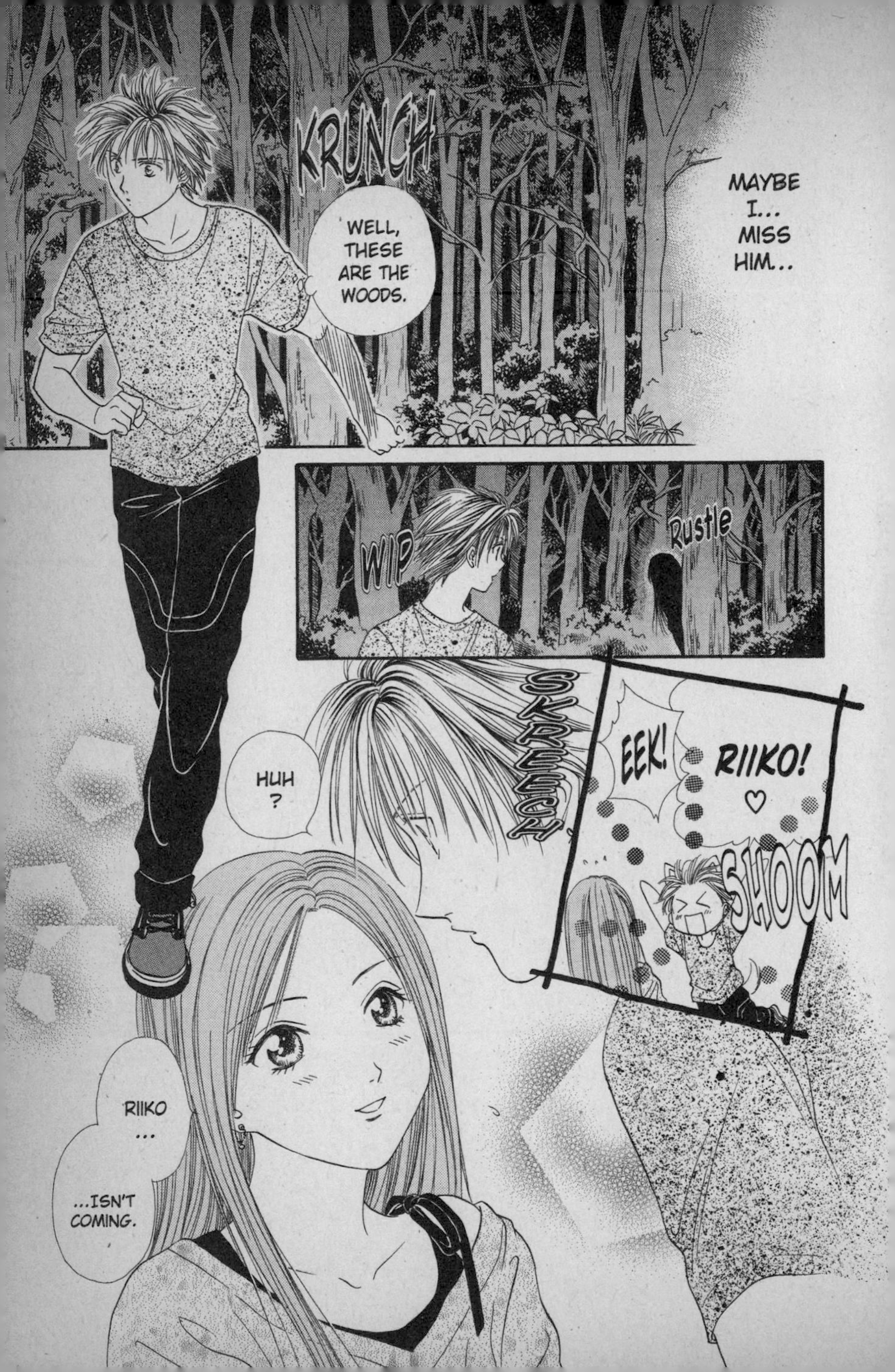
MAYBE I... MISS HIM...
KRUNCH
WELL, THESE ARE THE WOODS.
Rustle
WIP
RIIKO! ♡
EEK!
SHOOM
SKREECH
HUH?
RIIKO...
...ISN'T COMING.

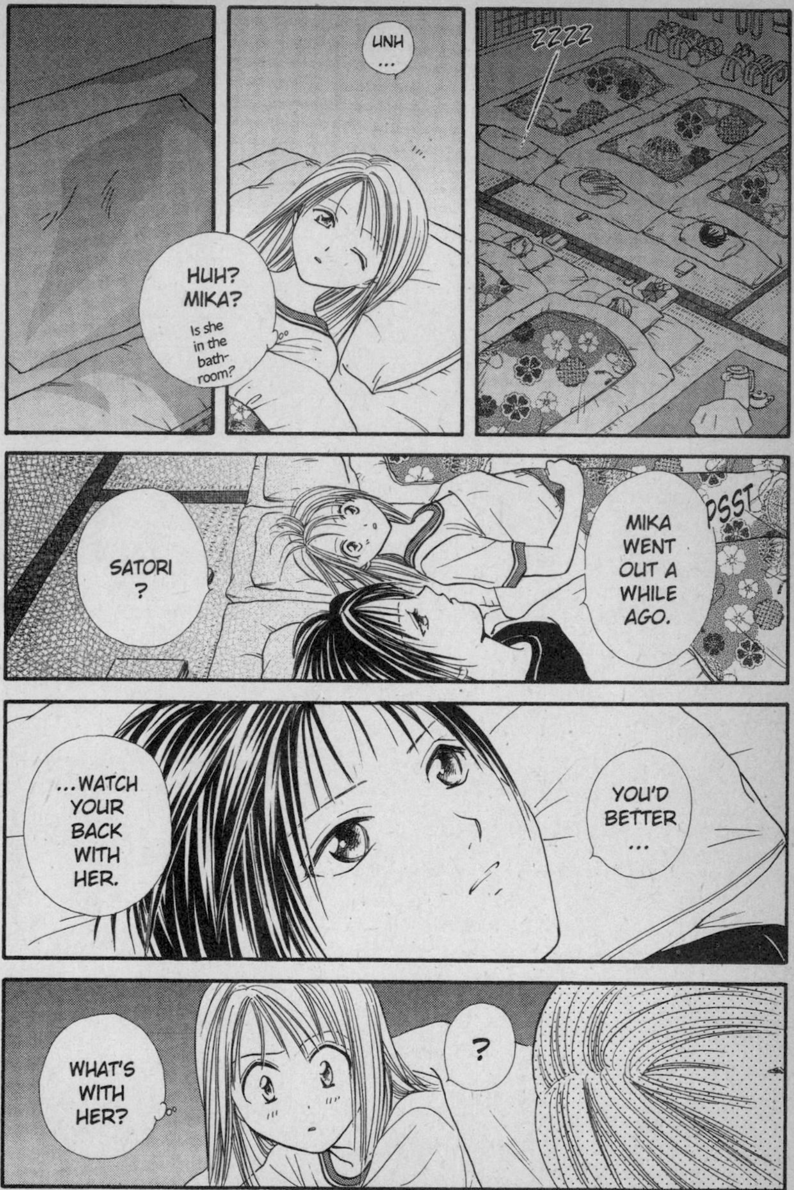
ZZZZ
UNH ...
HUH? MIKA?
Is she in the bathroom?
PSST
MIKA WENT OUT A WHILE AGO.
SATORI ?
YOU'D BETTER ...
...WATCH YOUR BACK WITH HER.
?
WHAT'S WITH HER?

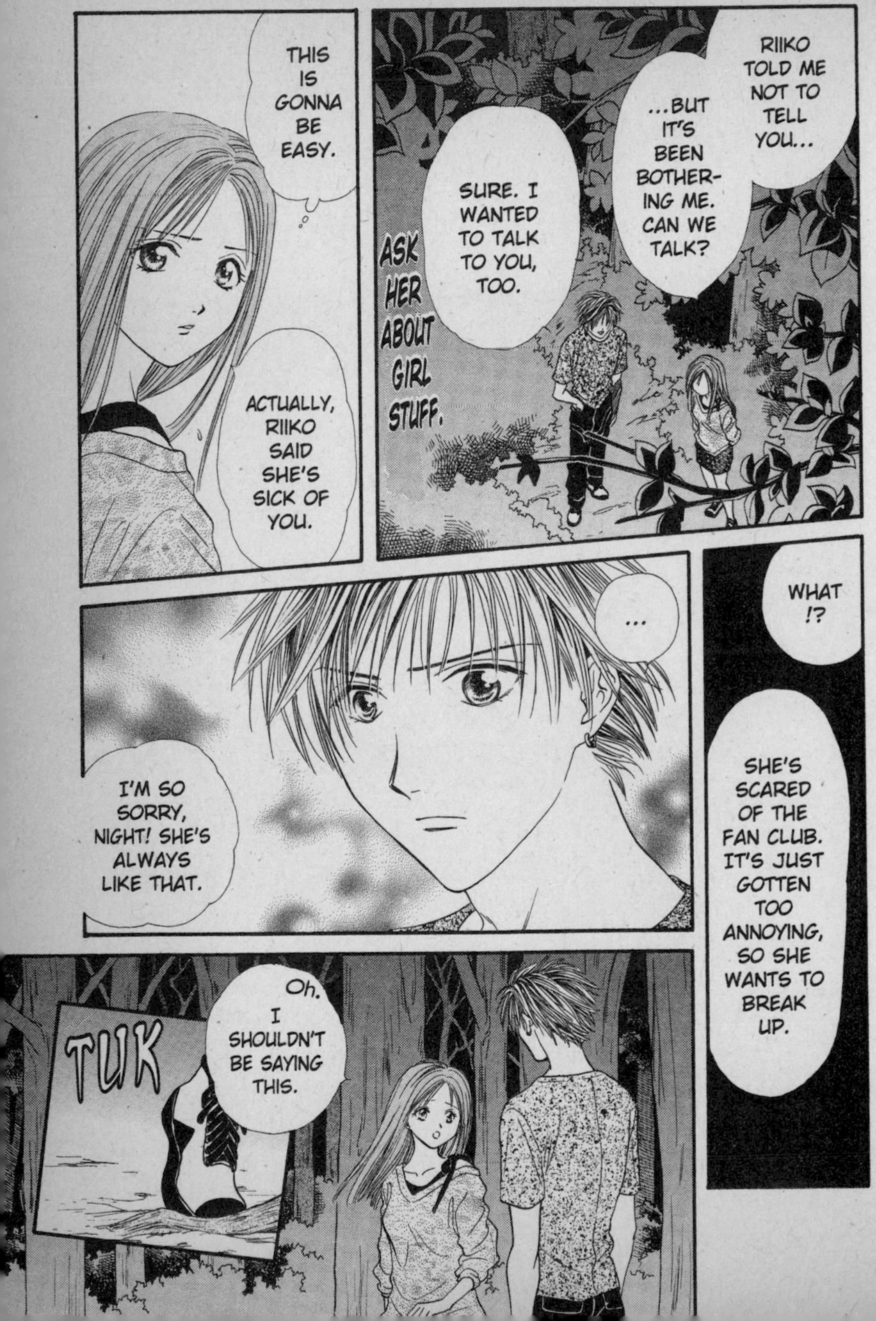
RIIKO TOLD ME NOT TO TELL YOU...
...BUT IT'S BEEN BOTHERING ME. CAN WE TALK?
SURE. I WANTED TO TALK TO YOU, TOO.
ASK HER ABOUT GIRL STUFF.
THIS IS GONNA BE EASY.
ACTUALLY, RIIKO SAID SHE'S SICK OF YOU.
WHAT !?
SHE'S SCARED OF THE FAN CLUB. IT'S JUST GOTTEN TOO ANNOYING, SO SHE WANTS TO BREAK UP.
...
I'M SO SORRY, NIGHT! SHE'S ALWAYS LIKE THAT.
Oh. I SHOULDN'T BE SAYING THIS.
TUK

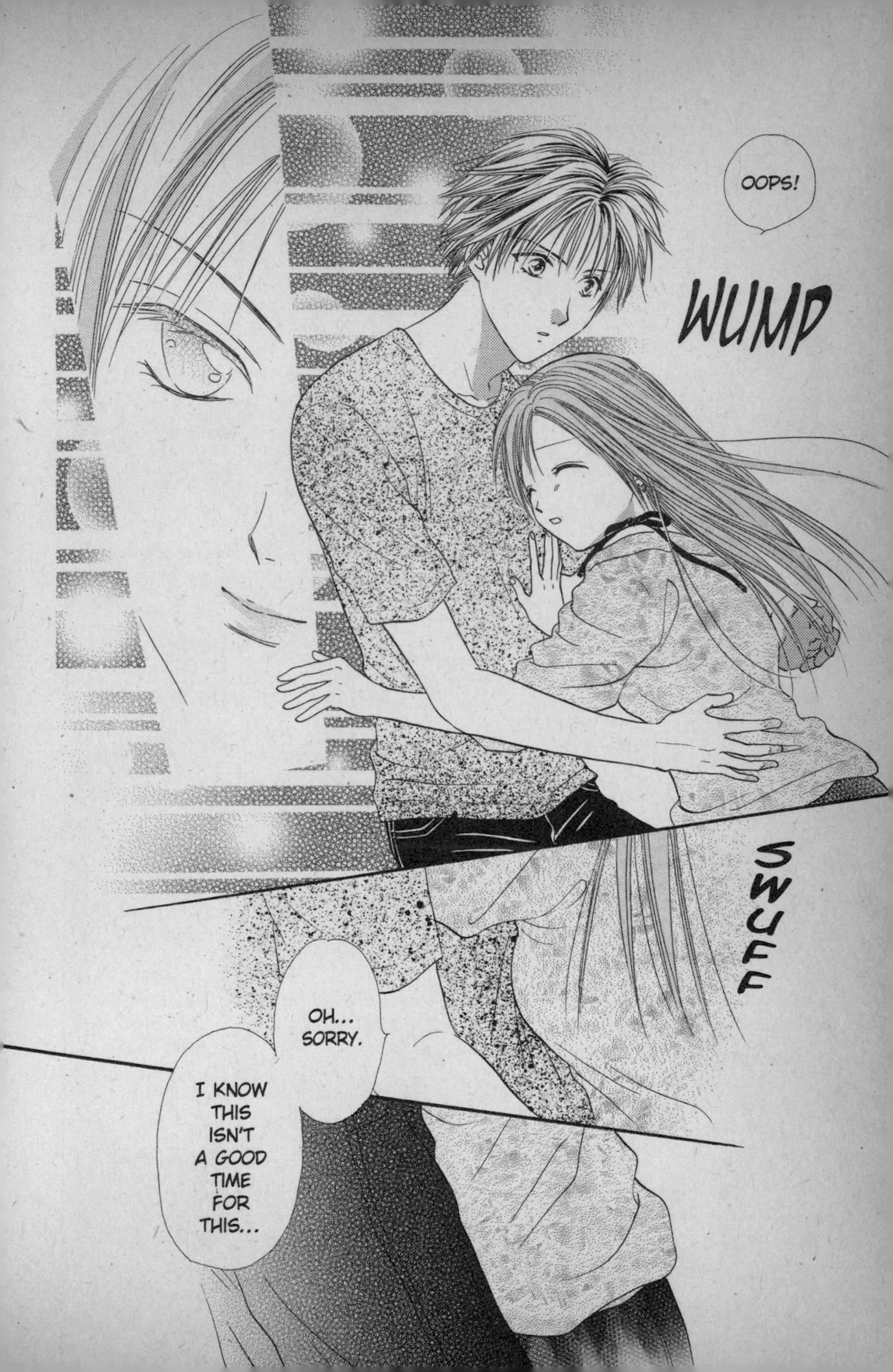
OOPS!
WUMP
SWUFF
OH... SORRY.
I KNOW THIS ISN'T A GOOD TIME FOR THIS...

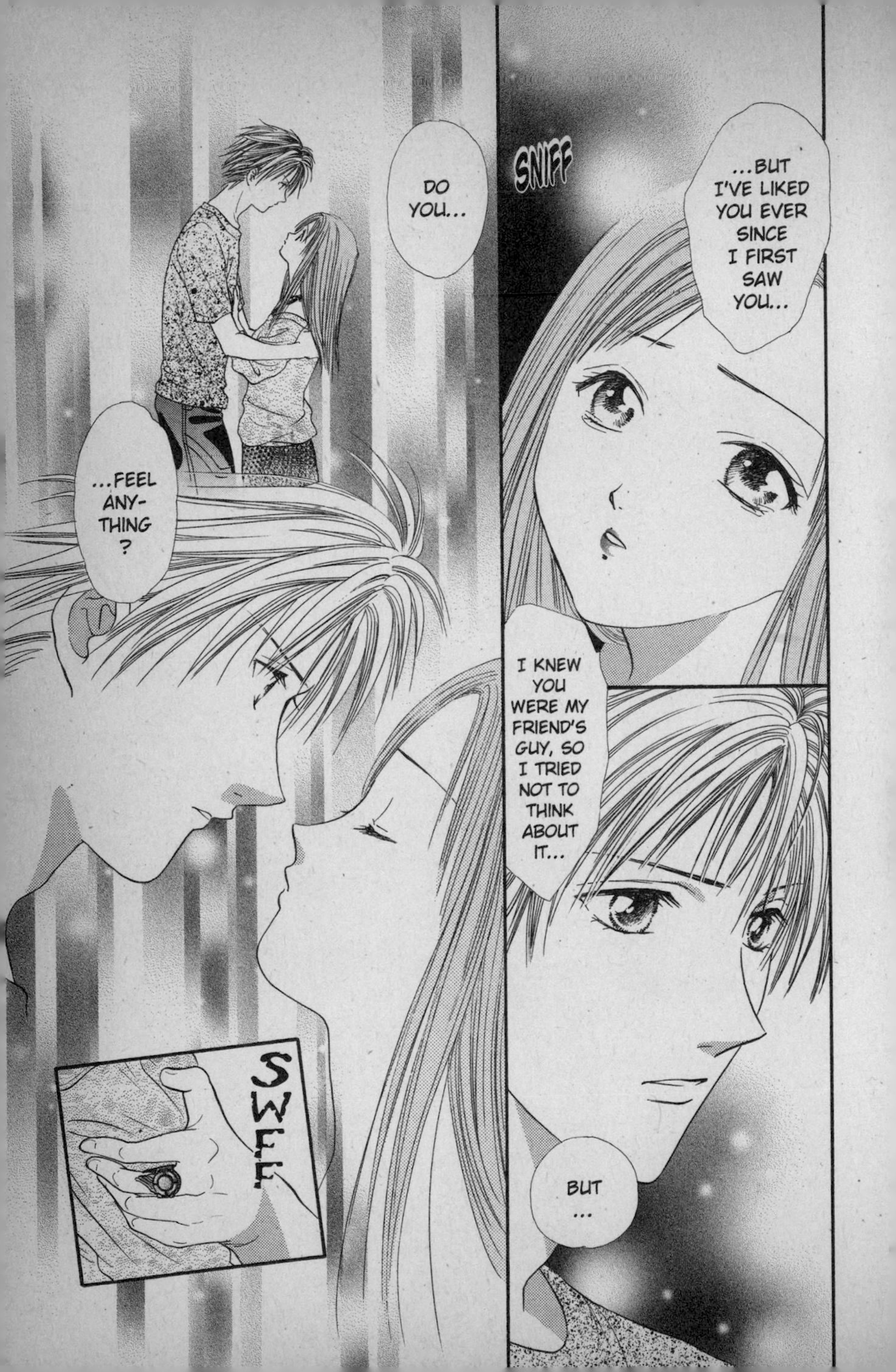
SNIFF
...BUT I'VE LIKED YOU EVER SINCE I FIRST SAW YOU...
I KNEW YOU WERE MY FRIEND'S GUY, SO I TRIED NOT TO THINK ABOUT IT...
BUT ...
DO YOU...
...FEEL ANY-THING?
SWFF

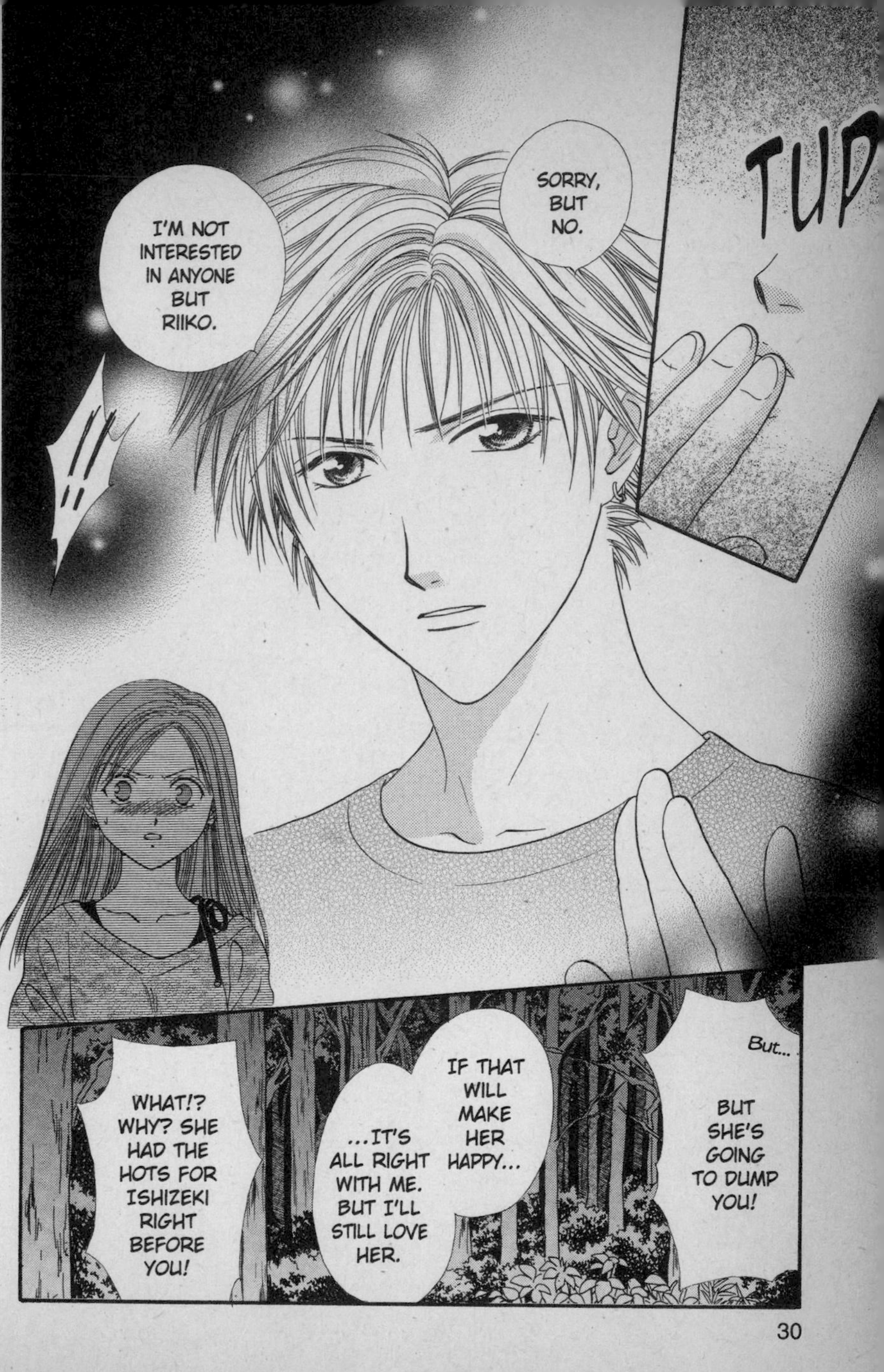
TUP
SORRY, BUT NO.
I'M NOT INTERESTED IN ANYONE BUT RIIKO.
!!
But...
BUT SHE'S GOING TO DUMP YOU!
IF THAT WILL MAKE HER HAPPY...
...IT'S ALL RIGHT WITH ME. BUT I'LL STILL LOVE HER.
WHAT!? WHY? SHE HAD THE HOTS FOR ISHIZEKI RIGHT BEFORE YOU!

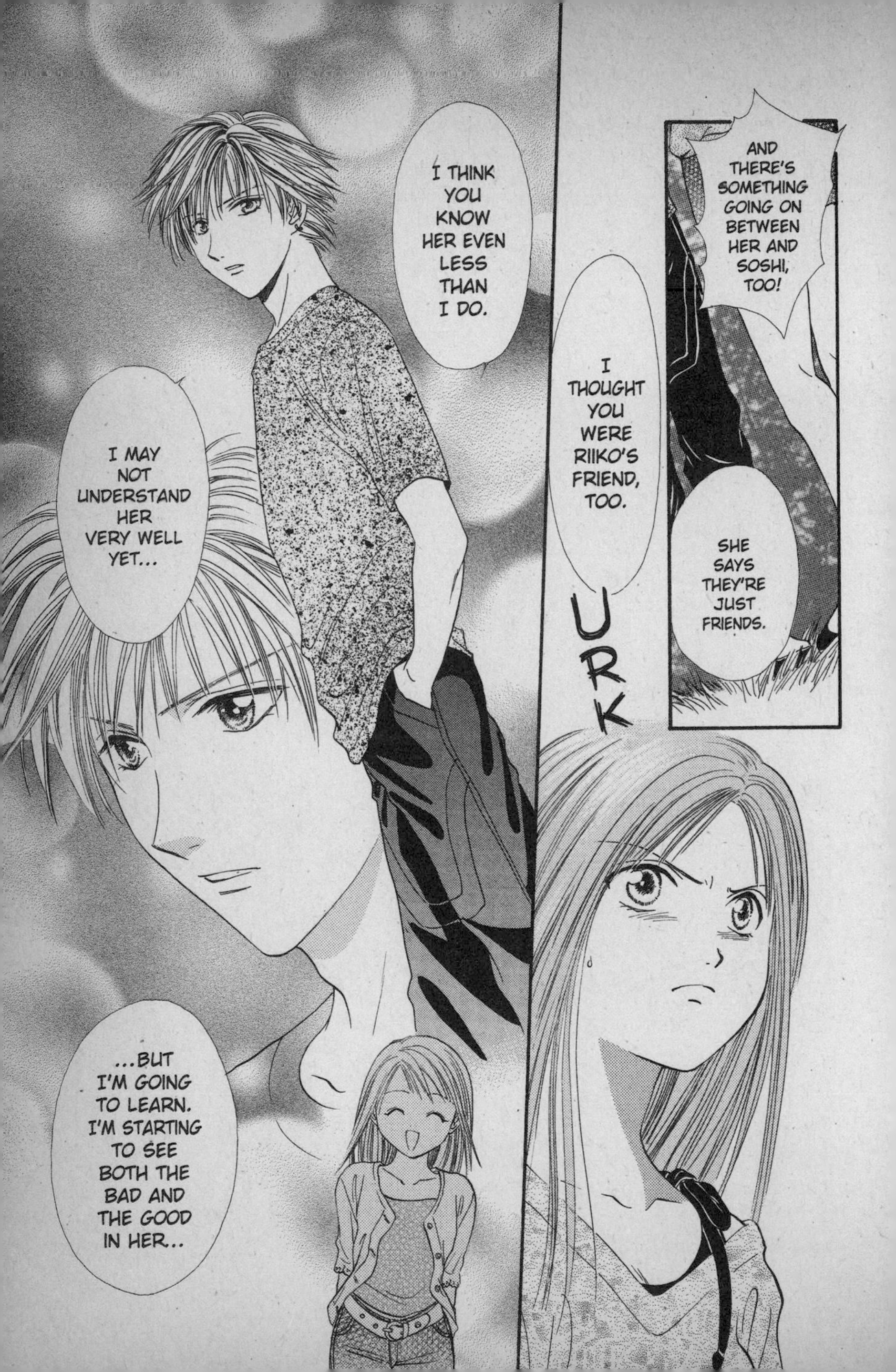
AND THERE'S SOMETHING GOING ON BETWEEN HER AND SOSHI, TOO!
SHE SAYS THEY'RE JUST FRIENDS.
I THOUGHT YOU WERE RIIKO'S FRIEND, TOO.
URK
I THINK YOU KNOW HER EVEN LESS THAN I DO.
I MAY NOT UNDERSTAND HER VERY WELL YET...
...BUT I'M GOING TO LEARN. I'M STARTING TO SEE BOTH THE BAD AND THE GOOD IN HER...

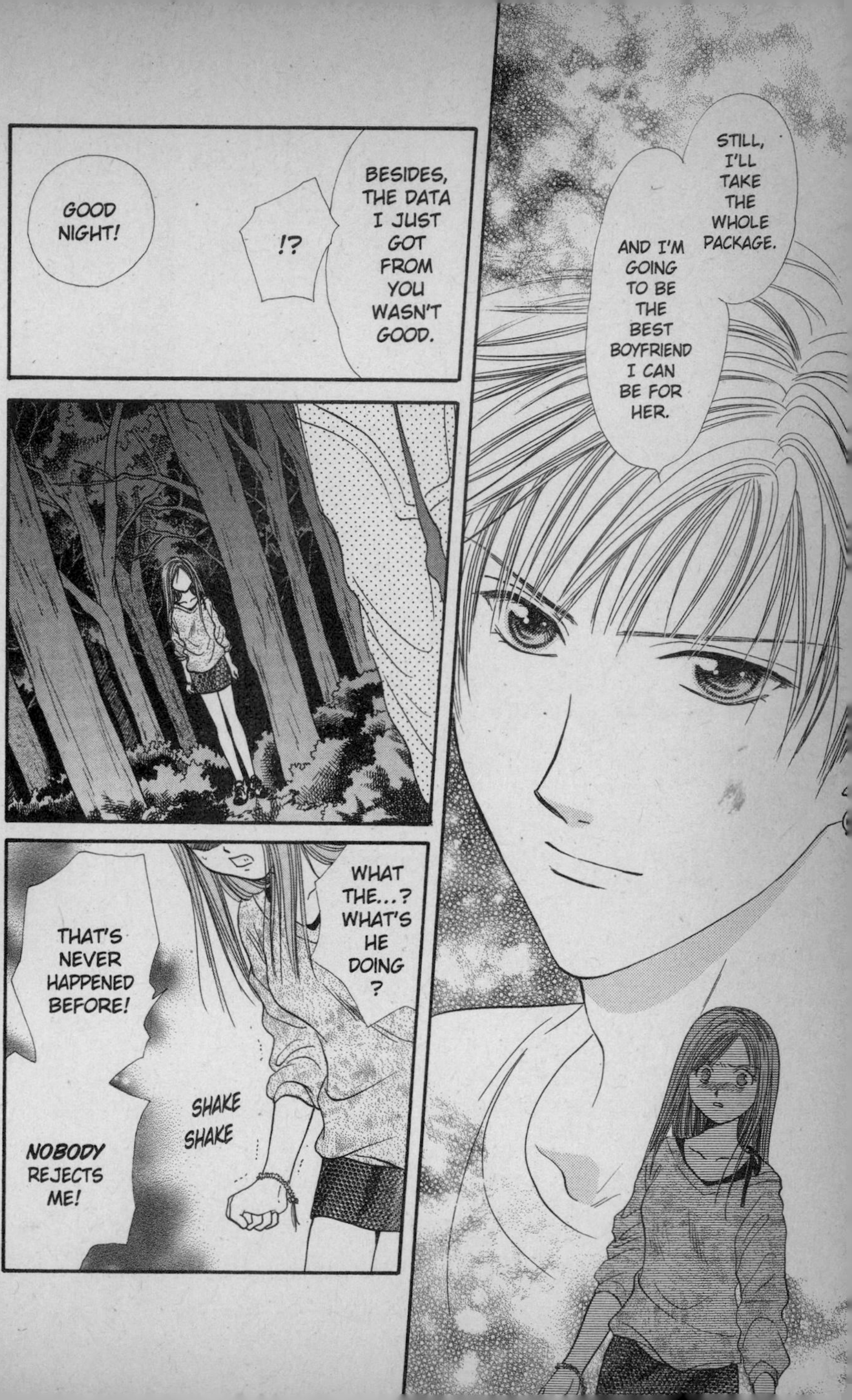
STILL, I'LL TAKE THE WHOLE PACKAGE.
AND I'M GOING TO BE THE BEST BOYFRIEND I CAN BE FOR HER.
BESIDES, THE DATA I JUST GOT FROM YOU WASN'T GOOD.
!?
GOOD NIGHT!
WHAT THE...? WHAT'S HE DOING?
SHAKE SHAKE
THAT'S NEVER HAPPENED BEFORE!
NOBODY REJECTS ME!

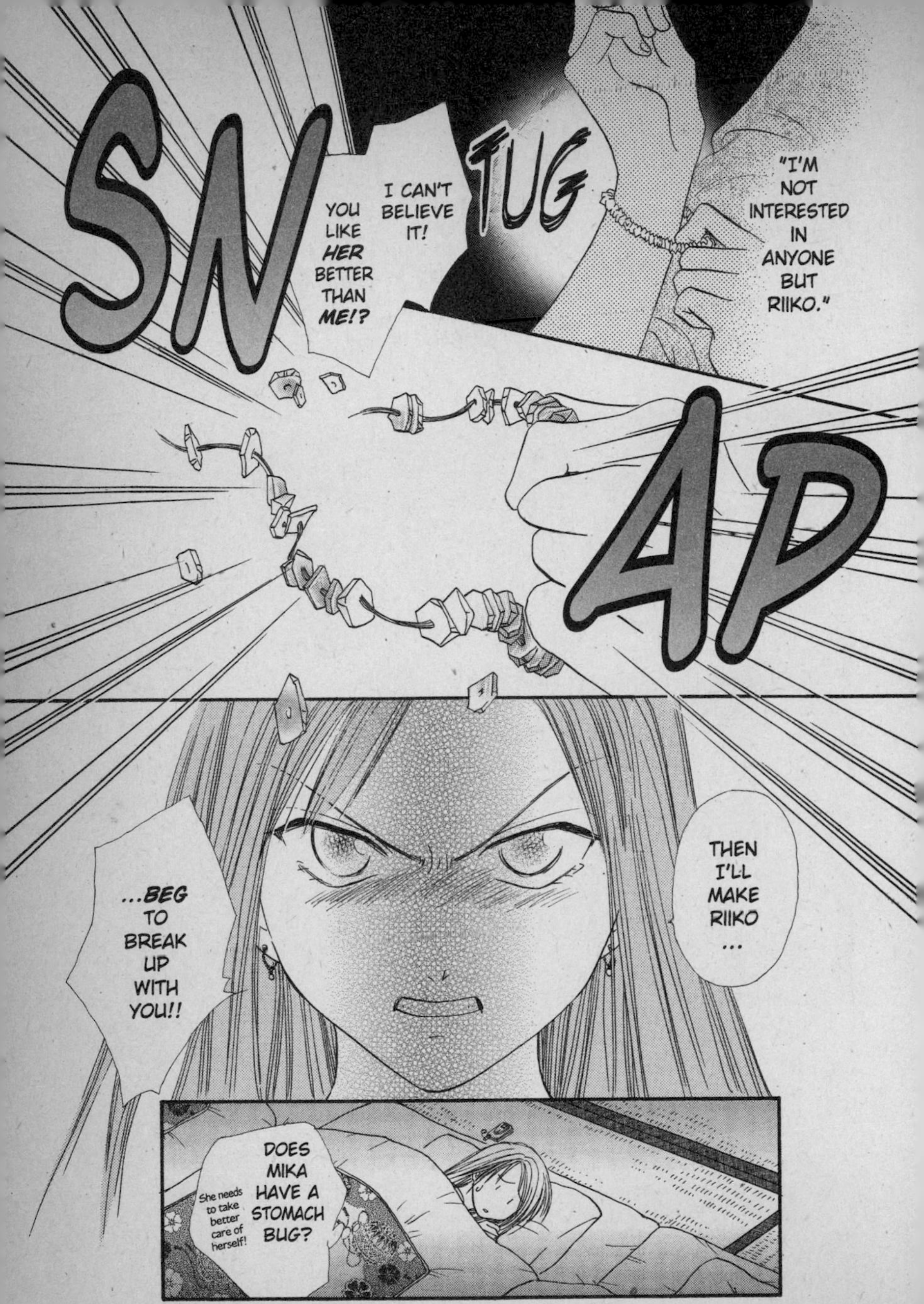
"I'M NOT INTERESTED IN ANYONE BUT RIIKO."
TUG
I CAN'T BELIEVE IT!
YOU LIKE *HER* BETTER THAN *ME!?*
SN
AP
THEN I'LL MAKE RIIKO ...
...*BEG* TO BREAK UP WITH YOU!!
DOES MIKA HAVE A STOMACH BUG?
She needs to take better care of herself!

Absolute Boyfriend

Act 8
Friends

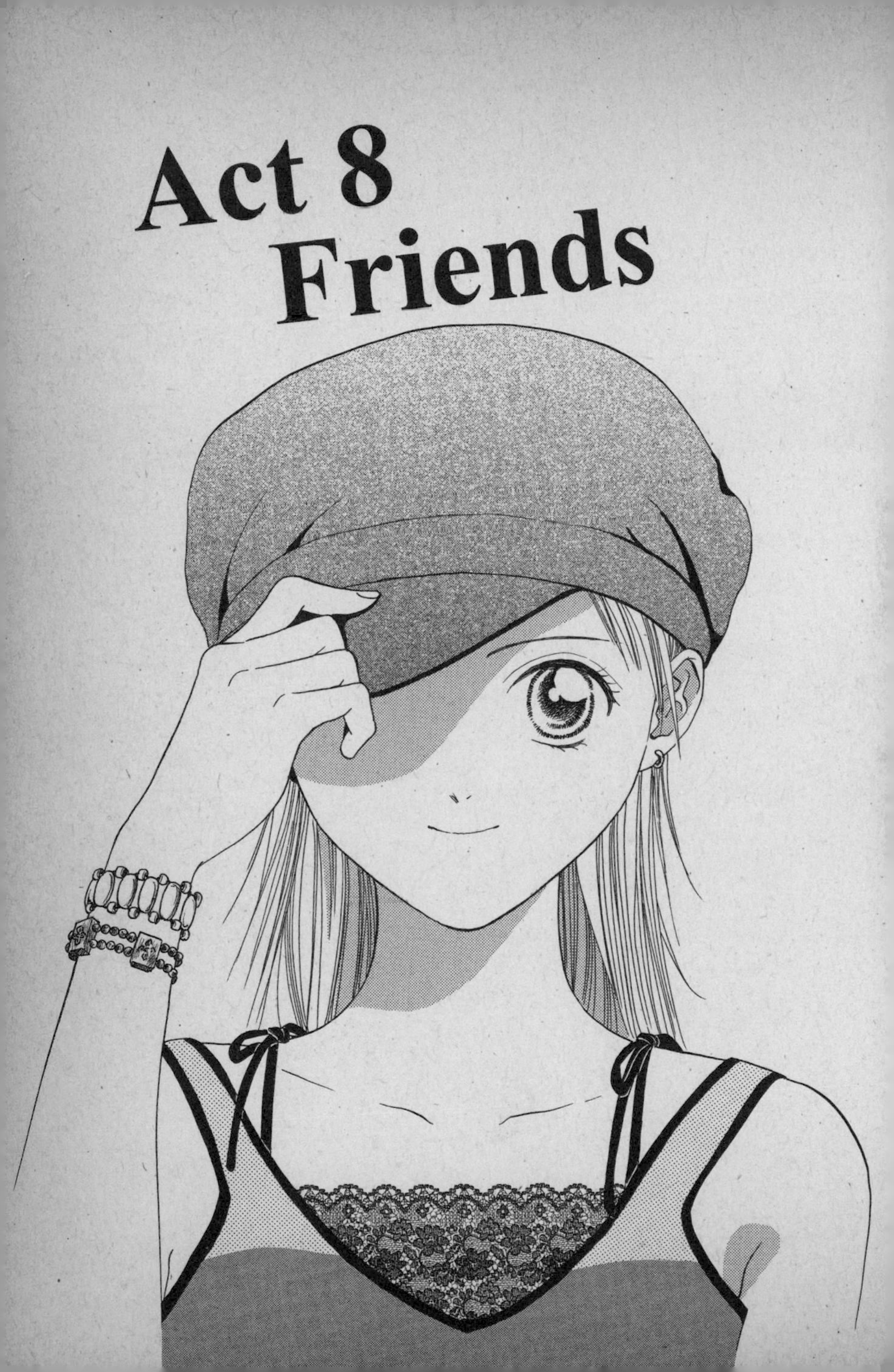

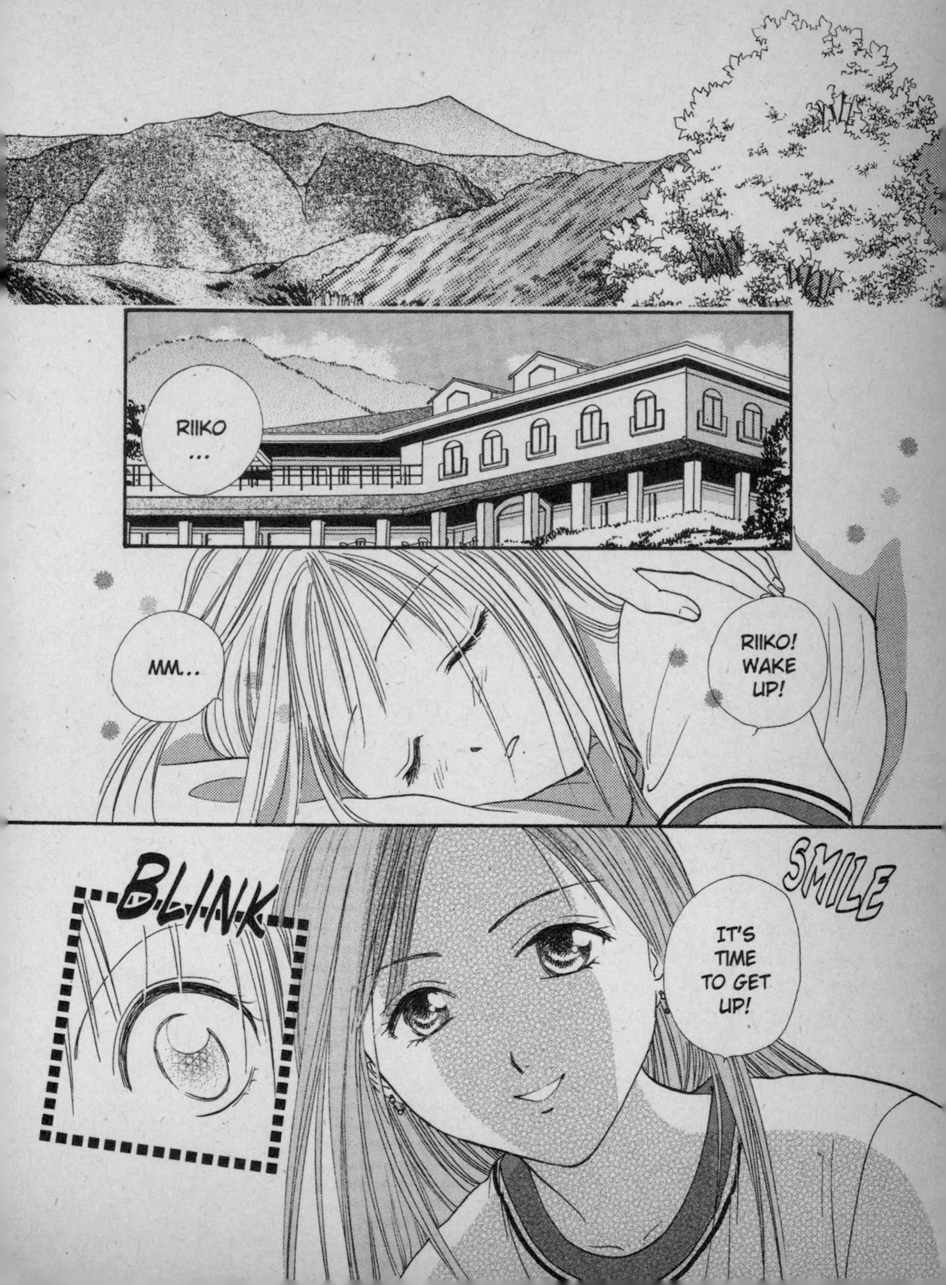
RIIKO ...
RIIKO! WAKE UP!
MM...
SMILE
IT'S TIME TO GET UP!
B.L.I.N.K

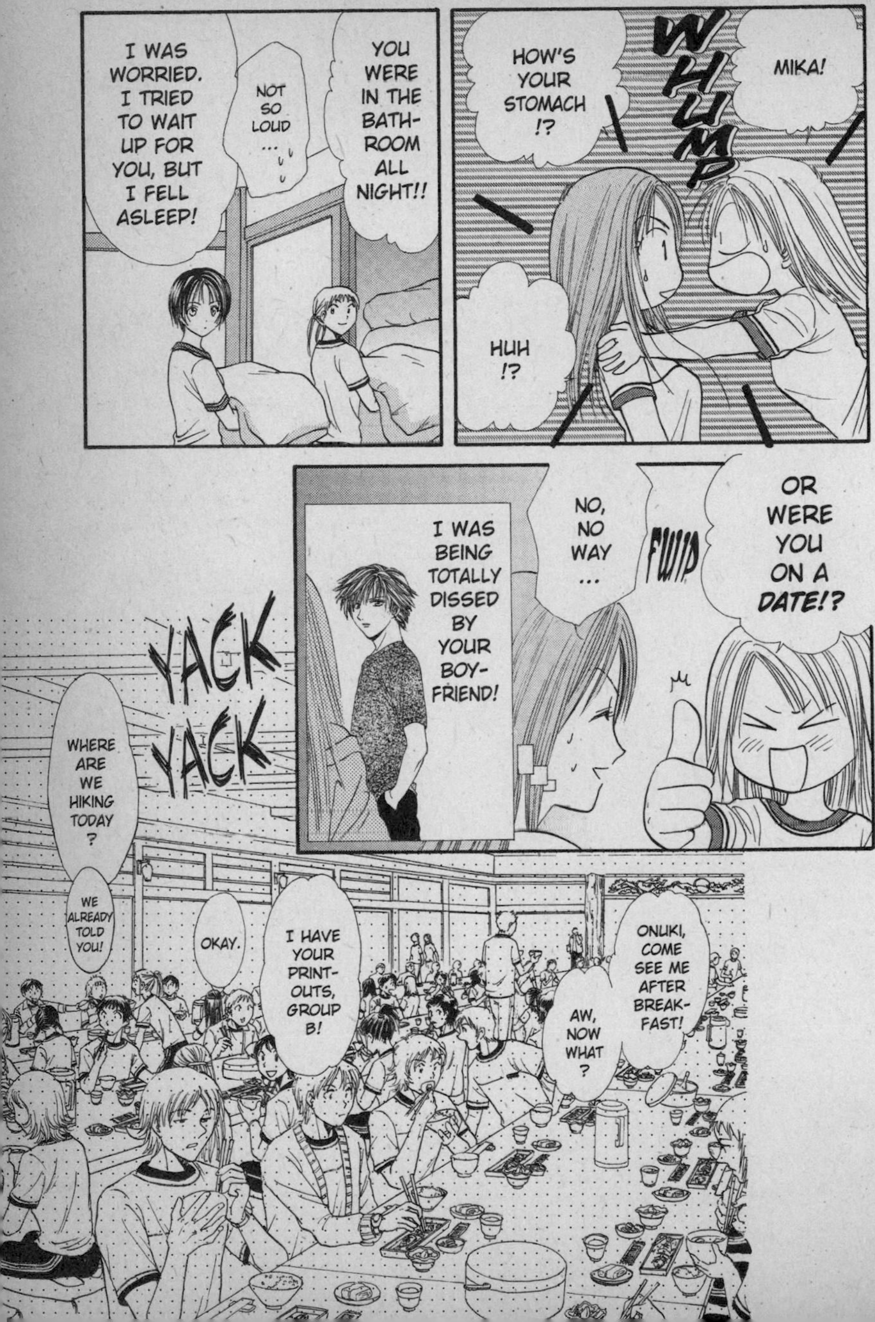
MIKA!
WHUMP
HOW'S YOUR STOMACH!?
HUH!?
YOU WERE IN THE BATH-ROOM ALL NIGHT!!
NOT SO LOUD...
I WAS WORRIED. I TRIED TO WAIT UP FOR YOU, BUT I FELL ASLEEP!
OR WERE YOU ON A *DATE!?*
FWIP
NO, NO WAY...
I WAS BEING TOTALLY DISSED BY YOUR BOY-FRIEND!
ONUKI, COME SEE ME AFTER BREAK-FAST!
AW, NOW WHAT?
I HAVE YOUR PRINT-OUTS, GROUP B!
OKAY.
YACK YACK
WHERE ARE WE HIKING TODAY?
WE ALREADY TOLD YOU!

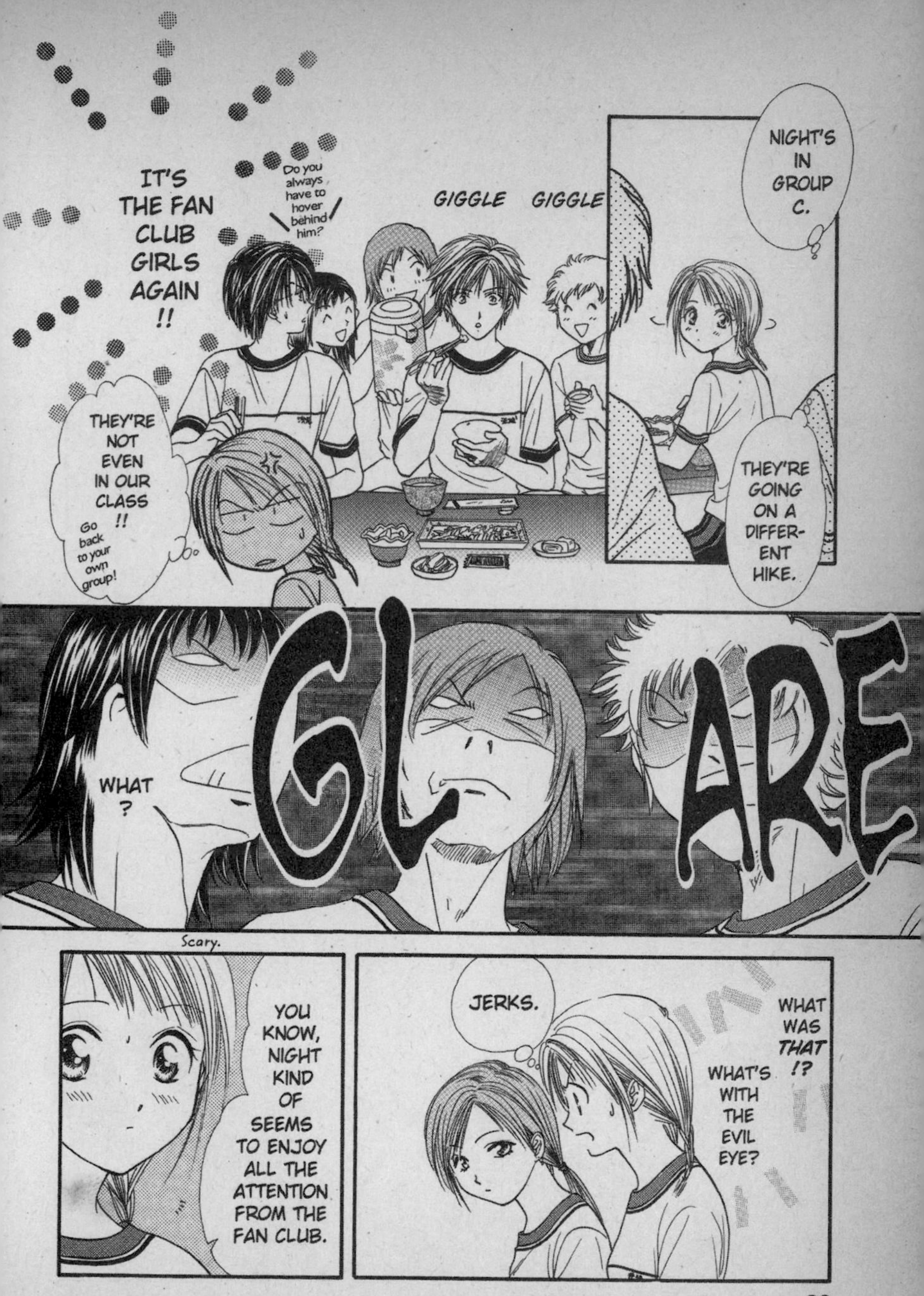
NIGHT'S IN GROUP C.
THEY'RE GOING ON A DIFFERENT HIKE.
GIGGLE GIGGLE
Do you always have to hover behind him?
IT'S THE FAN CLUB GIRLS AGAIN !!
THEY'RE NOT EVEN IN OUR CLASS !!
Go back to your own group!
GLARE
WHAT ?
JERKS.
WHAT WAS THAT !?
WHAT'S WITH THE EVIL EYE?
Scary.
YOU KNOW, NIGHT KIND OF SEEMS TO ENJOY ALL THE ATTENTION FROM THE FAN CLUB.

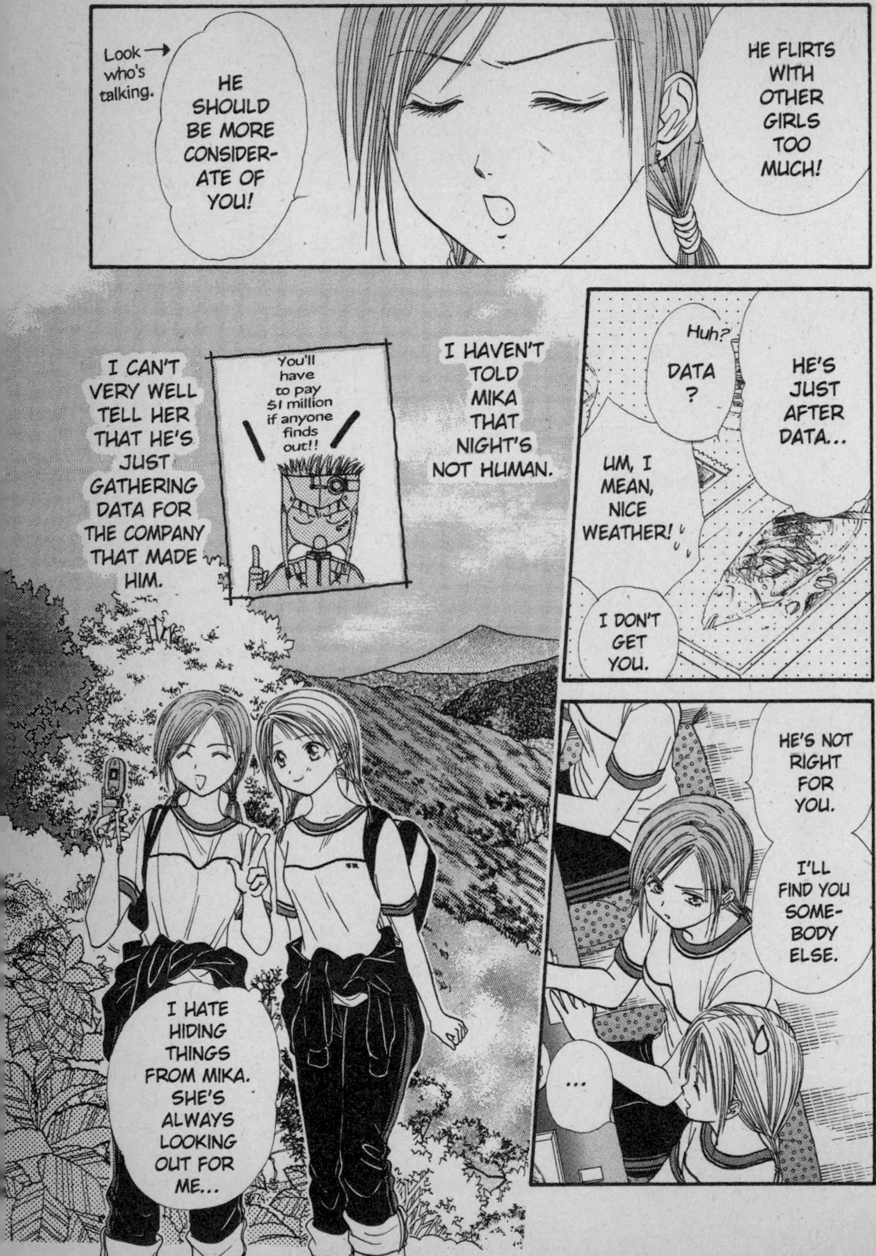
HE FLIRTS WITH OTHER GIRLS TOO MUCH!
HE SHOULD BE MORE CONSIDER-ATE OF YOU!
Look → who's talking.
HE'S JUST AFTER DATA...
Huh?
DATA?
UM, I MEAN, NICE WEATHER!
I DON'T GET YOU.
HE'S NOT RIGHT FOR YOU.
I'LL FIND YOU SOME-BODY ELSE.
...
I HAVEN'T TOLD MIKA THAT NIGHT'S NOT HUMAN.
You'll have to pay $1 million if anyone finds out!!
I CAN'T VERY WELL TELL HER THAT HE'S JUST GATHERING DATA FOR THE COMPANY THAT MADE HIM.
I HATE HIDING THINGS FROM MIKA. SHE'S ALWAYS LOOKING OUT FOR ME...

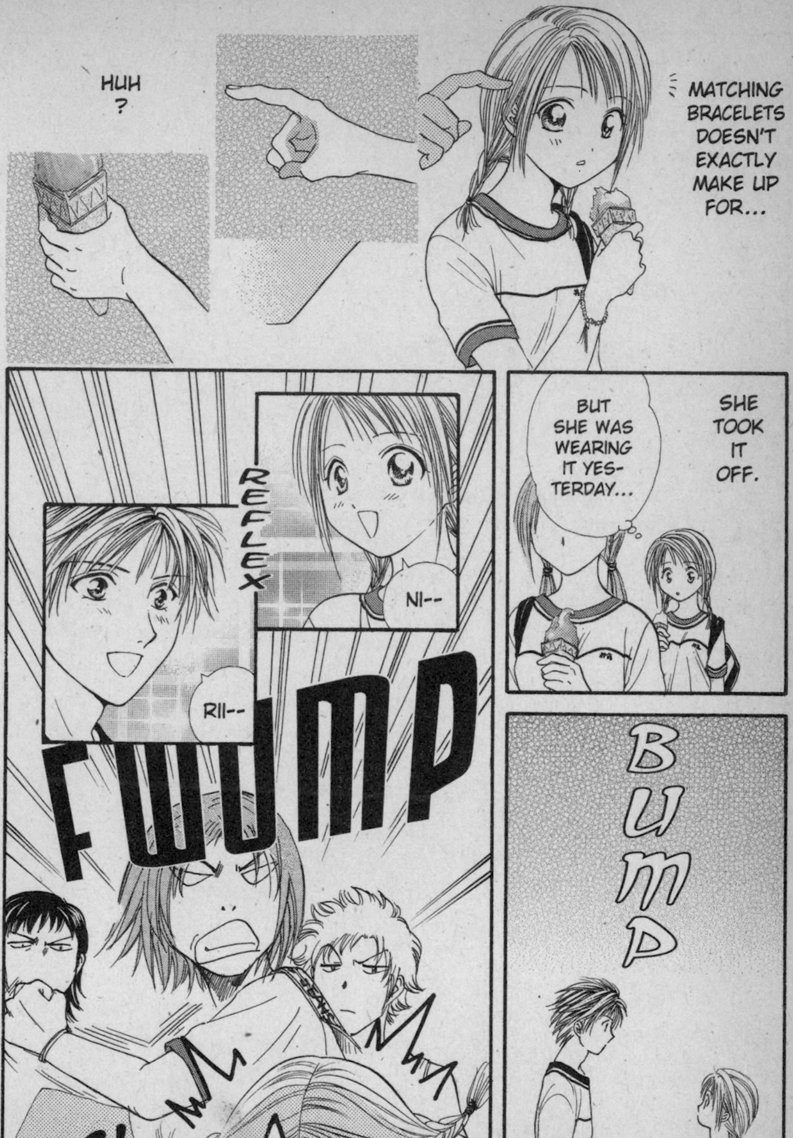
MATCHING BRACELETS DOESN'T EXACTLY MAKE UP FOR...
HUH ?
SHE TOOK IT OFF.
BUT SHE WAS WEARING IT YES-TERDAY...
BUMP
NI--
REFLEX
RII--
FWUMP
OOF!

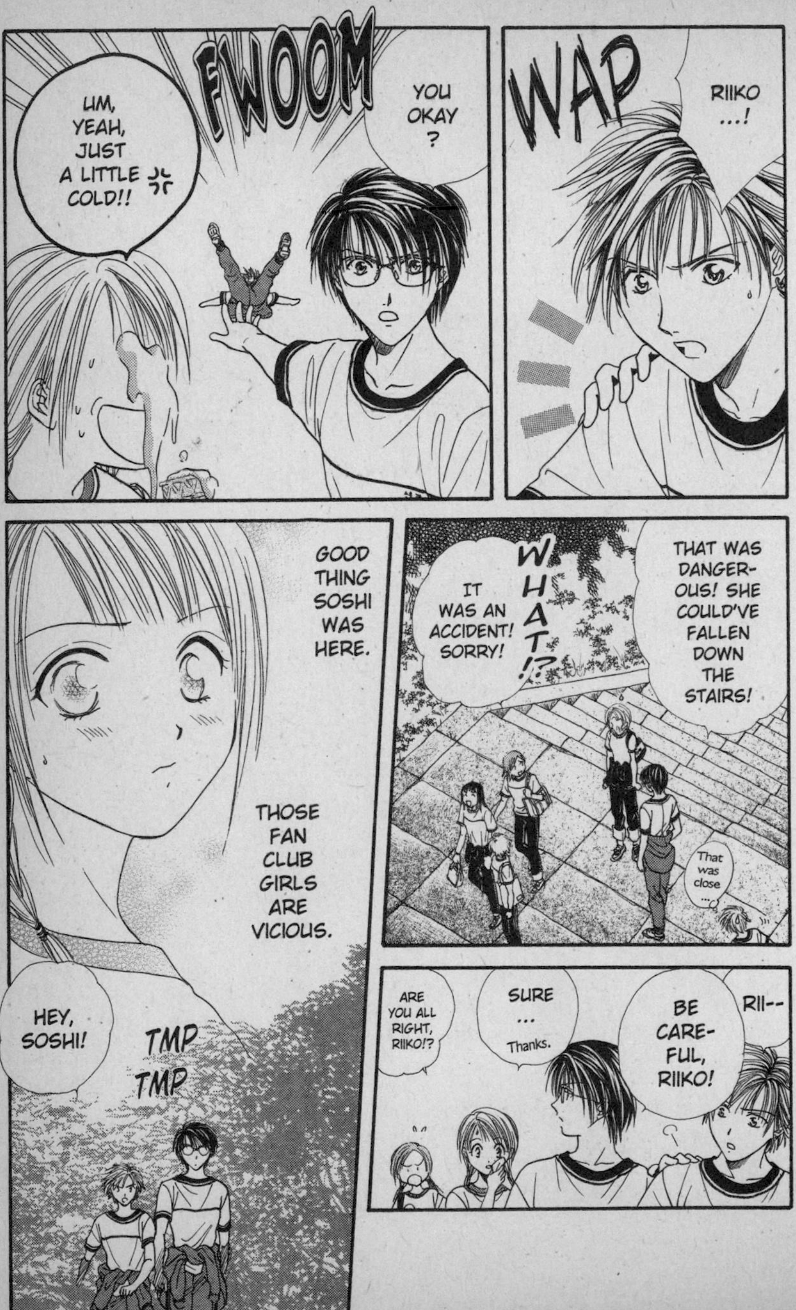
WAP
RIIKO ...!
FWOOM
YOU OKAY ?
UM, YEAH, JUST A LITTLE COLD!!
THAT WAS DANGER-OUS! SHE COULD'VE FALLEN DOWN THE STAIRS!
WHAT!?
IT WAS AN ACCIDENT! SORRY!
That was close ...
RII--
BE CARE-FUL, RIIKO!
SURE ... Thanks.
ARE YOU ALL RIGHT, RIIKO!?
GOOD THING SOSHI WAS HERE.
THOSE FAN CLUB GIRLS ARE VICIOUS.
TMP TMP
HEY, SOSHI!

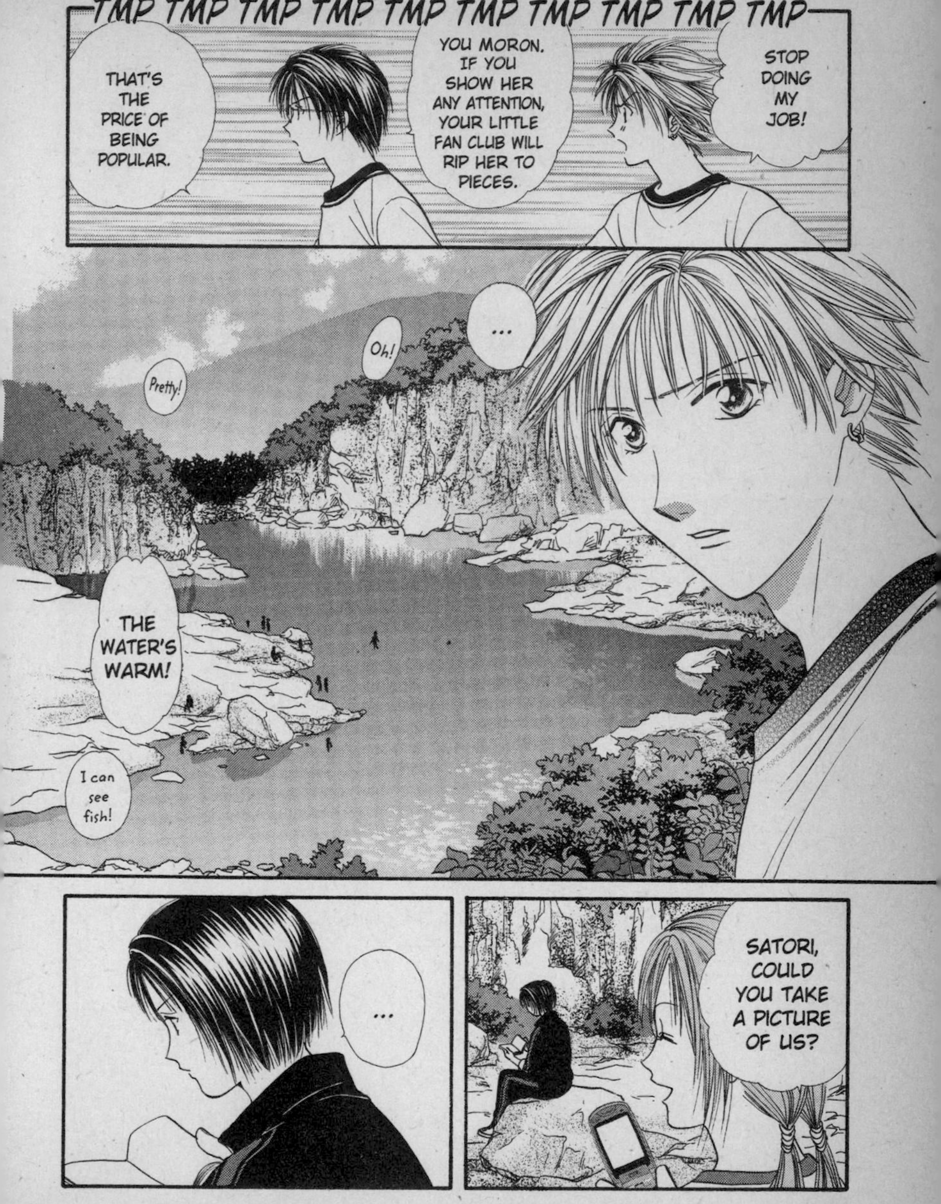
TMP TMP TMP TMP TMP TMP TMP TMP TMP TMP
STOP DOING MY JOB!
YOU MORON. IF YOU SHOW HER ANY ATTENTION, YOUR LITTLE FAN CLUB WILL RIP HER TO PIECES.
THAT'S THE PRICE OF BEING POPULAR.
...
Oh!
Pretty!
THE WATER'S WARM!
I can see fish!
SATORI, COULD YOU TAKE A PICTURE OF US?
...

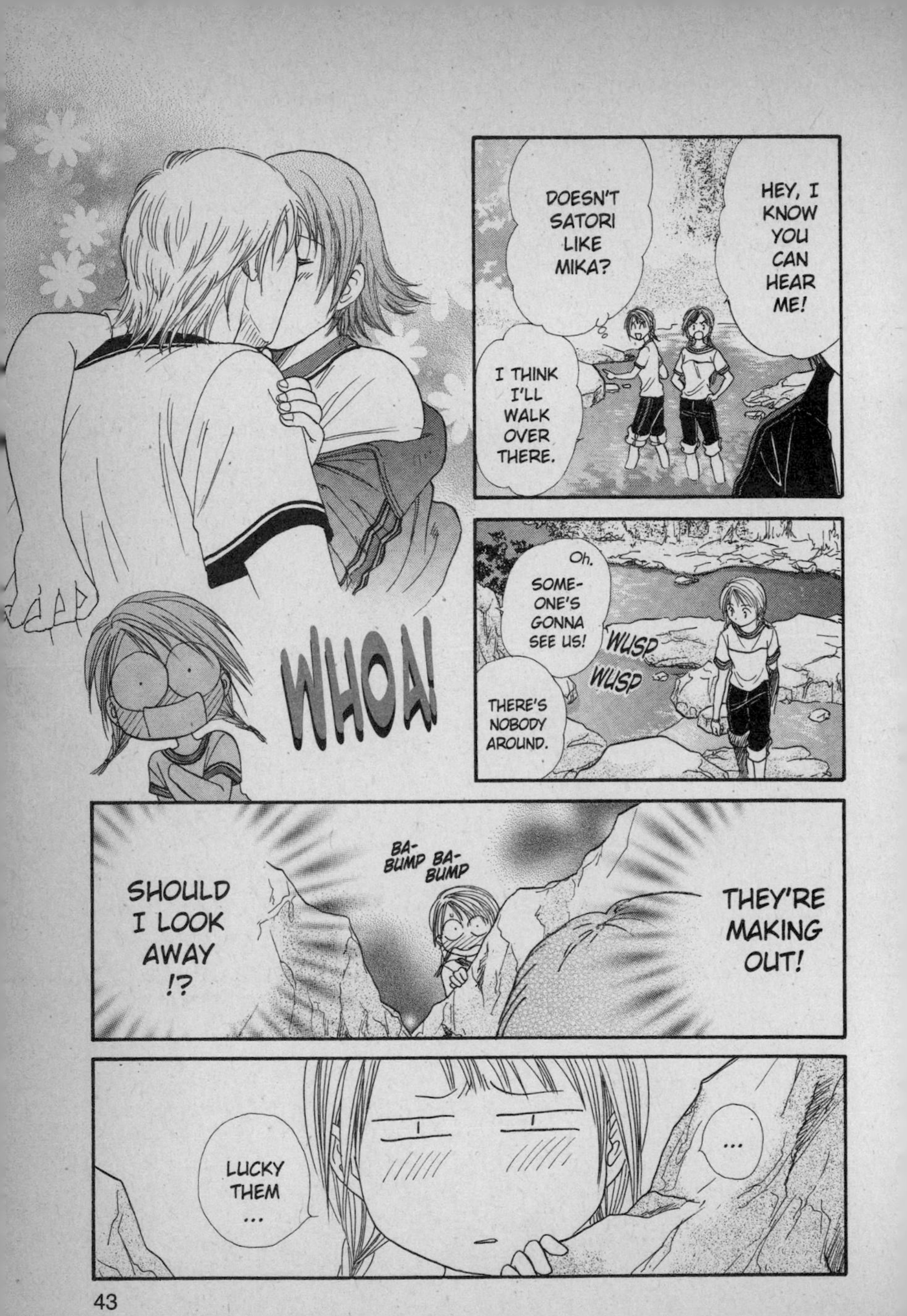
HEY, I KNOW YOU CAN HEAR ME!
DOESN'T SATORI LIKE MIKA?
I THINK I'LL WALK OVER THERE.
Oh.
SOME-ONE'S GONNA SEE US!
WUSP WUSP
THERE'S NOBODY AROUND.
WHOA!
THEY'RE MAKING OUT!
BA-BUMP BA-BUMP
SHOULD I LOOK AWAY !?
...
LUCKY THEM ...

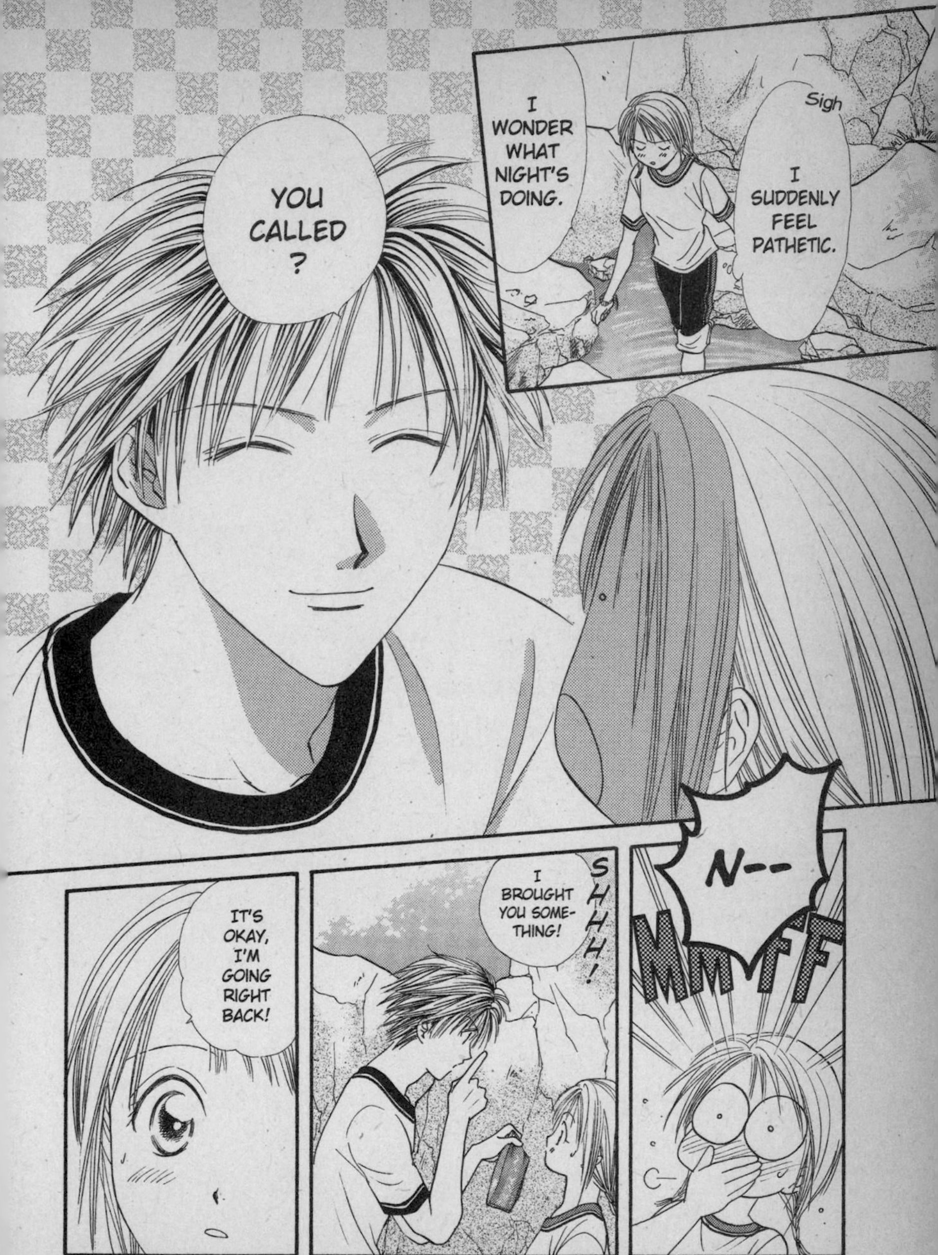
Sigh
I SUDDENLY FEEL PATHETIC.
I WONDER WHAT NIGHT'S DOING.
YOU CALLED?
N--
MMFF
SHHH!
I BROUGHT YOU SOMETHING!
IT'S OKAY, I'M GOING RIGHT BACK!

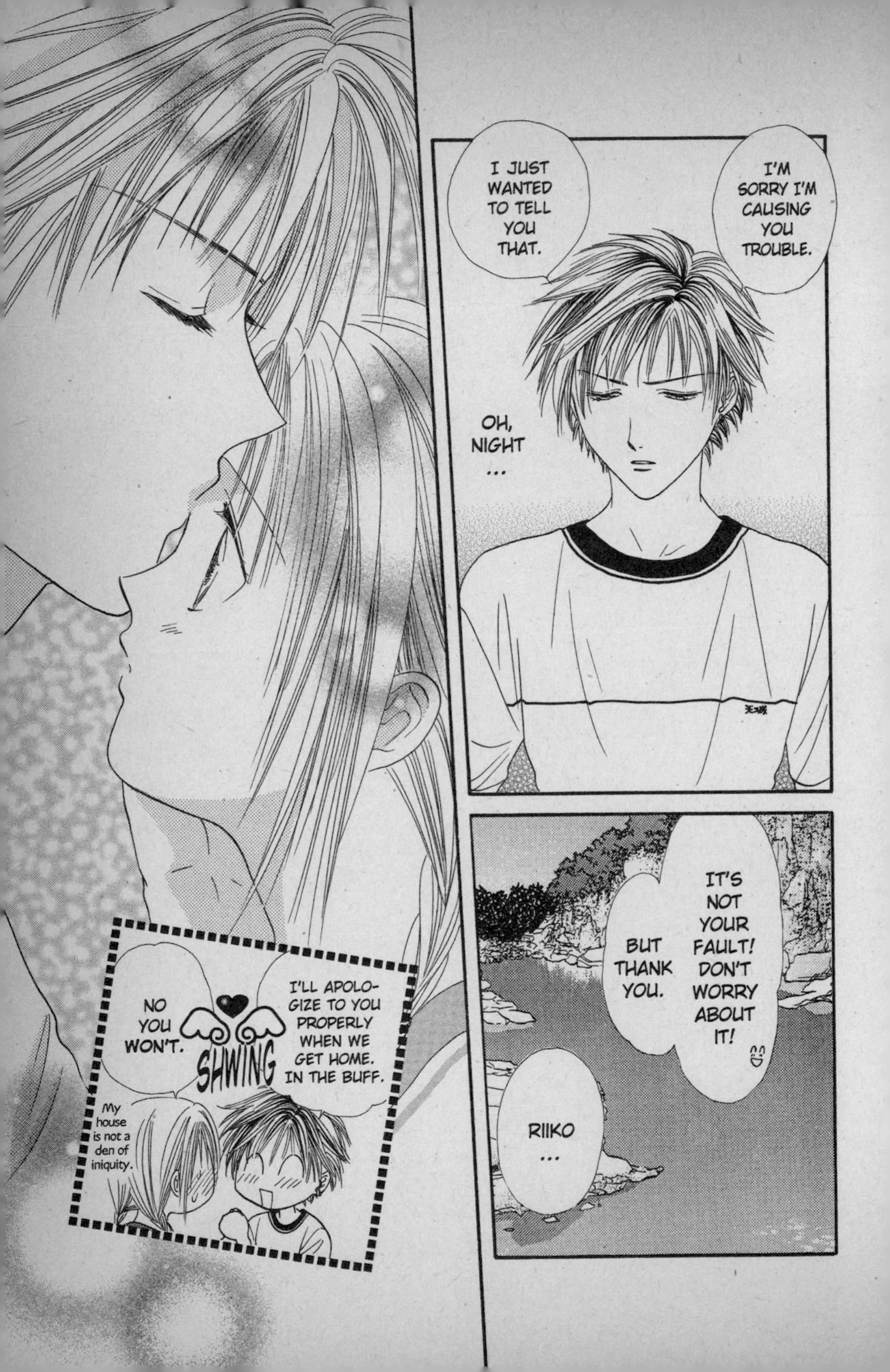
I'M SORRY I'M CAUSING YOU TROUBLE.
I JUST WANTED TO TELL YOU THAT.
OH, NIGHT ...
IT'S NOT YOUR FAULT! DON'T WORRY ABOUT IT!
BUT THANK YOU.
RIIKO ...
I'LL APOLOGIZE TO YOU PROPERLY WHEN WE GET HOME. IN THE BUFF.
SHWING
NO YOU WON'T.
My house is not a den of iniquity.

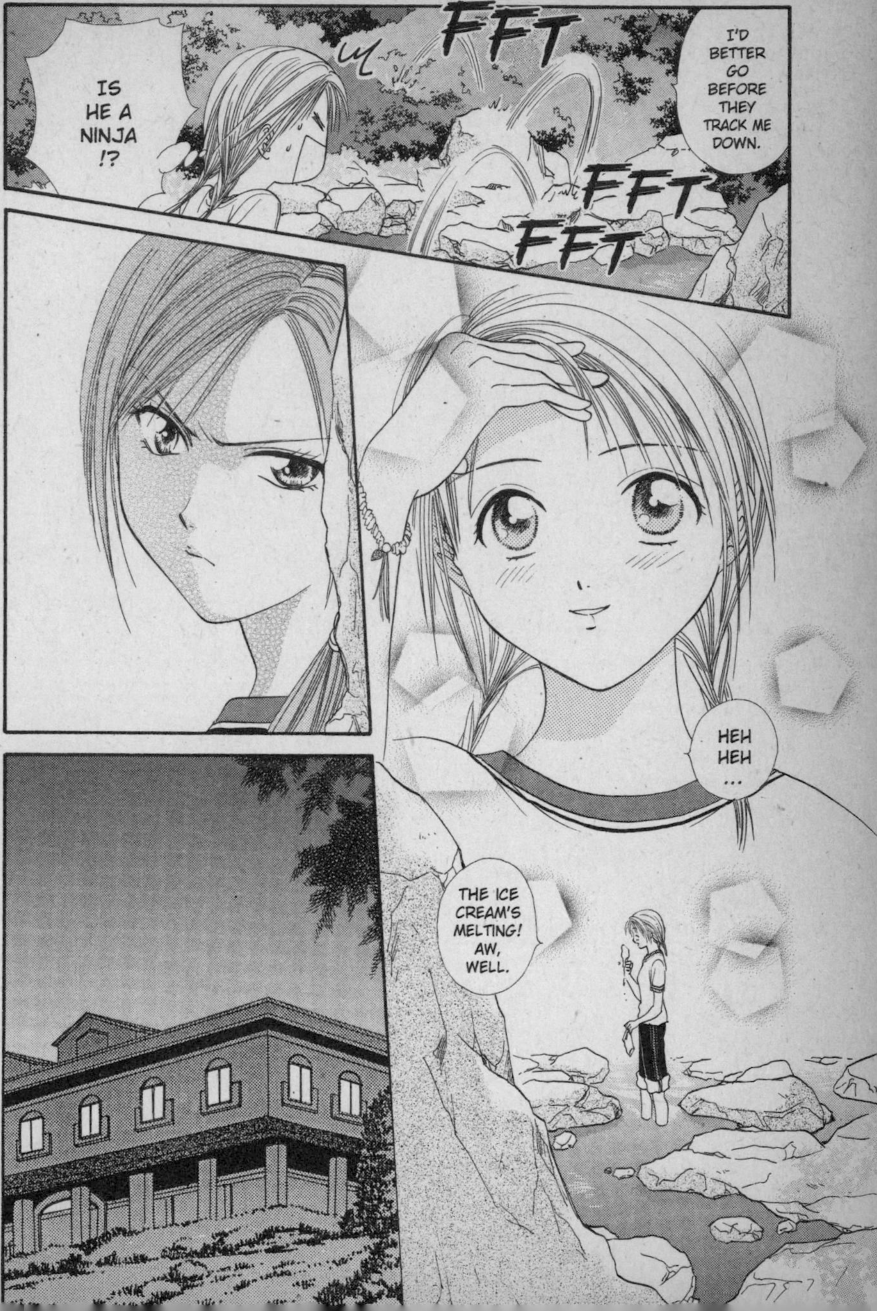
I'D BETTER GO BEFORE THEY TRACK ME DOWN.
FFT
FFT
FFT
IS HE A NINJA!?
HEH HEH...
THE ICE CREAM'S MELTING! AW, WELL.

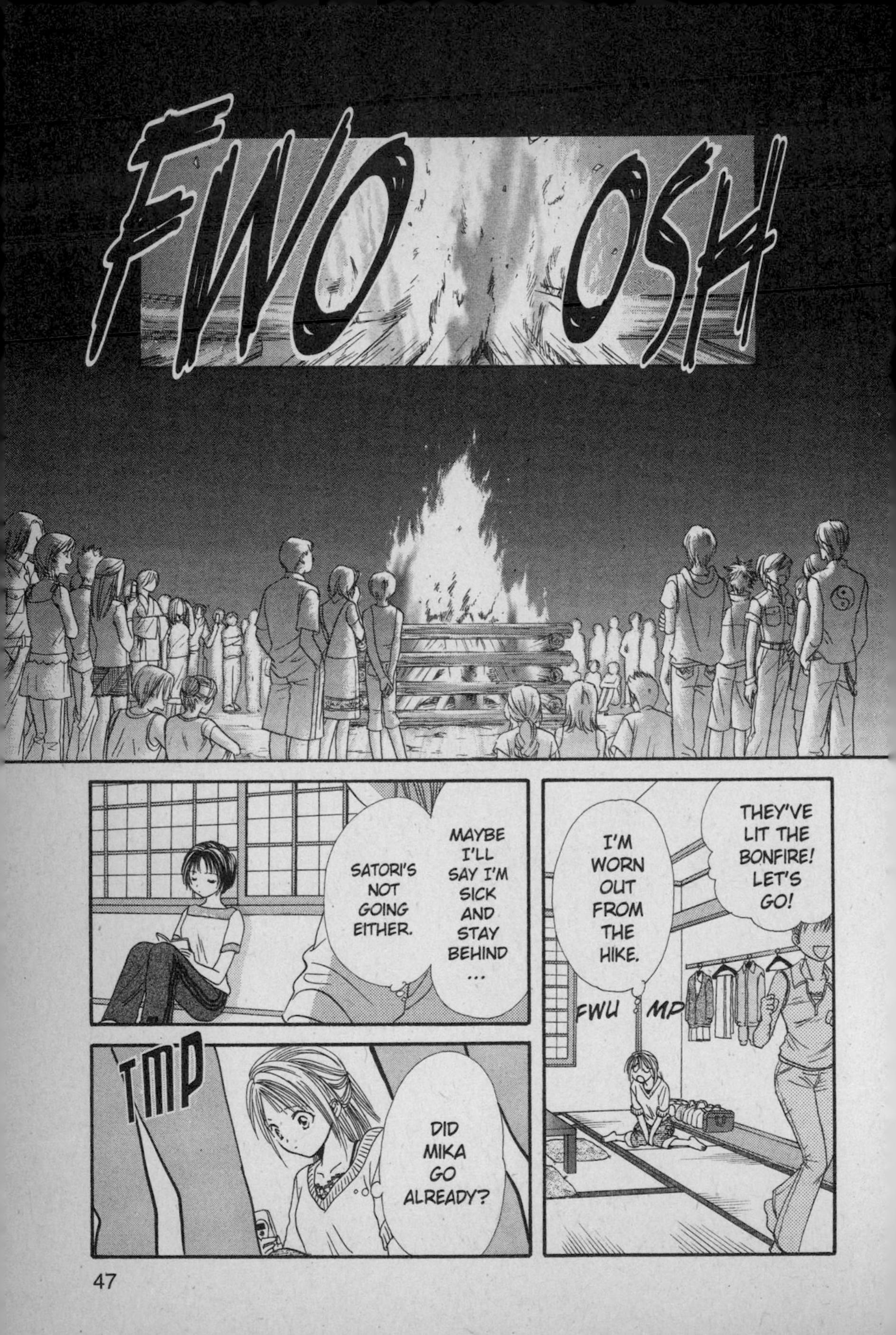
FWOOSH
THEY'VE LIT THE BONFIRE! LET'S GO!
I'M WORN OUT FROM THE HIKE.
FWUMP
MAYBE I'LL SAY I'M SICK AND STAY BEHIND...
SATORI'S NOT GOING EITHER.
TMP
DID MIKA GO ALREADY?

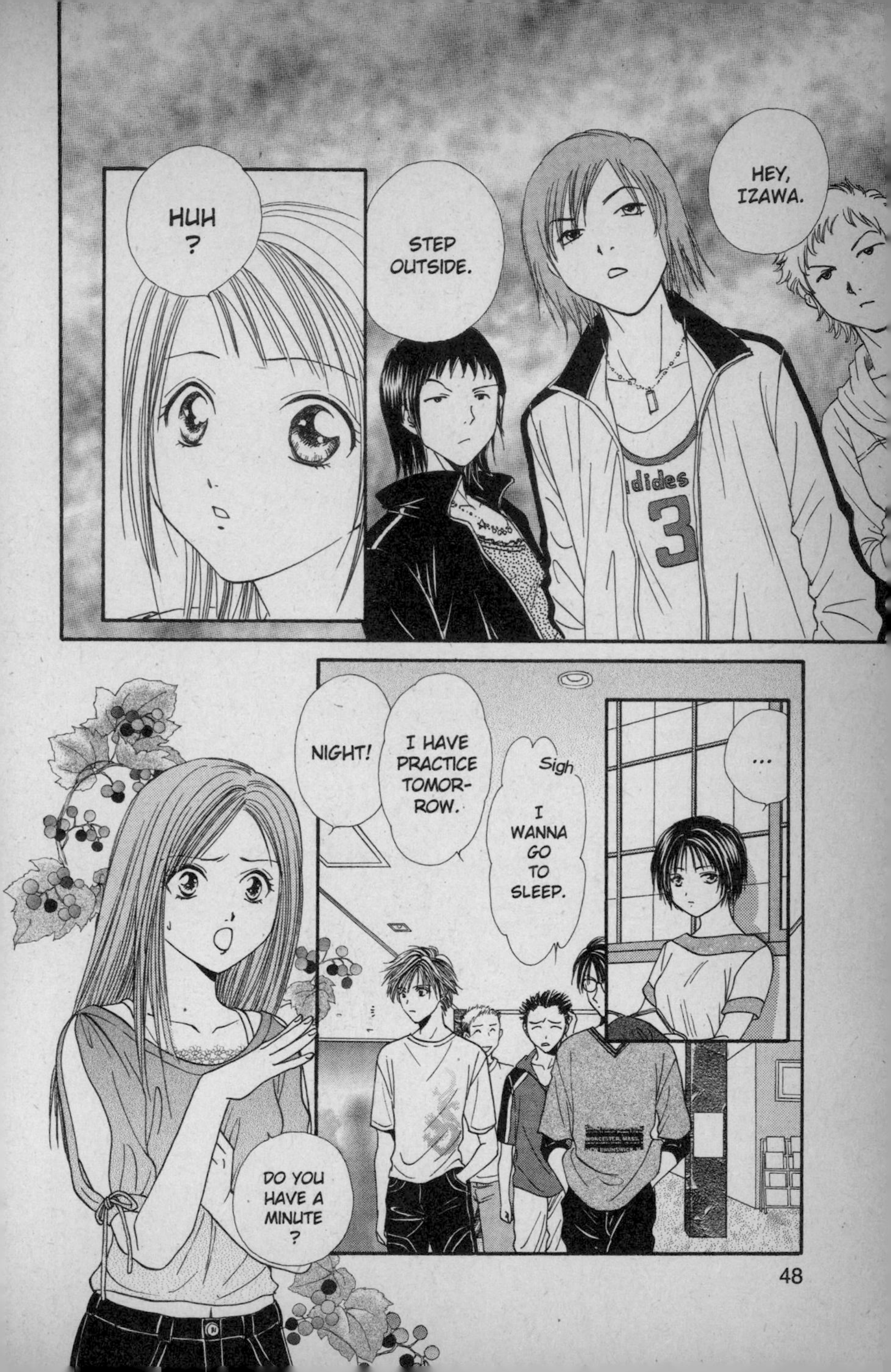
HEY, IZAWA.
STEP OUTSIDE.
HUH ?
...
Sigh
I WANNA GO TO SLEEP.
I HAVE PRACTICE TOMOR-ROW.
NIGHT!
DO YOU HAVE A MINUTE ?

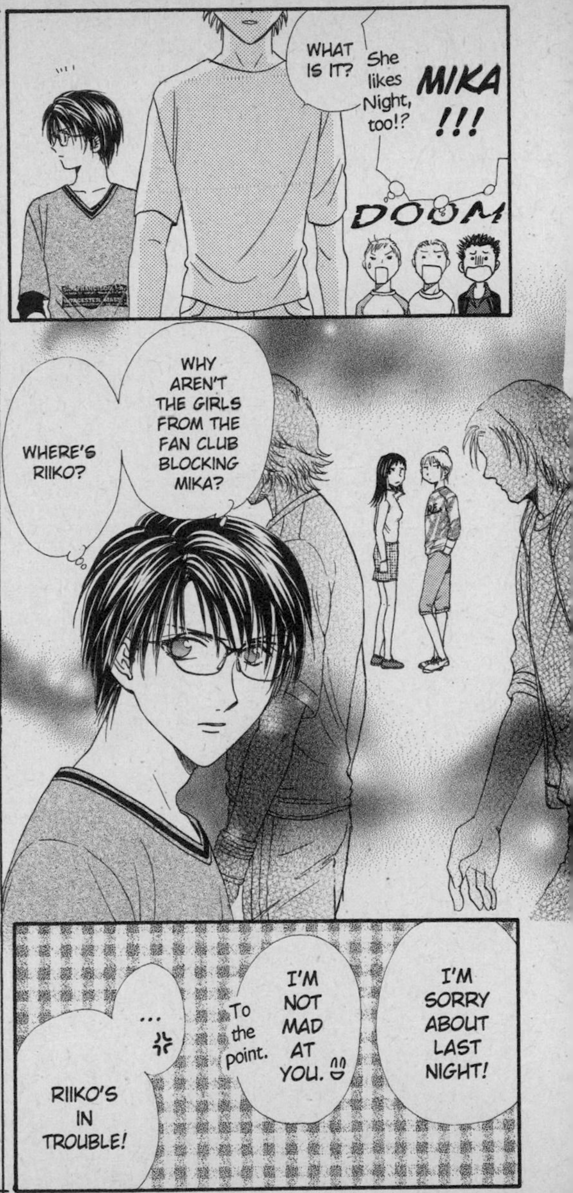

MIKA !!!
She likes Night, too!?
WHAT IS IT?
DOOM
WHY AREN'T THE GIRLS FROM THE FAN CLUB BLOCKING MIKA?
WHERE'S RIIKO?
I'M SORRY ABOUT LAST NIGHT!
I'M NOT MAD AT YOU.
To the point.
...
RIIKO'S IN TROUBLE!

I'm going to do an autograph tour in Taiwan in January '04. The last time I was there, I didn't take many pictures. Well, I took pictures for research but no personal ones to show my family and stuff. My schedule's so full. Anyway, Taiwan's not far from Japan.

So Soshi made the cover of volume 2. When will the protagonist get her own cover?

Glasses: there sure are a lot of people who like guys in glasses. I don't go totally ga-ga over them, but I get it. Well, the guy would still have to be good-looking (smile). I've never had to wear glasses myself. I had 20/10 vision in both eyes back in high school. Even now, hunched over my desk all the time, I have eyesight that's pretty good. I think they're 20/16 or 20/20 right now... I'm not sure.

I'm dreading old age and farsightedness.

All of my assistants have bad eyesight. Two of them wear glasses. I think most of my friends do too. Actually, most people seem to have bad eyesight! Why? A lot of people wear contacts, so you can't tell a lot of the time. Is that why they like guys in glasses? (Probably not.)

I've always wondered why some guys have a fetish for girls in glasses. Is it because they look intellectual? It's a mystery to me, just like that fetish for girls with cat ears. A passing fancy is okay, but when it becomes a fetish... Someone please tell me what's so great about them. I'd really like to know (smile). Although I think I'd be weirded out if someone were to go on and on about it. But I do think good-looking people can look great in glasses.

Glasses are a fashion statement on them.

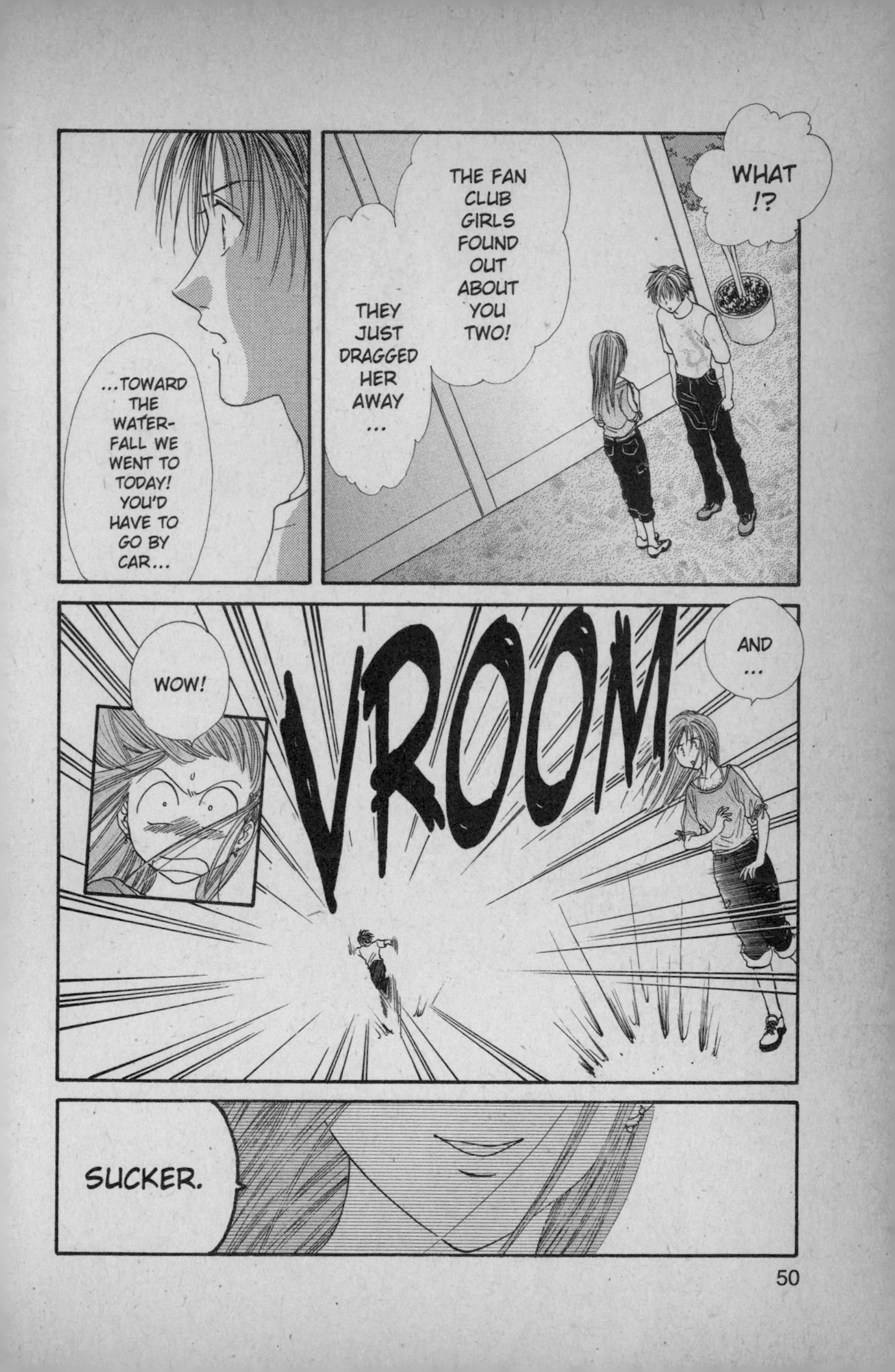
WHAT !?
THE FAN CLUB GIRLS FOUND OUT ABOUT YOU TWO!
THEY JUST DRAGGED HER AWAY ...
...TOWARD THE WATER-FALL WE WENT TO TODAY! YOU'D HAVE TO GO BY CAR...
AND ...
VROOM
WOW!
SUCKER.

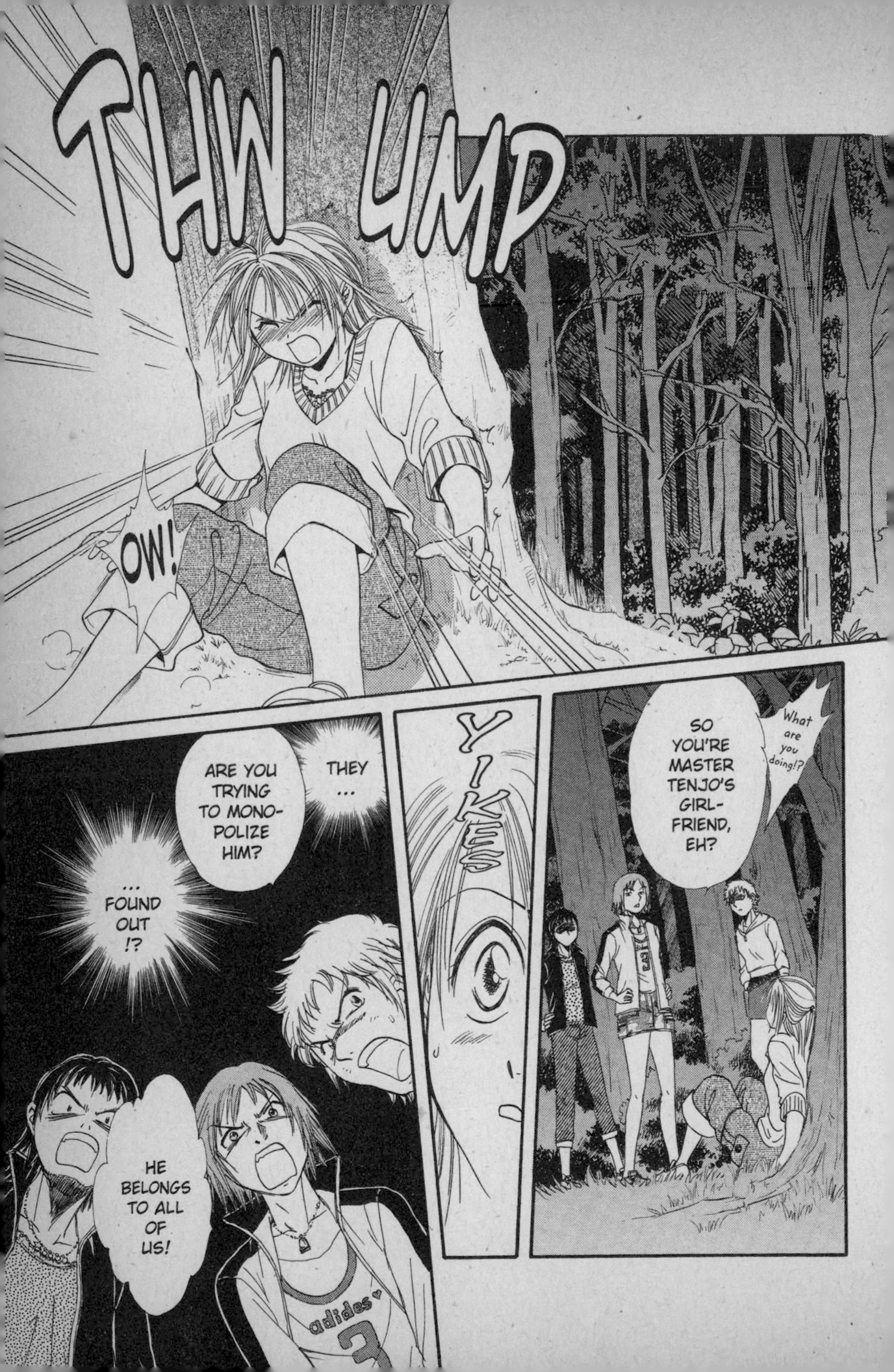
THWUMP
OW!
What are you doing!?
SO YOU'RE MASTER TENJO'S GIRL-FRIEND, EH?
YIKES
THEY ...
ARE YOU TRYING TO MONO-POLIZE HIM?
... FOUND OUT !?
HE BELONGS TO ALL OF US!

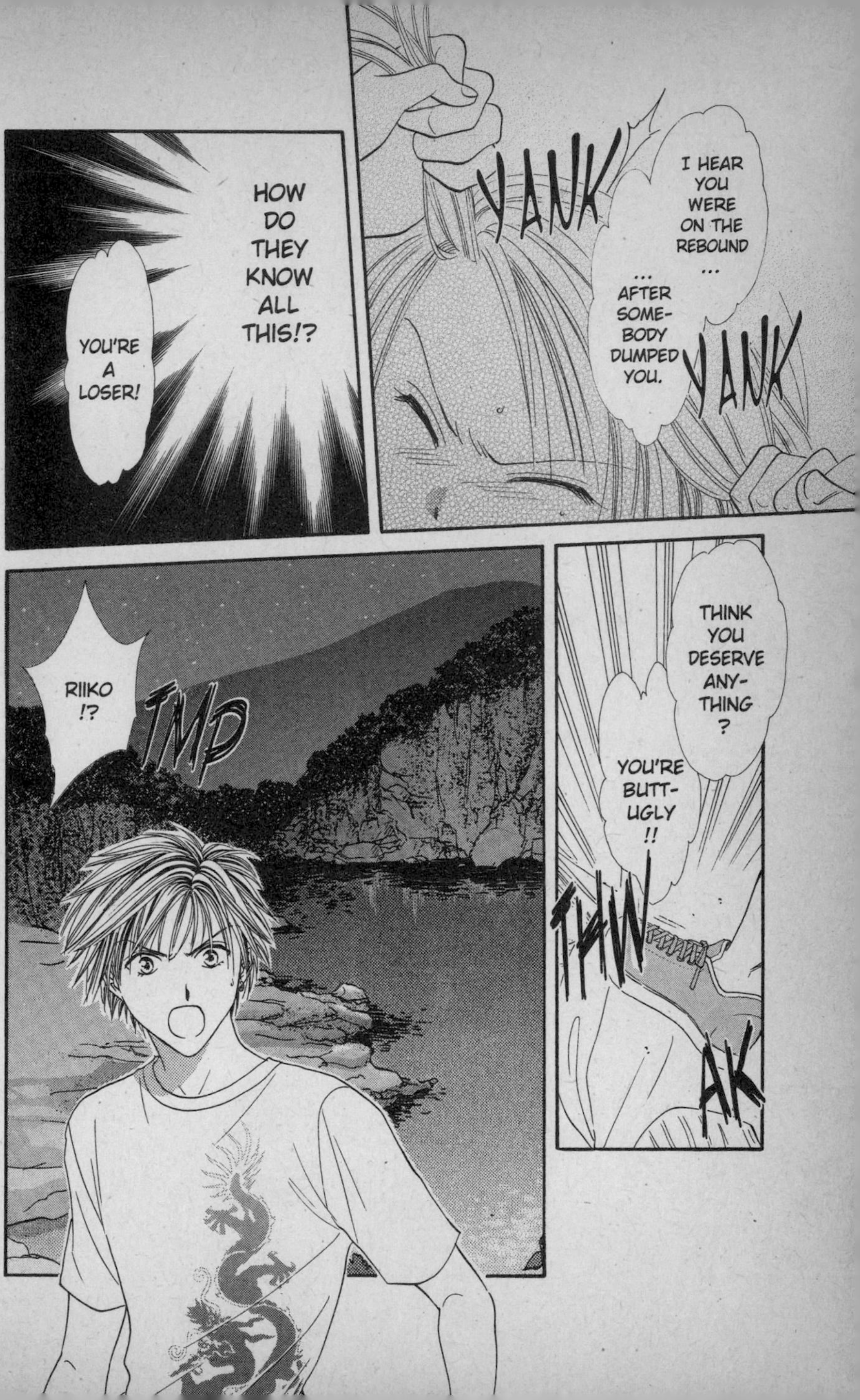
YANK
I HEAR YOU WERE ON THE REBOUND...
...AFTER SOMEBODY DUMPED YOU.
YANK
HOW DO THEY KNOW ALL THIS!?
YOU'RE A LOSER!
THINK YOU DESERVE ANYTHING?
YOU'RE BUTT-UGLY!!
THWAK
RIIKO!?
TMP

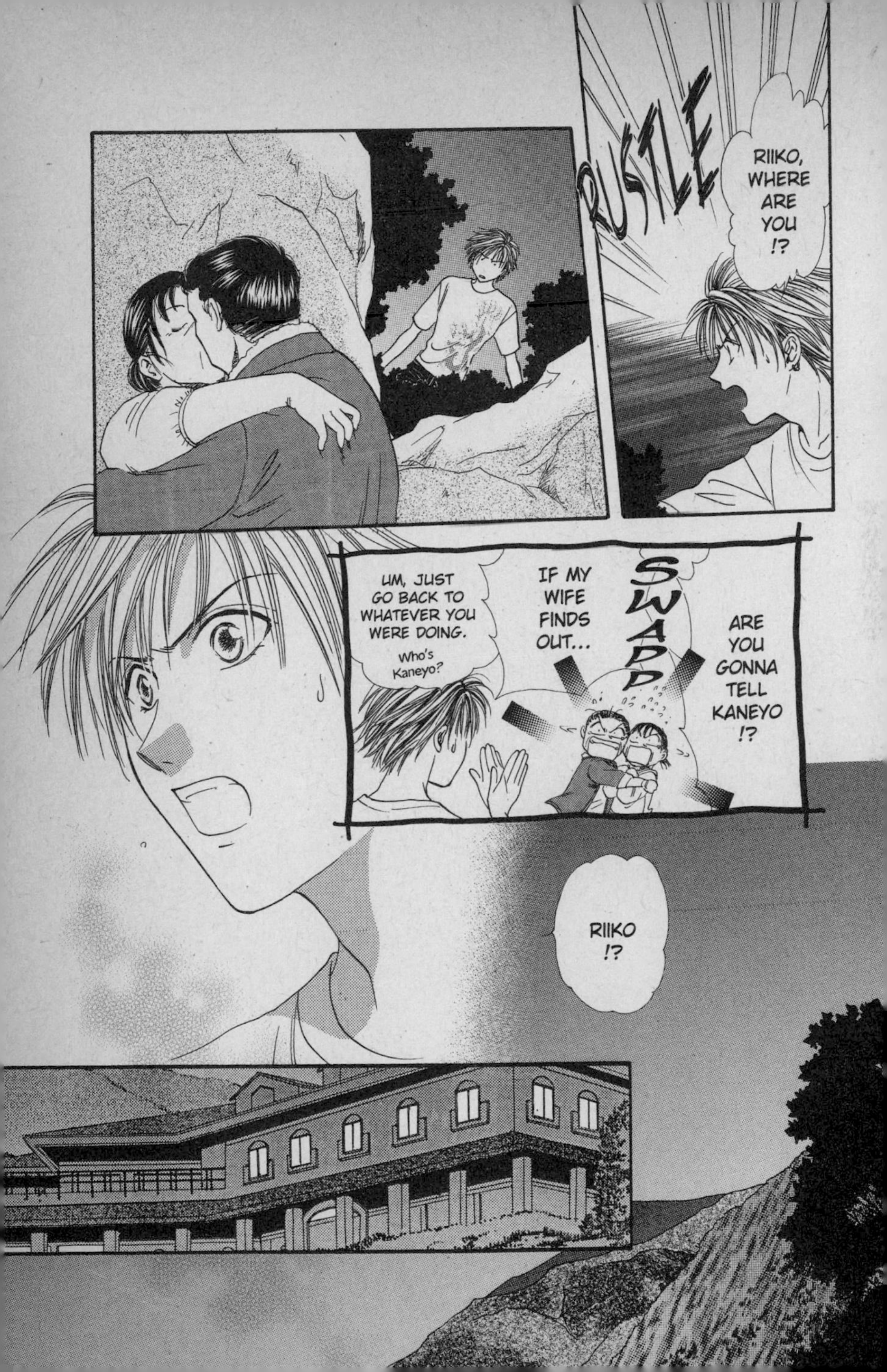
RUSTLE
RIIKO, WHERE ARE YOU !?
ARE YOU GONNA TELL KANEYO !?
SWAPP
IF MY WIFE FINDS OUT...
UM, JUST GO BACK TO WHATEVER YOU WERE DOING.
Who's Kaneyo?
RIIKO !?

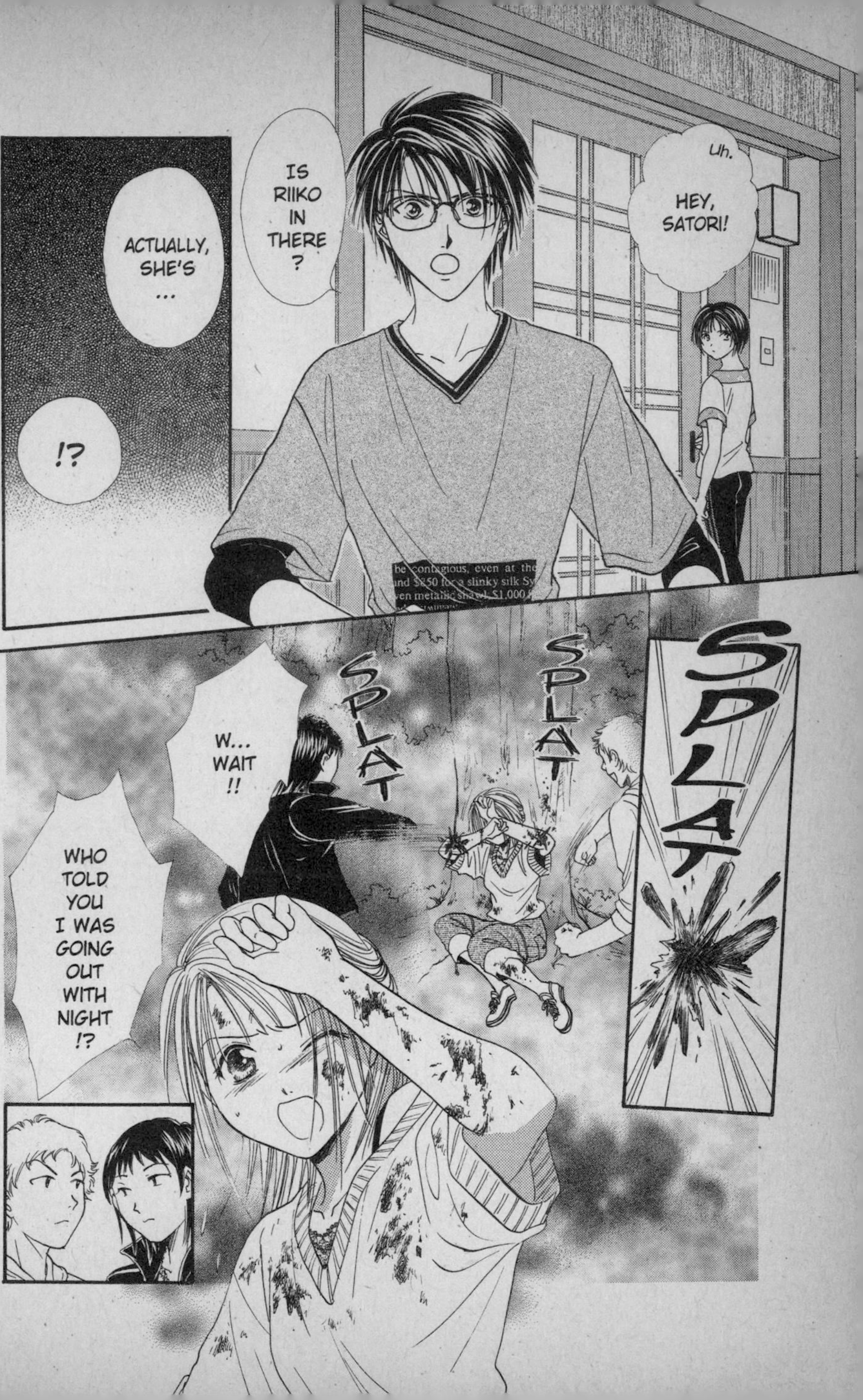
Uh.
HEY, SATORI!
IS RIIKO IN THERE?
ACTUALLY, SHE'S ...
!?
SPLAT
SPLAT
SPLAT
W... WAIT!!
WHO TOLD YOU I WAS GOING OUT WITH NIGHT!?

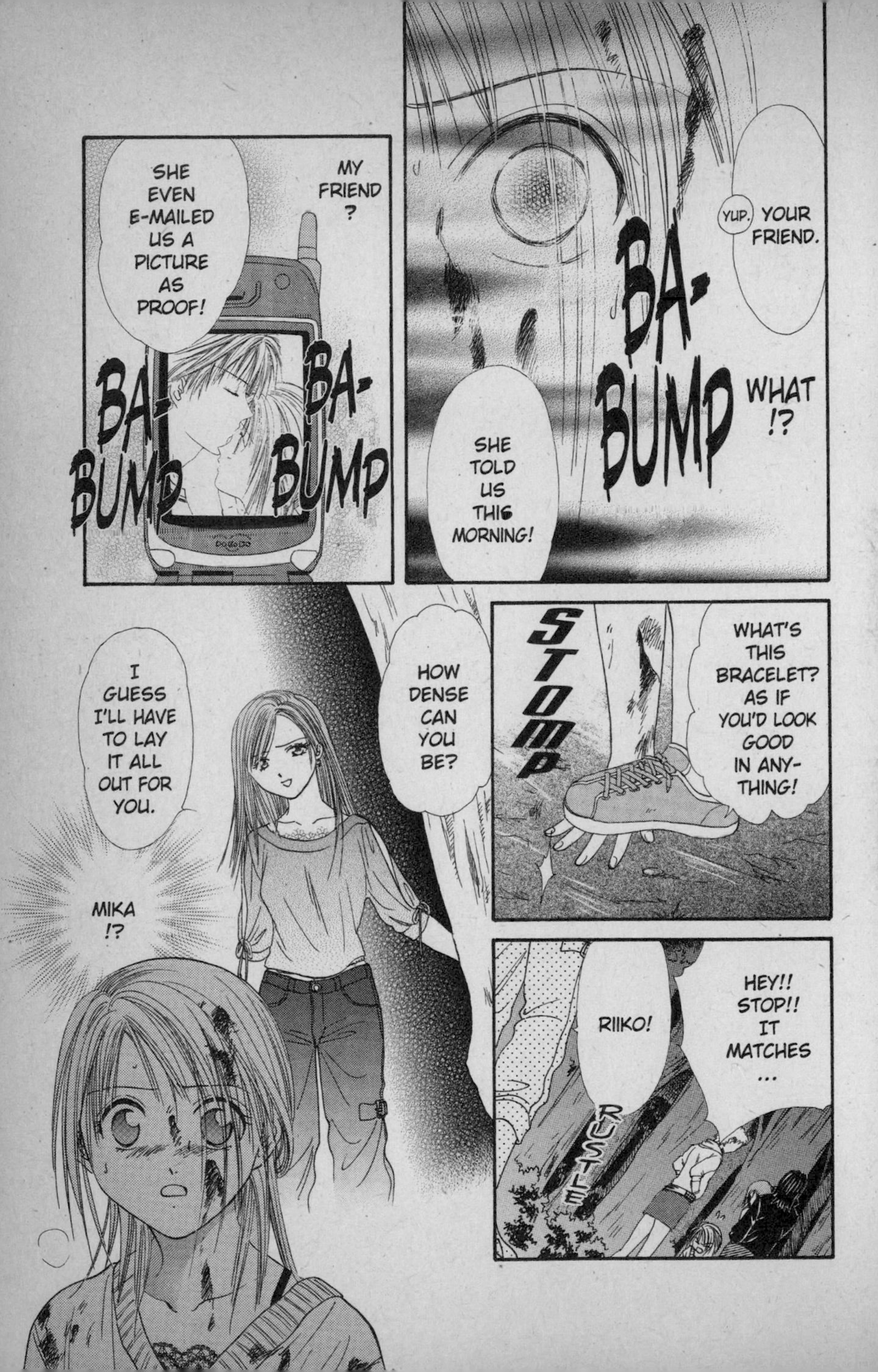
YUP.
YOUR FRIEND.
WHAT !?
BA-BUMP
SHE TOLD US THIS MORNING!
MY FRIEND ?
SHE EVEN E-MAILED US A PICTURE AS PROOF!
BA-BUMP
BA-BUMP
WHAT'S THIS BRACELET? AS IF YOU'D LOOK GOOD IN ANY-THING!
STOMP
HEY!! STOP!! IT MATCHES ...
RIIKO!
RUSTLE
HOW DENSE CAN YOU BE?
I GUESS I'LL HAVE TO LAY IT ALL OUT FOR YOU.
MIKA !?

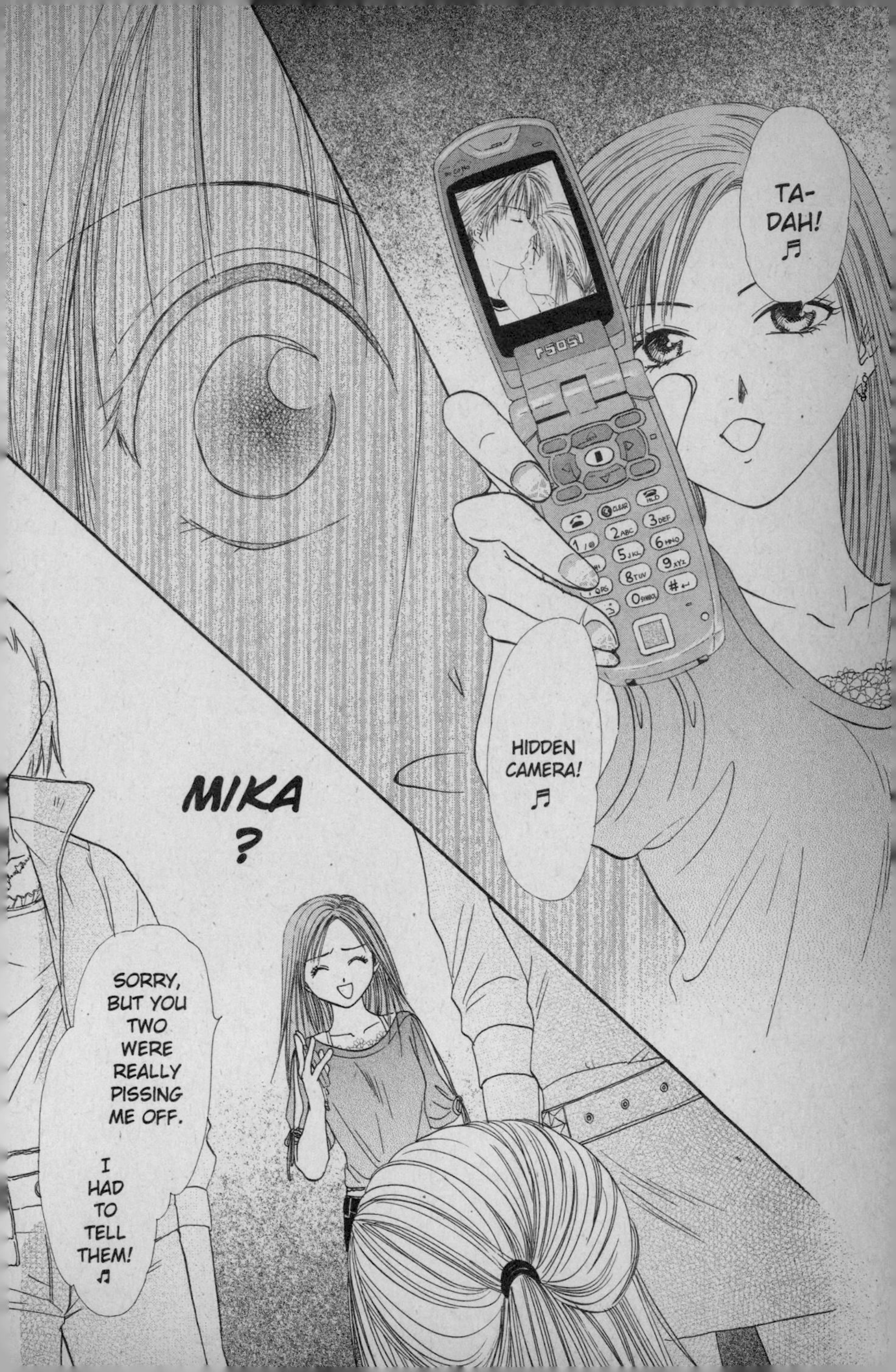
TA-DAH! ♫
HIDDEN CAMERA! ♫
MIKA?
SORRY, BUT YOU TWO WERE REALLY PISSING ME OFF.
I HAD TO TELL THEM! ♫

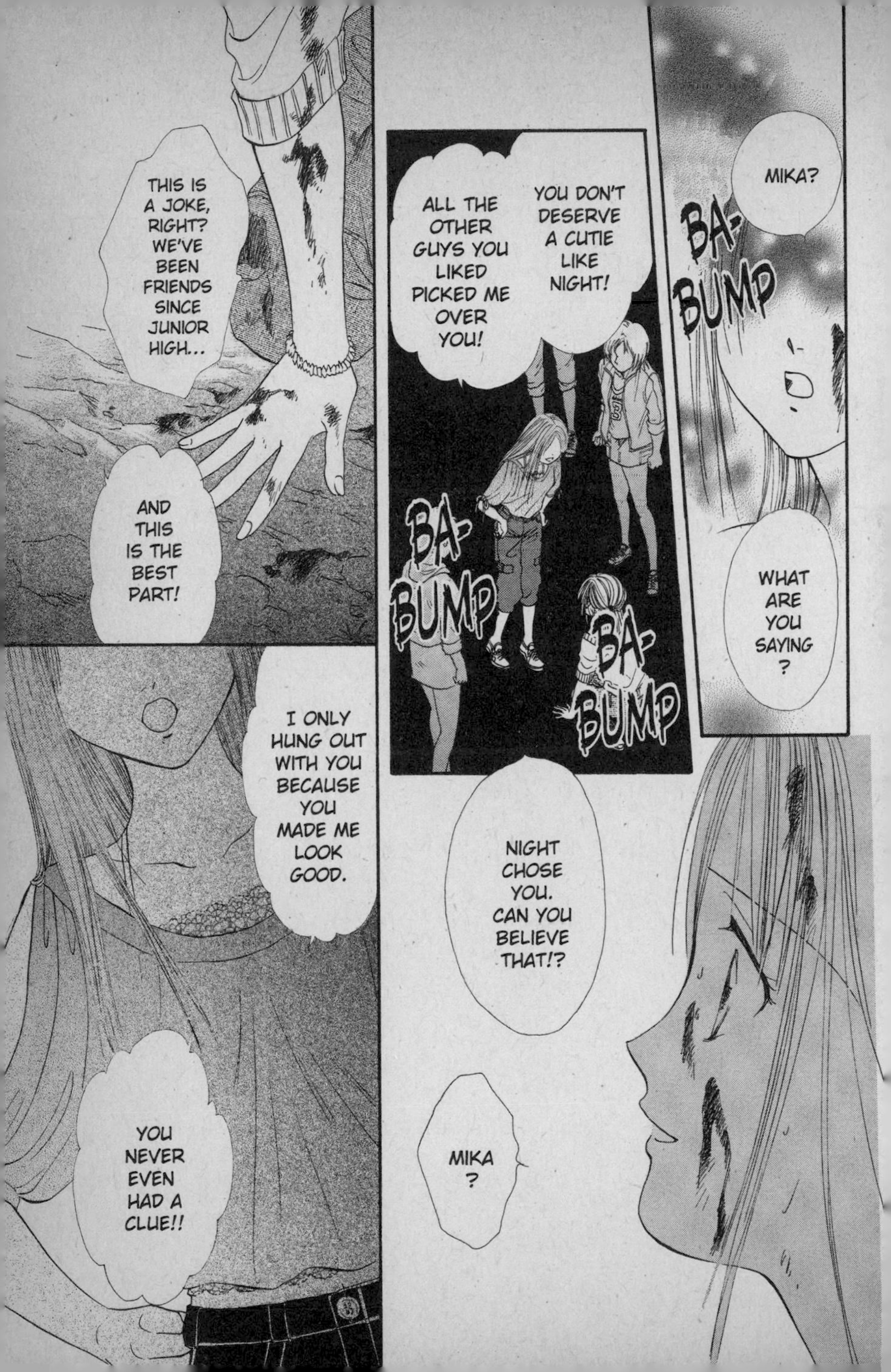
MIKA?
BA-BUMP
WHAT ARE YOU SAYING?
YOU DON'T DESERVE A CUTIE LIKE NIGHT!
ALL THE OTHER GUYS YOU LIKED PICKED ME OVER YOU!
BA-BUMP
BA-BUMP
BA-BUMP
NIGHT CHOSE YOU. CAN YOU BELIEVE THAT!?
MIKA?
THIS IS A JOKE, RIGHT? WE'VE BEEN FRIENDS SINCE JUNIOR HIGH...
AND THIS IS THE BEST PART!
I ONLY HUNG OUT WITH YOU BECAUSE YOU MADE ME LOOK GOOD.
YOU NEVER EVEN HAD A CLUE!!

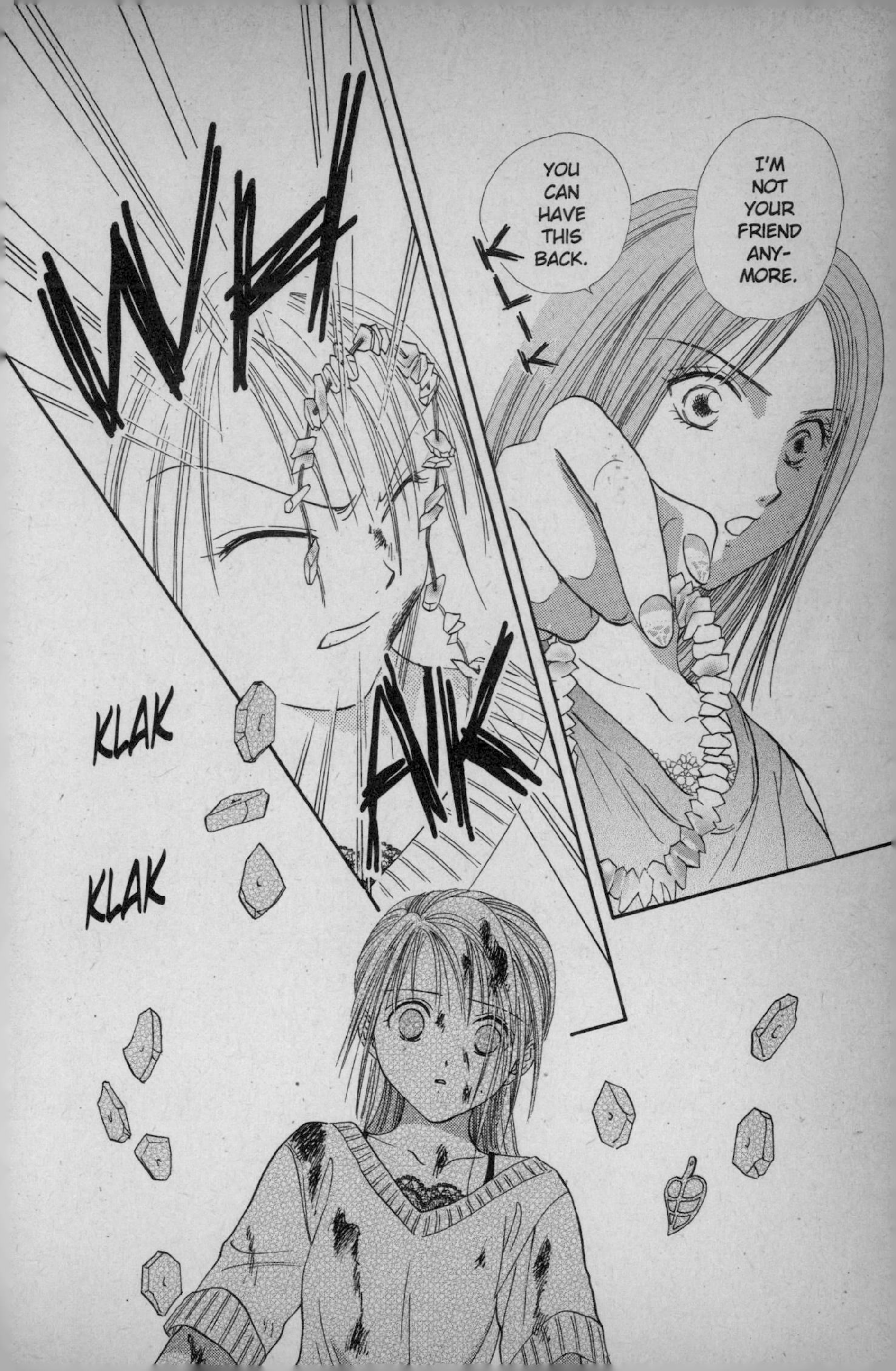
I'M NOT YOUR FRIEND ANY-MORE.
YOU CAN HAVE THIS BACK.
KLIK
WH
AK
KLAK
KLAK

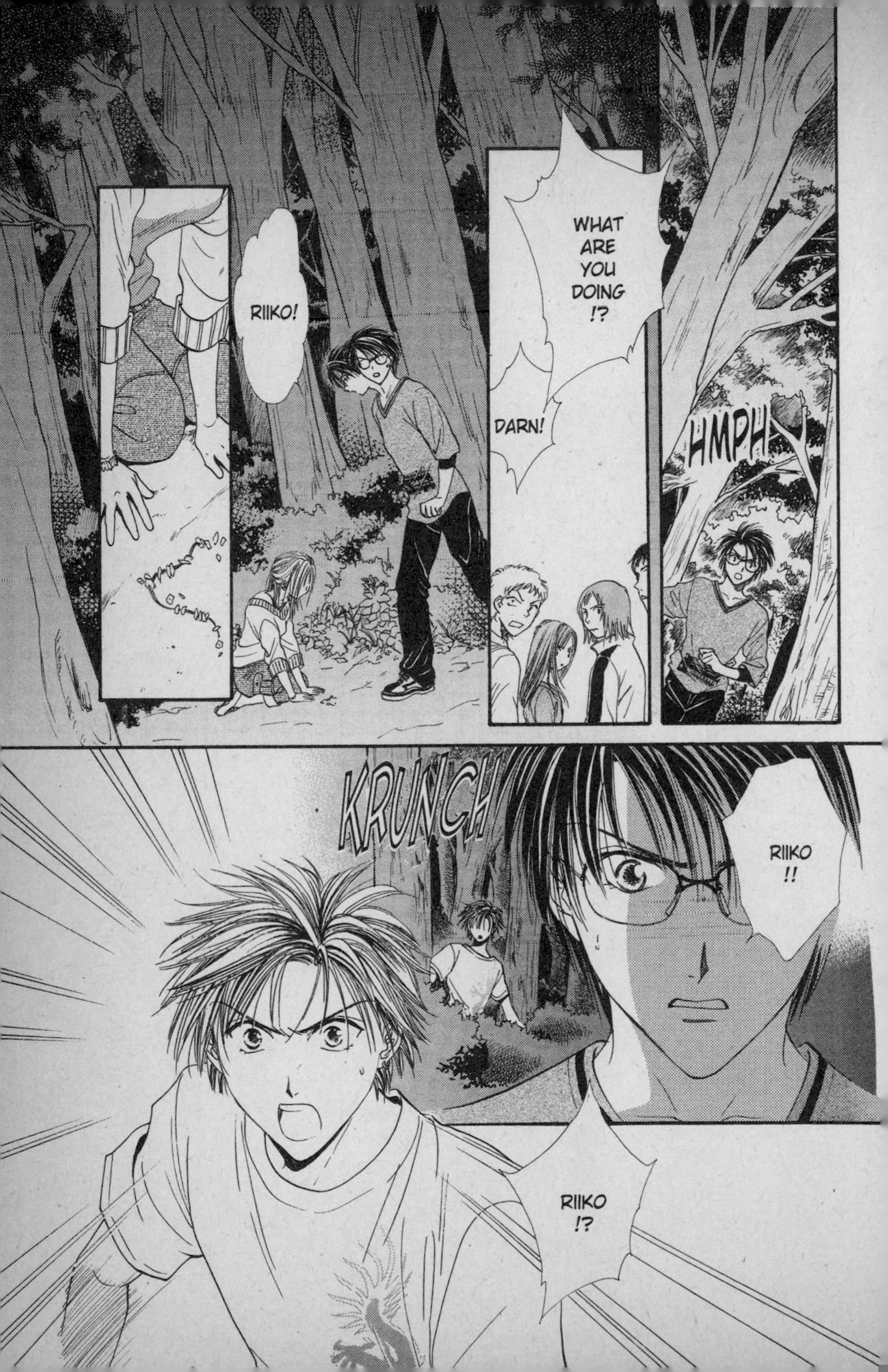
HMPH
WHAT ARE YOU DOING !?
DARN!
RIIKO!
KRUNCH
RIIKO !!
RIIKO !?

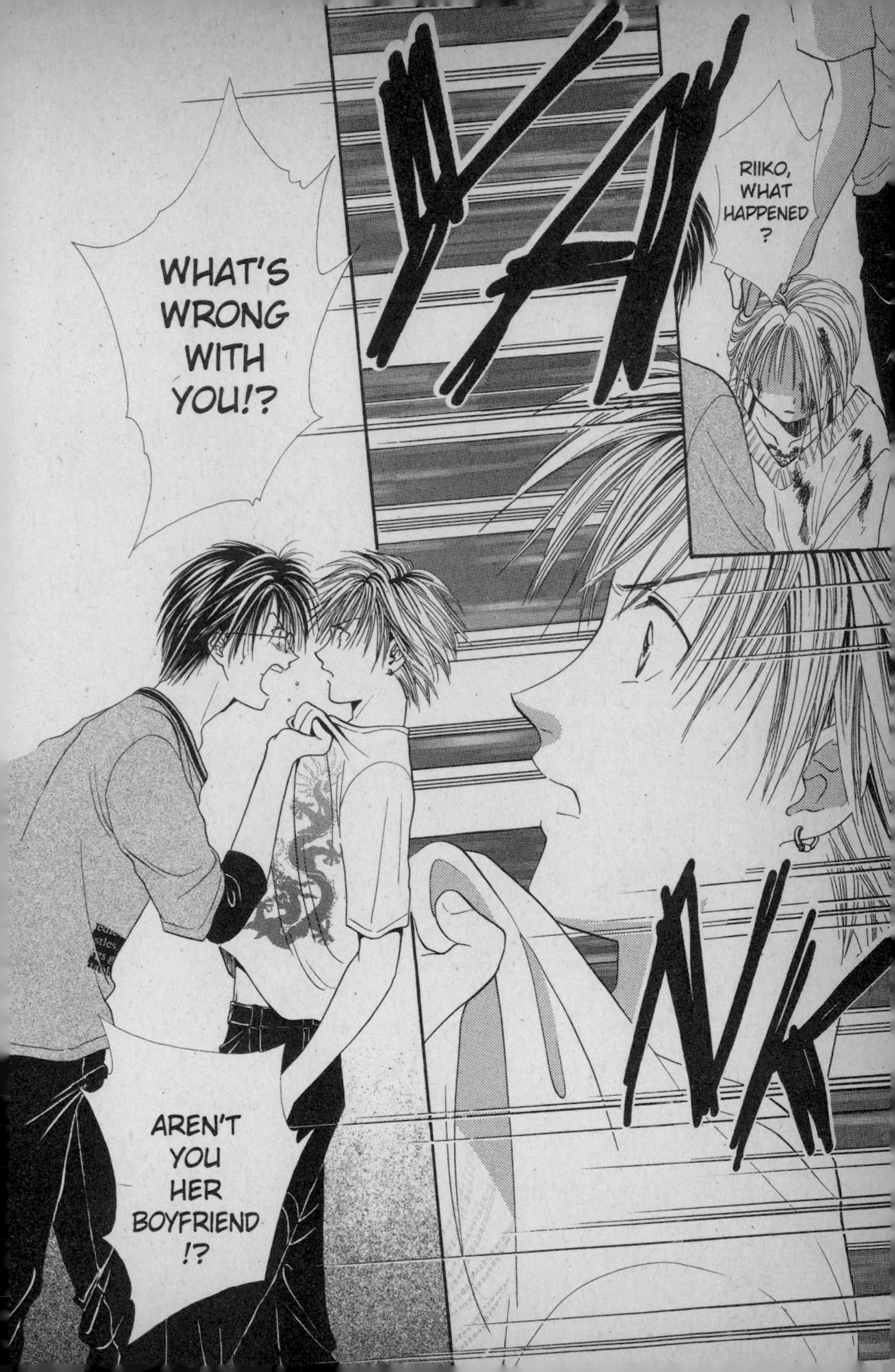
RIIKO, WHAT HAPPENED ?
WHAT'S WRONG WITH YOU!?
AREN'T YOU HER BOYFRIEND !?

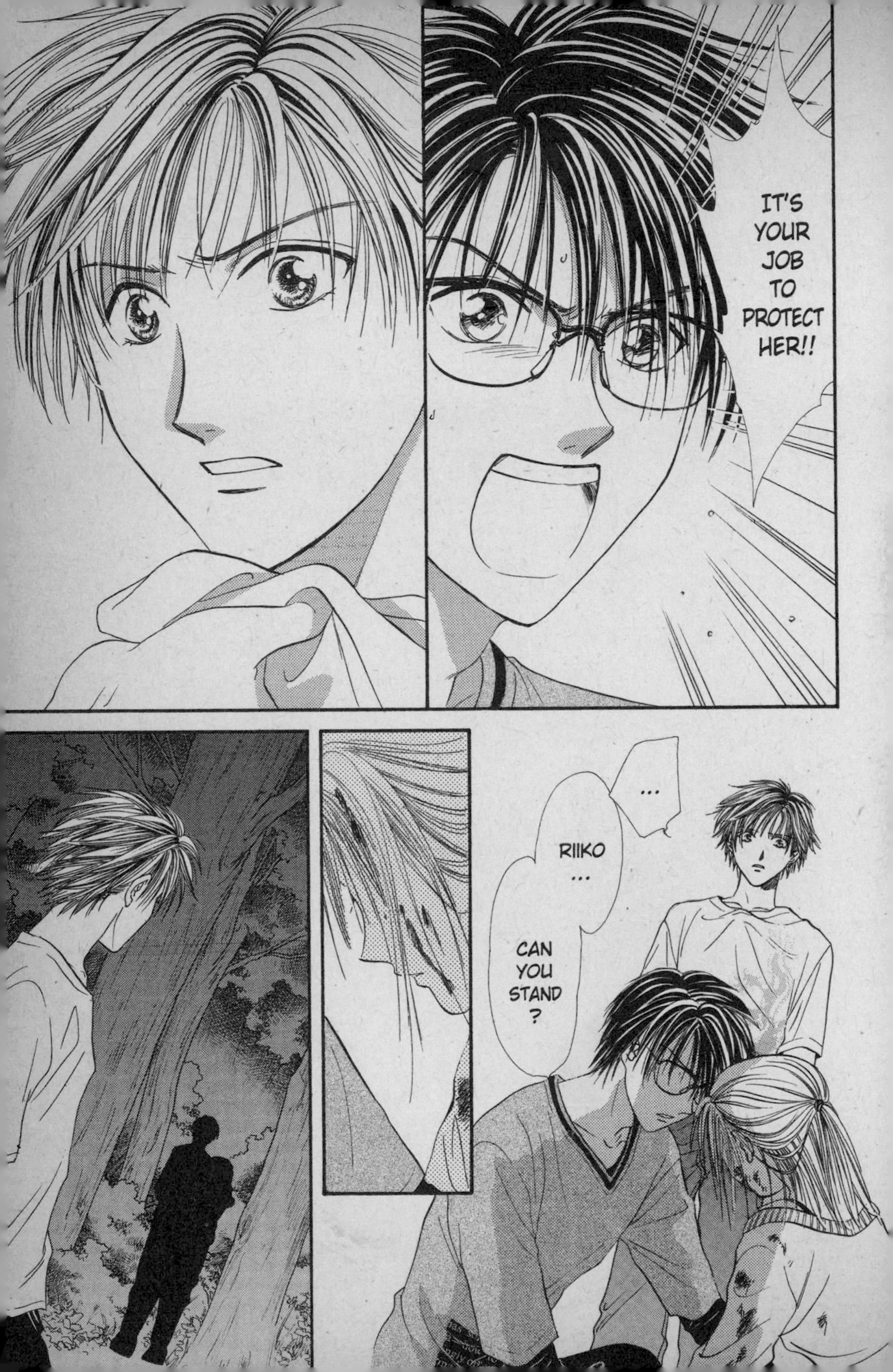
IT'S YOUR JOB TO PROTECT HER!!
...
RIIKO ...
CAN YOU STAND ?

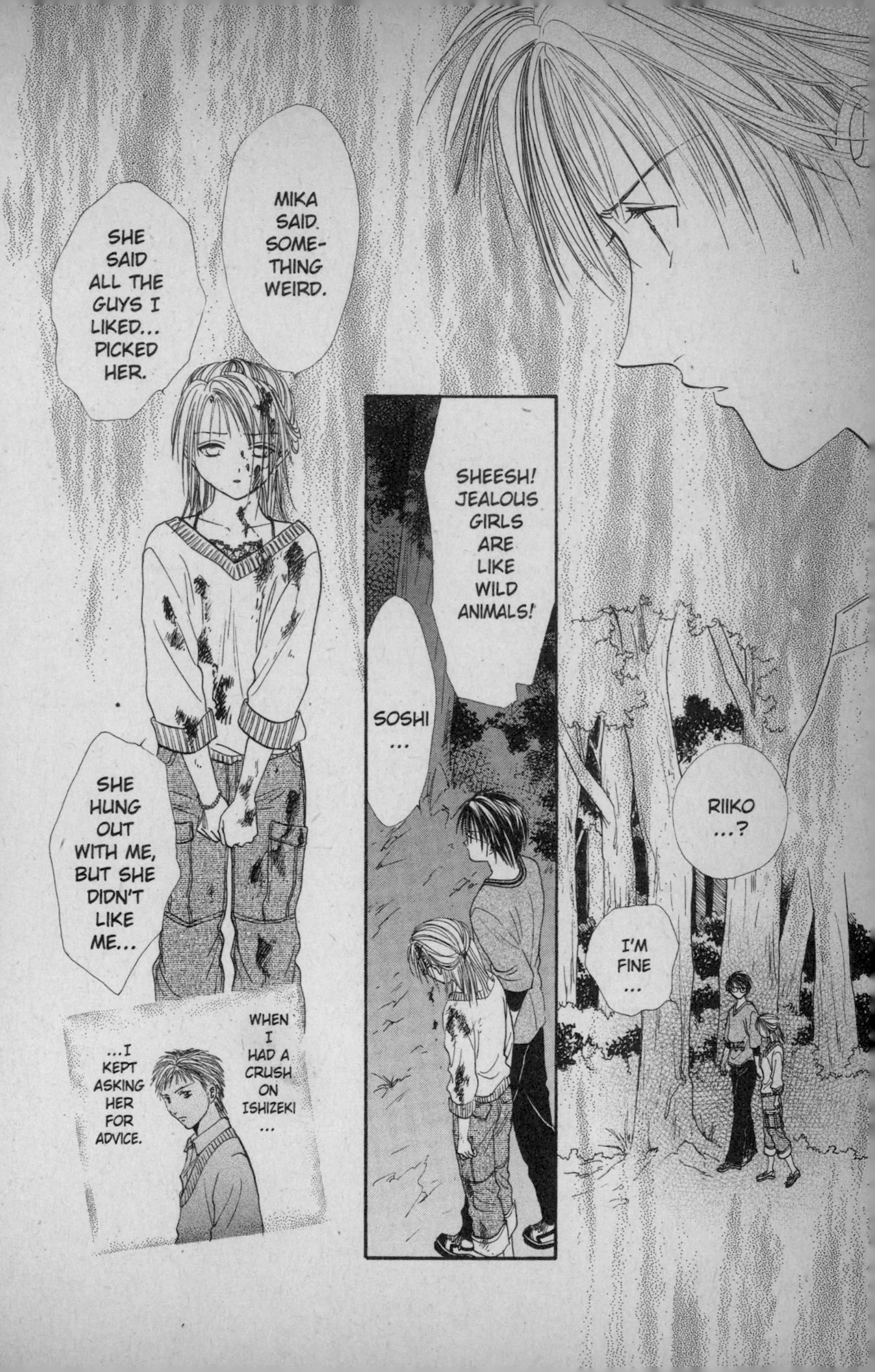
RIIKO ...?
I'M FINE ...
SHEESH! JEALOUS GIRLS ARE LIKE WILD ANIMALS!
SOSHI ...
MIKA SAID SOME-THING WEIRD.
SHE SAID ALL THE GUYS I LIKED... PICKED HER.
SHE HUNG OUT WITH ME, BUT SHE DIDN'T LIKE ME...
WHEN I HAD A CRUSH ON ISHIZEKI ...
...I KEPT ASKING HER FOR ADVICE.

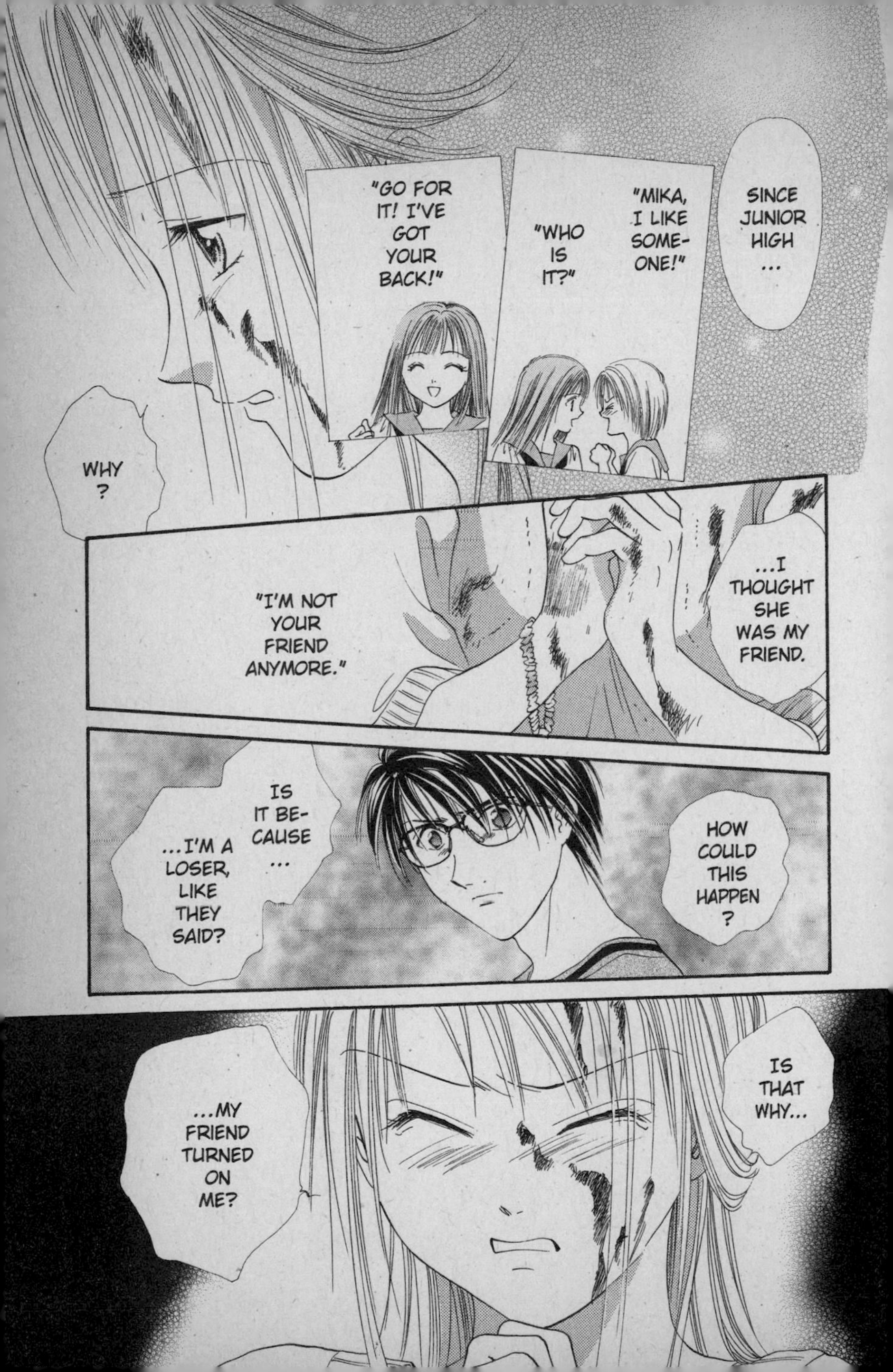
SINCE JUNIOR HIGH ...
"MIKA, I LIKE SOME-ONE!"
"WHO IS IT?"
"GO FOR IT! I'VE GOT YOUR BACK!"
WHY ?
...I THOUGHT SHE WAS MY FRIEND.
"I'M NOT YOUR FRIEND ANYMORE."
HOW COULD THIS HAPPEN ?
IS IT BE-CAUSE ...
...I'M A LOSER, LIKE THEY SAID?
IS THAT WHY...
...MY FRIEND TURNED ON ME?

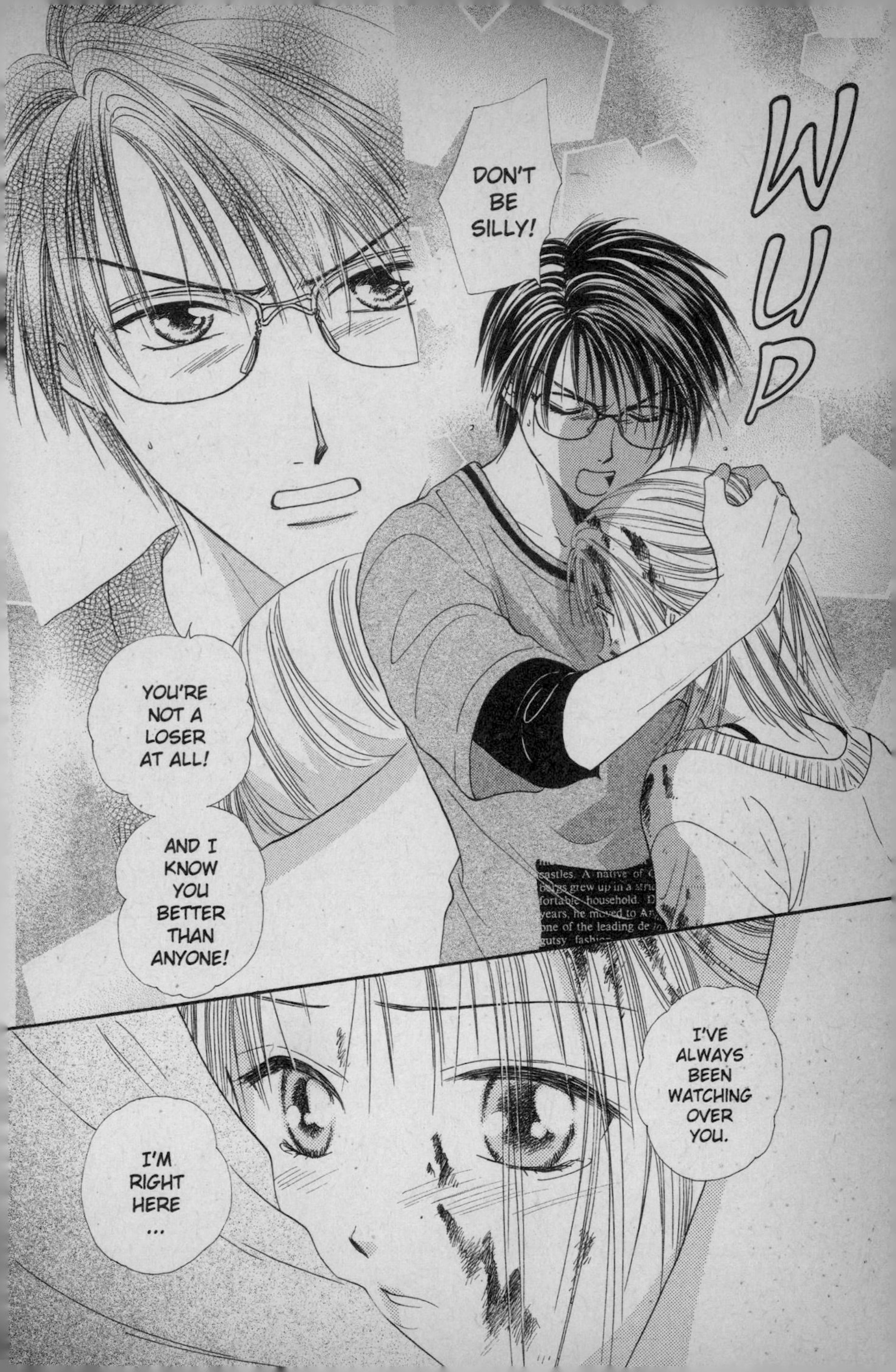
WUP
DON'T BE SILLY!
YOU'RE NOT A LOSER AT ALL!
AND I KNOW YOU BETTER THAN ANYONE!
I'VE ALWAYS BEEN WATCHING OVER YOU.
I'M RIGHT HERE ...

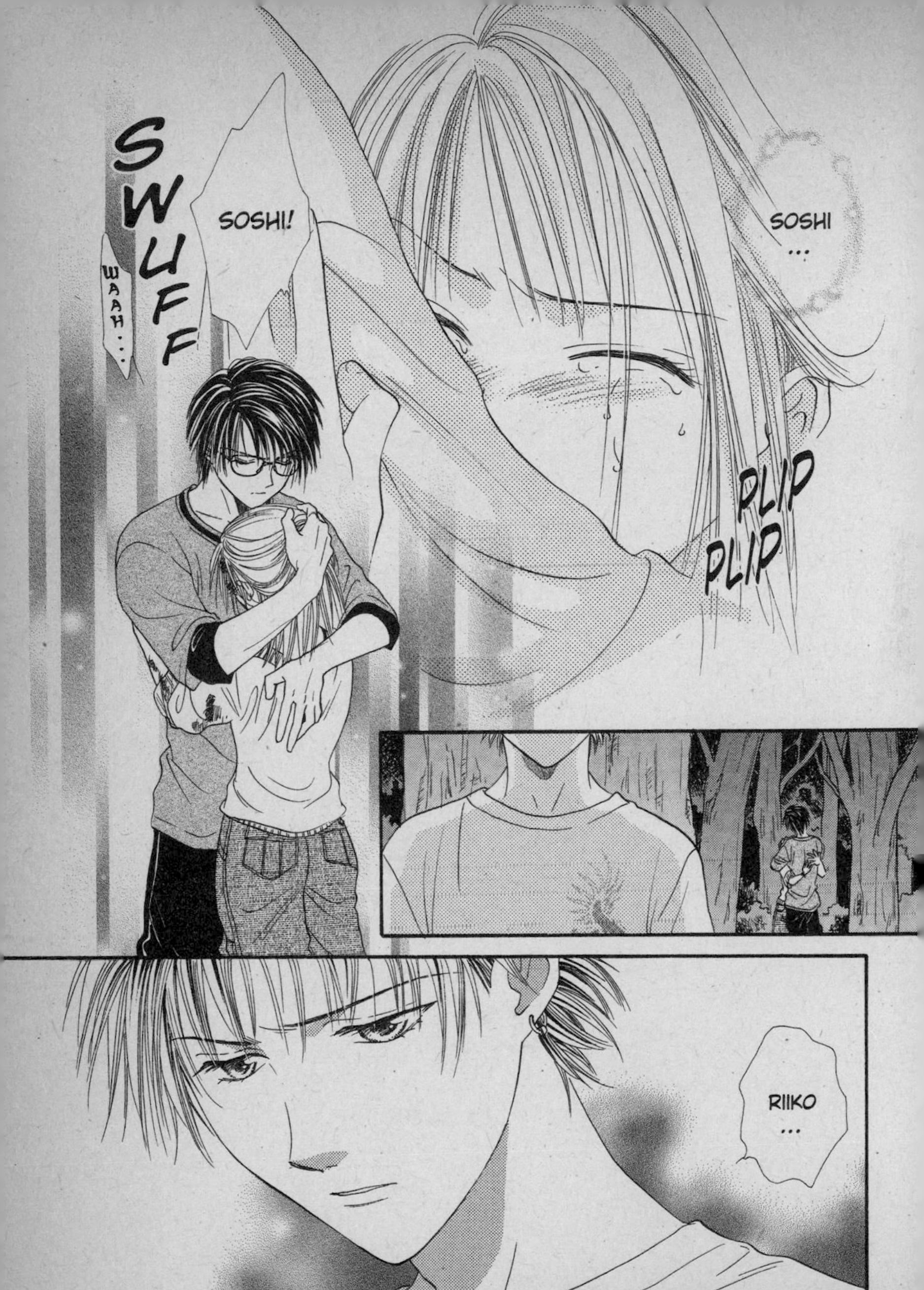
SOSHI ...
PLIP PLIP
SOSHI!
SWUFF
WAAAH...
RIIKO ...

Absolute Boyfriend

Act 9 Thank You

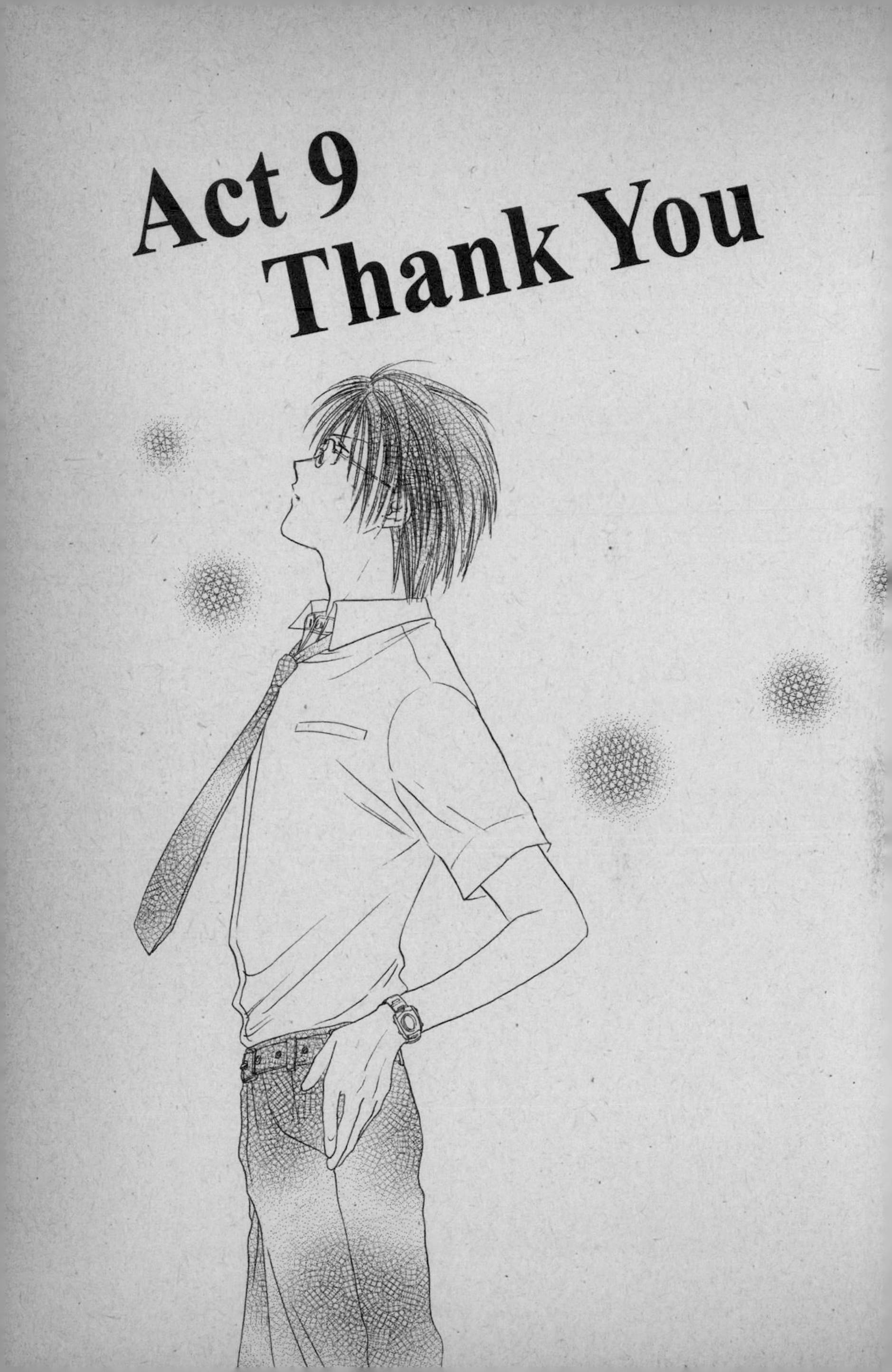

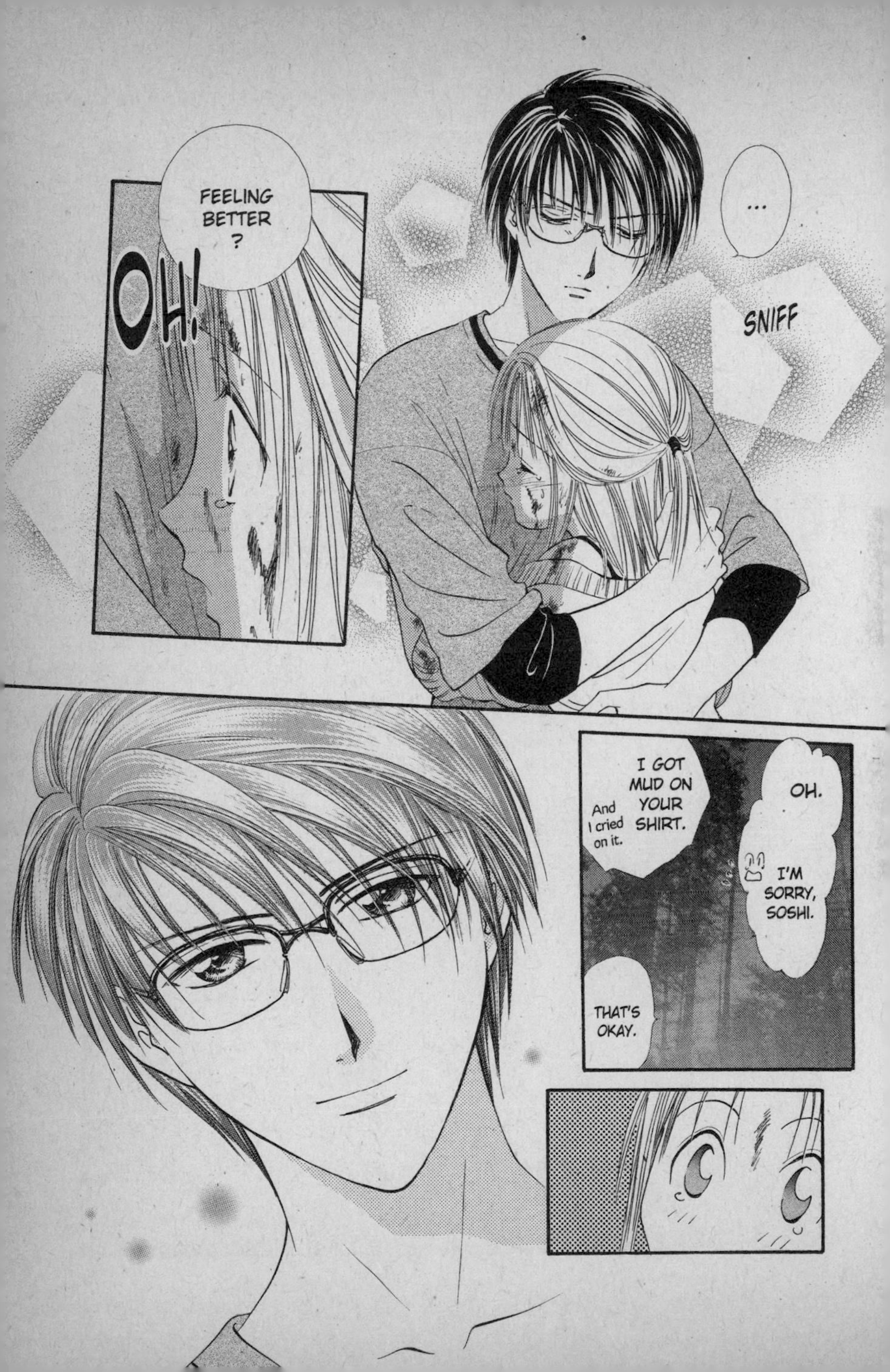
...
SNIFF
FEELING BETTER ?
OH!
OH.
I'M SORRY, SOSHI.
I GOT MUD ON YOUR SHIRT.
And I cried on it.
THAT'S OKAY.

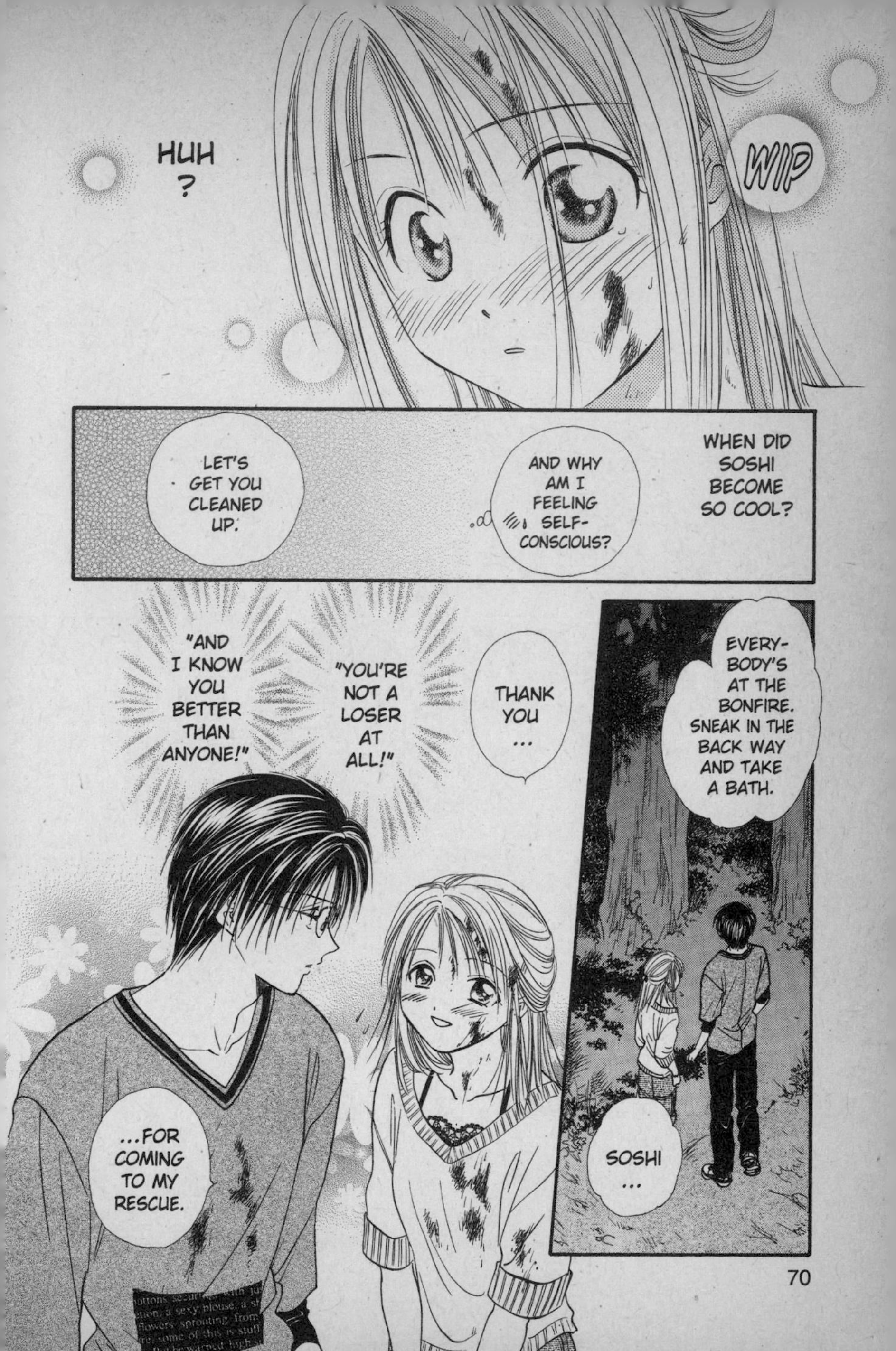
WIP
HUH ?
WHEN DID SOSHI BECOME SO COOL?
AND WHY AM I FEELING SELF-CONSCIOUS?
LET'S GET YOU CLEANED UP.
EVERY-BODY'S AT THE BONFIRE. SNEAK IN THE BACK WAY AND TAKE A BATH.
SOSHI ...
THANK YOU ...
"YOU'RE NOT A LOSER AT ALL!"
"AND I KNOW YOU BETTER THAN ANYONE!"
...FOR COMING TO MY RESCUE.

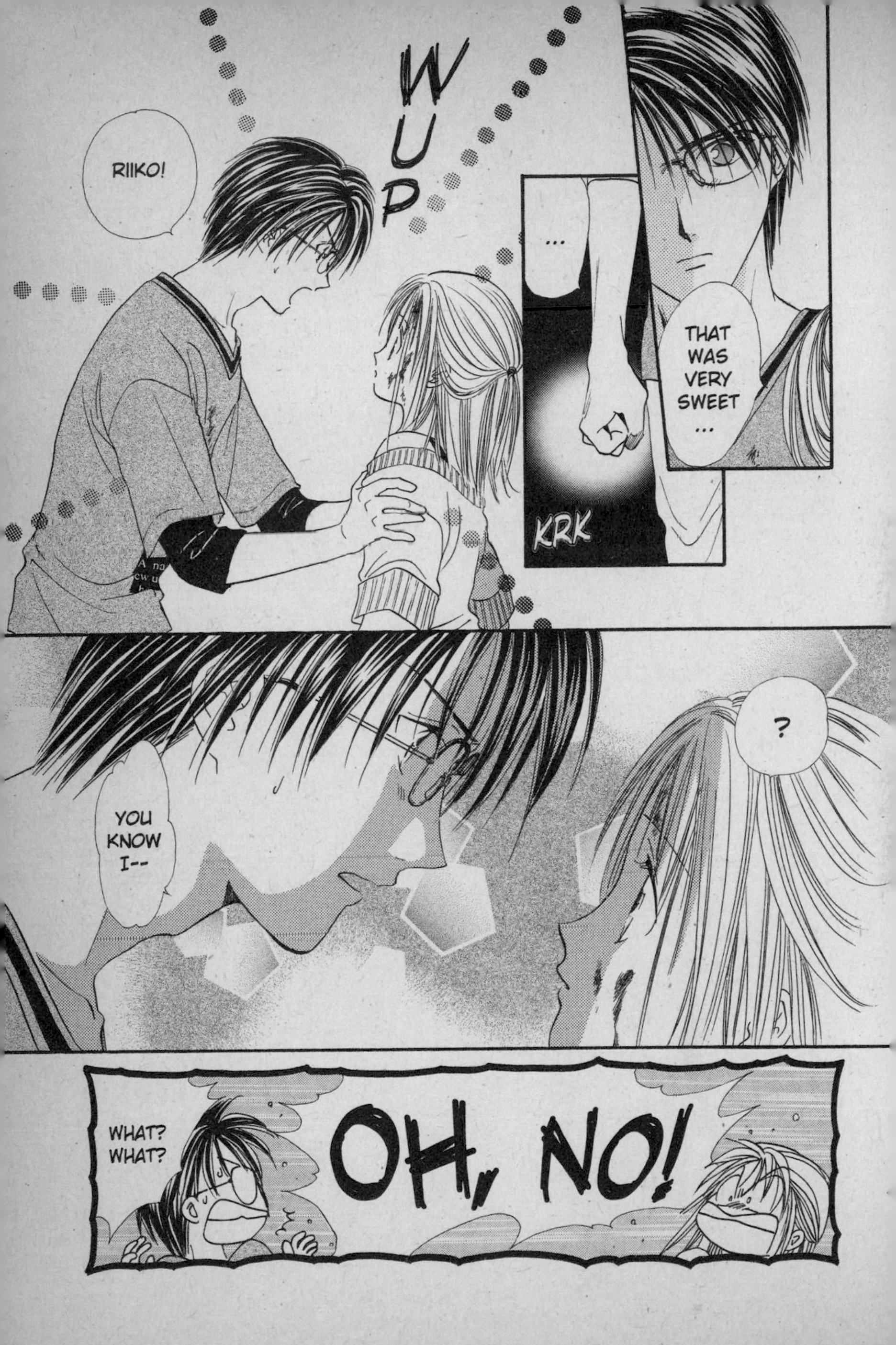
THAT WAS VERY SWEET ...
...
KRK
WUP
RIIKO!
?
YOU KNOW I--
OH, NO!
WHAT? WHAT?

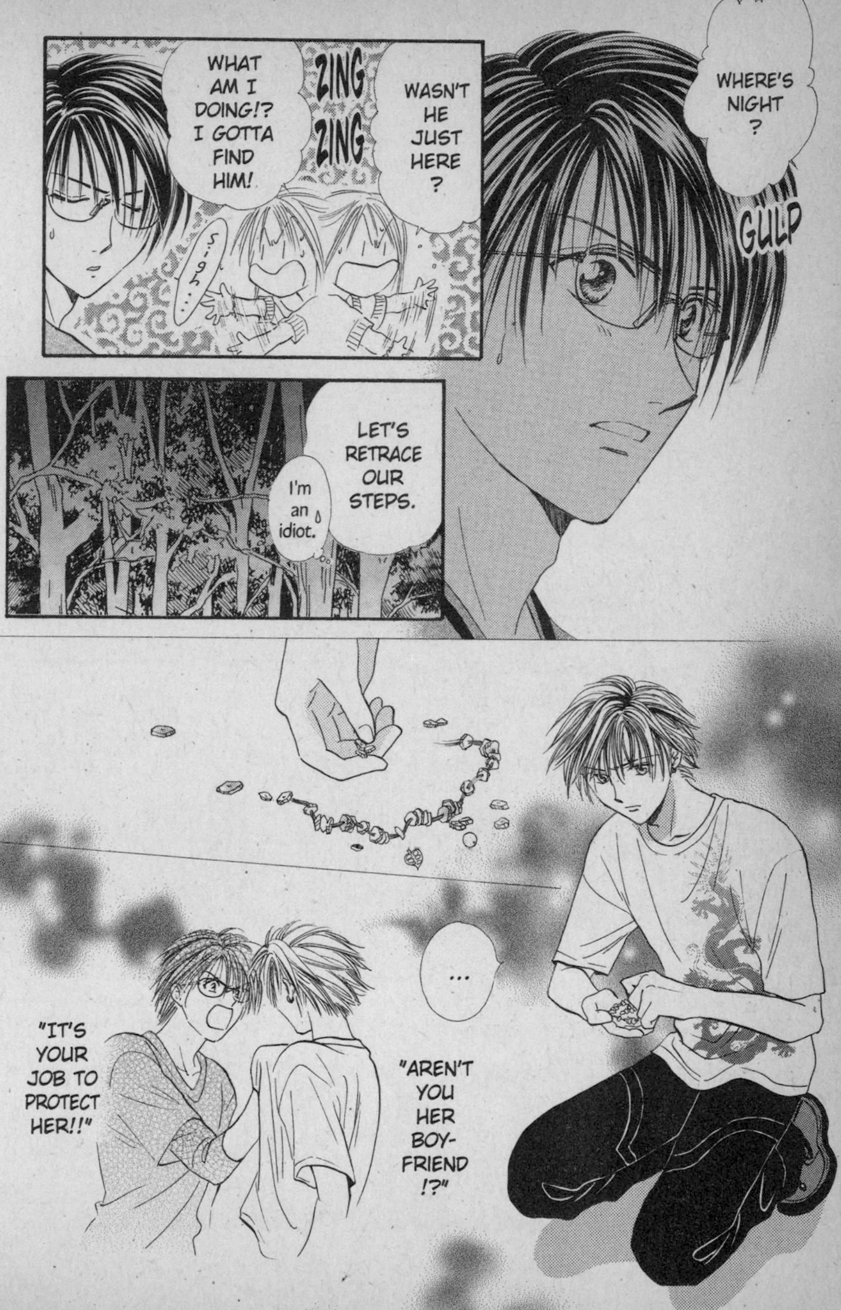
WHERE'S NIGHT ?
GULP
WASN'T HE JUST HERE ?
ZING ZING
WHAT AM I DOING!? I GOTTA FIND HIM!
sigh...
LET'S RETRACE OUR STEPS.
I'm an idiot.
...
"AREN'T YOU HER BOY-FRIEND !?"
"IT'S YOUR JOB TO PROTECT HER!!"

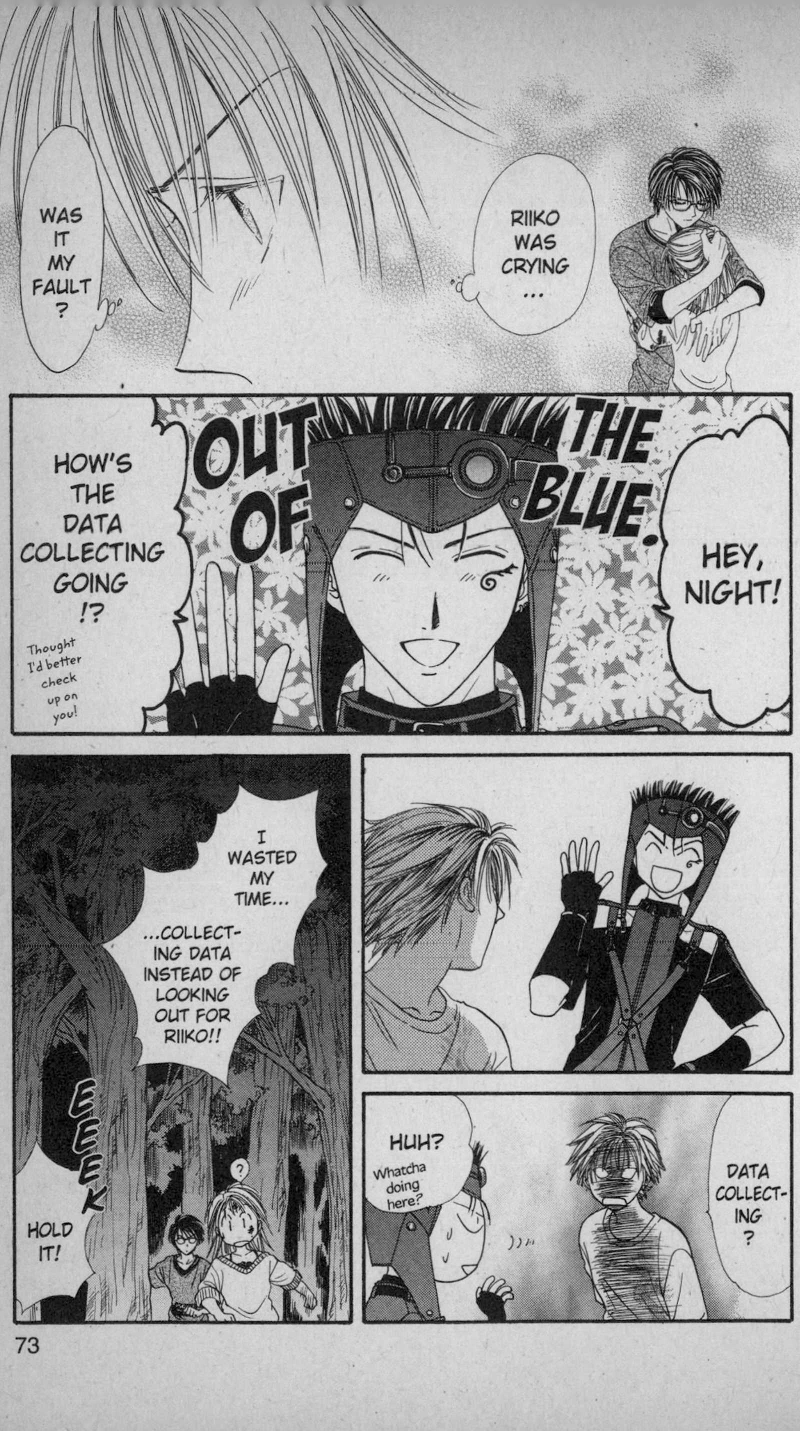
RIIKO WAS CRYING...
WAS IT MY FAULT?
HEY, NIGHT!
OUT OF THE BLUE.
HOW'S THE DATA COLLECTING GOING!?
Thought I'd better check up on you!
DATA COLLECT-ING?
HUH?
Whatcha doing here?
I WASTED MY TIME...
...COLLECT-ING DATA INSTEAD OF LOOKING OUT FOR RIIKO!!
EEEEK
HOLD IT!

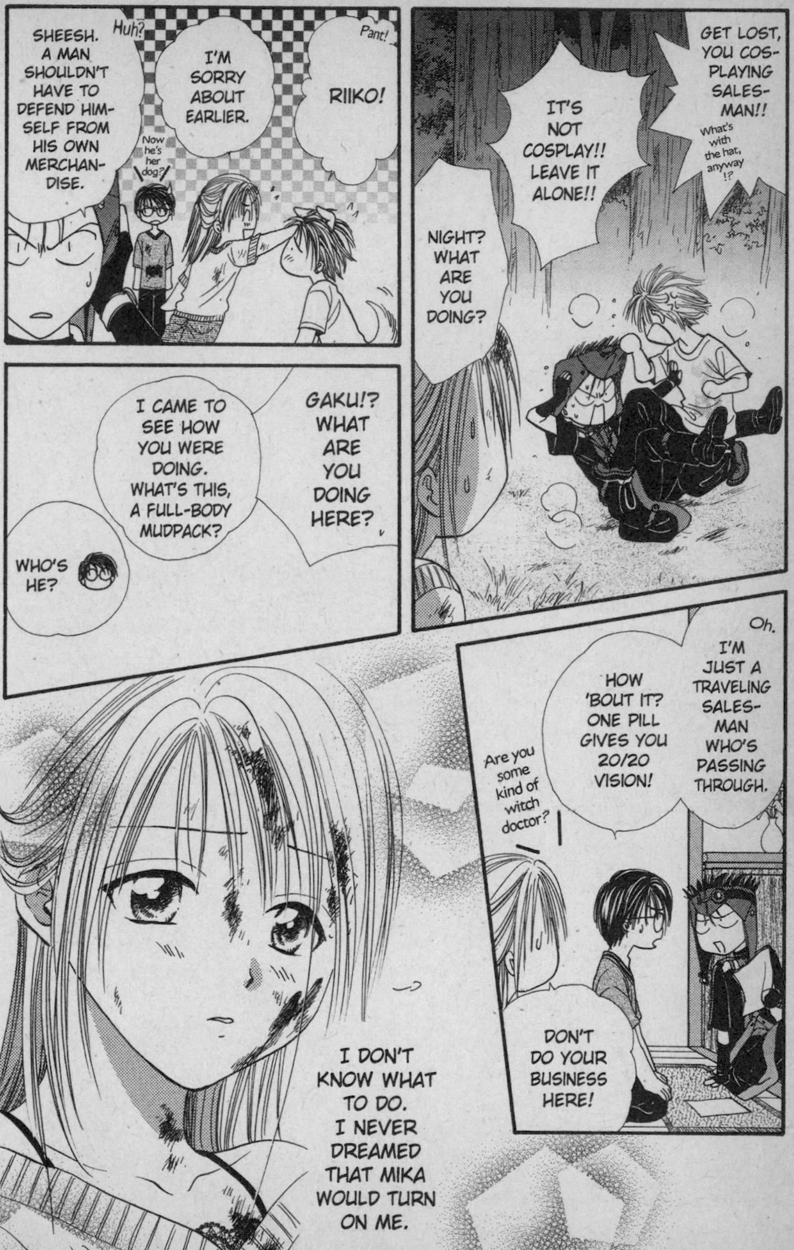
GET LOST, YOU COS-PLAYING SALES-MAN!!
What's with the hat, anyway!?
IT'S NOT COSPLAY!! LEAVE IT ALONE!!
NIGHT? WHAT ARE YOU DOING?
Pant!
RIIKO!
I'M SORRY ABOUT EARLIER.
Huh?
SHEESH. A MAN SHOULDN'T HAVE TO DEFEND HIM-SELF FROM HIS OWN MERCHAN-DISE.
Now he's her dog?
GAKU!? WHAT ARE YOU DOING HERE?
I CAME TO SEE HOW YOU WERE DOING. WHAT'S THIS, A FULL-BODY MUDPACK?
WHO'S HE?
Oh.
I'M JUST A TRAVELING SALES-MAN WHO'S PASSING THROUGH.
HOW 'BOUT IT? ONE PILL GIVES YOU 20/20 VISION!
Are you some kind of witch doctor?
DON'T DO YOUR BUSINESS HERE!
I DON'T KNOW WHAT TO DO. I NEVER DREAMED THAT MIKA WOULD TURN ON ME.

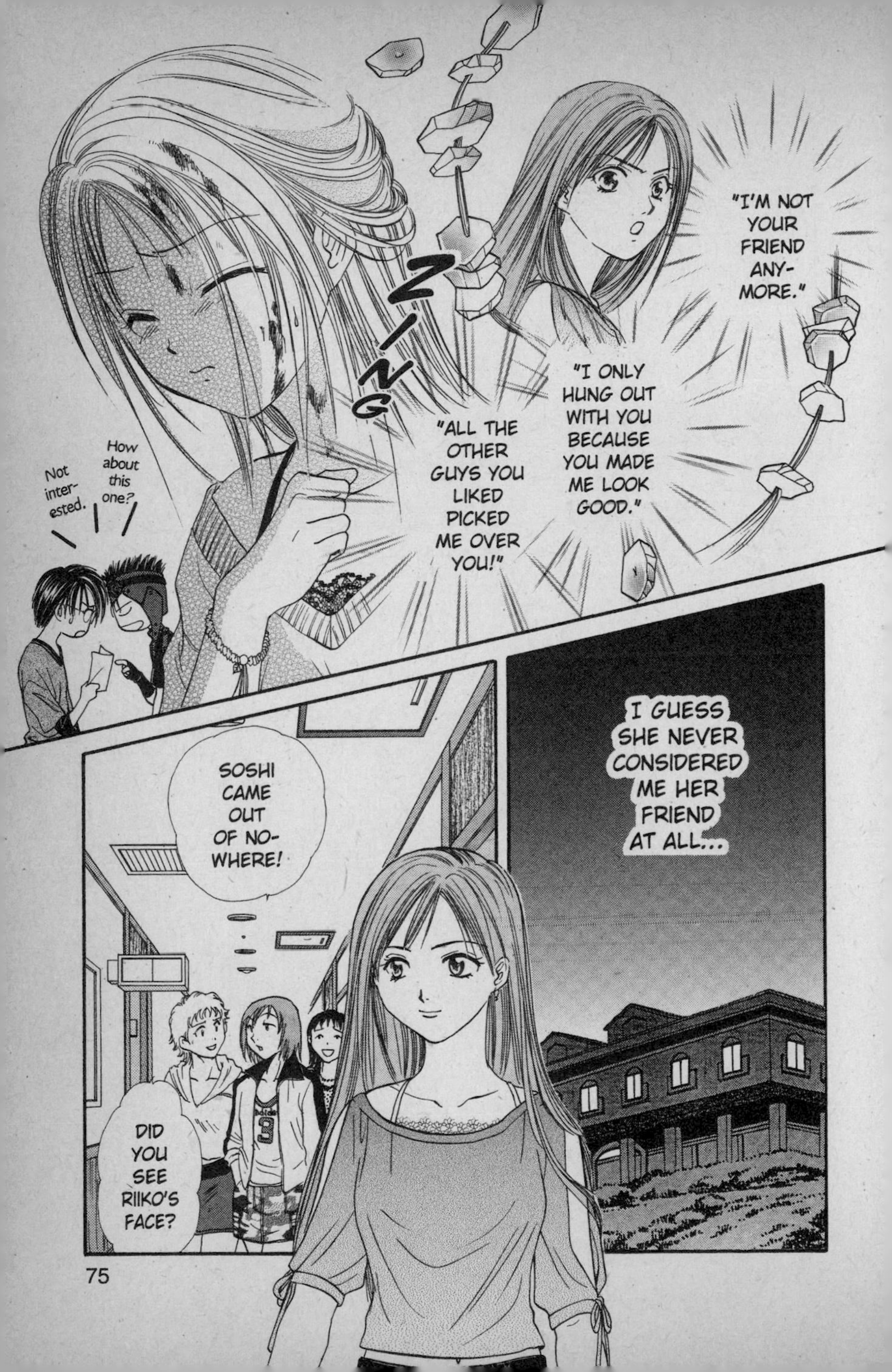
"I'M NOT YOUR FRIEND ANY-MORE."
"I ONLY HUNG OUT WITH YOU BECAUSE YOU MADE ME LOOK GOOD."
ZING
"ALL THE OTHER GUYS YOU LIKED PICKED ME OVER YOU!"
How about this one?
Not inter-ested.
I GUESS SHE NEVER CONSIDERED ME HER FRIEND AT ALL...
SOSHI CAME OUT OF NO-WHERE!
...
DID YOU SEE RIIKO'S FACE?

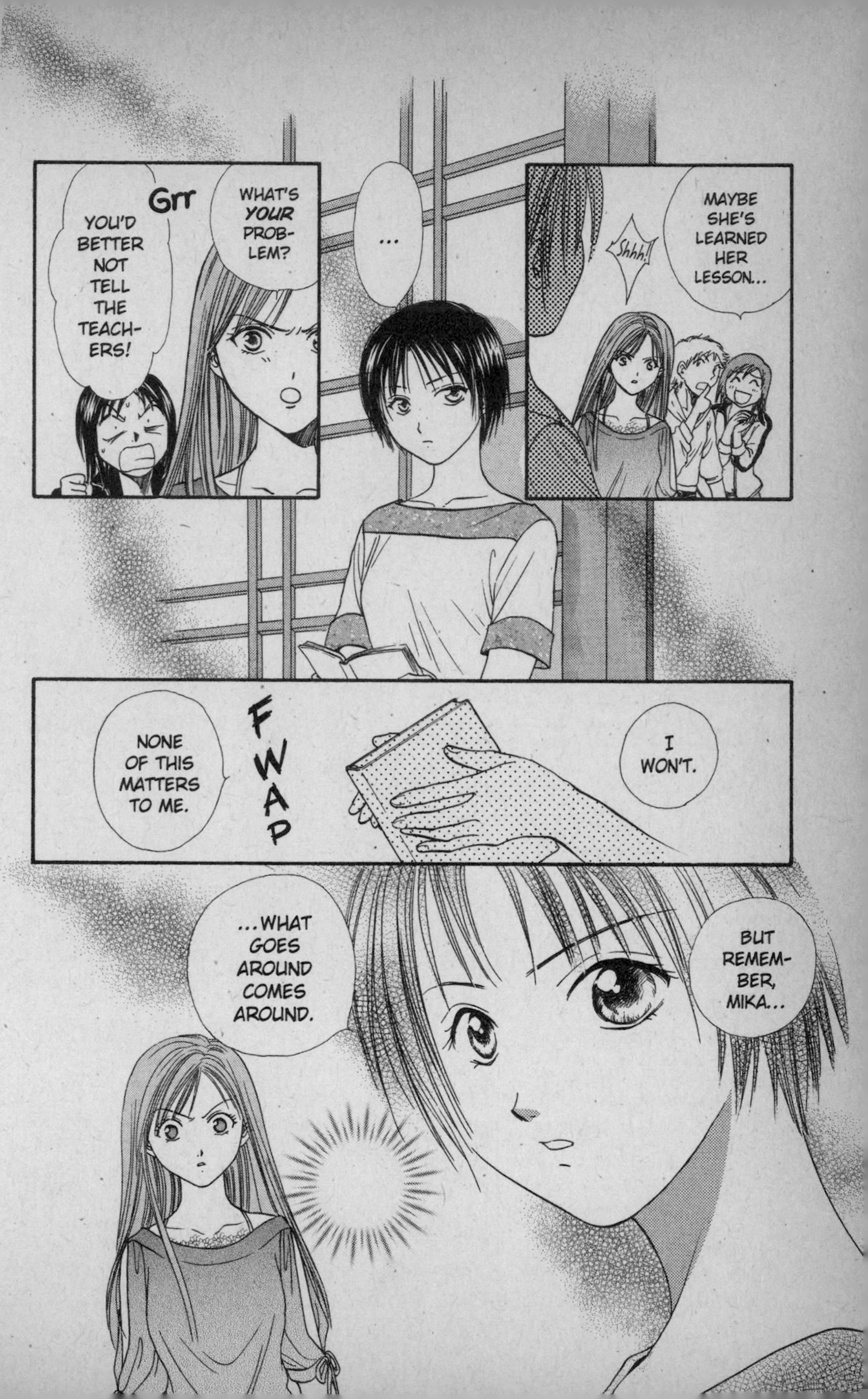
MAYBE SHE'S LEARNED HER LESSON...
Shhh!
...
WHAT'S YOUR PROBLEM?
Grr
YOU'D BETTER NOT TELL THE TEACHERS!
I WON'T.
FWAP
NONE OF THIS MATTERS TO ME.
BUT REMEMBER, MIKA...
...WHAT GOES AROUND COMES AROUND.

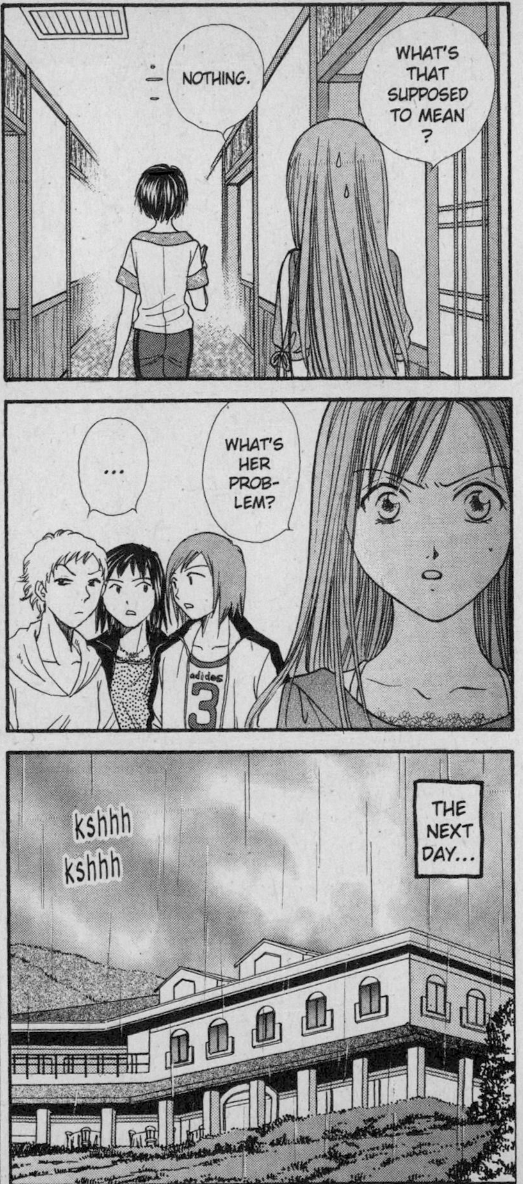
WHAT'S THAT SUPPOSED TO MEAN ?
NOTHING.
WHAT'S HER PROB-LEM?
...
THE NEXT DAY...
kshhh
kshhh

I've been pretty cruel to Riiko in this volume. But let's talk about Mika. A lot of people wrote to say they hate her. I can't blame them, but isn't there a girl like her in every school? Something like that even happened in my own high school. One girl was using another to boost her own popularity. Well, she was cute, but what she did was wrong.

Girls can be really scary. Friendships can easily be destroyed when a guy comes into the picture.

I don't really understand the minds of girls like Mika, so she hasn't been an easy character for me. Actually, even in my past titles, I don't really understand how the bad guys work. I don't know why people do mean things (there is some degree of meanness in everyone, though). But doesn't it feel awful to hurt others? I feel bad for days if I think I might've insulted someone. Well, everyone has a dark side, I guess (smile). I can be cold sometimes, too, but blatant schemers amaze me.

I was surfing the Net one day and stumbled on some nasty sites. It makes me physically sick when I see such concentrated evil (smile). But when I see **real** brutal people, what I feel is beyond anger--it makes me sad as a human being and it makes me want to cry. Good kids should stay away from sites like those (smile). The malice will get to you. I used to take a peek once in a while out of curiosity (why do I do this when I know what'll happen?), but I always end up getting really mad!! Sure, everyone has a dark side, but that's no reason to give yourself over to it! Don't they feel miserable about themselves? Those people tend to blame others for their problems, too. It makes me wonder.

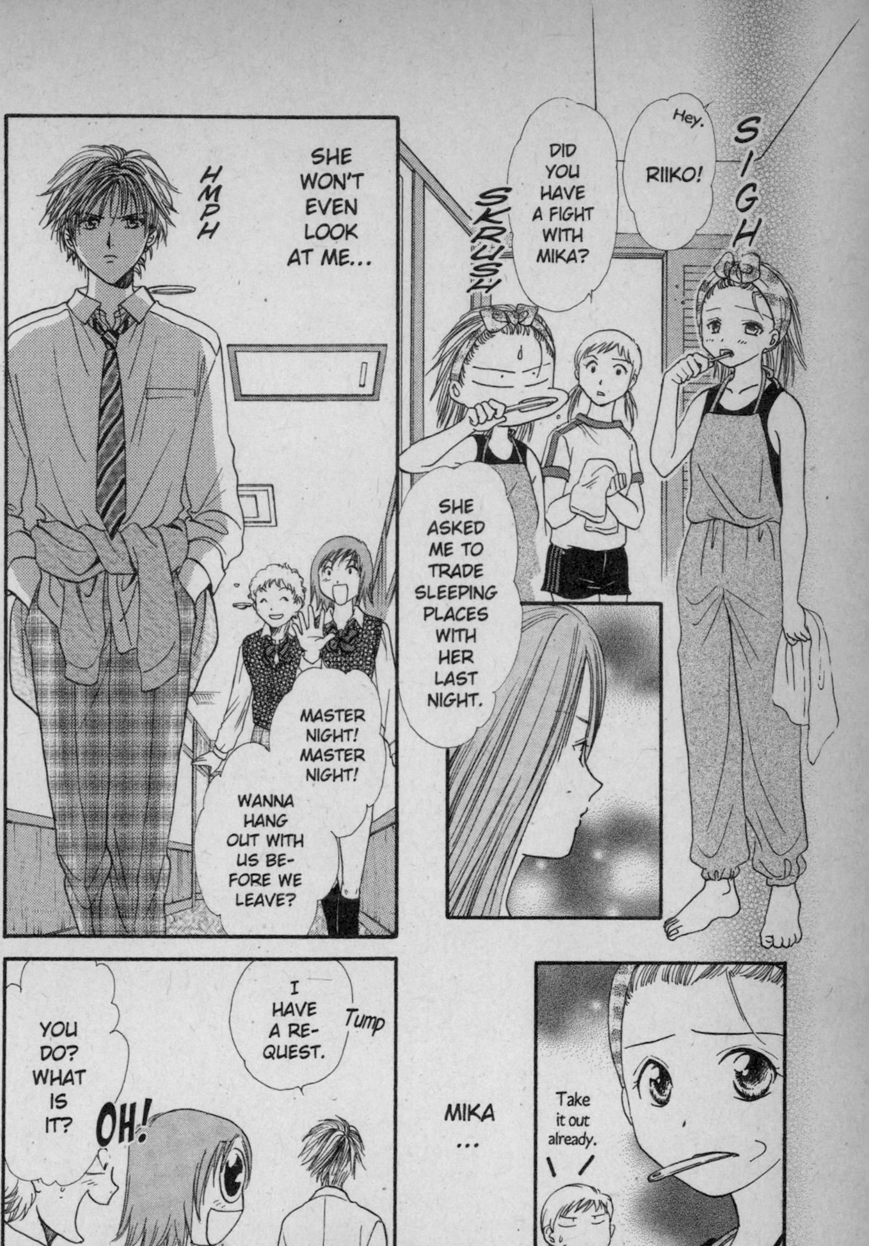
SIGH
Hey.
RIIKO!
DID YOU HAVE A FIGHT WITH MIKA?
SKRUSH
SHE ASKED ME TO TRADE SLEEPING PLACES WITH HER LAST NIGHT.
SHE WON'T EVEN LOOK AT ME...
HMPH
MASTER NIGHT! MASTER NIGHT!
WANNA HANG OUT WITH US BE-FORE WE LEAVE?
MIKA ...
Take it out already.
I HAVE A RE-QUEST.
Tump
YOU DO? WHAT IS IT?
OH!

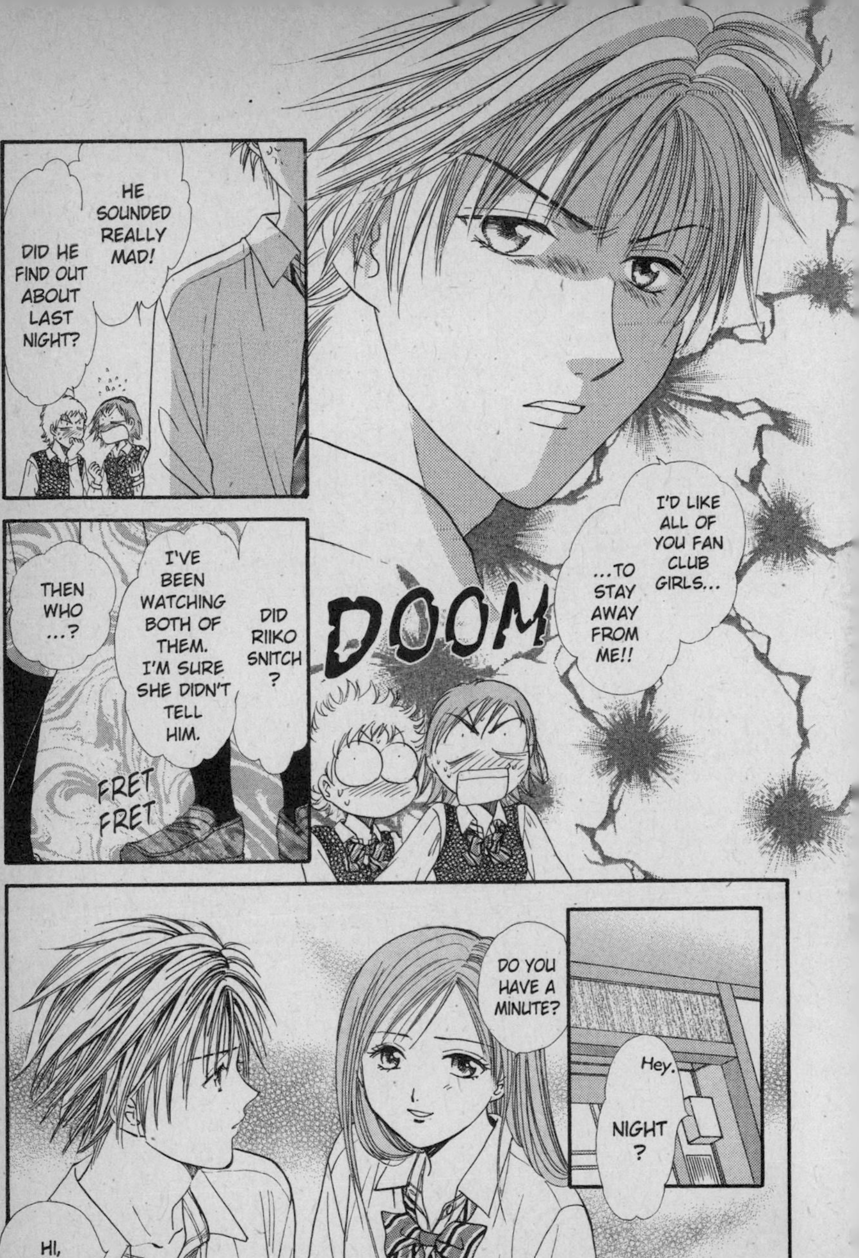
I'D LIKE ALL OF YOU FAN CLUB GIRLS...
...TO STAY AWAY FROM ME!!
DOOM
HE SOUNDED REALLY MAD!
DID HE FIND OUT ABOUT LAST NIGHT?
DID RIIKO SNITCH?
I'VE BEEN WATCHING BOTH OF THEM. I'M SURE SHE DIDN'T TELL HIM.
THEN WHO ...?
FRET FRET
Hey.
NIGHT?
DO YOU HAVE A MINUTE?
HI, MIKA.

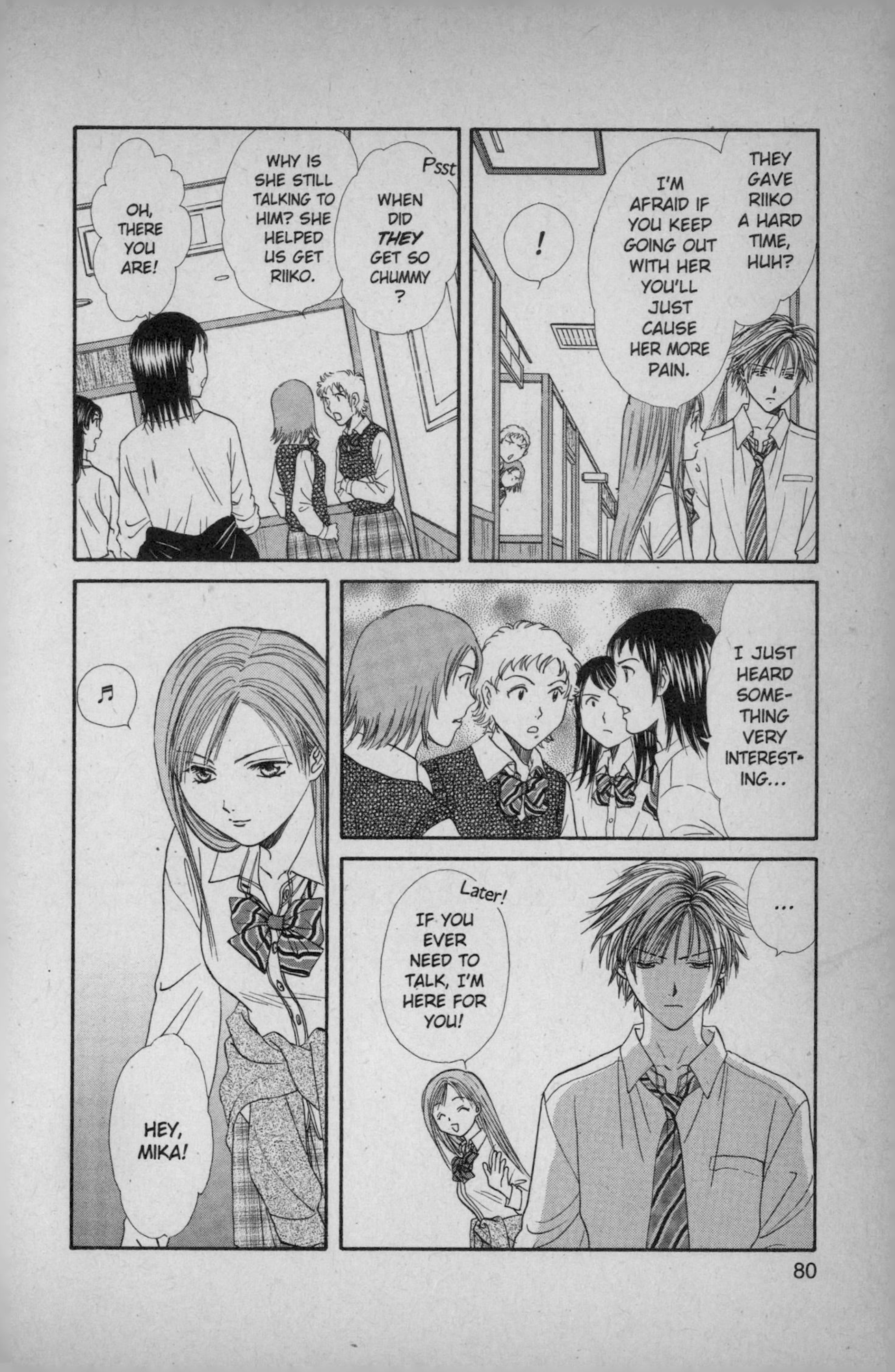
THEY GAVE RIIKO A HARD TIME, HUH?
I'M AFRAID IF YOU KEEP GOING OUT WITH HER YOU'LL JUST CAUSE HER MORE PAIN.
!
Psst
WHEN DID *THEY* GET SO CHUMMY?
WHY IS SHE STILL TALKING TO HIM? SHE HELPED US GET RIIKO.
OH, THERE YOU ARE!
I JUST HEARD SOMETHING VERY INTERESTING...
...
Later!
IF YOU EVER NEED TO TALK, I'M HERE FOR YOU!
♫
HEY, MIKA!

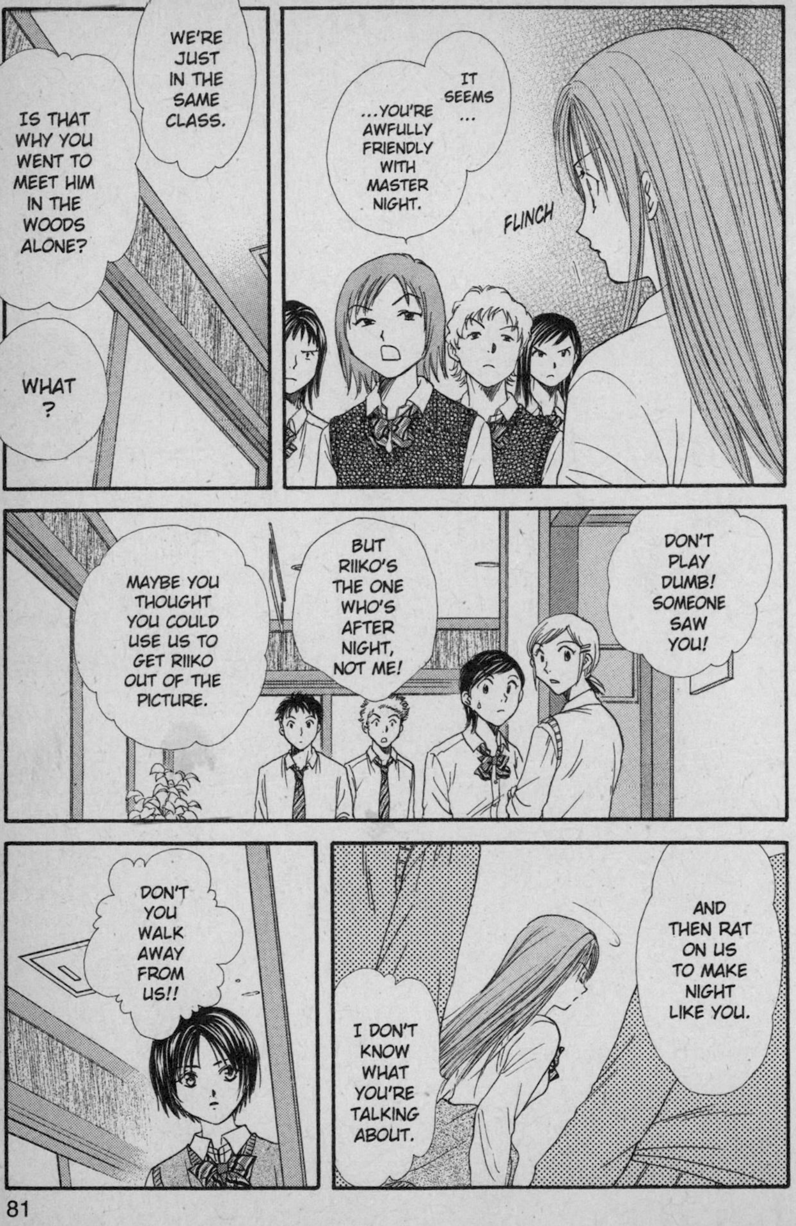
IT SEEMS ...
...YOU'RE AWFULLY FRIENDLY WITH MASTER NIGHT.
FLINCH
WE'RE JUST IN THE SAME CLASS.
IS THAT WHY YOU WENT TO MEET HIM IN THE WOODS ALONE?
WHAT ?
DON'T PLAY DUMB! SOMEONE SAW YOU!
BUT RIIKO'S THE ONE WHO'S AFTER NIGHT, NOT ME!
MAYBE YOU THOUGHT YOU COULD USE US TO GET RIIKO OUT OF THE PICTURE.
AND THEN RAT ON US TO MAKE NIGHT LIKE YOU.
I DON'T KNOW WHAT YOU'RE TALKING ABOUT.
DON'T YOU WALK AWAY FROM US!!

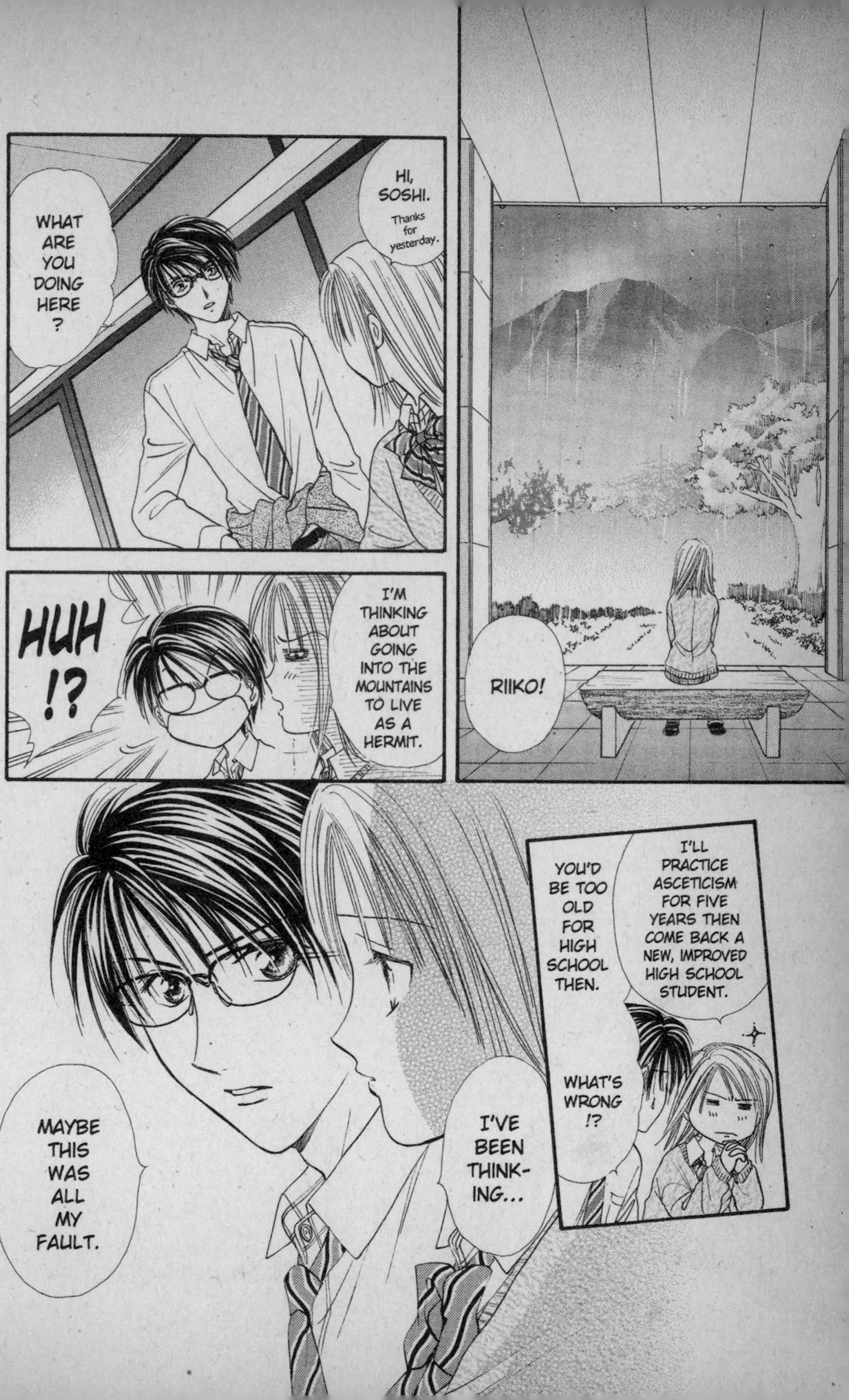
RIIKO!
HI, SOSHI.
Thanks for yesterday.
WHAT ARE YOU DOING HERE?
I'M THINKING ABOUT GOING INTO THE MOUNTAINS TO LIVE AS A HERMIT.
HUH!?
I'LL PRACTICE ASCETICISM FOR FIVE YEARS THEN COME BACK A NEW, IMPROVED HIGH SCHOOL STUDENT.
YOU'D BE TOO OLD FOR HIGH SCHOOL THEN.
WHAT'S WRONG!?
I'VE BEEN THINK-ING...
MAYBE THIS WAS ALL MY FAULT.

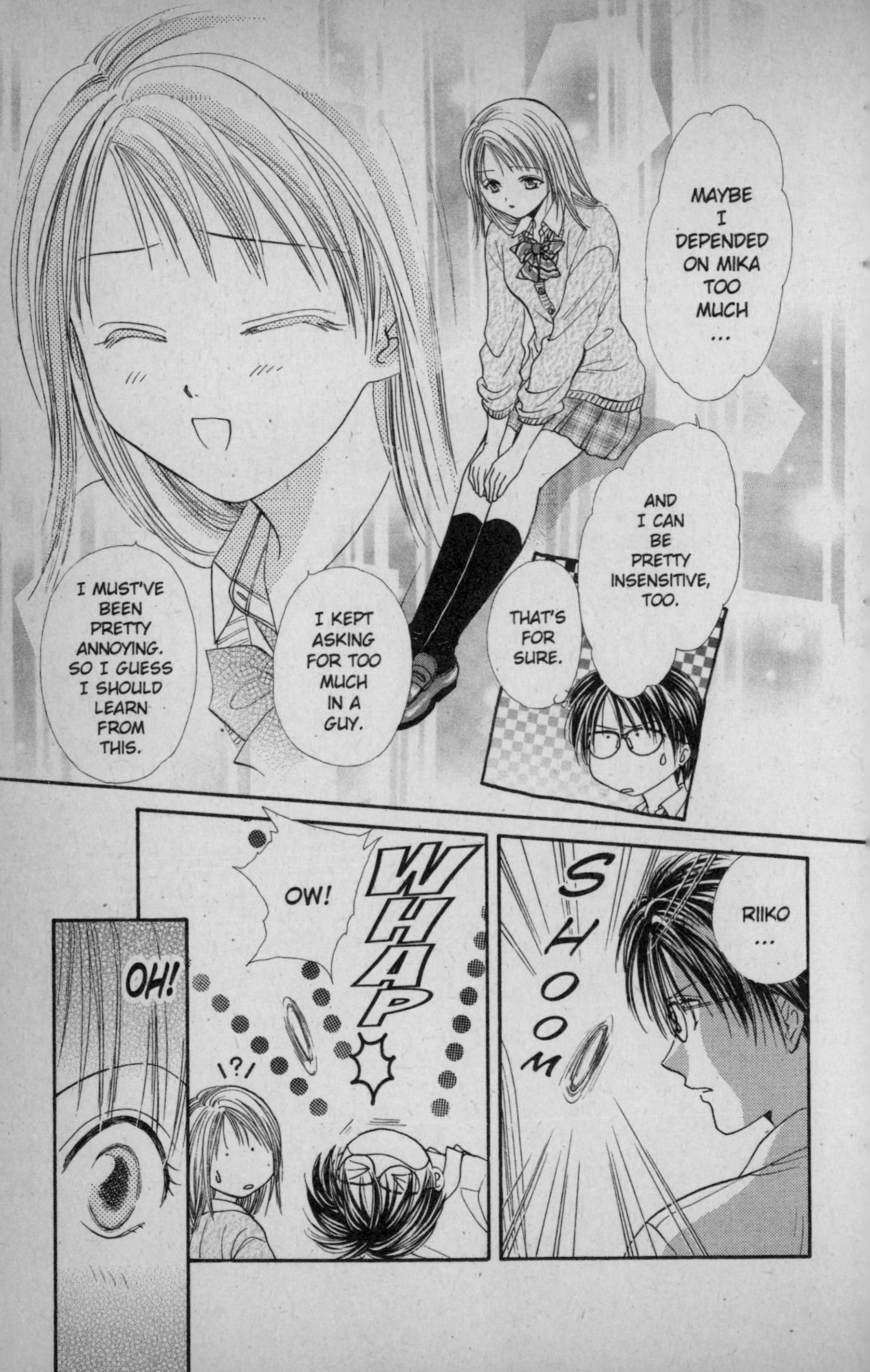
MAYBE I DEPENDED ON MIKA TOO MUCH...
AND I CAN BE PRETTY INSENSITIVE, TOO.
THAT'S FOR SURE.
I KEPT ASKING FOR TOO MUCH IN A GUY.
I MUST'VE BEEN PRETTY ANNOYING. SO I GUESS I SHOULD LEARN FROM THIS.
RIIKO...
SHOOOM
WHAP
OW!
!?!
OH!

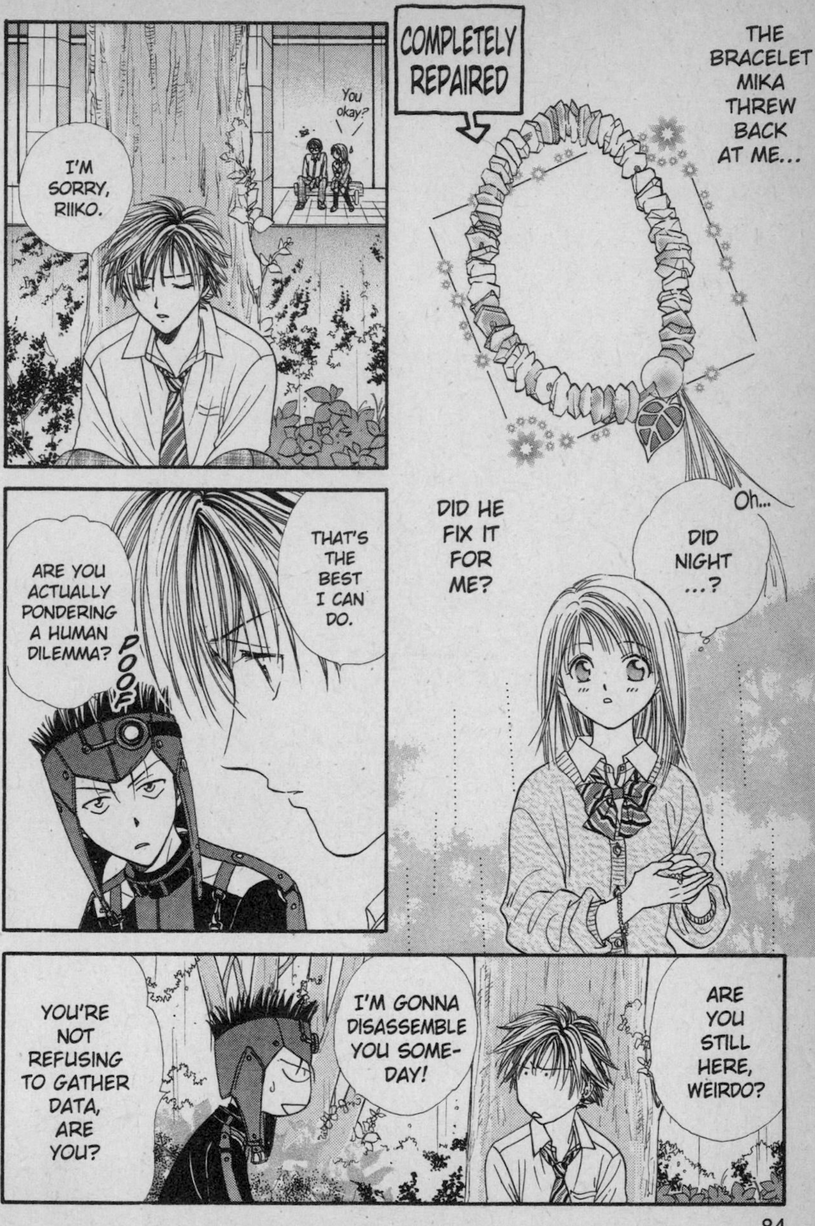
THE BRACELET MIKA THREW BACK AT ME...
COMPLETELY REPAIRED
You okay?
I'M SORRY, RIIKO.
Oh...
DID NIGHT ...?
DID HE FIX IT FOR ME?
THAT'S THE BEST I CAN DO.
ARE YOU ACTUALLY PONDERING A HUMAN DILEMMA?
POOF
ARE YOU STILL HERE, WEIRDO?
I'M GONNA DISASSEMBLE YOU SOME-DAY!
YOU'RE NOT REFUSING TO GATHER DATA, ARE YOU?

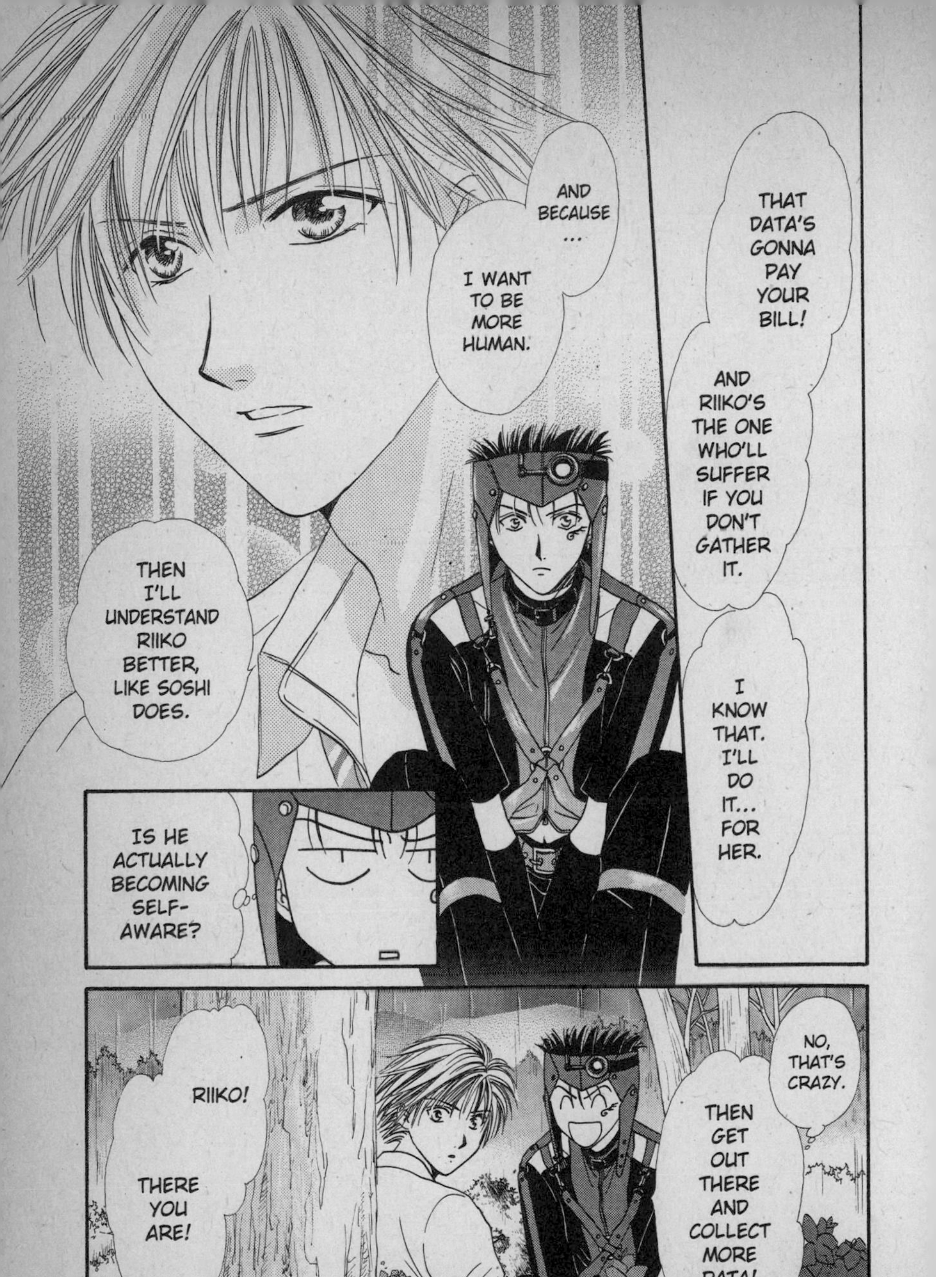
THAT DATA'S GONNA PAY YOUR BILL!
AND RIIKO'S THE ONE WHO'LL SUFFER IF YOU DON'T GATHER IT.
I KNOW THAT. I'LL DO IT... FOR HER.
AND BECAUSE ...
I WANT TO BE MORE HUMAN.
THEN I'LL UNDERSTAND RIIKO BETTER, LIKE SOSHI DOES.
IS HE ACTUALLY BECOMING SELF-AWARE?
NO, THAT'S CRAZY.
THEN GET OUT THERE AND COLLECT MORE DATA!
RIIKO!
THERE YOU ARE!

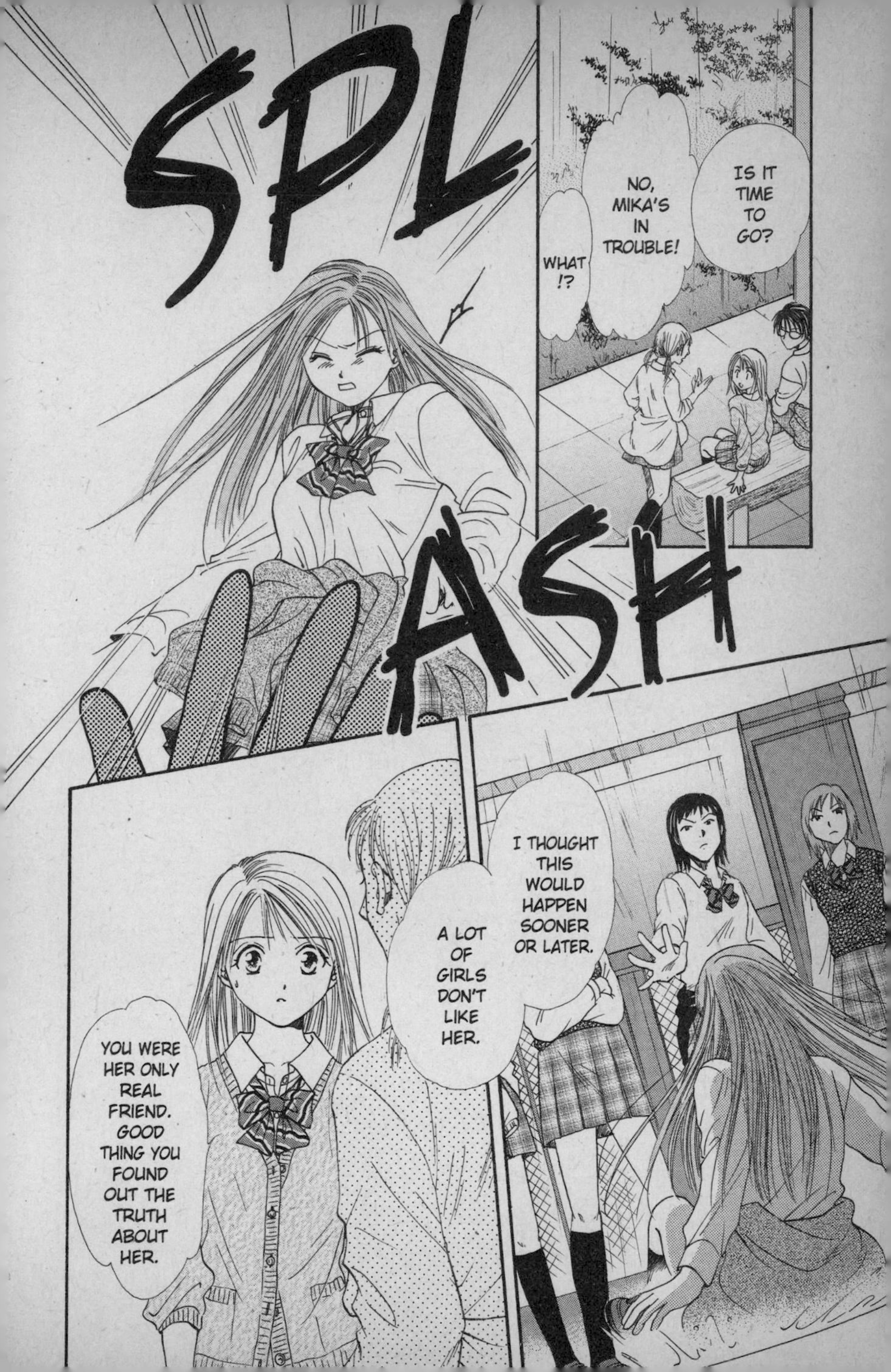
IS IT TIME TO GO?
NO, MIKA'S IN TROUBLE!
WHAT!?
SPLASH
I THOUGHT THIS WOULD HAPPEN SOONER OR LATER.
A LOT OF GIRLS DON'T LIKE HER.
YOU WERE HER ONLY REAL FRIEND. GOOD THING YOU FOUND OUT THE TRUTH ABOUT HER.

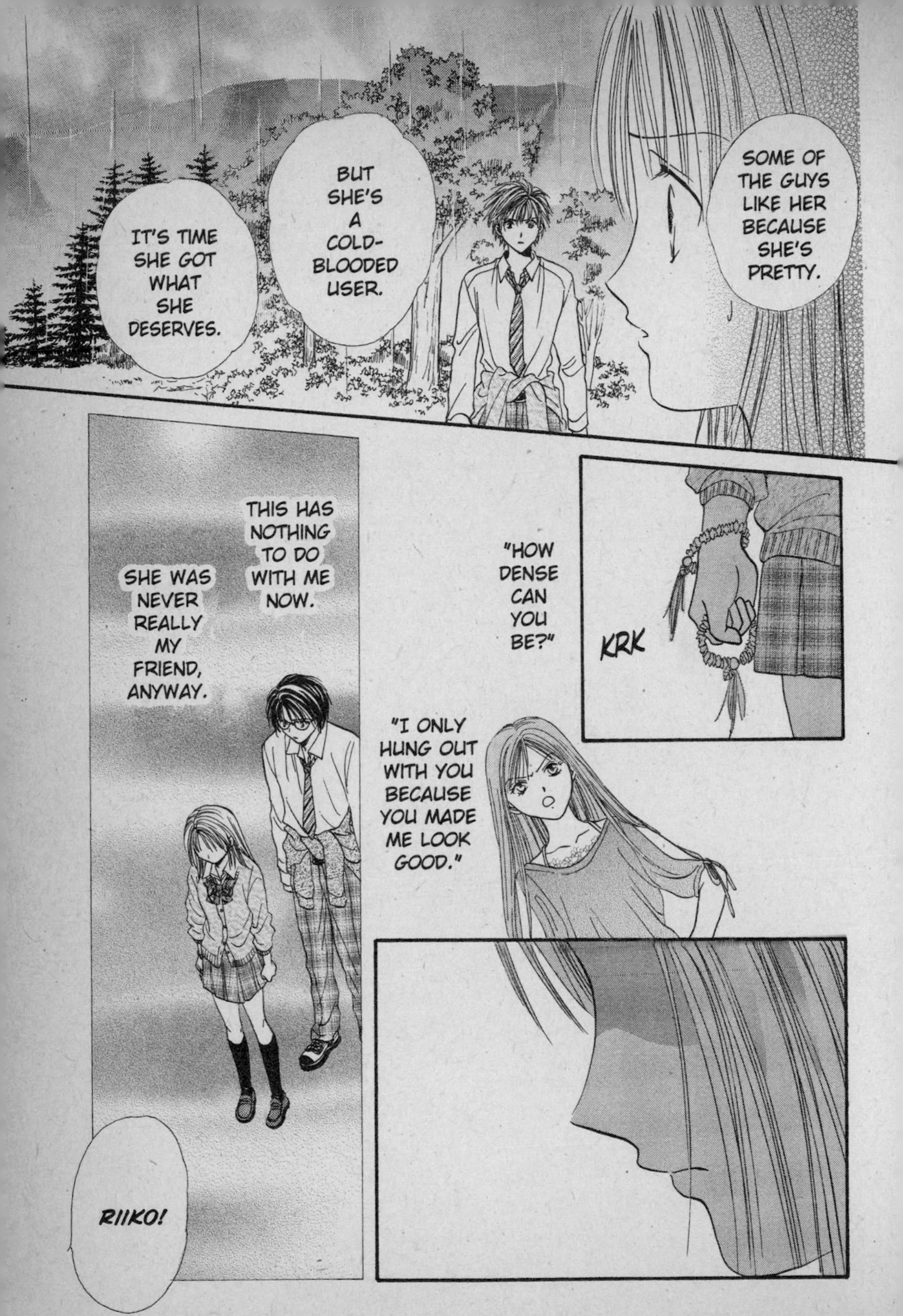
SOME OF THE GUYS LIKE HER BECAUSE SHE'S PRETTY.
BUT SHE'S A COLD-BLOODED USER.
IT'S TIME SHE GOT WHAT SHE DESERVES.
KRK
"HOW DENSE CAN YOU BE?"
"I ONLY HUNG OUT WITH YOU BECAUSE YOU MADE ME LOOK GOOD."
THIS HAS NOTHING TO DO WITH ME NOW.
SHE WAS NEVER REALLY MY FRIEND, ANYWAY.
RIIKO!

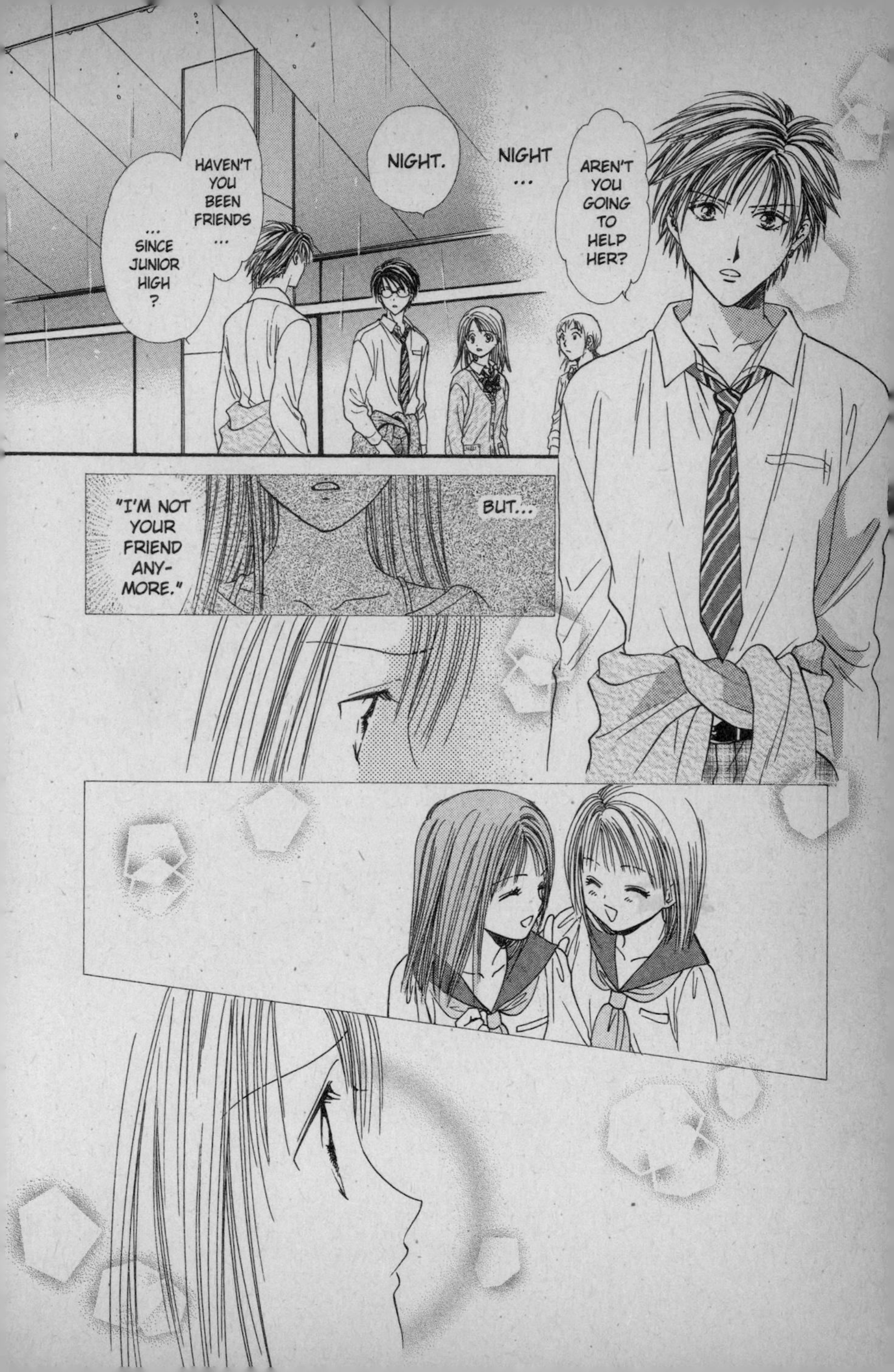
AREN'T YOU GOING TO HELP HER?
NIGHT ...
NIGHT.
HAVEN'T YOU BEEN FRIENDS ...
... SINCE JUNIOR HIGH ?
BUT...
"I'M NOT YOUR FRIEND ANY-MORE."

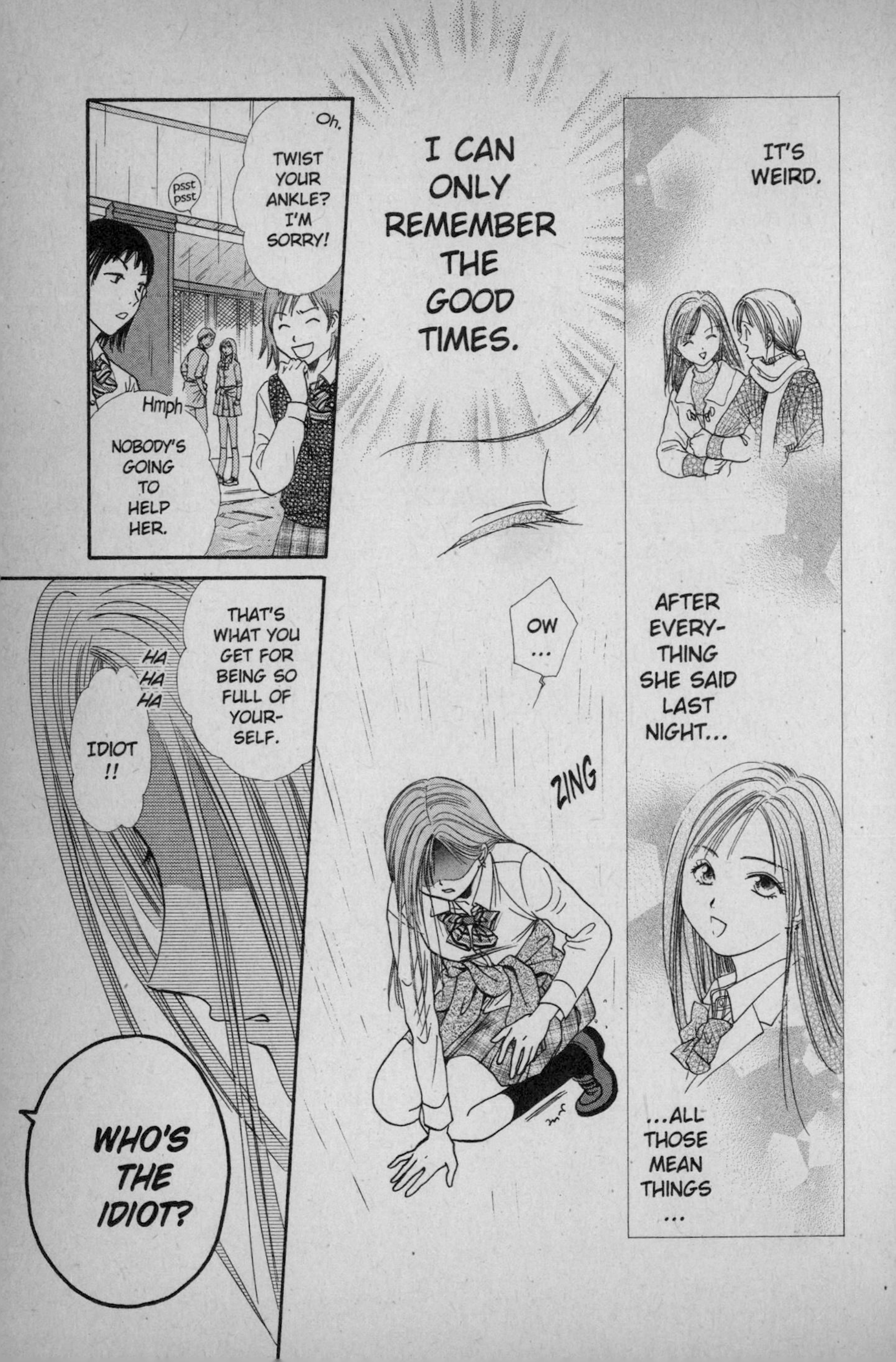

IT'S WEIRD.
I CAN ONLY REMEMBER THE GOOD TIMES.
AFTER EVERYTHING SHE SAID LAST NIGHT...
...ALL THOSE MEAN THINGS...
Oh.
TWIST YOUR ANKLE? I'M SORRY!
psst psst
Hmph
NOBODY'S GOING TO HELP HER.
OW...
ZING
THAT'S WHAT YOU GET FOR BEING SO FULL OF YOUR-SELF.
HA HA HA
IDIOT !!
WHO'S THE IDIOT?

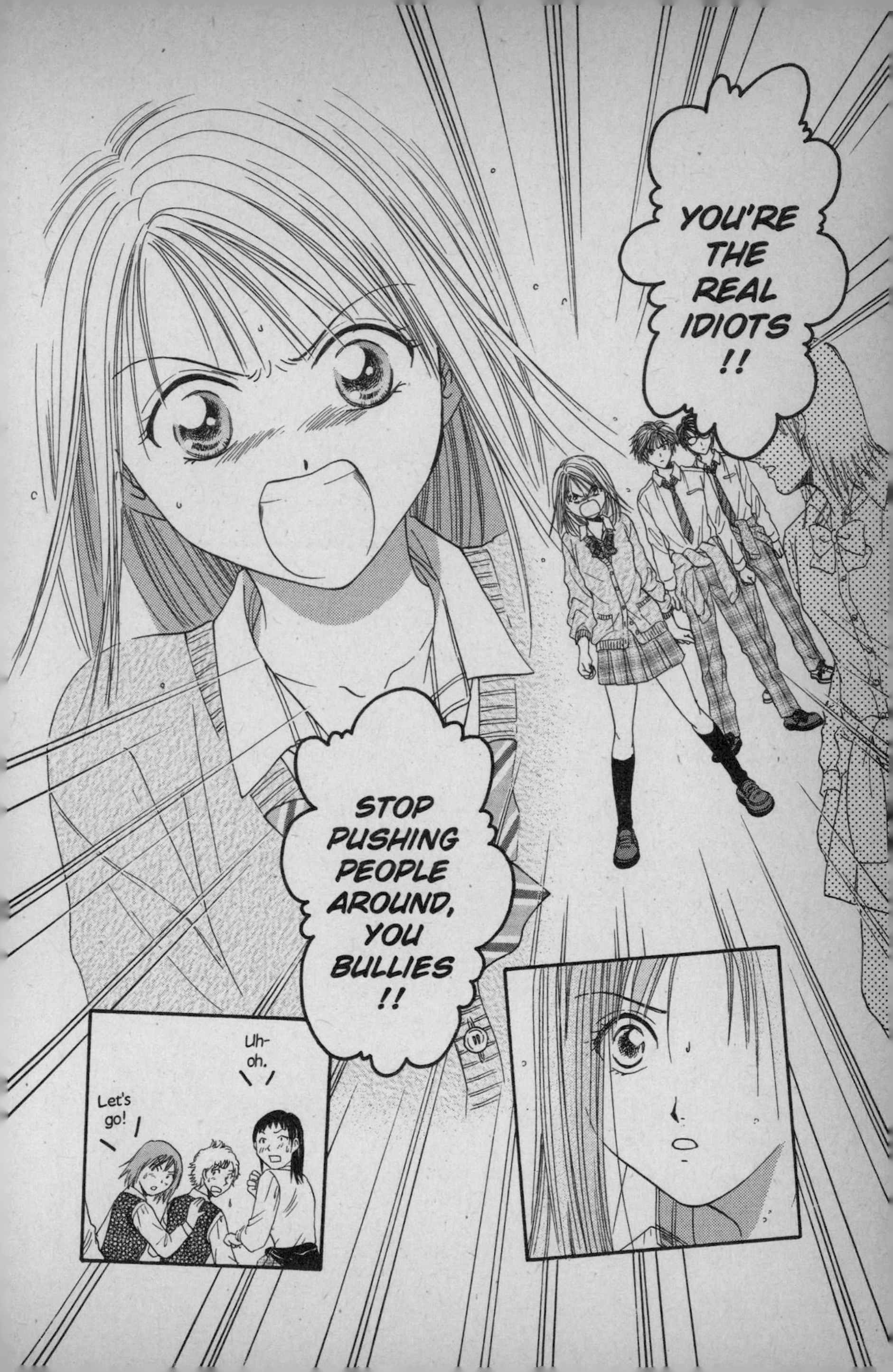
YOU'RE THE REAL IDIOTS !!
STOP PUSHING PEOPLE AROUND, YOU BULLIES !!
Uh-oh.
Let's go!

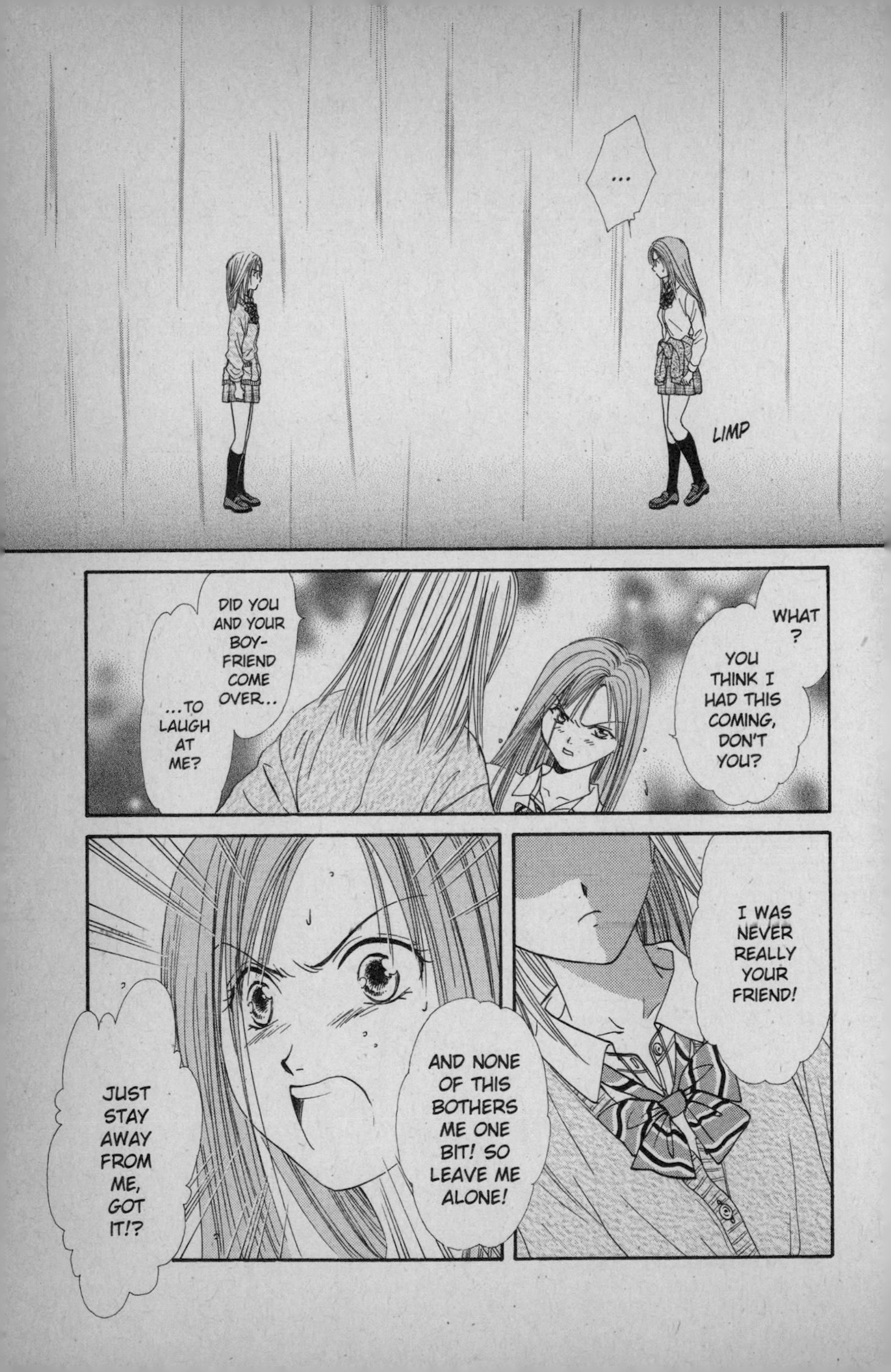
...
LIMP
WHAT?
YOU THINK I HAD THIS COMING, DON'T YOU?
DID YOU AND YOUR BOY-FRIEND COME OVER...
...TO LAUGH AT ME?
I WAS NEVER REALLY YOUR FRIEND!
AND NONE OF THIS BOTHERS ME ONE BIT! SO LEAVE ME ALONE!
JUST STAY AWAY FROM ME, GOT IT!?

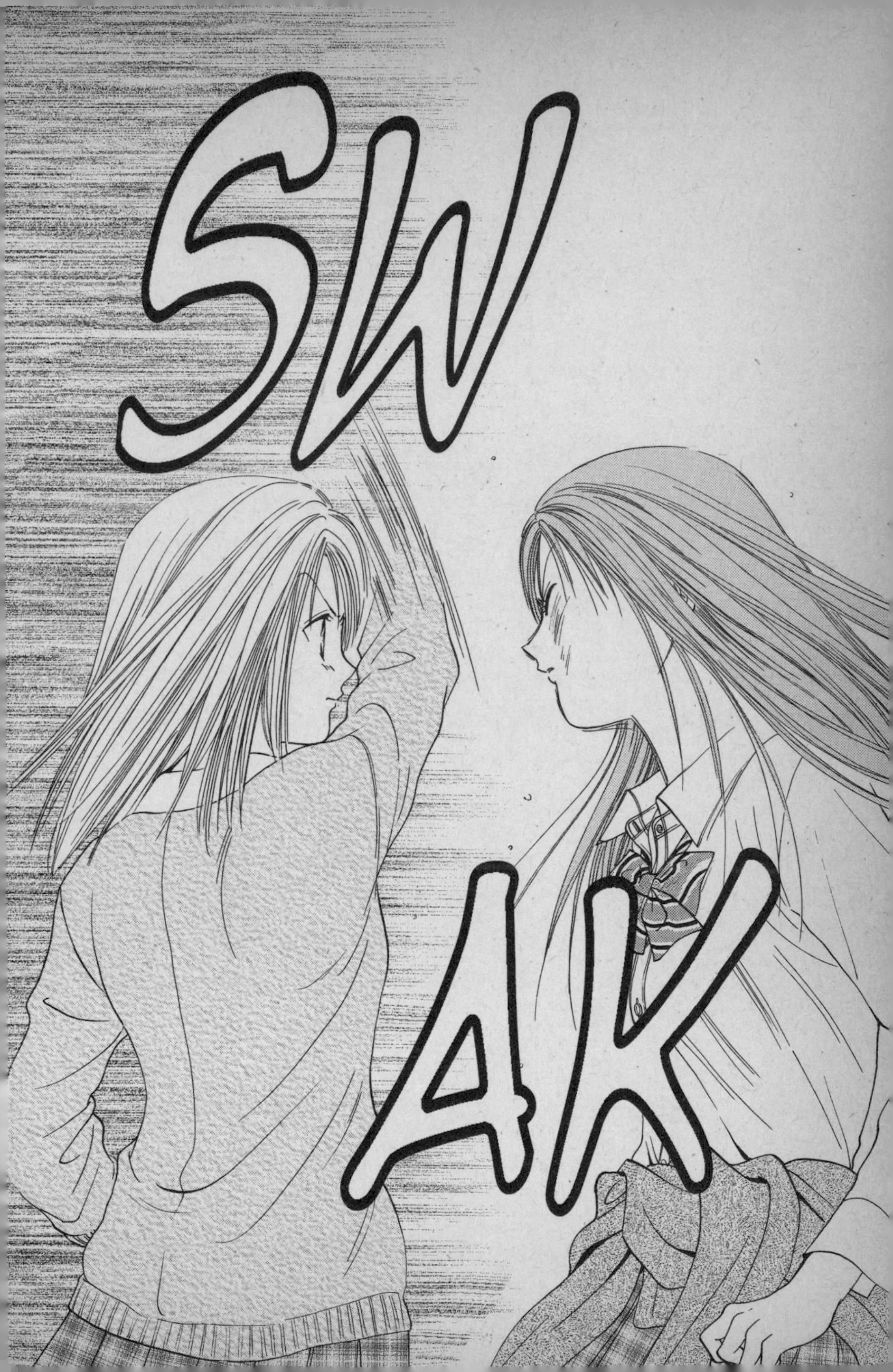
SWAK

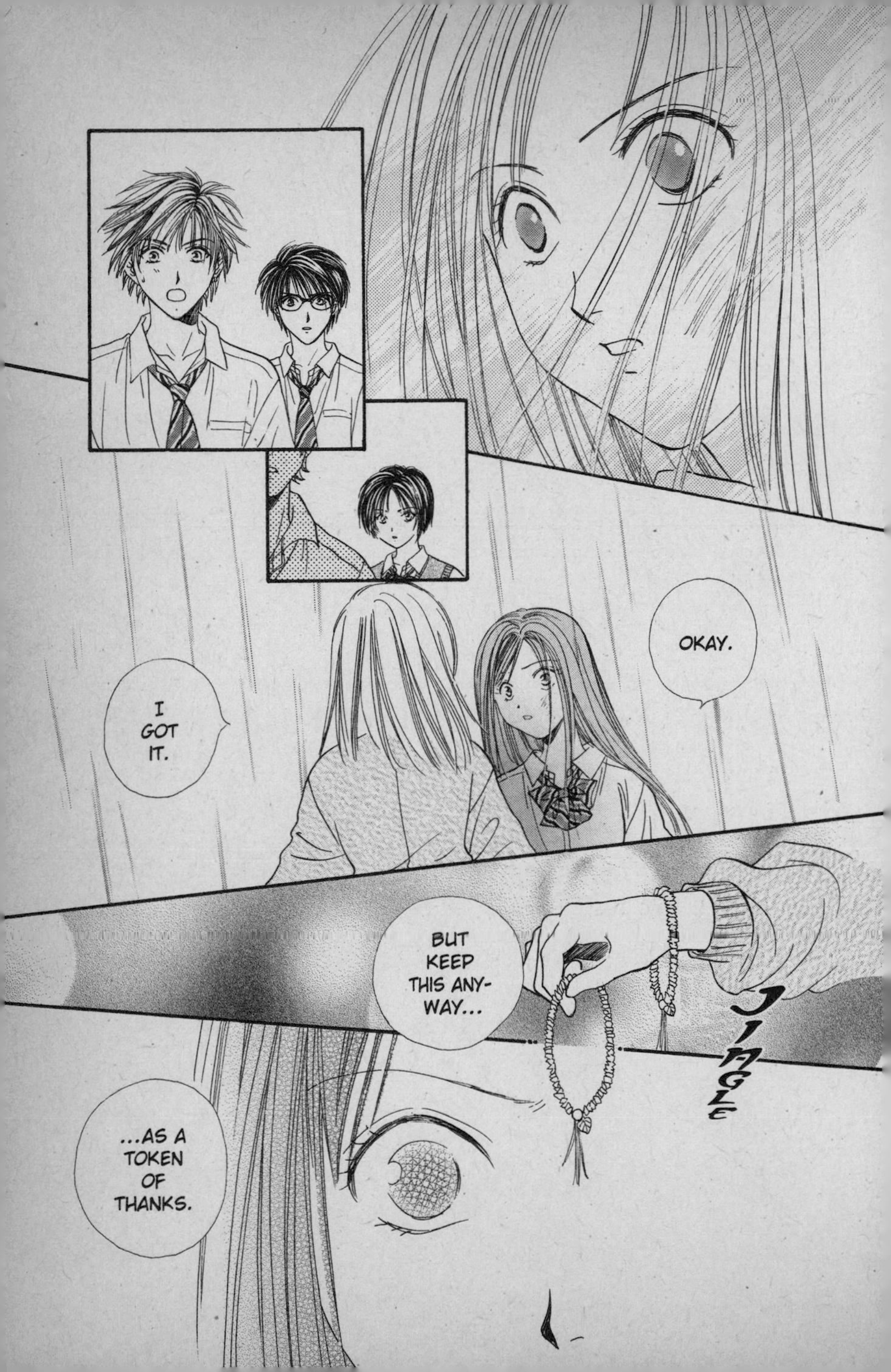
OKAY.
I GOT IT.
BUT KEEP THIS ANY-WAY...
JINGLE
...AS A TOKEN OF THANKS.

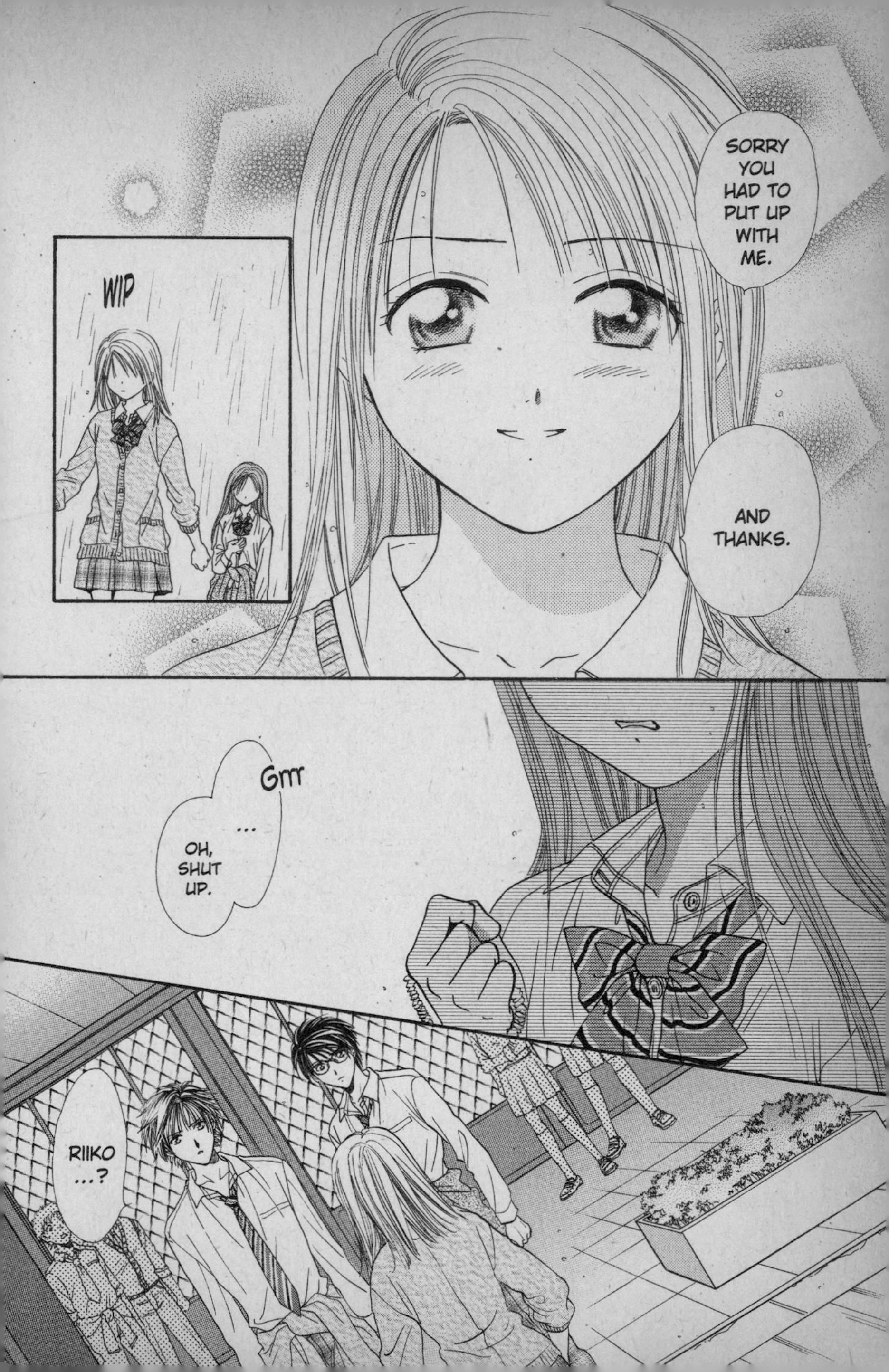
SORRY YOU HAD TO PUT UP WITH ME.
AND THANKS.
WIP
Grrr
... OH, SHUT UP.
RIIKO ...?

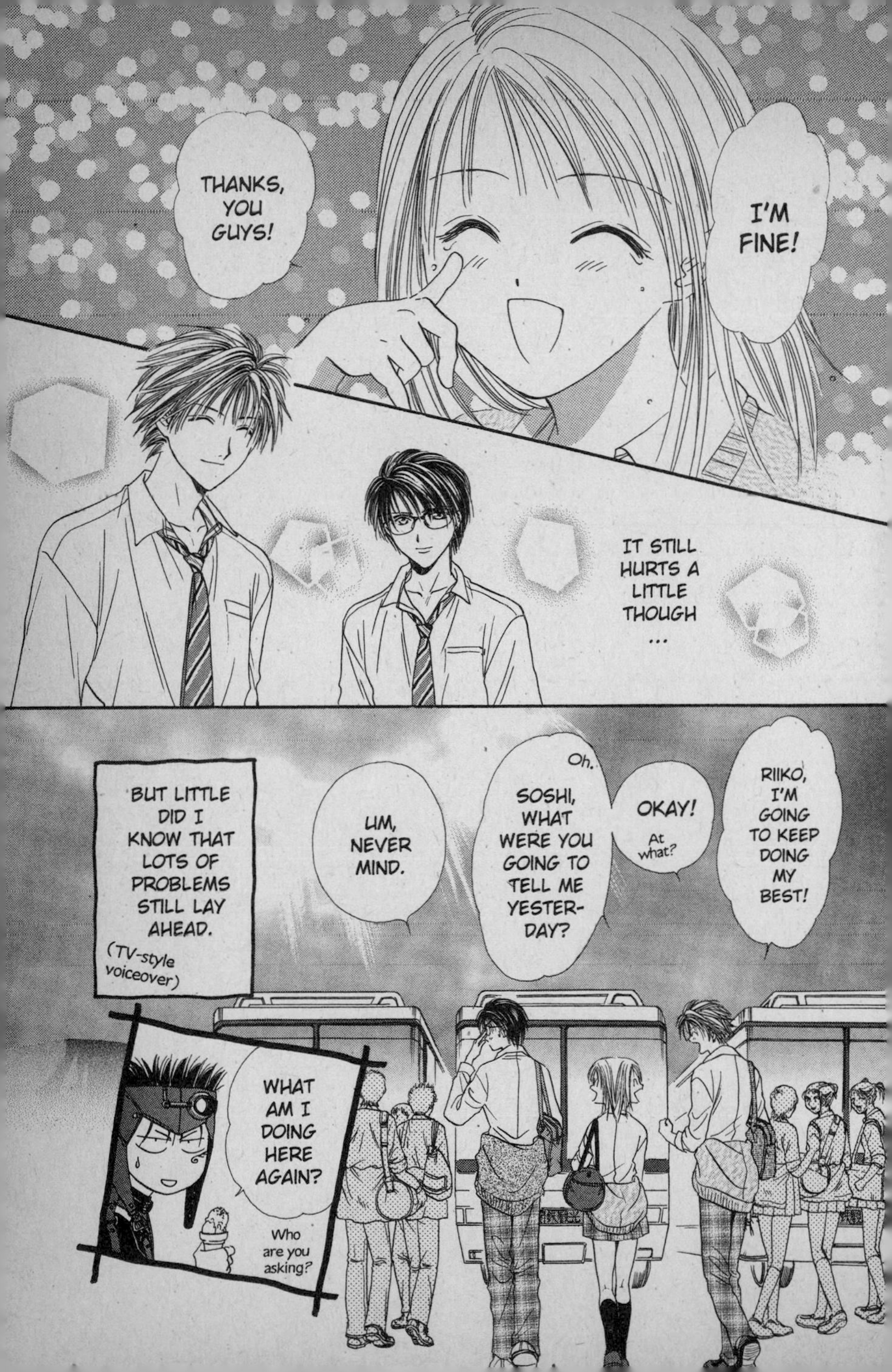
I'M FINE!
THANKS, YOU GUYS!
IT STILL HURTS A LITTLE THOUGH ...
RIIKO, I'M GOING TO KEEP DOING MY BEST!
OKAY!
At what?
Oh.
SOSHI, WHAT WERE YOU GOING TO TELL ME YESTER-DAY?
UM, NEVER MIND.
BUT LITTLE DID I KNOW THAT LOTS OF PROBLEMS STILL LAY AHEAD.
(TV-style voiceover)
WHAT AM I DOING HERE AGAIN?
Who are you asking?

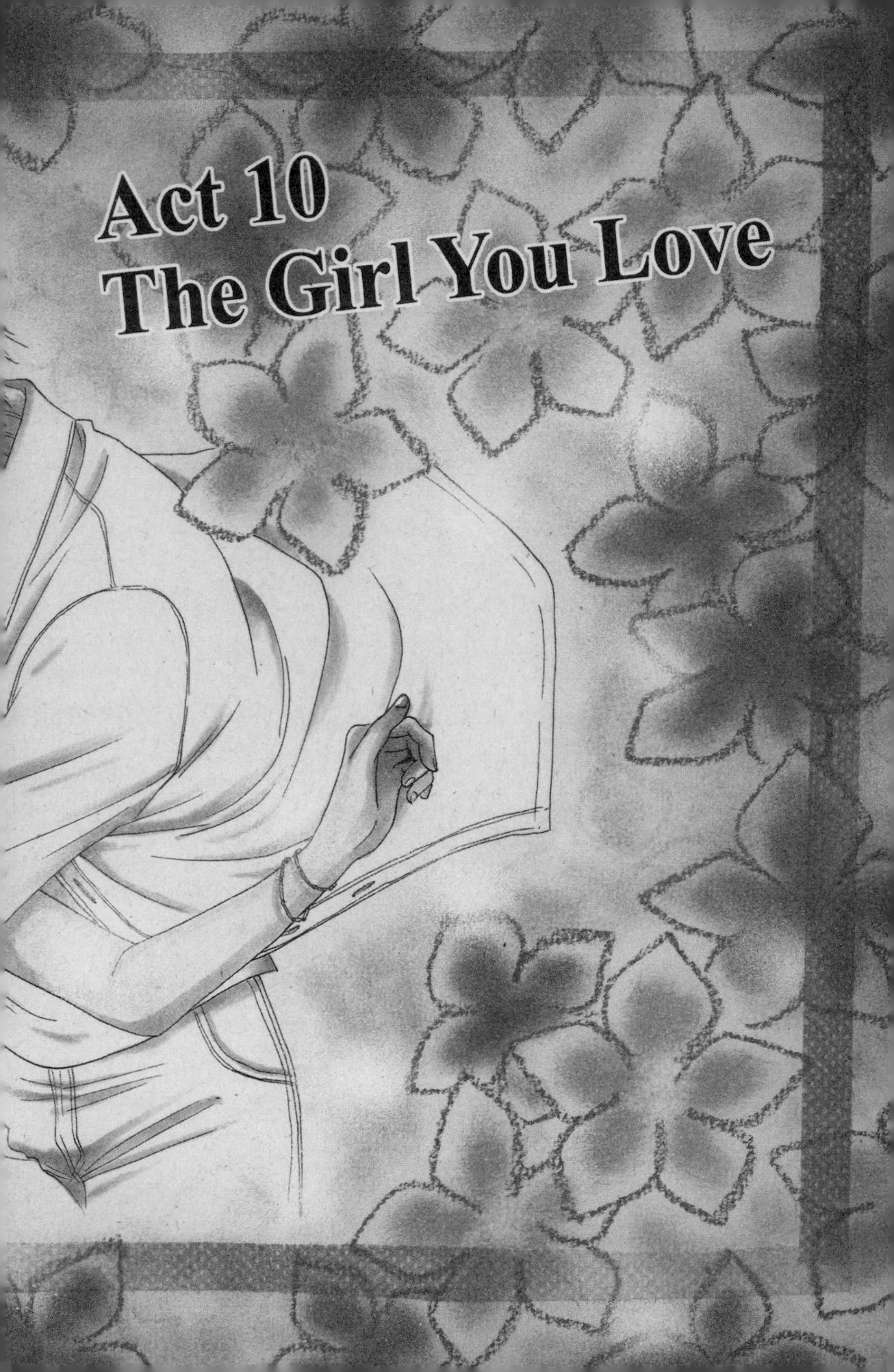
Act 10
The Girl You Love

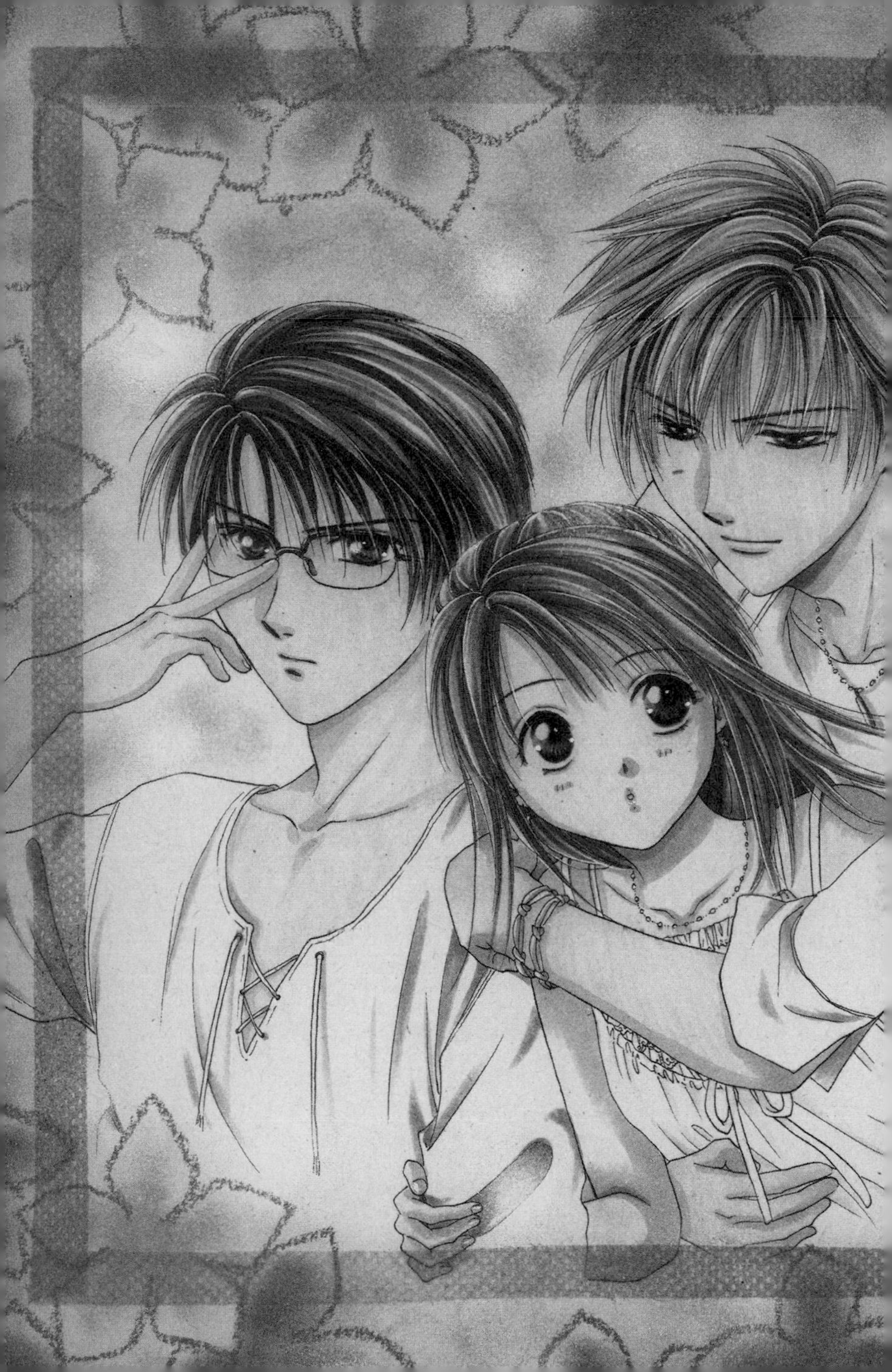

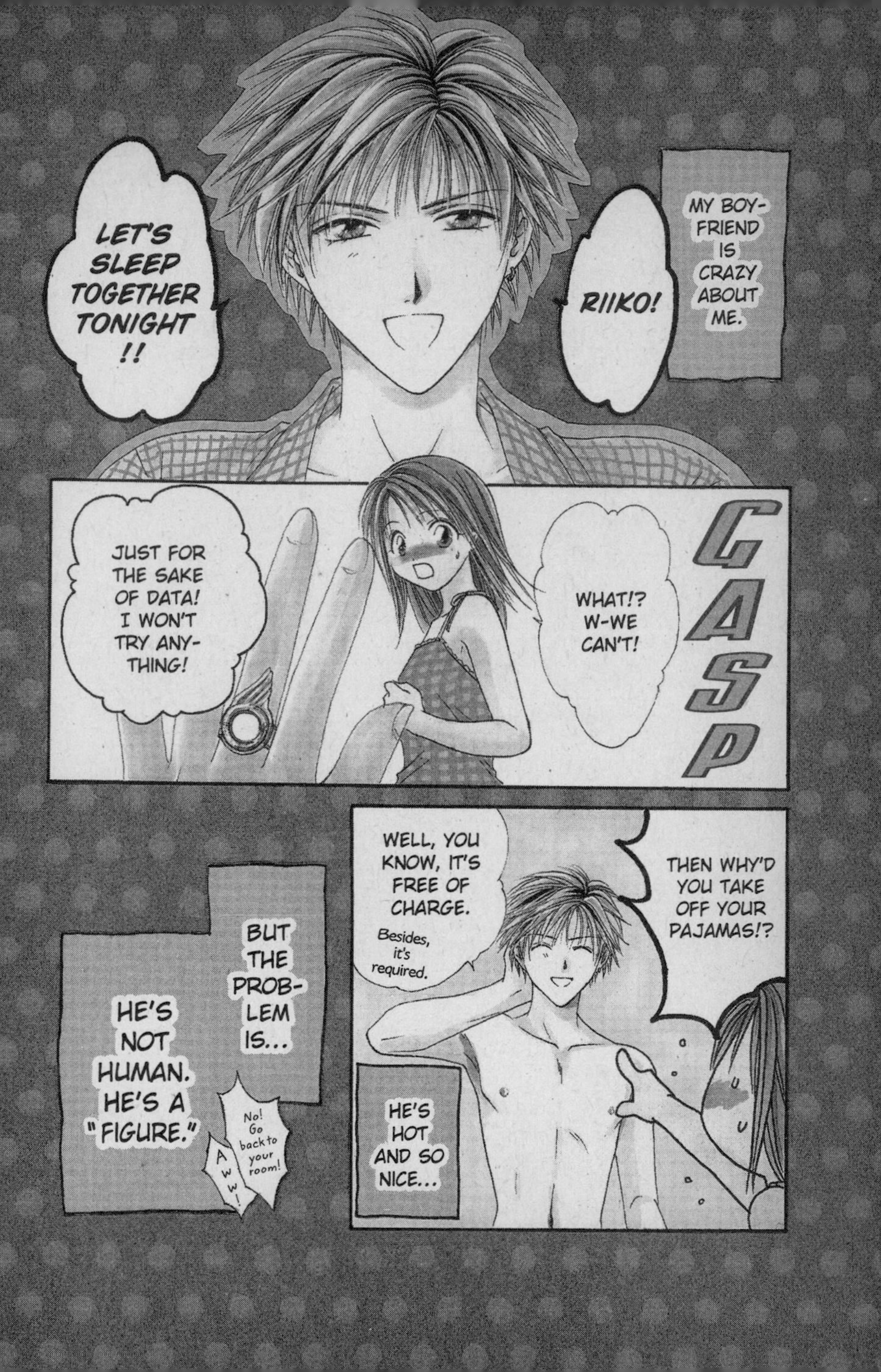
MY BOY-FRIEND IS CRAZY ABOUT ME.
RIIKO!
LET'S SLEEP TOGETHER TONIGHT!!
GASP
WHAT!? W-WE CAN'T!
JUST FOR THE SAKE OF DATA! I WON'T TRY ANY-THING!
THEN WHY'D YOU TAKE OFF YOUR PAJAMAS!?
WELL, YOU KNOW, IT'S FREE OF CHARGE.
Besides, it's required.
HE'S HOT AND SO NICE...
BUT THE PROB-LEM IS...
HE'S NOT HUMAN. HE'S A "FIGURE."
No! Go back to your room!
Aww!

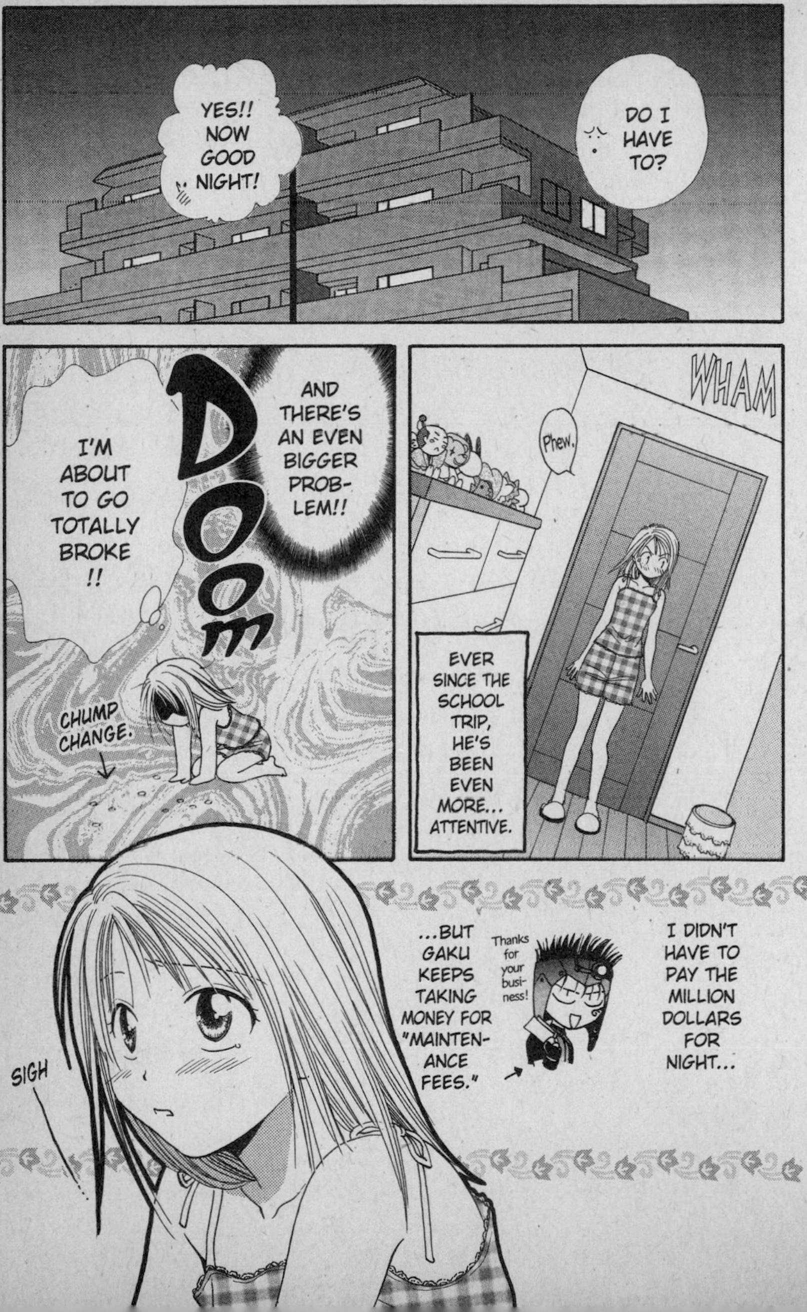

DO I HAVE TO?
YES!! NOW GOOD NIGHT!
WHAM
Phew.
EVER SINCE THE SCHOOL TRIP, HE'S BEEN EVEN MORE... ATTENTIVE.
AND THERE'S AN EVEN BIGGER PROB-LEM!!
DOOM
I'M ABOUT TO GO TOTALLY BROKE !!
CHUMP CHANGE.
I DIDN'T HAVE TO PAY THE MILLION DOLLARS FOR NIGHT...
...BUT GAKU KEEPS TAKING MONEY FOR "MAINTEN-ANCE FEES."
Thanks for your busi-ness!
SIGH

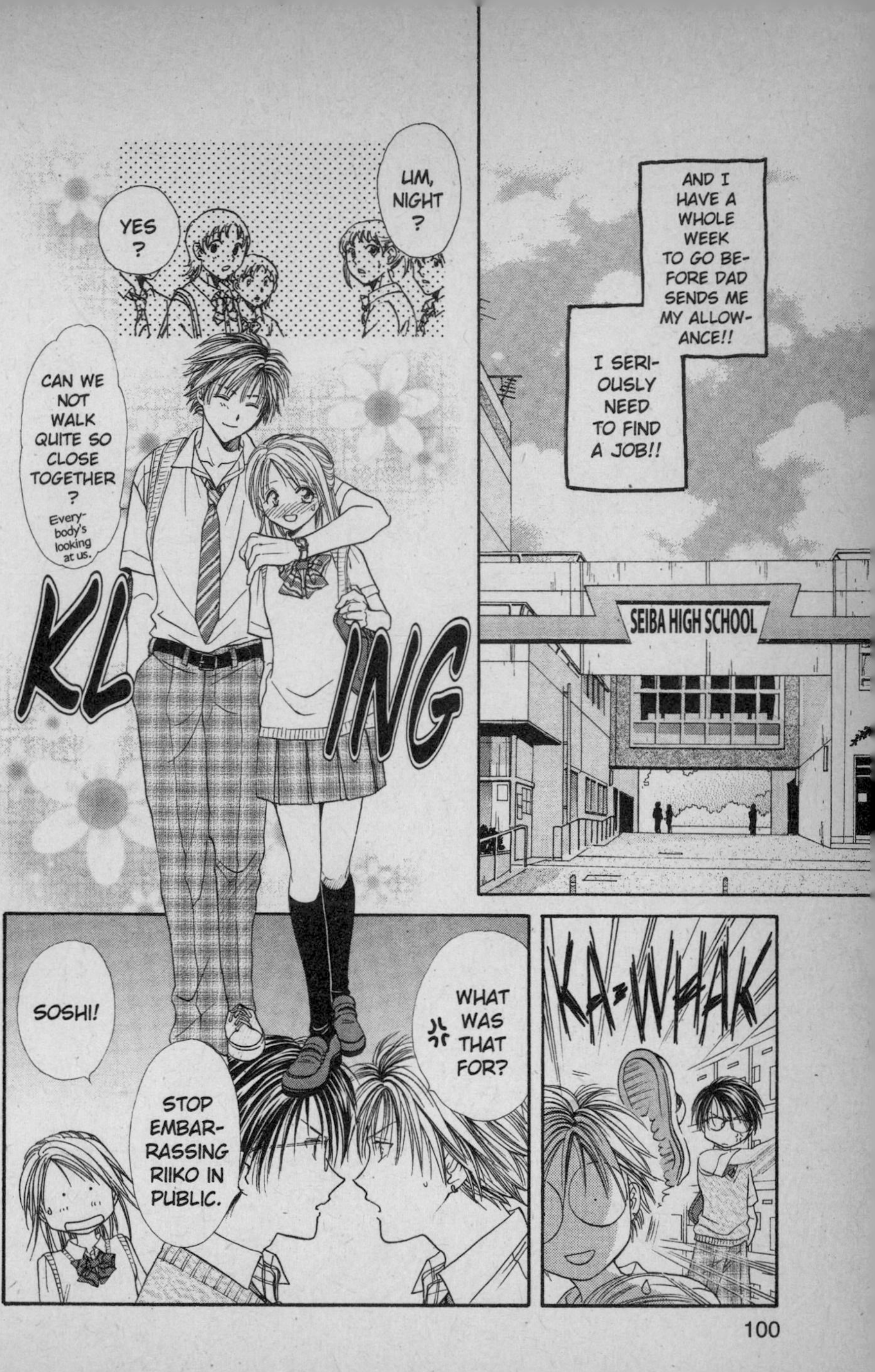
AND I HAVE A WHOLE WEEK TO GO BEFORE DAD SENDS ME MY ALLOWANCE!!
I SERIOUSLY NEED TO FIND A JOB!!
SEIBA HIGH SCHOOL
UM, NIGHT?
YES?
CAN WE NOT WALK QUITE SO CLOSE TOGETHER?
Everybody's looking at us.
KLING
KA-WHAK
WHAT WAS THAT FOR?
SOSHI!
STOP EMBARRASSING RIIKO IN PUBLIC.

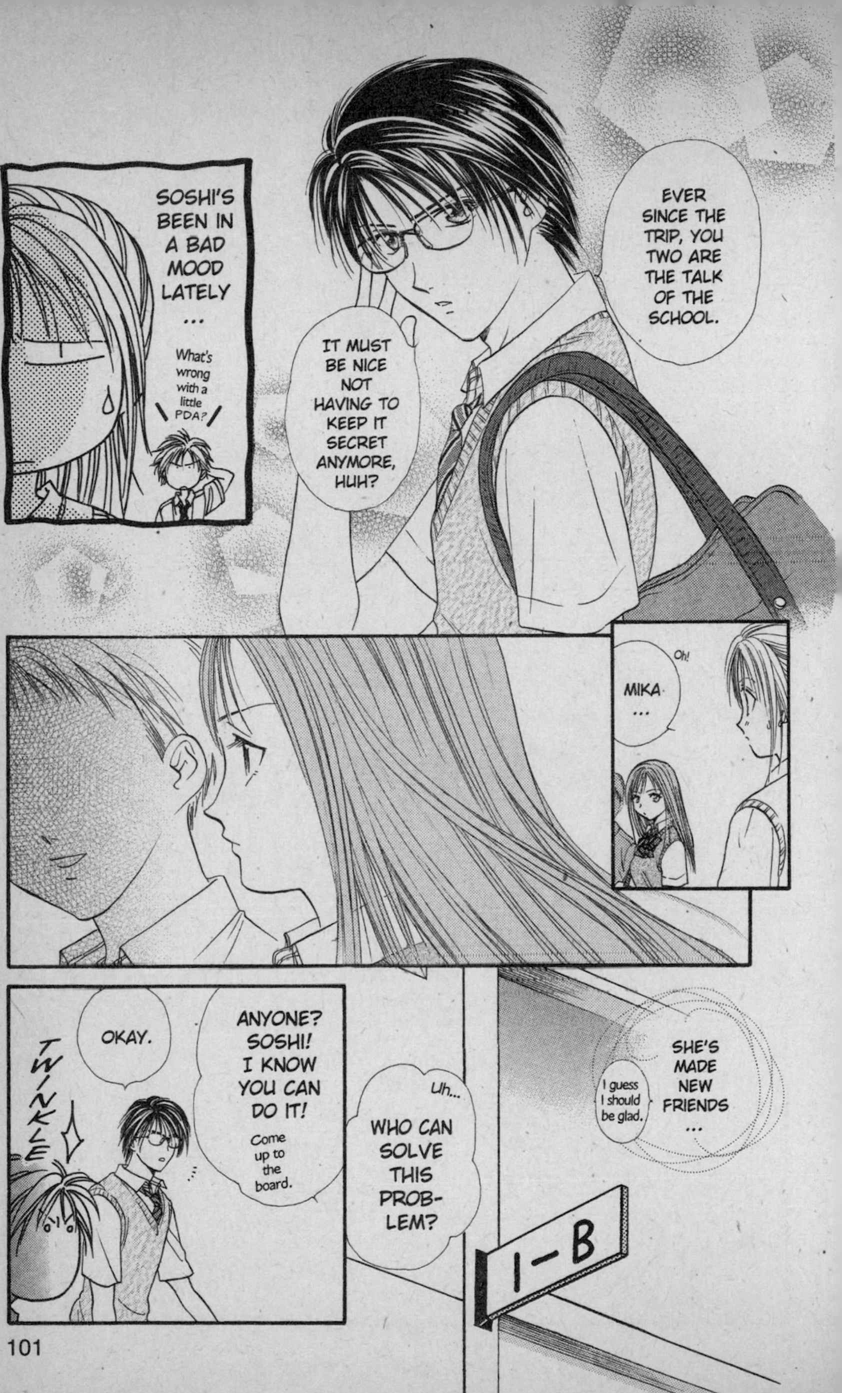
EVER SINCE THE TRIP, YOU TWO ARE THE TALK OF THE SCHOOL.
IT MUST BE NICE NOT HAVING TO KEEP IT SECRET ANYMORE, HUH?
SOSHI'S BEEN IN A BAD MOOD LATELY ...
What's wrong with a little PDA?
Oh!
MIKA ...
SHE'S MADE NEW FRIENDS ...
I guess I should be glad.
I-B
WHO CAN SOLVE THIS PROB-LEM?
Uh...
ANYONE? SOSHI! I KNOW YOU CAN DO IT!
Come up to the board.
OKAY.
TWINKLE

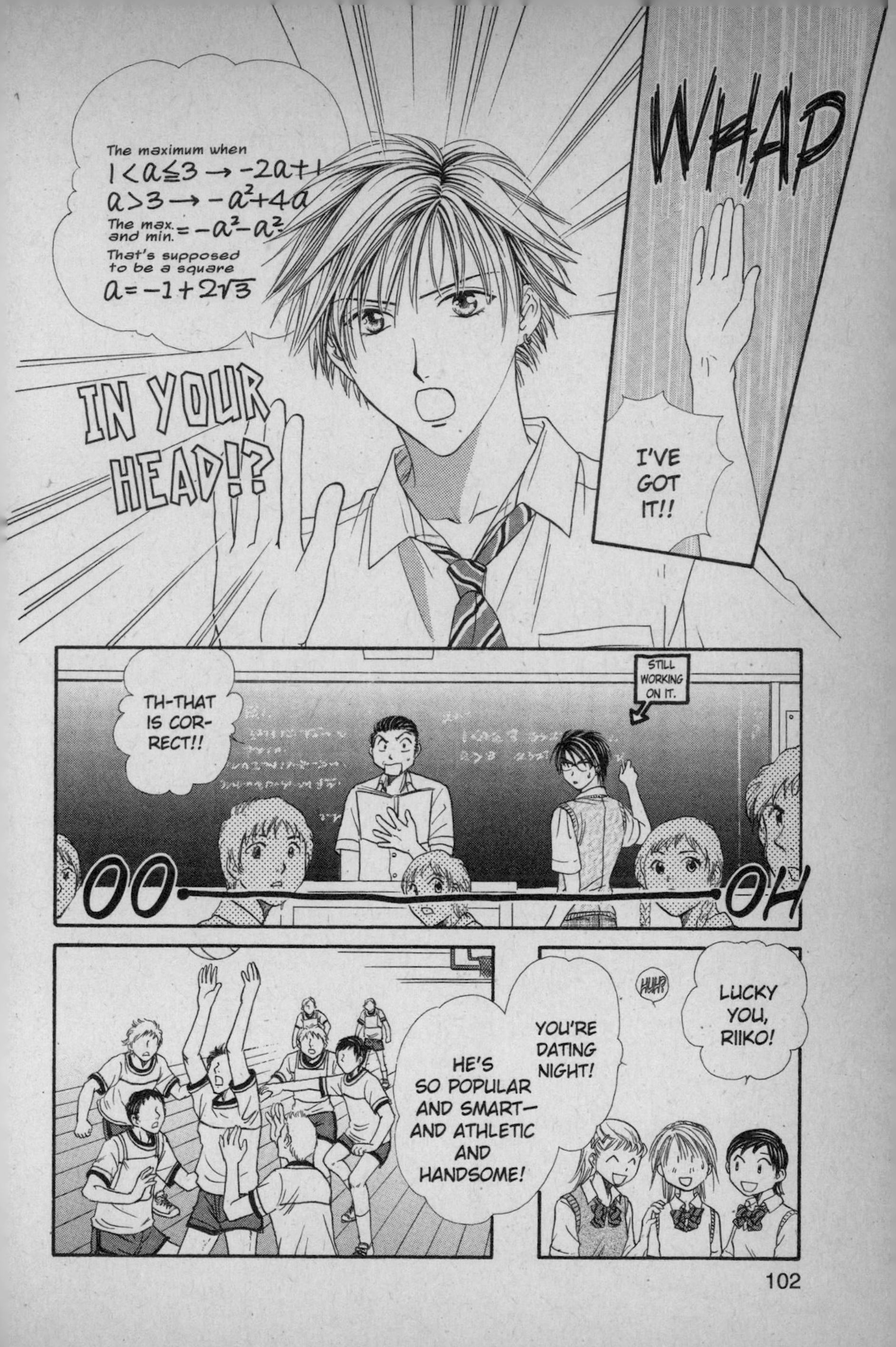
WHAD
I'VE GOT IT!!
The maximum when
$1 < a \leqq 3 \rightarrow -2a+1$
$a > 3 \rightarrow -a^2+4a$
The max. and min. $= -a^2 - a^2$
That's supposed to be a square
$a = -1 + 2\sqrt{3}$
IN YOUR HEAD!?
STILL WORKING ON IT.
TH-THAT IS CORRECT!!
OO—OH
LUCKY YOU, RIIKO!
HUH?
YOU'RE DATING NIGHT!
HE'S SO POPULAR AND SMART—AND ATHLETIC AND HANDSOME!

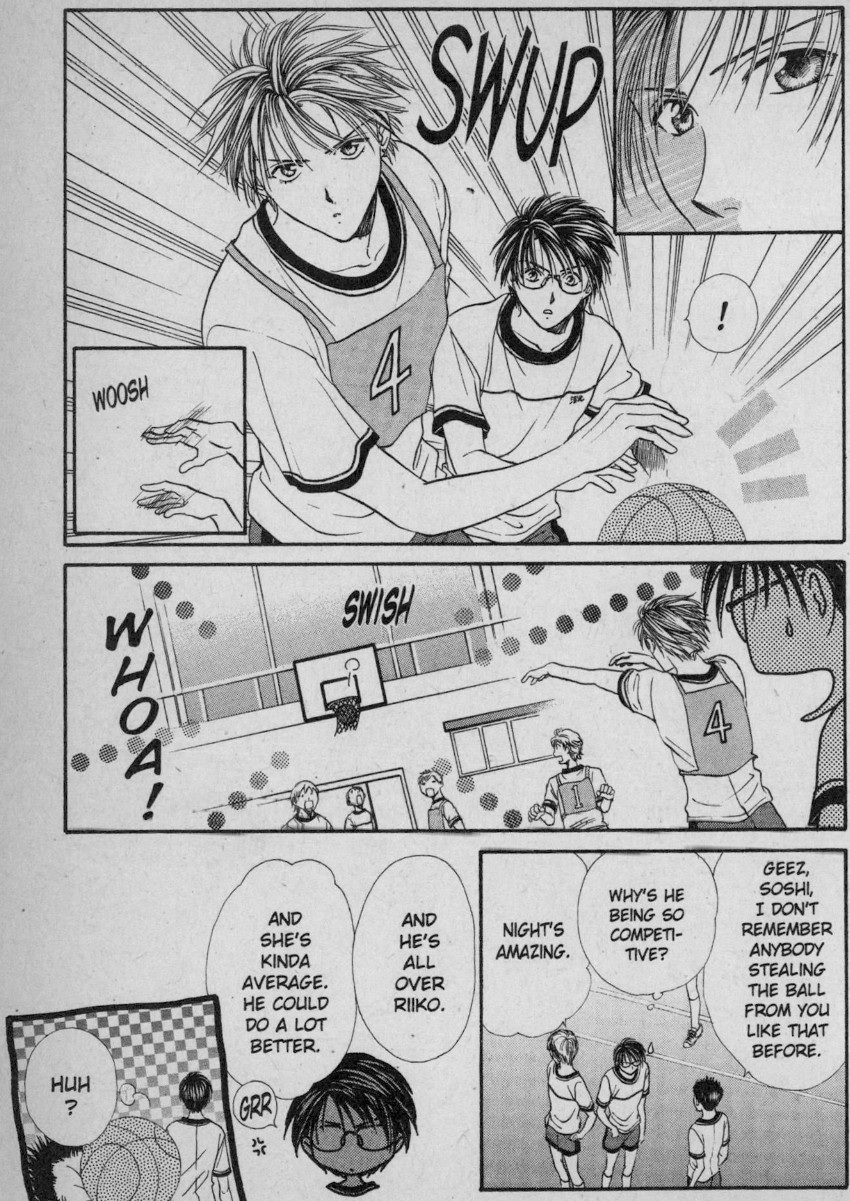

SWUP
!
WOOSH
SWISH
WHOA!
GEEZ, SOSHI, I DON'T REMEMBER ANYBODY STEALING THE BALL FROM YOU LIKE THAT BEFORE.
WHY'S HE BEING SO COMPETI-TIVE?
NIGHT'S AMAZING.
AND HE'S ALL OVER RIIKO.
AND SHE'S KINDA AVERAGE. HE COULD DO A LOT BETTER.
GRR
HUH ?

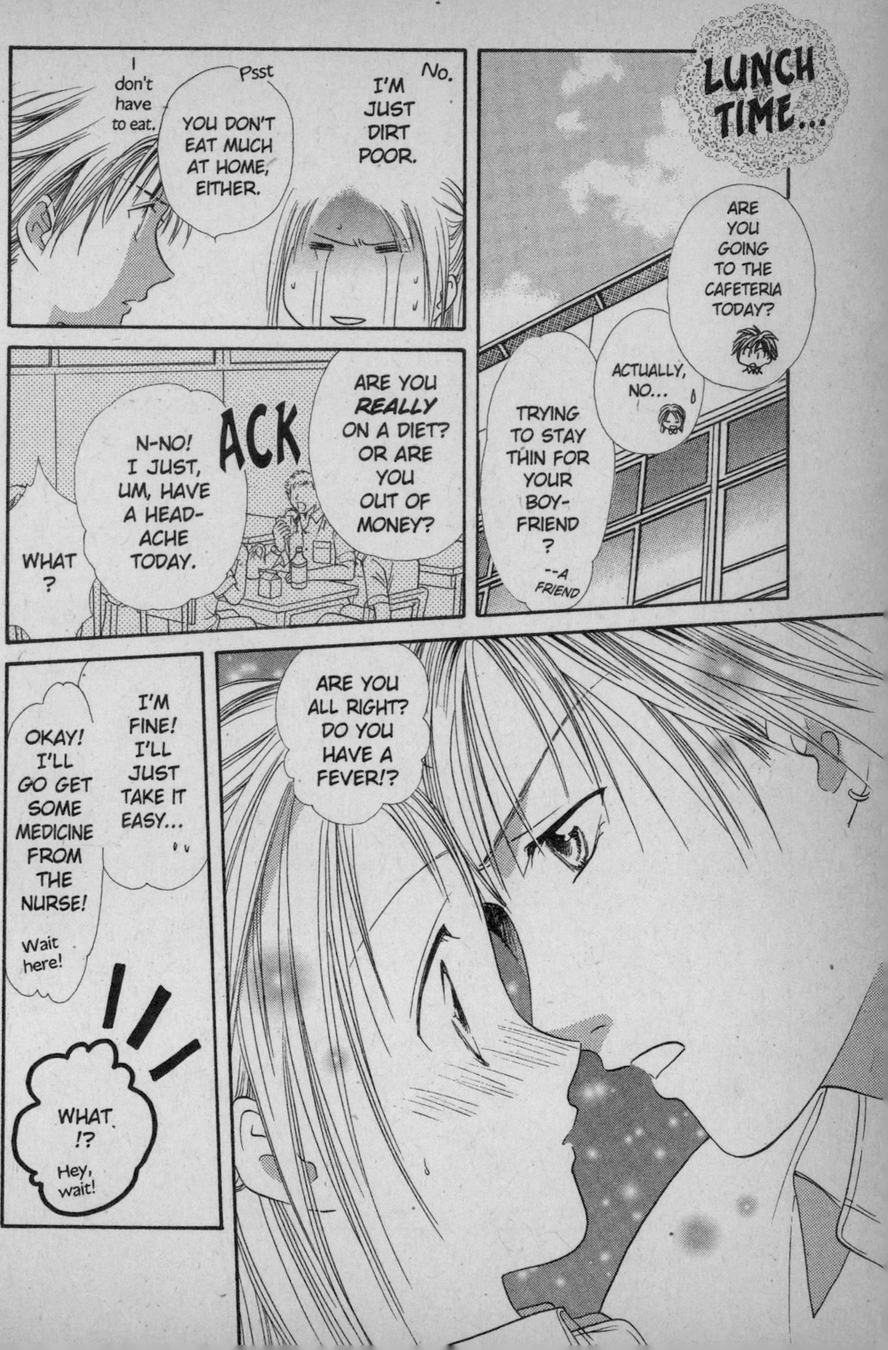
LUNCH TIME...
ARE YOU GOING TO THE CAFETERIA TODAY?
ACTUALLY, NO...
TRYING TO STAY THIN FOR YOUR BOY-FRIEND?
--A FRIEND
No.
I'M JUST DIRT POOR.
Psst
YOU DON'T EAT MUCH AT HOME, EITHER.
I don't have to eat.
ARE YOU REALLY ON A DIET? OR ARE YOU OUT OF MONEY?
ACK
N-NO! I JUST, UM, HAVE A HEAD-ACHE TODAY.
WHAT?
ARE YOU ALL RIGHT? DO YOU HAVE A FEVER!?
I'M FINE! I'LL JUST TAKE IT EASY...
OKAY! I'LL GO GET SOME MEDICINE FROM THE NURSE!
Wait here!
WHAT!?
Hey, wait!

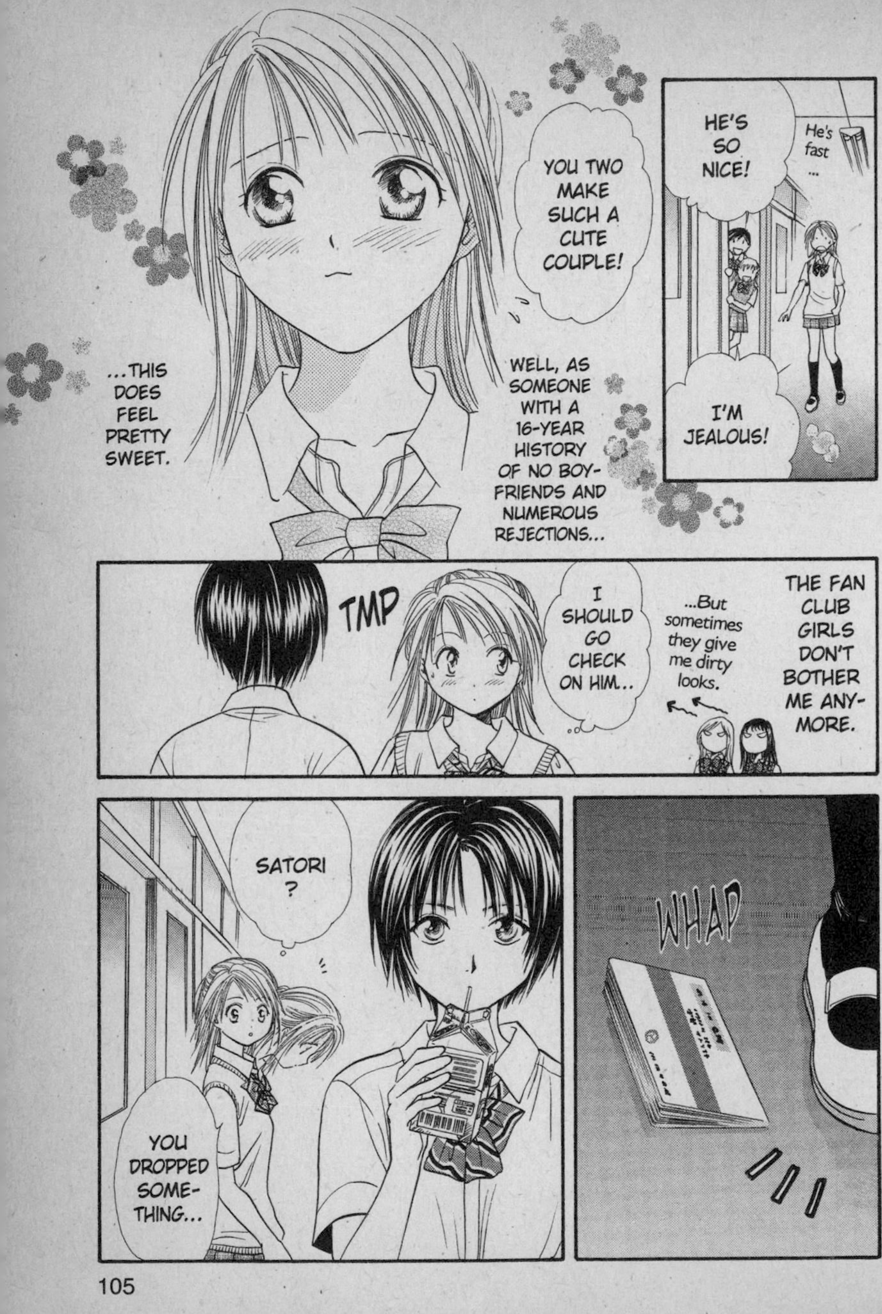

HE'S SO NICE!
He's fast ...
I'M JEALOUS!
YOU TWO MAKE SUCH A CUTE COUPLE!
WELL, AS SOMEONE WITH A 16-YEAR HISTORY OF NO BOY-FRIENDS AND NUMEROUS REJECTIONS...
...THIS DOES FEEL PRETTY SWEET.
THE FAN CLUB GIRLS DON'T BOTHER ME ANY-MORE.
...But sometimes they give me dirty looks.
I SHOULD GO CHECK ON HIM...
TMP
WHAP
SATORI ?
YOU DROPPED SOME-THING...

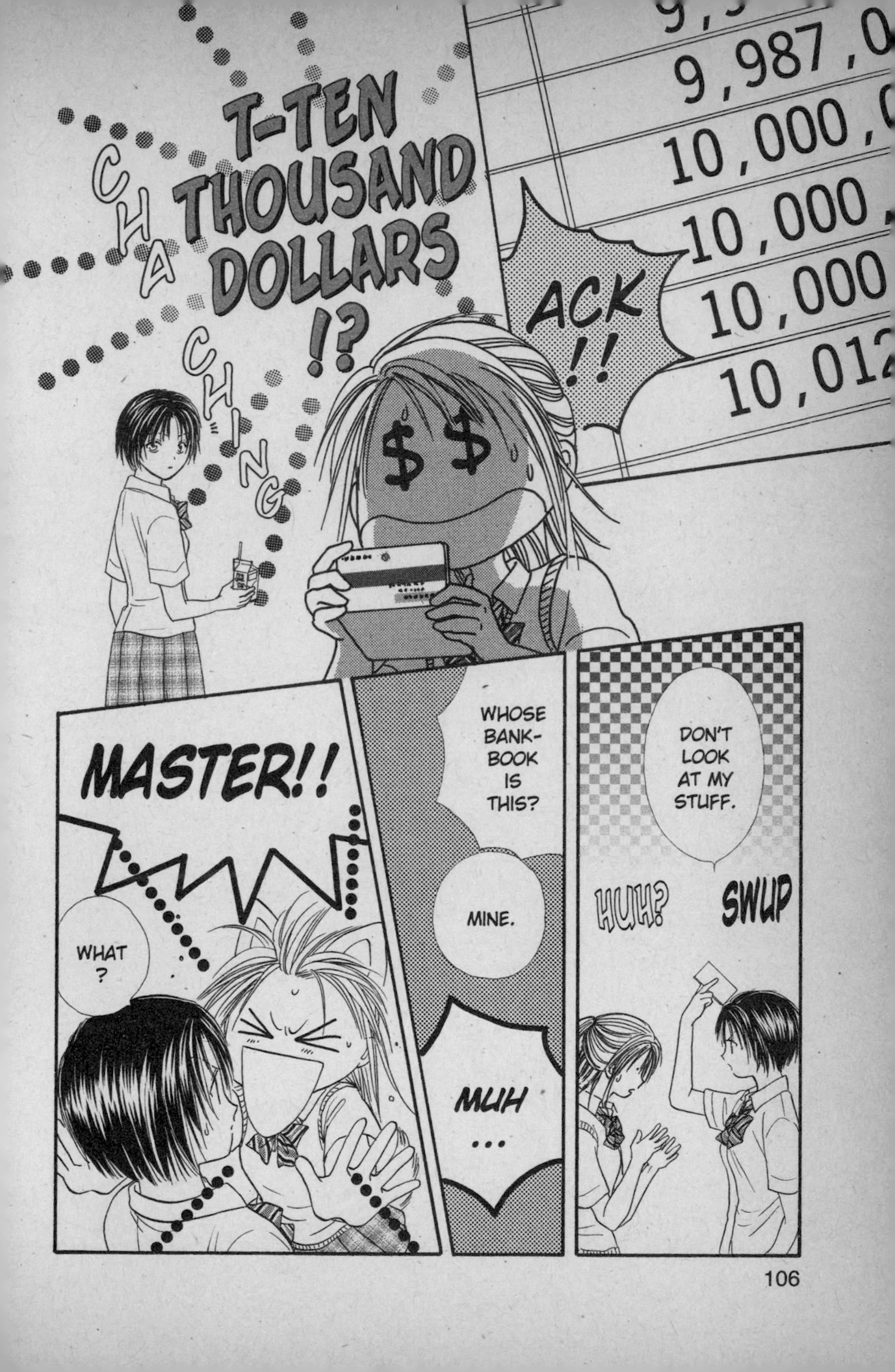

9,987,0
10,000,0
10,000,
10,000
10,012
ACK !!
T-TEN THOUSAND DOLLARS !?
CHA CHING
DON'T LOOK AT MY STUFF.
SWUP
HUH?
WHOSE BANK-BOOK IS THIS?
MINE.
MUH ...
MASTER!!
WHAT ?

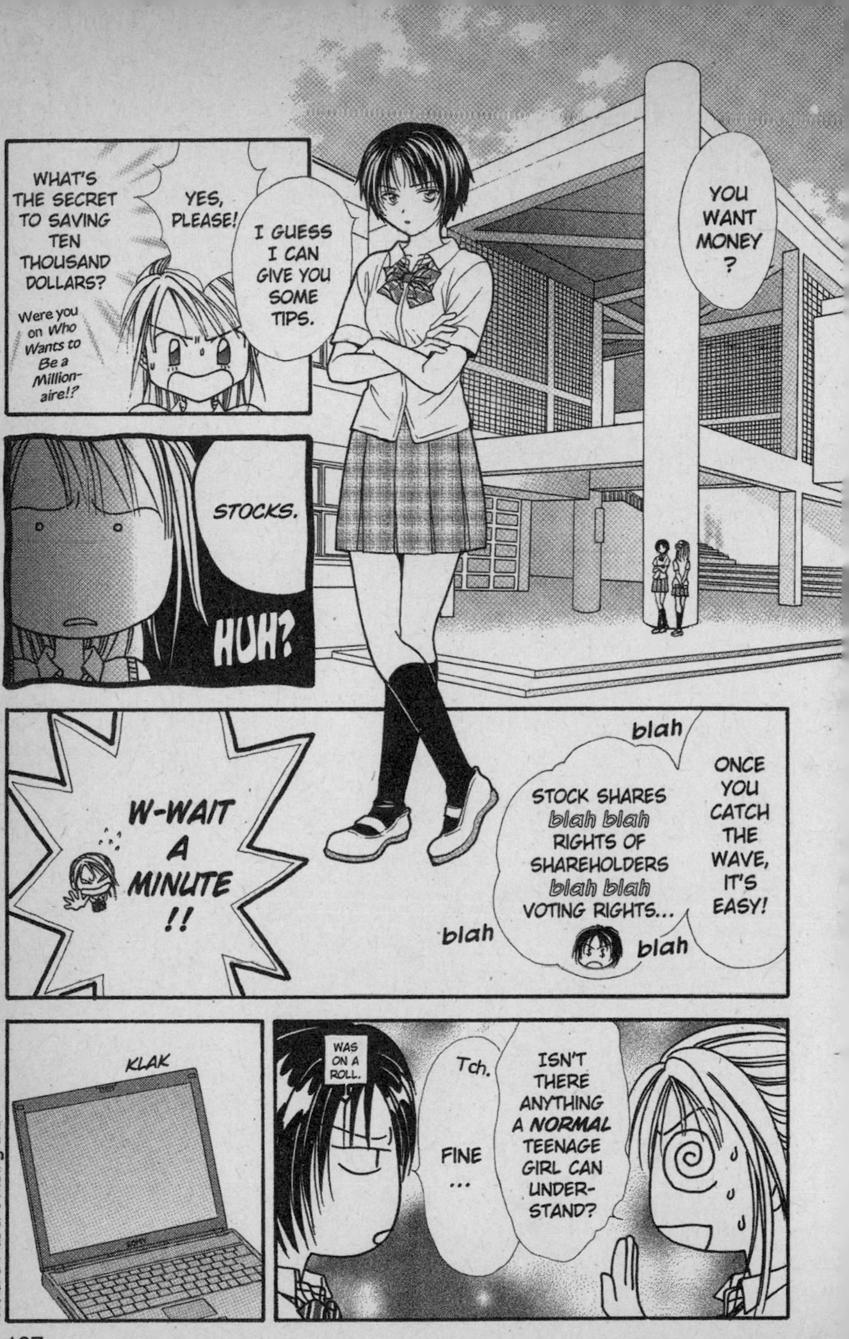
YOU WANT MONEY?
I GUESS I CAN GIVE YOU SOME TIPS.
YES, PLEASE!
WHAT'S THE SECRET TO SAVING TEN THOUSAND DOLLARS?
Were you on *Who Wants to Be a Millionaire*!?
STOCKS.
HUH?
ONCE YOU CATCH THE WAVE, IT'S EASY!
blah
STOCK SHARES *blah blah* RIGHTS OF SHAREHOLDERS *blah blah* VOTING RIGHTS...
blah
blah
W-WAIT A MINUTE!!
ISN'T THERE ANYTHING A ***NORMAL*** TEENAGE GIRL CAN UNDERSTAND?
Tch.
FINE...
WAS ON A ROLL.
KLAK

Where was she hiding this?

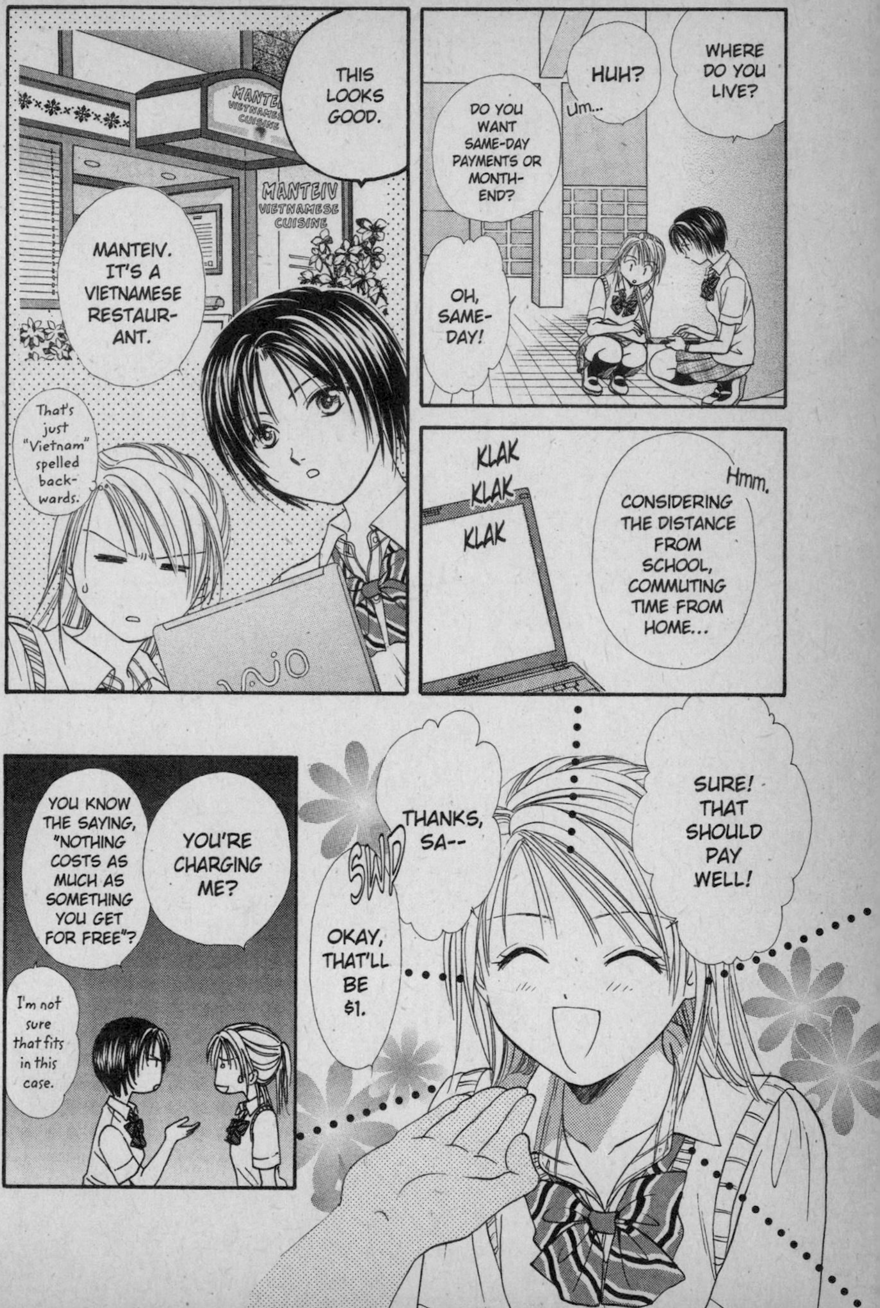
WHERE DO YOU LIVE?
HUH?
Um...
DO YOU WANT SAME-DAY PAYMENTS OR MONTH-END?
OH, SAME-DAY!
Hmm.
CONSIDERING THE DISTANCE FROM SCHOOL, COMMUTING TIME FROM HOME...
KLAK
KLAK
KLAK
THIS LOOKS GOOD.
MANTEIV VIETNAMESE CUISINE
MANTEIV VIETNAMESE CUISINE
MANTEIV. IT'S A VIETNAMESE RESTAURANT.
That's just "Vietnam" spelled backwards.
SURE! THAT SHOULD PAY WELL!
THANKS, SA--
SWP
OKAY, THAT'LL BE $1.
YOU'RE CHARGING ME?
YOU KNOW THE SAYING, "NOTHING COSTS AS MUCH AS SOMETHING YOU GET FOR FREE"?
I'm not sure that fits in this case.

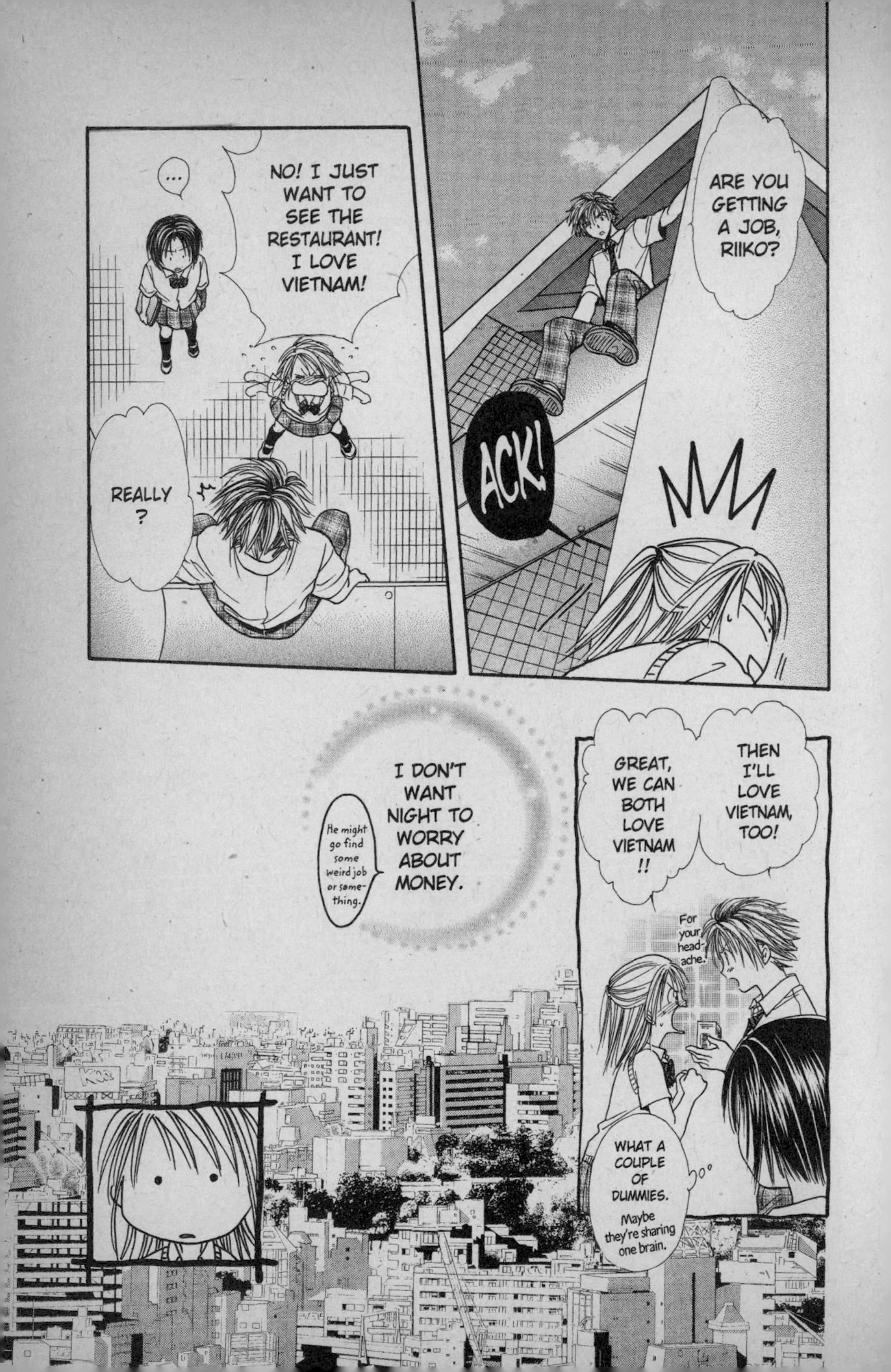

ARE YOU GETTING A JOB, RIIKO?
ACK!
NO! I JUST WANT TO SEE THE RESTAURANT! I LOVE VIETNAM!
...
REALLY?
THEN I'LL LOVE VIETNAM, TOO!
GREAT, WE CAN BOTH LOVE VIETNAM!!
For your headache.
WHAT A COUPLE OF DUMMIES.
Maybe they're sharing one brain.
I DON'T WANT NIGHT TO WORRY ABOUT MONEY.
He might go find some weird job or something.

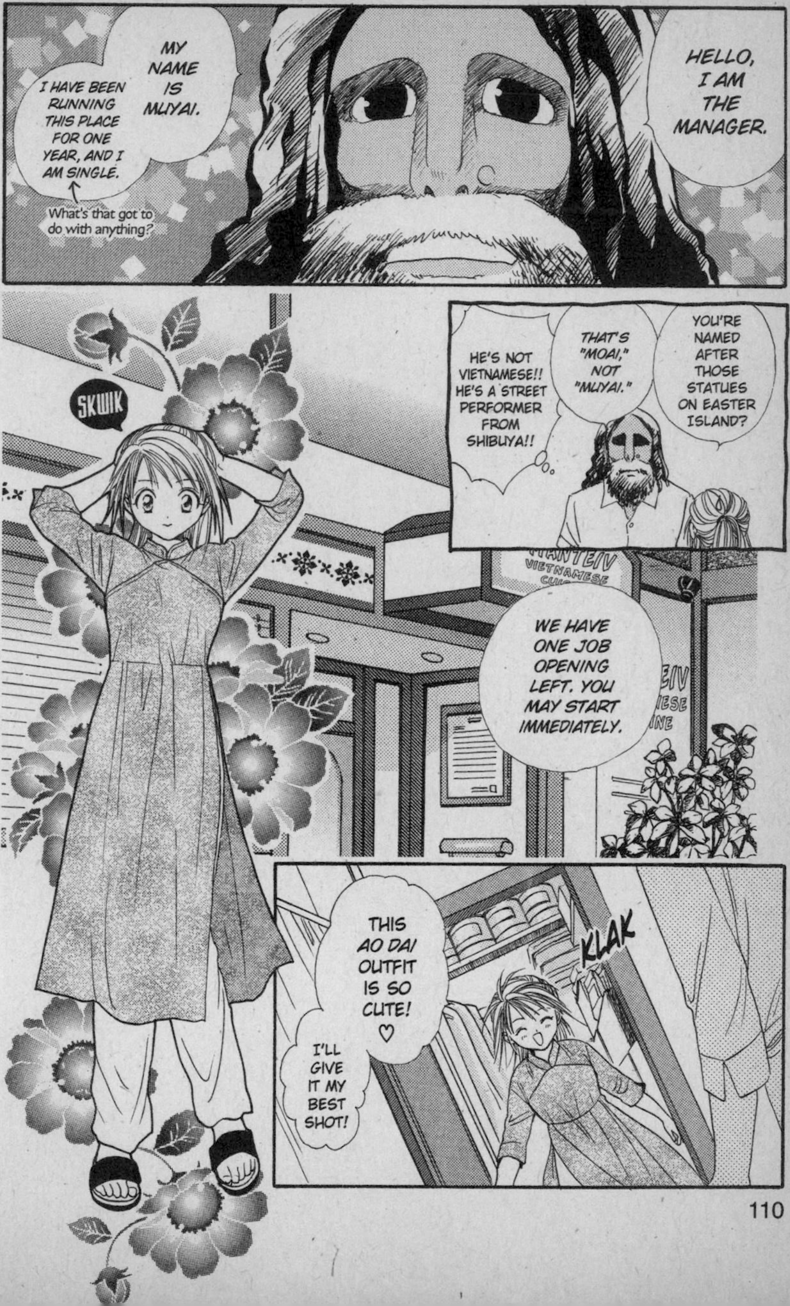
HELLO, I AM THE MANAGER.
MY NAME IS MUYAI.
I HAVE BEEN RUNNING THIS PLACE FOR ONE YEAR, AND I AM SINGLE.
What's that got to do with anything?
YOU'RE NAMED AFTER THOSE STATUES ON EASTER ISLAND?
THAT'S "MOAI," NOT "MUYAI."
HE'S NOT VIETNAMESE!! HE'S A STREET PERFORMER FROM SHIBUYA!!
WE HAVE ONE JOB OPENING LEFT. YOU MAY START IMMEDIATELY.
SKWIK
KLAK
THIS AO DAI OUTFIT IS SO CUTE! ♡
I'LL GIVE IT MY BEST SHOT!

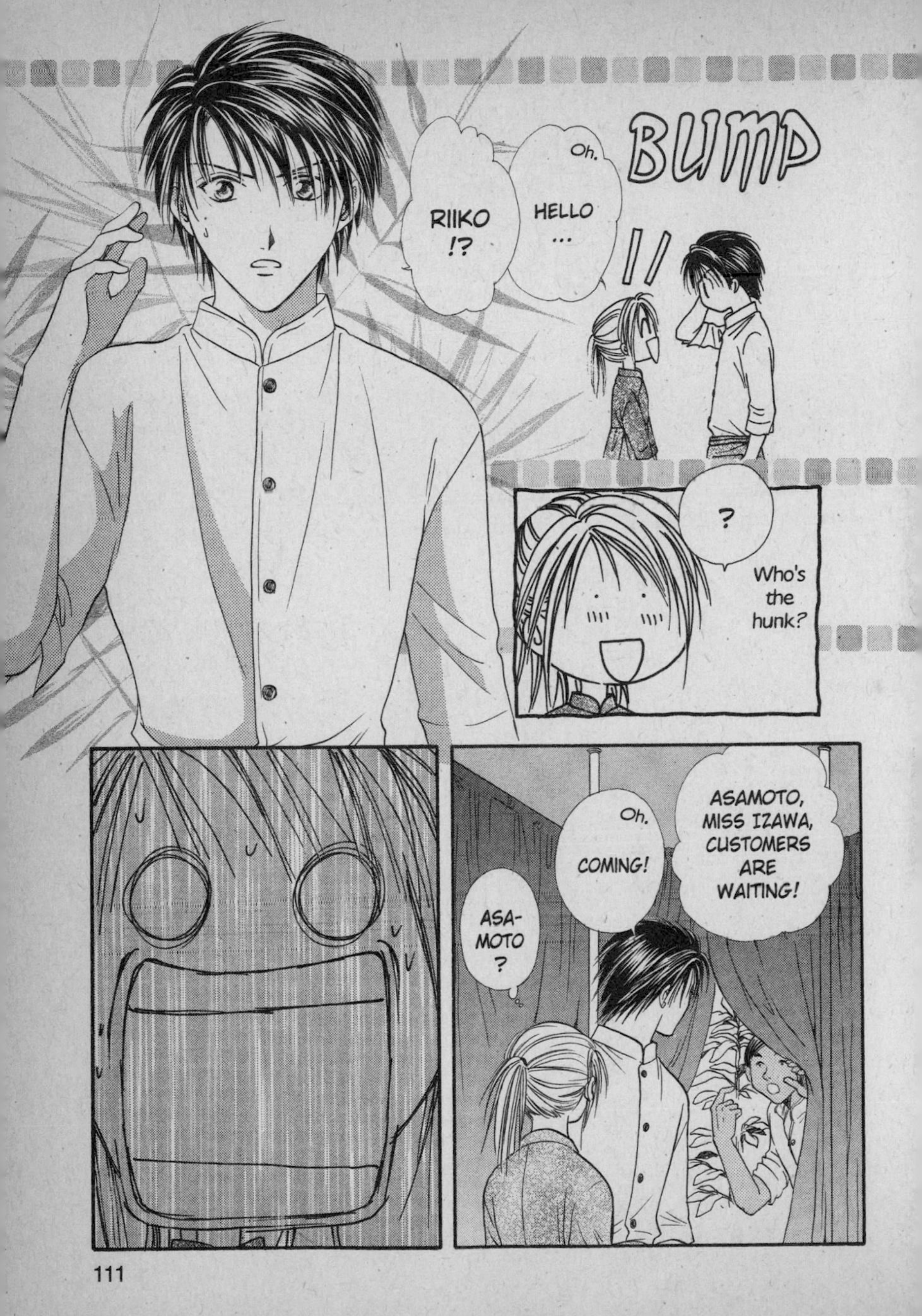
BUMP
Oh.
HELLO ...
RIIKO !?
?
Who's the hunk?
ASAMOTO, MISS IZAWA, CUSTOMERS ARE WAITING!
Oh.
COMING!
ASAMOTO ?

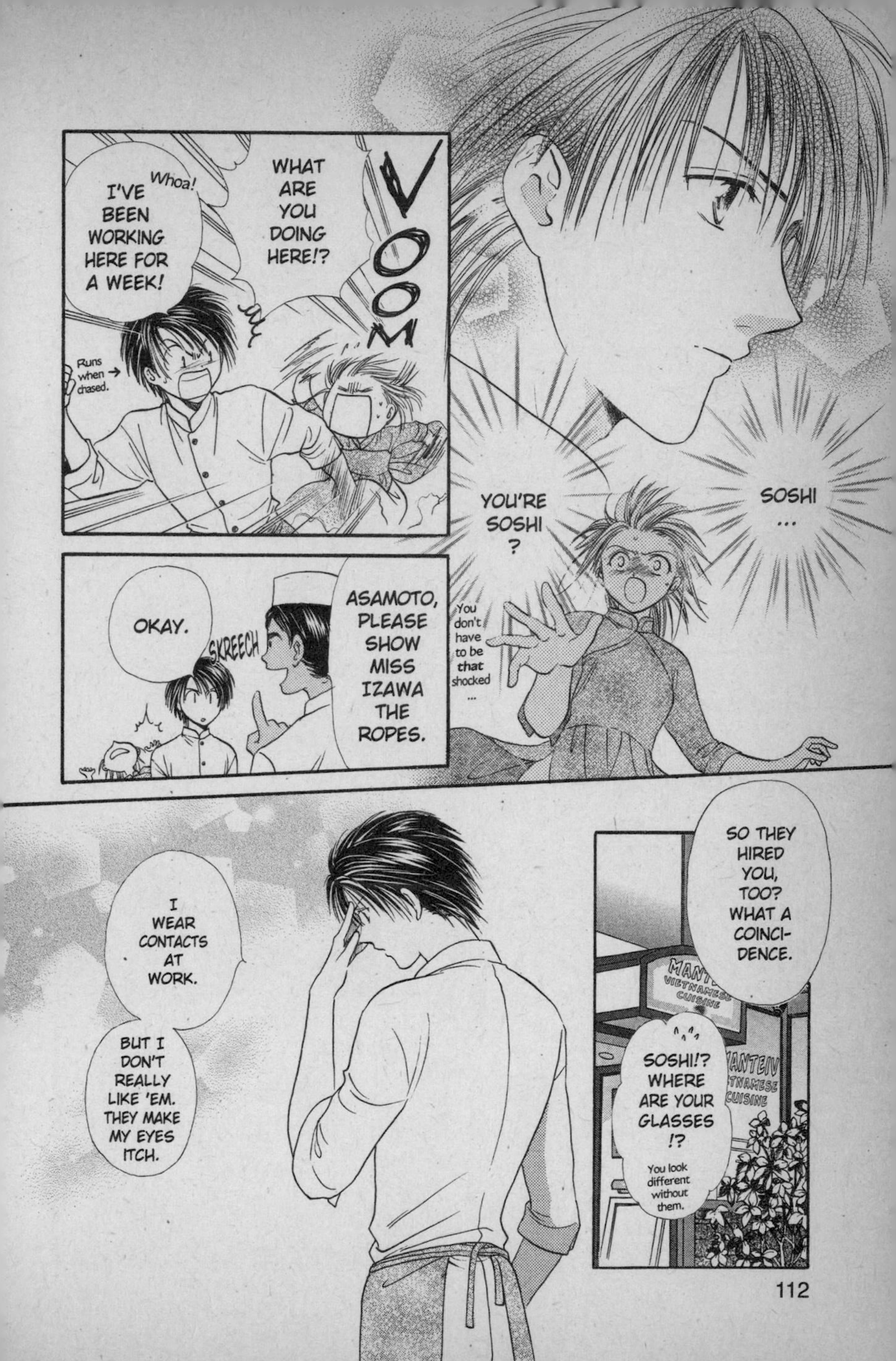
SOSHI ...
YOU'RE SOSHI ?
You don't have to be that shocked ...
WHAT ARE YOU DOING HERE!?
VOOM
Whoa!
I'VE BEEN WORKING HERE FOR A WEEK!
Runs when chased.
ASAMOTO, PLEASE SHOW MISS IZAWA THE ROPES.
SKREECH
OKAY.
SO THEY HIRED YOU, TOO? WHAT A COINCIDENCE.
VIETNAMESE CUISINE
SOSHI!? WHERE ARE YOUR GLASSES !?
You look different without them.
I WEAR CONTACTS AT WORK.
BUT I DON'T REALLY LIKE 'EM. THEY MAKE MY EYES ITCH.

So, that's what happened to Mika. The way you treat others comes back around to you someday. That's karma. If you ask, "Why is this happening to me?" and you can't remember what you did to deserve it, it must've been something you did in your previous life (smile). So don't go around blithely bad-mouthing people or doing bad things. I heard once that everything you say, do, and think are all permanently carved into the record of your life. It all gets recorded like a video. Murder and crime are the worst. Who knows how they might come back to you? Scary. It's better not to kill anything at all! ♪ Not even animals! ♪ Even cows and chickens are part of the chain of life, so you should be thankful whenever you eat meat. What am I rambling about now? I used to love this manga called *Parasyte*. It made me cry. Anyway, everyone, please watch what you do with your life.

What a moralistic column (smile). Every day I regret something I've done...
I need to be a better person.

Oh, I got a letter pointing out that bullying shows up a lot in my work. Come to think of it, that's true (smile). It's probably because the problem is so common and close to home (for readers). And it never goes away. Social critics have discussed the causes, but I think it stems from a lack of compassion. I wrote earlier that everyone has a dark side, but bullying is going too far. I can't imagine how many people are suffering even as I write this. Frankly, the bullies are 100 percent at fault. Some argue that people who get bullied tend to have problems already, but that doesn't mean it's all right to pick on them. I read a book about a rape case that mentioned the argument that it was the woman's fault for walking home alone late at night. Sure, a woman should be careful, but it's not her fault if someone rapes her.

WELCOME!

I DIDN'T RECOGNIZE HIM AT FIRST!

HE LOOKS SO DIFFERENT!

W-WELCOME!!

ACK

SMILE, MISS IZAWA!

TAKE THE WATER.

THROB
THROB

113

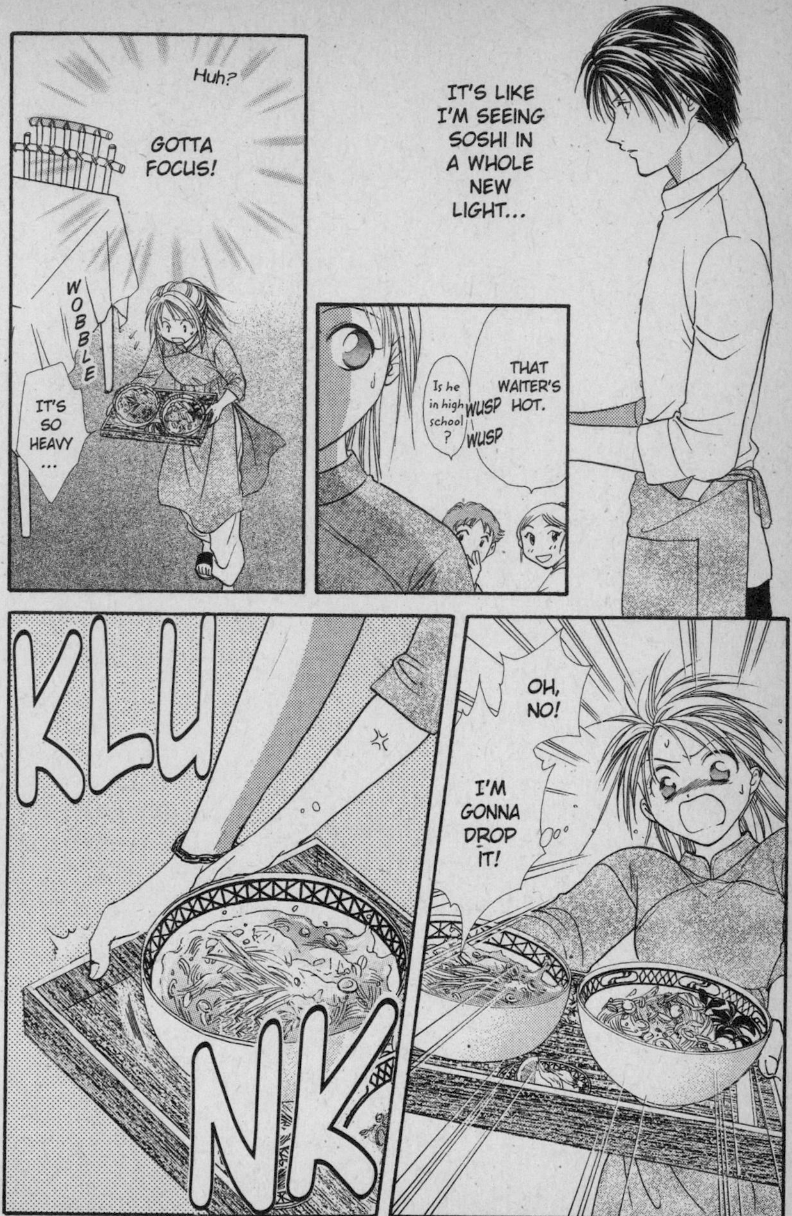
IT'S LIKE I'M SEEING SOSHI IN A WHOLE NEW LIGHT...
THAT WAITER'S HOT.
Is he in high school?
WUSP
WUSP
Huh?
GOTTA FOCUS!
WOBBLE
IT'S SO HEAVY...
OH, NO!
I'M GONNA DROP IT!
KLUNK

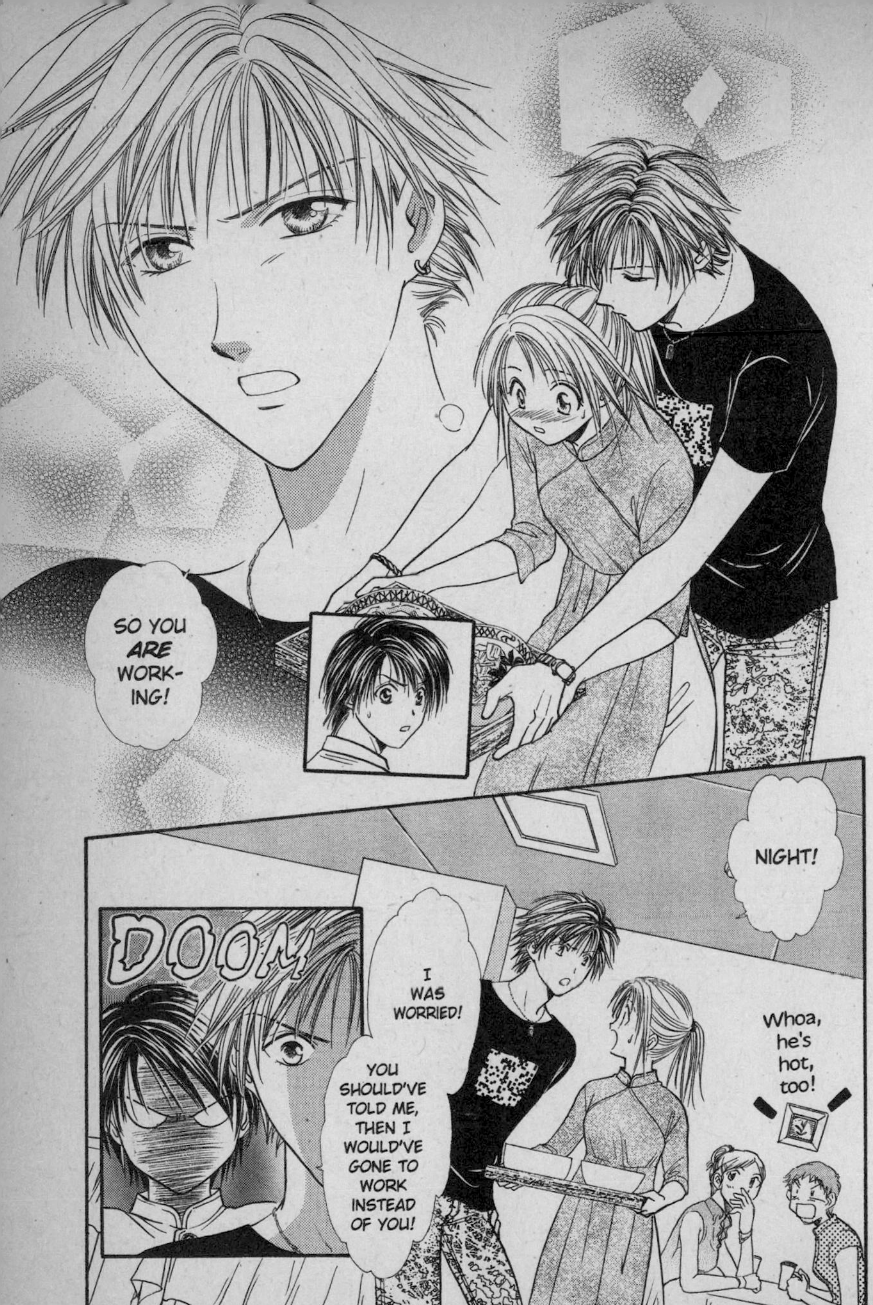
SO YOU ARE WORKING!
NIGHT!
I WAS WORRIED!
YOU SHOULD'VE TOLD ME, THEN I WOULD'VE GONE TO WORK INSTEAD OF YOU!
Whoa, he's hot, too!
DOOM

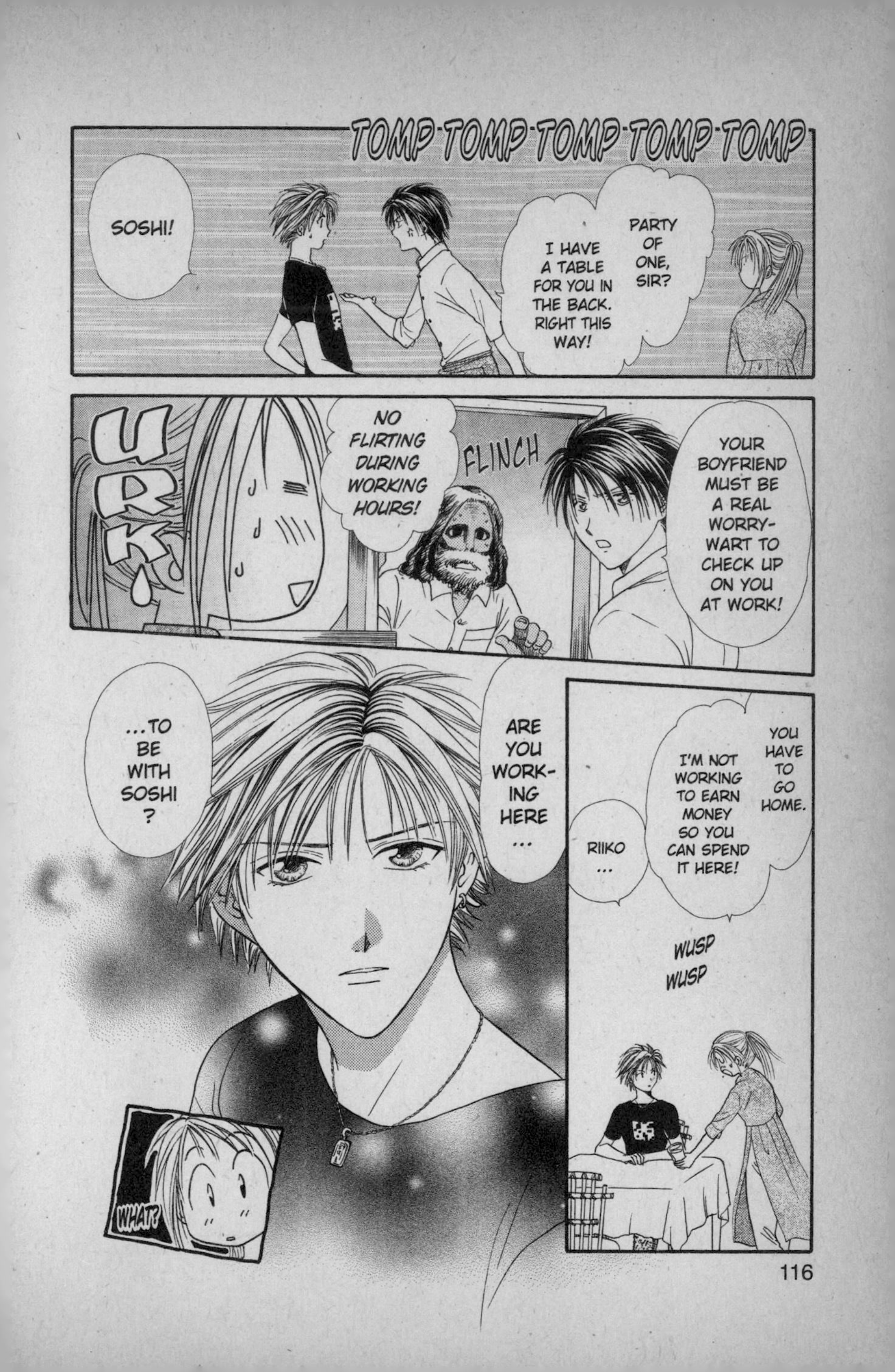
TOMP TOMP TOMP TOMP TOMP
PARTY OF ONE, SIR?
I HAVE A TABLE FOR YOU IN THE BACK. RIGHT THIS WAY!
SOSHI!
YOUR BOYFRIEND MUST BE A REAL WORRY-WART TO CHECK UP ON YOU AT WORK!
FLINCH
NO FLIRTING DURING WORKING HOURS!
URK
YOU HAVE TO GO HOME.
I'M NOT WORKING TO EARN MONEY SO YOU CAN SPEND IT HERE!
RIIKO...
WUSP WUSP
ARE YOU WORKING HERE...
...TO BE WITH SOSHI?
WHAT?

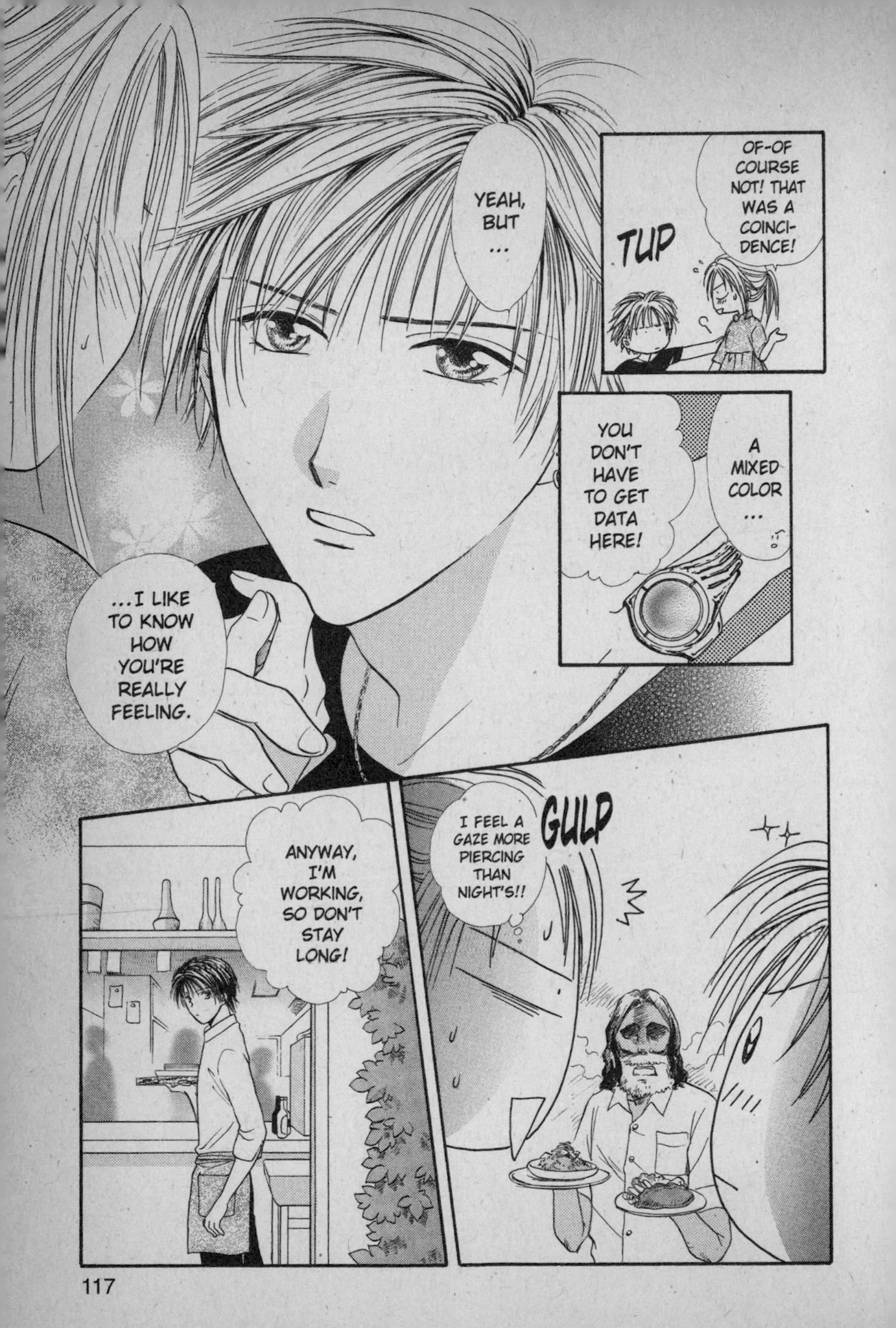

OF-OF COURSE NOT! THAT WAS A COINCI-DENCE!
TUP
A MIXED COLOR ...
YOU DON'T HAVE TO GET DATA HERE!
YEAH, BUT ...
...I LIKE TO KNOW HOW YOU'RE REALLY FEELING.
GULP
I FEEL A GAZE MORE PIERCING THAN NIGHT'S!!
ANYWAY, I'M WORKING, SO DON'T STAY LONG!

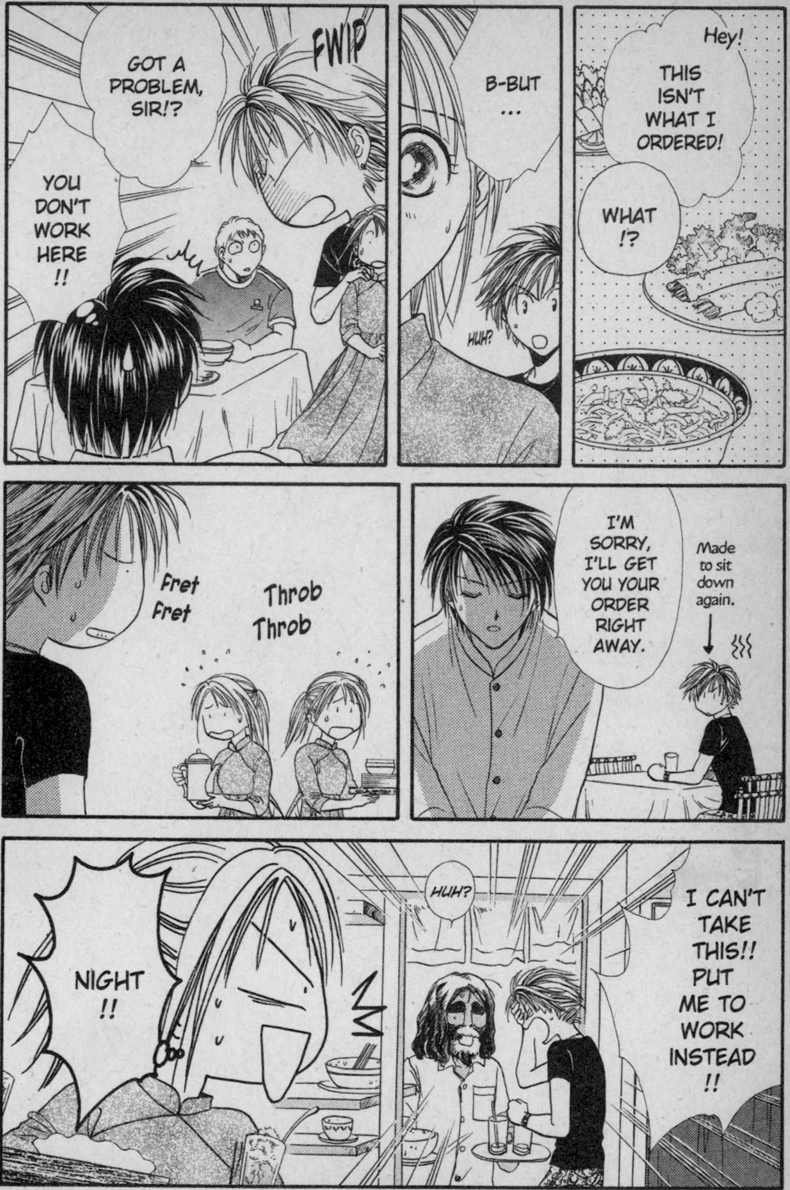
Hey!
THIS ISN'T WHAT I ORDERED!
WHAT !?
B-BUT ...
HUH?
FWIP
GOT A PROBLEM, SIR!?
YOU DON'T WORK HERE !!
I'M SORRY, I'LL GET YOU YOUR ORDER RIGHT AWAY.
Made to sit down again.
Throb Throb
Fret Fret
I CAN'T TAKE THIS!! PUT ME TO WORK INSTEAD !!
HUH?
NIGHT !!

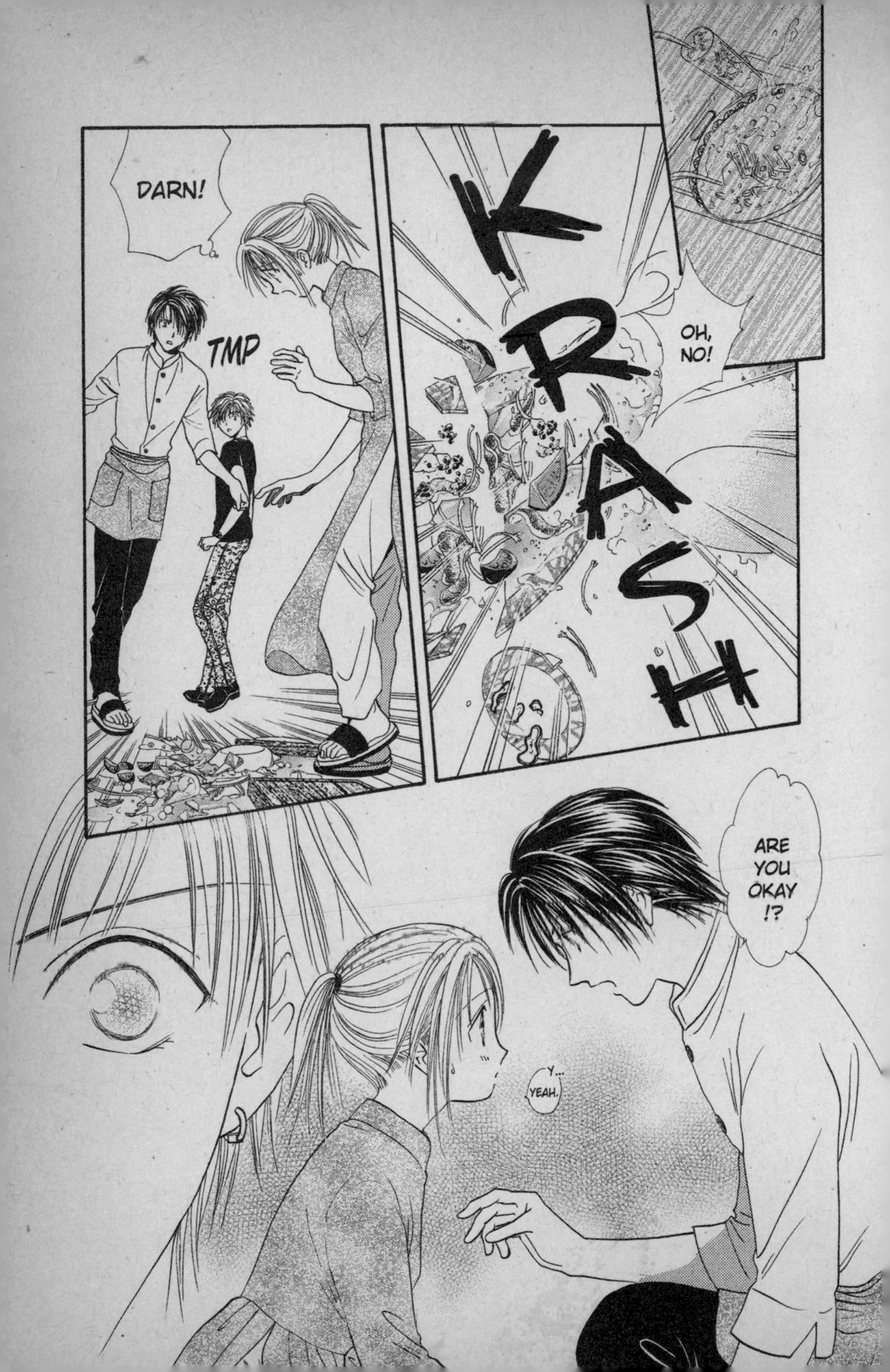
KRASH
OH, NO!
DARN!
TMP
ARE YOU OKAY!?
Y... YEAH.

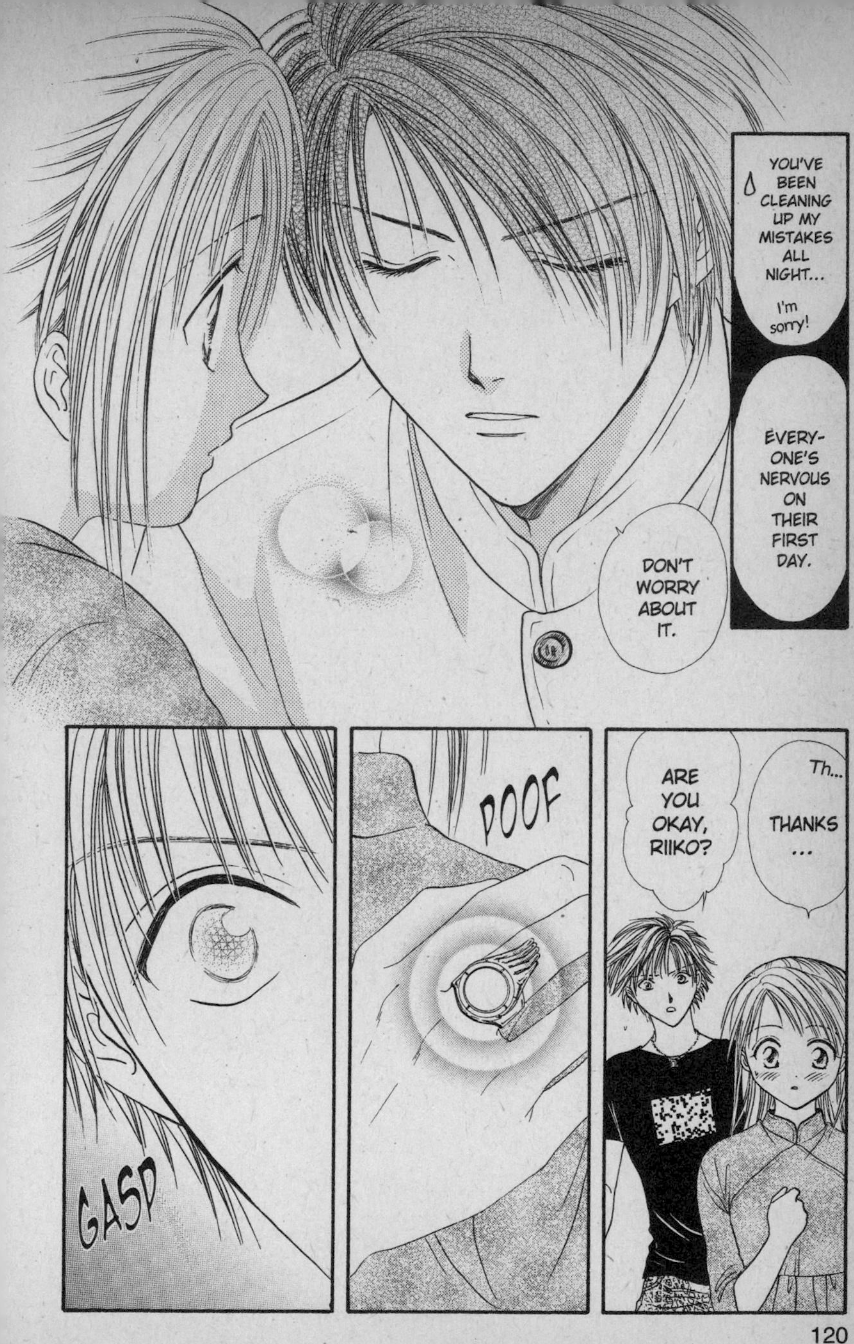
YOU'VE BEEN CLEANING UP MY MISTAKES ALL NIGHT...
I'm sorry!
EVERY-ONE'S NERVOUS ON THEIR FIRST DAY.
DON'T WORRY ABOUT IT.
Th... THANKS ...
ARE YOU OKAY, RIIKO?
POOF
GASP

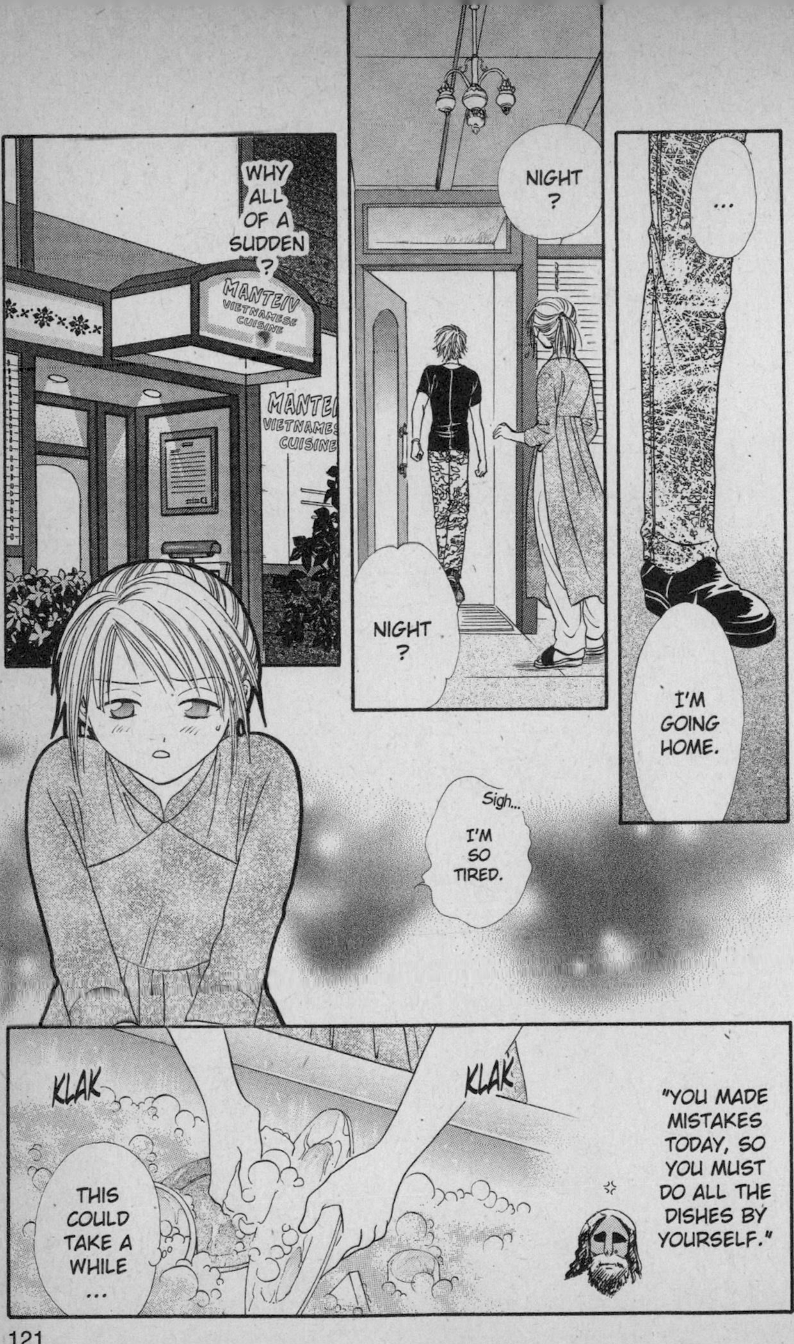

...
I'M GOING HOME.
NIGHT?
NIGHT?
WHY ALL OF A SUDDEN?
MANTEIV VIETNAMESE CUISINE
Sigh... I'M SO TIRED.
"YOU MADE MISTAKES TODAY, SO YOU MUST DO ALL THE DISHES BY YOURSELF."
KLAK
KLAK
THIS COULD TAKE A WHILE ...

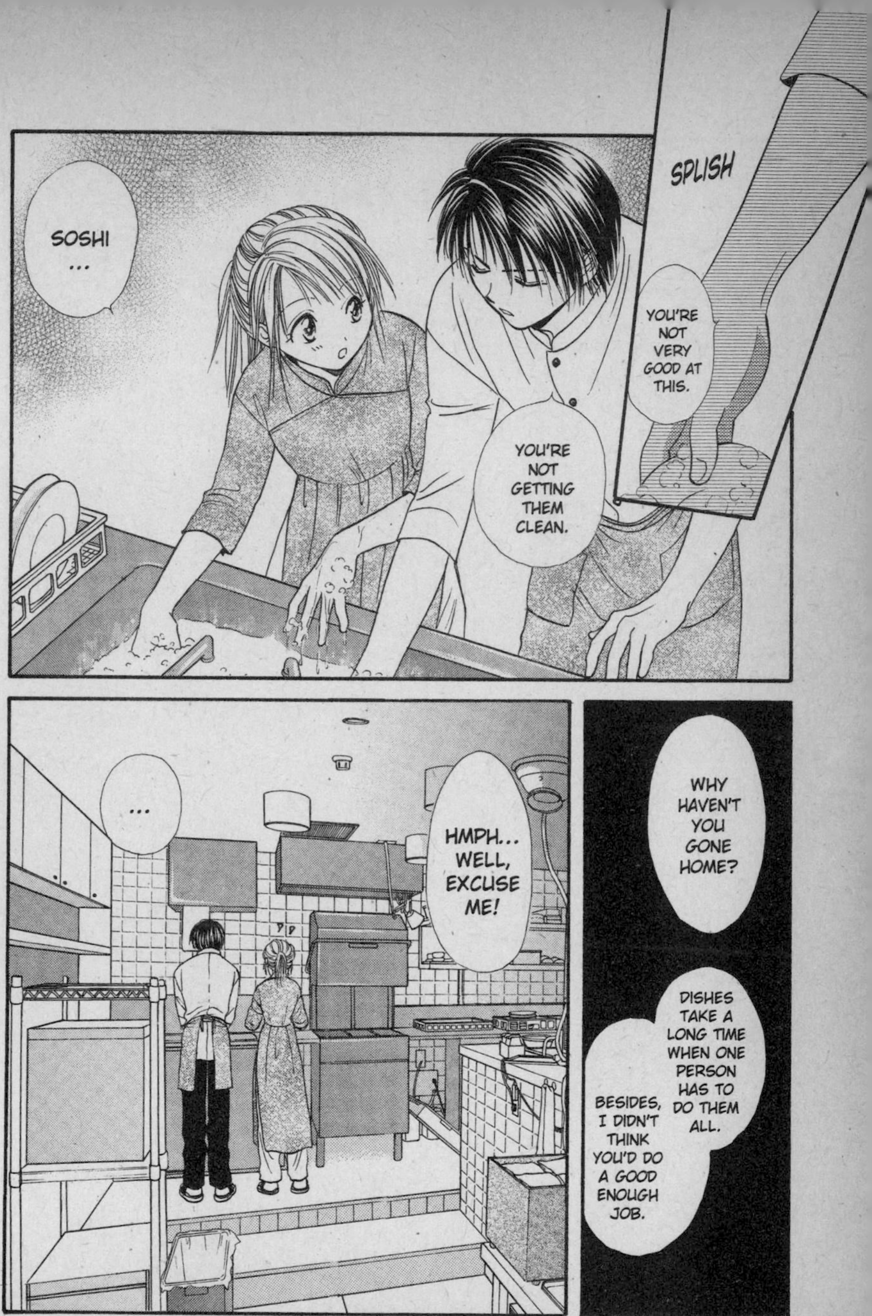
SPLISH
YOU'RE NOT VERY GOOD AT THIS.
YOU'RE NOT GETTING THEM CLEAN.
SOSHI ...
WHY HAVEN'T YOU GONE HOME?
DISHES TAKE A LONG TIME WHEN ONE PERSON HAS TO DO THEM ALL.
BESIDES, I DIDN'T THINK YOU'D DO A GOOD ENOUGH JOB.
HMPH... WELL, EXCUSE ME!
...

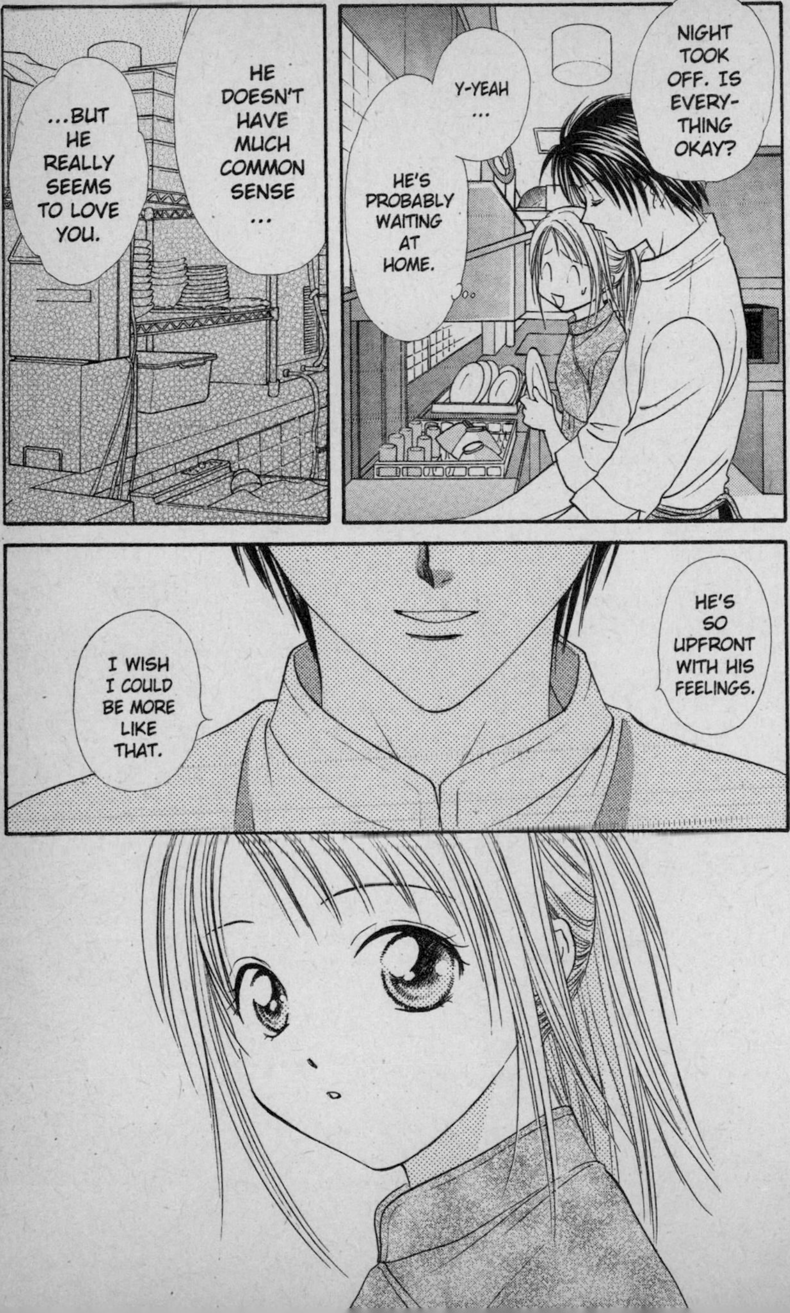
NIGHT TOOK OFF. IS EVERY-THING OKAY?
Y-YEAH ...
HE'S PROBABLY WAITING AT HOME.
HE DOESN'T HAVE MUCH COMMON SENSE ...
...BUT HE REALLY SEEMS TO LOVE YOU.
HE'S SO UPFRONT WITH HIS FEELINGS.
I WISH I COULD BE MORE LIKE THAT.

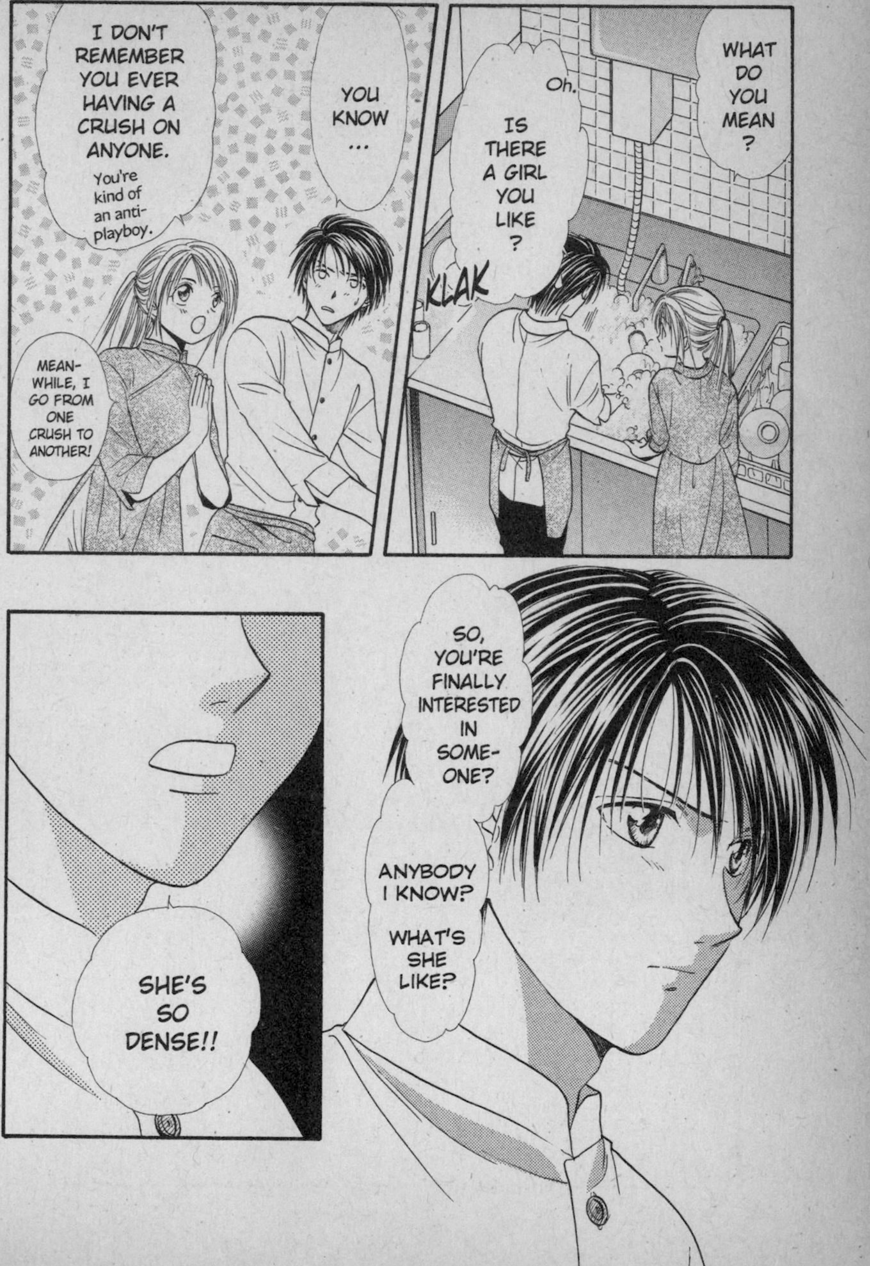
WHAT DO YOU MEAN?
Oh.
IS THERE A GIRL YOU LIKE?
KLAK
YOU KNOW ...
I DON'T REMEMBER YOU EVER HAVING A CRUSH ON ANYONE.
You're kind of an anti-playboy.
MEAN-WHILE, I GO FROM ONE CRUSH TO ANOTHER!
SO, YOU'RE FINALLY INTERESTED IN SOME-ONE?
ANYBODY I KNOW?
WHAT'S SHE LIKE?
SHE'S SO DENSE!!

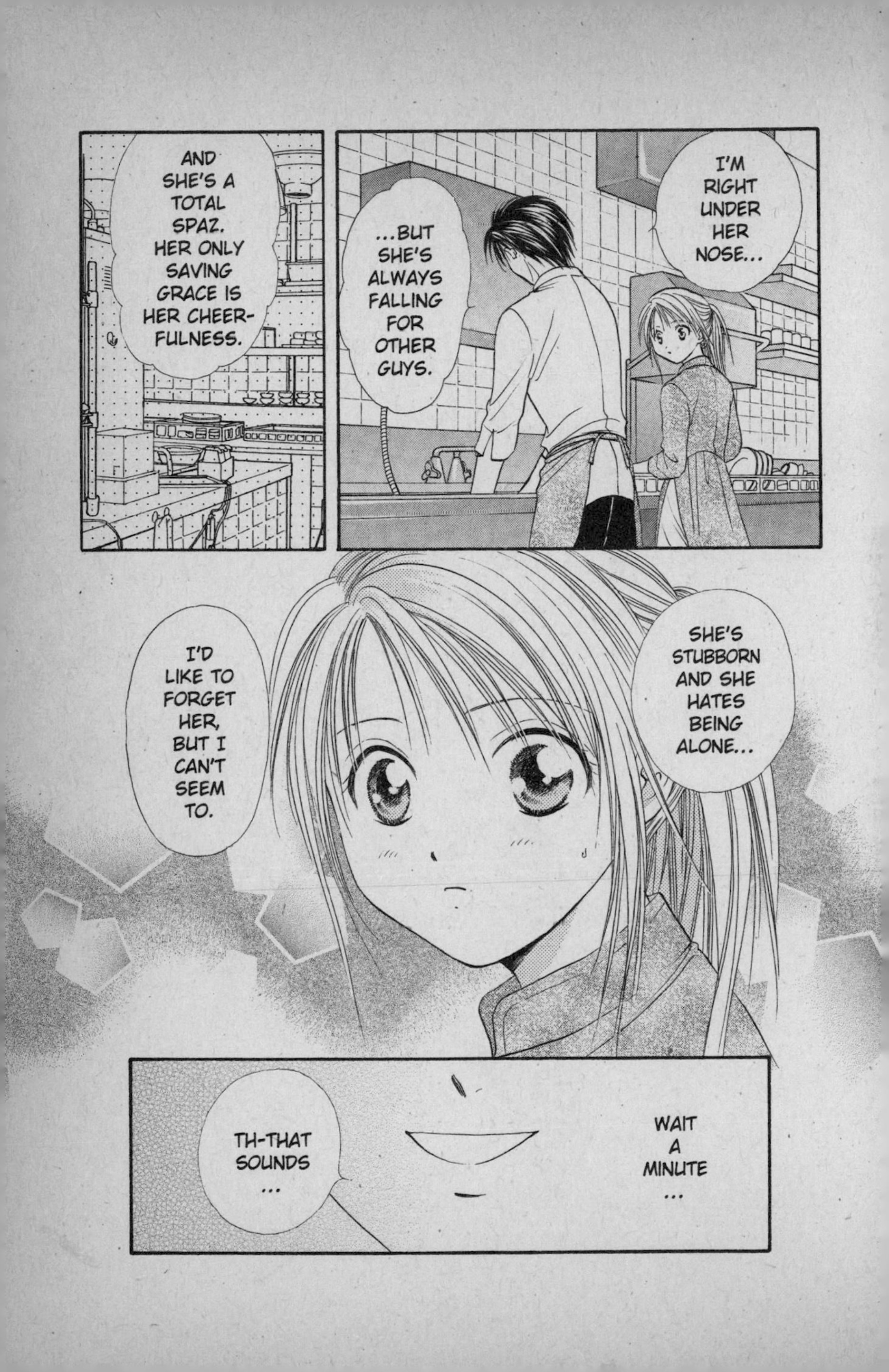
I'M RIGHT UNDER HER NOSE...
...BUT SHE'S ALWAYS FALLING FOR OTHER GUYS.
AND SHE'S A TOTAL SPAZ. HER ONLY SAVING GRACE IS HER CHEER-FULNESS.
SHE'S STUBBORN AND SHE HATES BEING ALONE...
I'D LIKE TO FORGET HER, BUT I CAN'T SEEM TO.
WAIT A MINUTE ...
TH-THAT SOUNDS ...

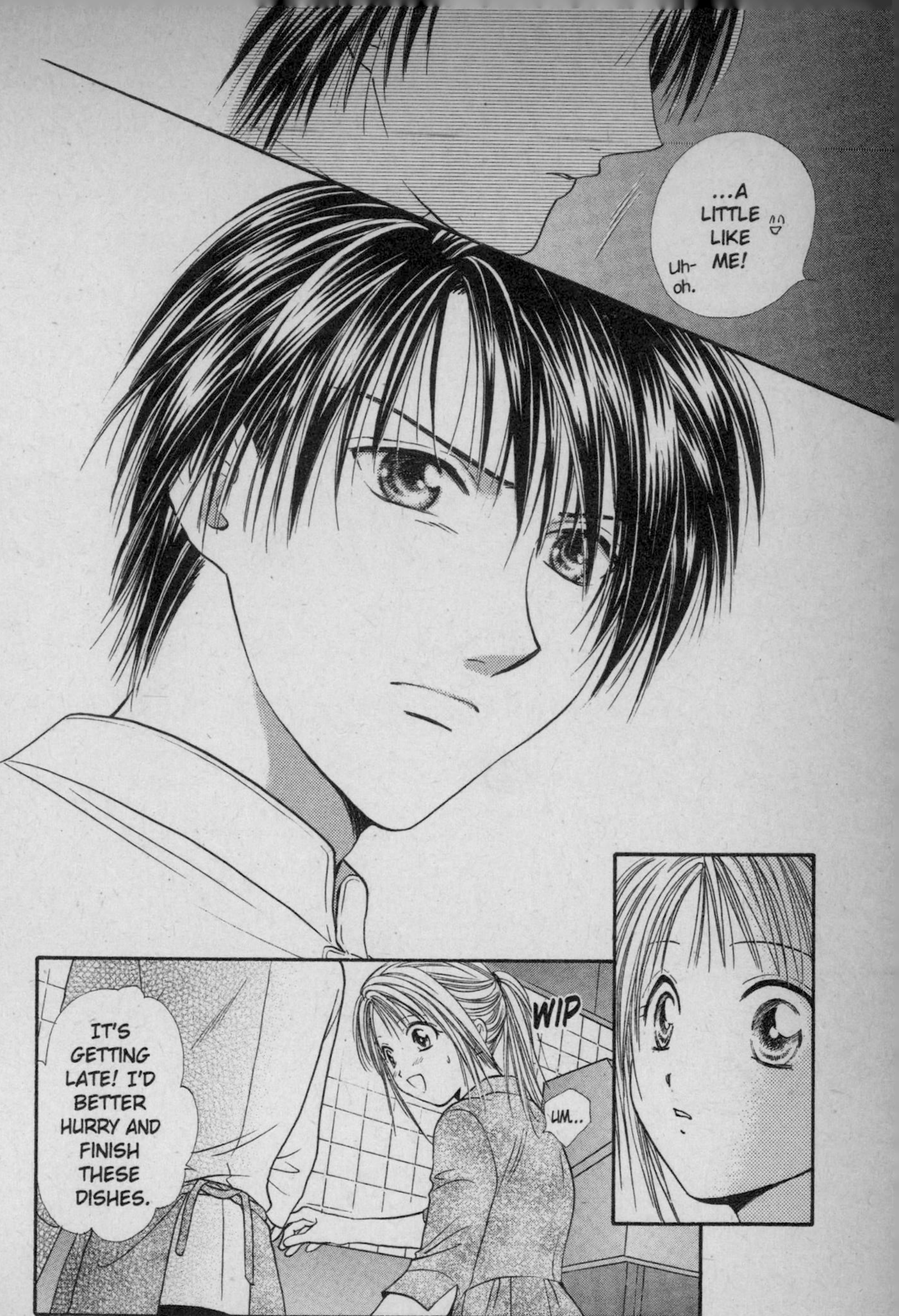
...A LITTLE LIKE ME!
Uh-oh.
WIP
UM...
IT'S GETTING LATE! I'D BETTER HURRY AND FINISH THESE DISHES.

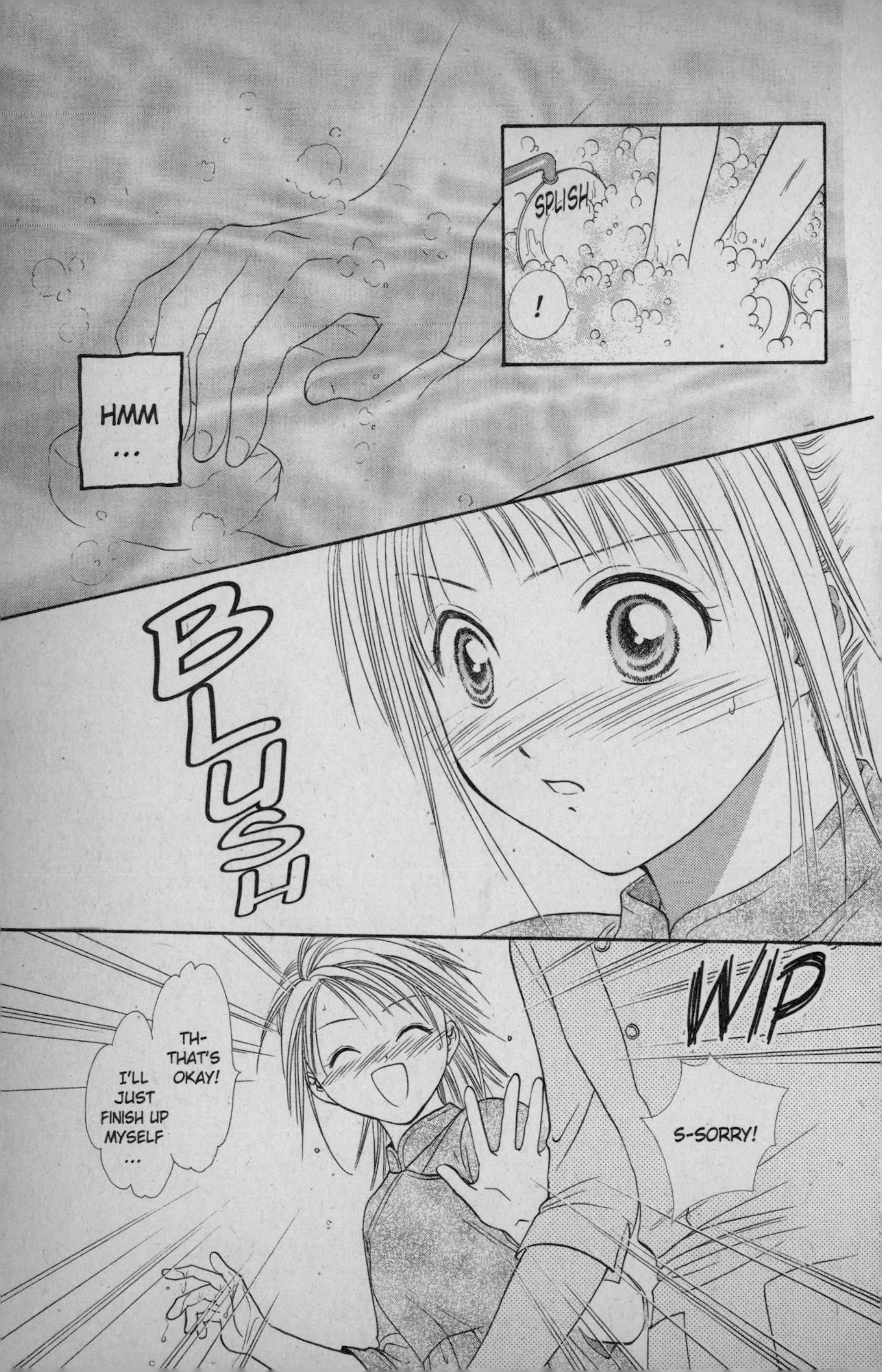
SPLISH
!
HMM ...
BLUSH
WIP
S-SORRY!
TH-THAT'S OKAY!
I'LL JUST FINISH UP MYSELF ...

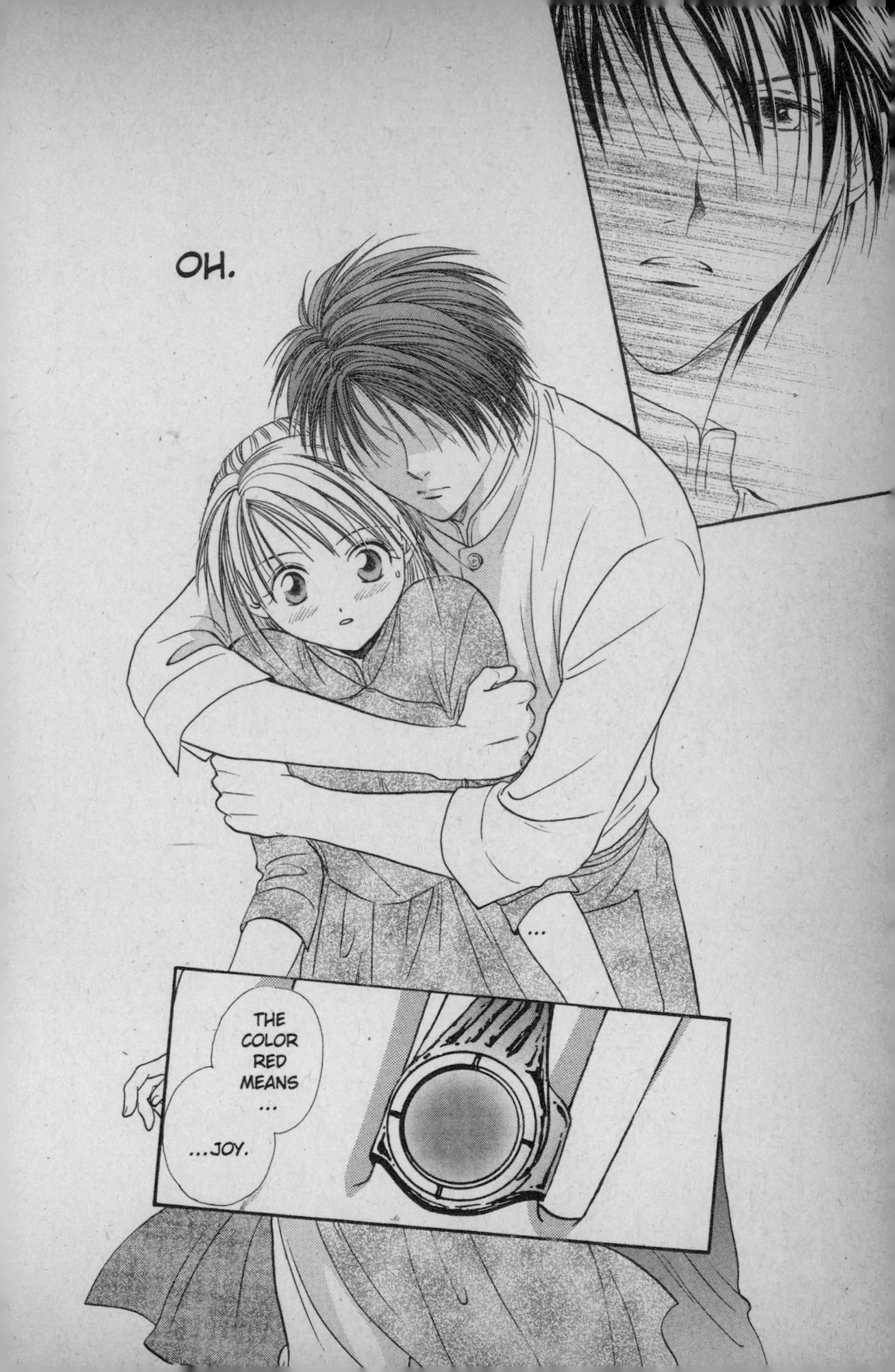
OH.
...
THE COLOR RED MEANS ...
...JOY.

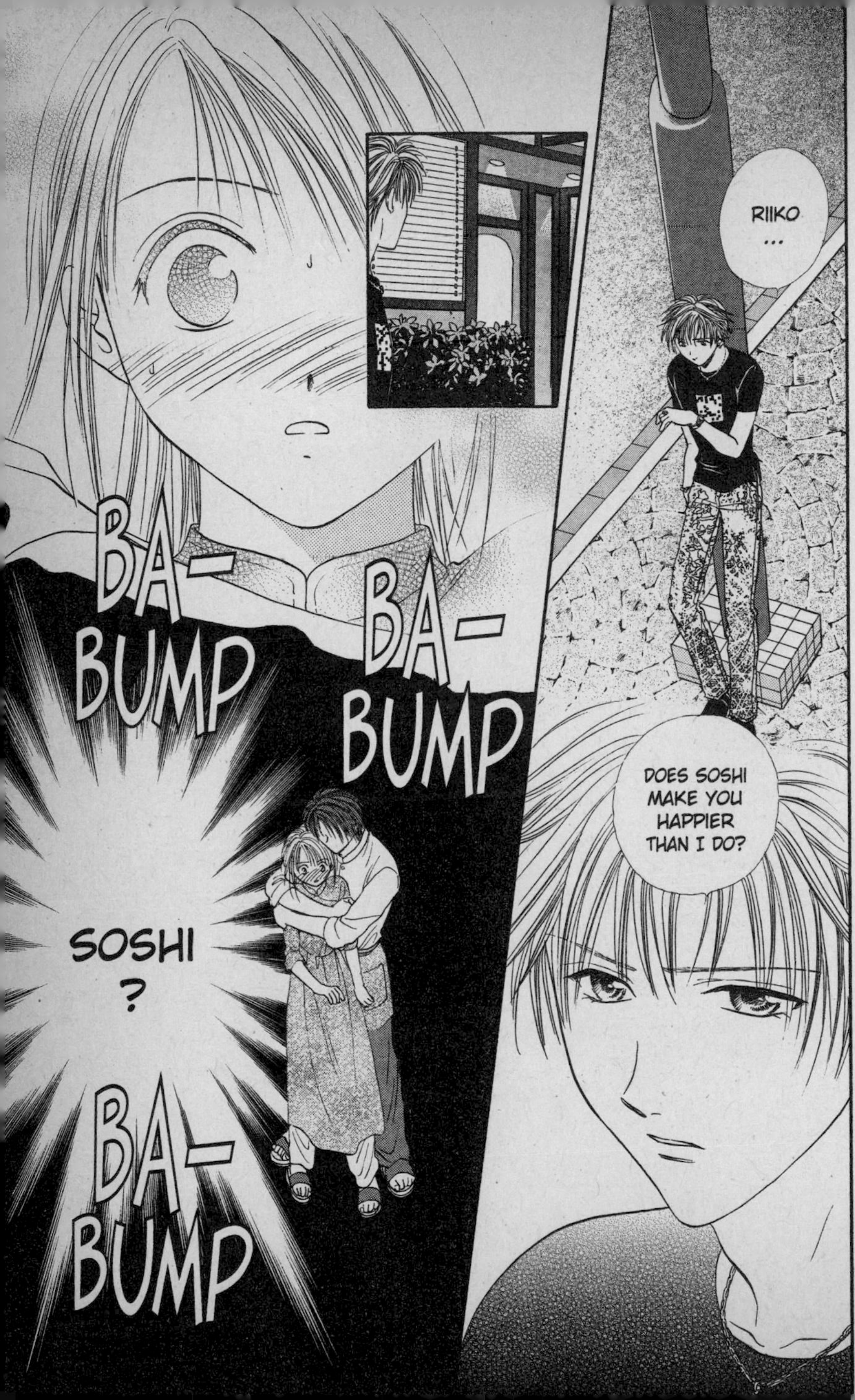
RIIKO ...
DOES SOSHI MAKE YOU HAPPIER THAN I DO?
BA-BUMP
BA-BUMP
SOSHI ?
BA-BUMP

Absolute Boyfriend

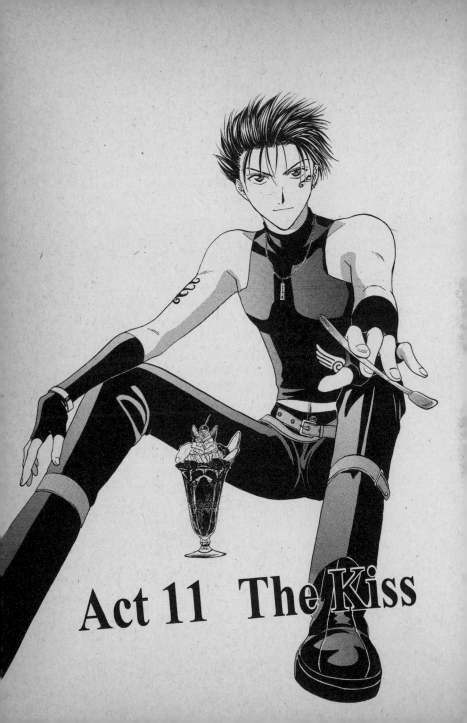

Act 11　The Kiss

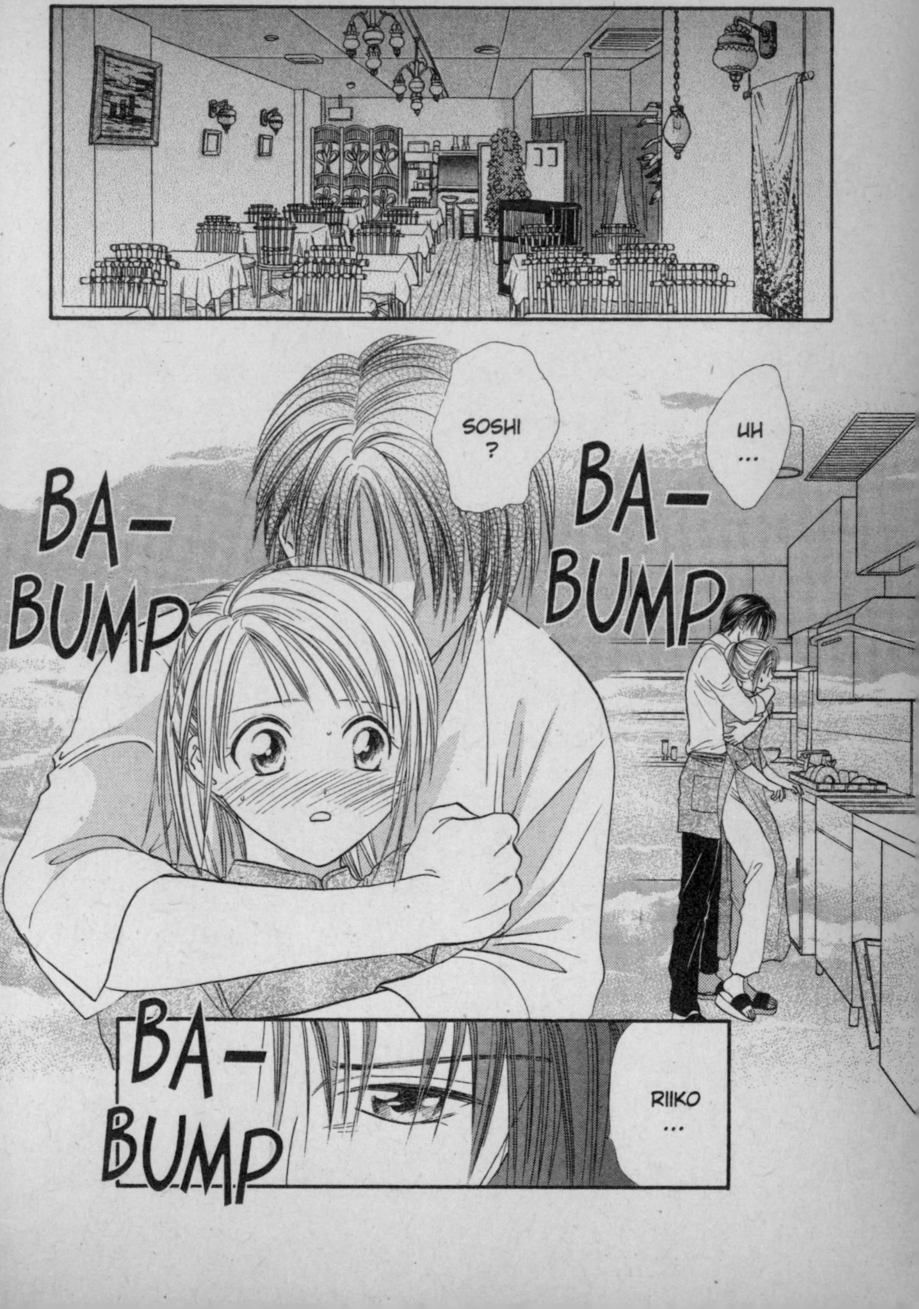
UH ...
BA-BUMP
SOSHI ?
BA-BUMP
RIIKO ...
BA-BUMP

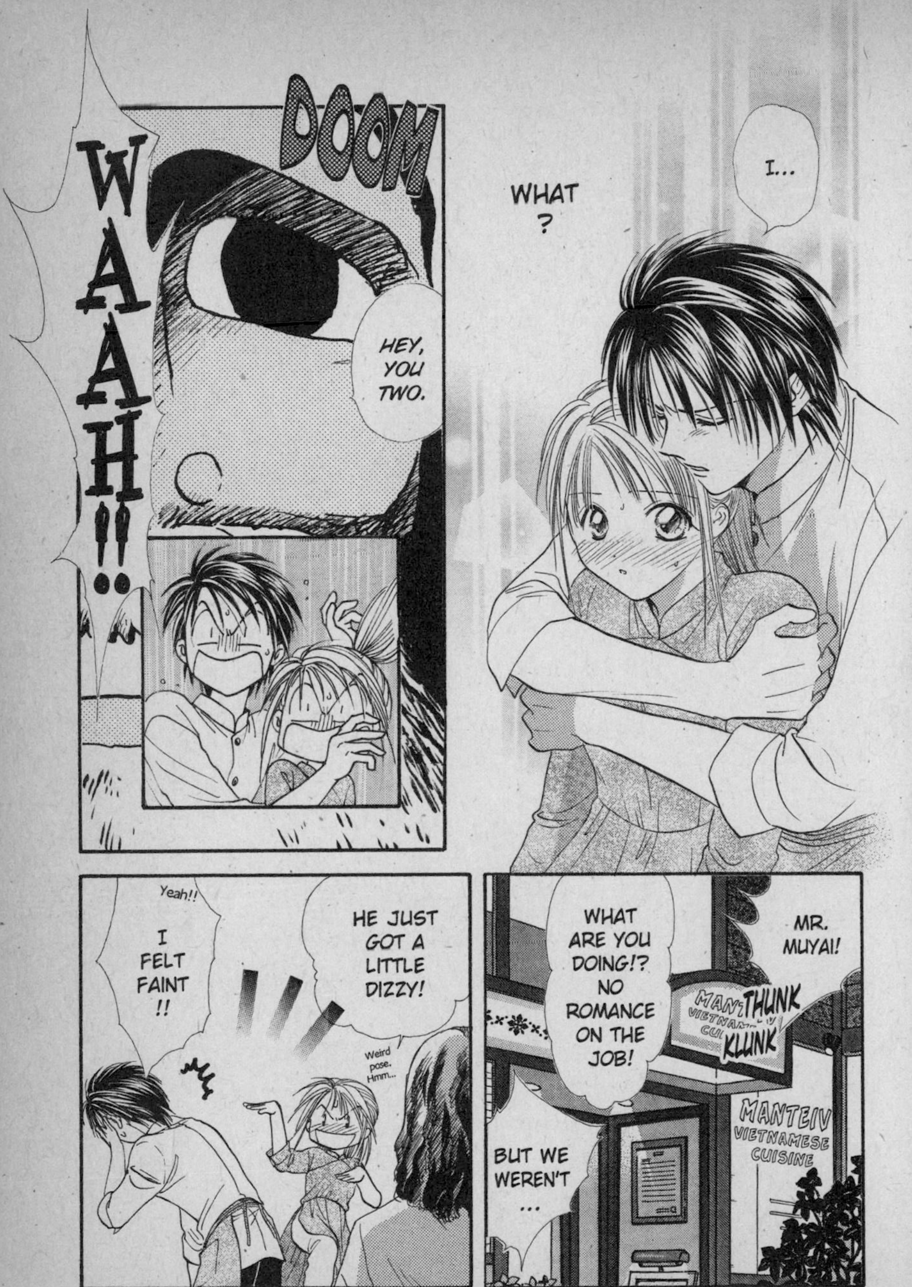
I...
WHAT ?
DOOM
HEY, YOU TWO.
WAAAH!!
MR. MUYAI!
WHAT ARE YOU DOING!? NO ROMANCE ON THE JOB!
THUNK
KLUNK
MANTEIV VIETNAMESE CUISINE
BUT WE WEREN'T ...
HE JUST GOT A LITTLE DIZZY!
Yeah!!
I FELT FAINT !!
Weird pose. Hmm...

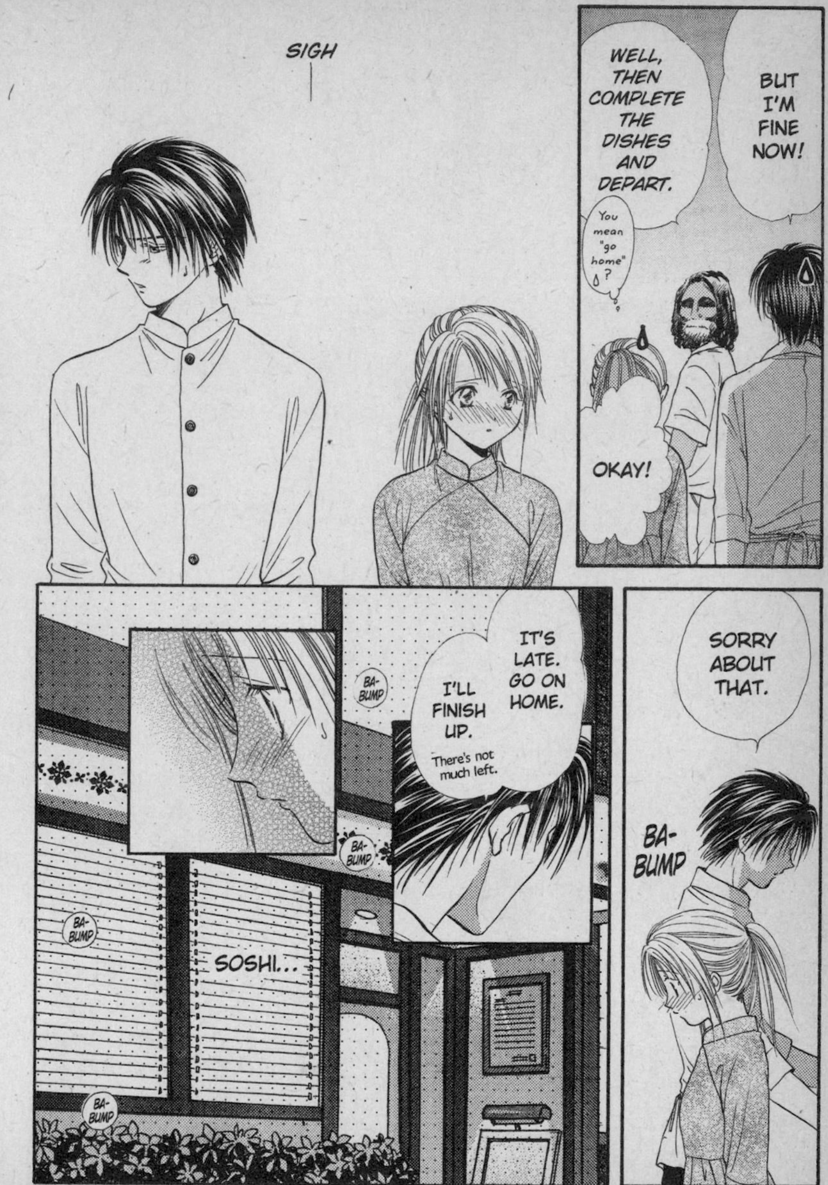
BUT I'M FINE NOW!
WELL, THEN COMPLETE THE DISHES AND DEPART.
You mean "go home"?
OKAY!
SIGH
SORRY ABOUT THAT.
BA-BUMP
IT'S LATE. GO ON HOME.
I'LL FINISH UP.
There's not much left.
BA-BUMP
BA-BUMP
BA-BUMP
SOSHI...
BA-BUMP

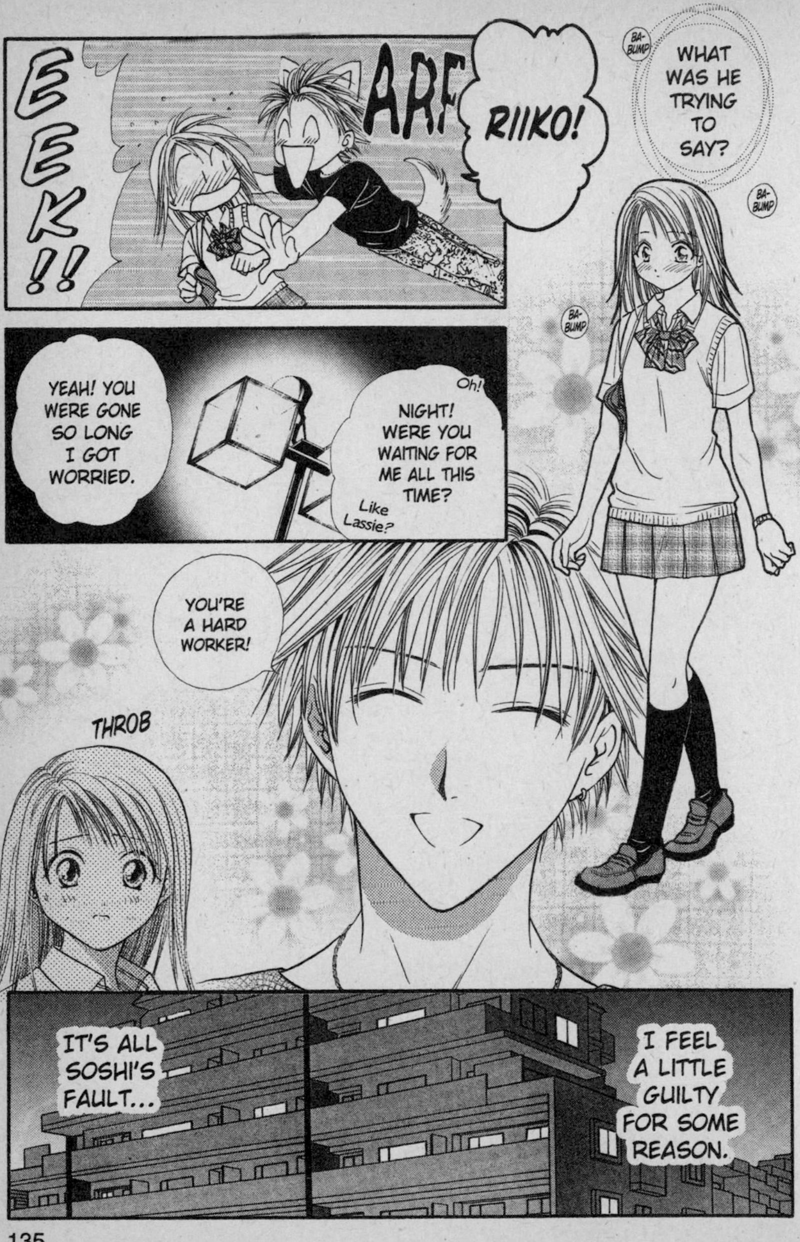
BA-BUMP
WHAT WAS HE TRYING TO SAY?
RIIKO!
ARF
EEK!!
BA-BUMP
BA-BUMP
Oh!
NIGHT! WERE YOU WAITING FOR ME ALL THIS TIME?
Like Lassie?
YEAH! YOU WERE GONE SO LONG I GOT WORRIED.
YOU'RE A HARD WORKER!
THROB
I FEEL A LITTLE GUILTY FOR SOME REASON.
IT'S ALL SOSHI'S FAULT...

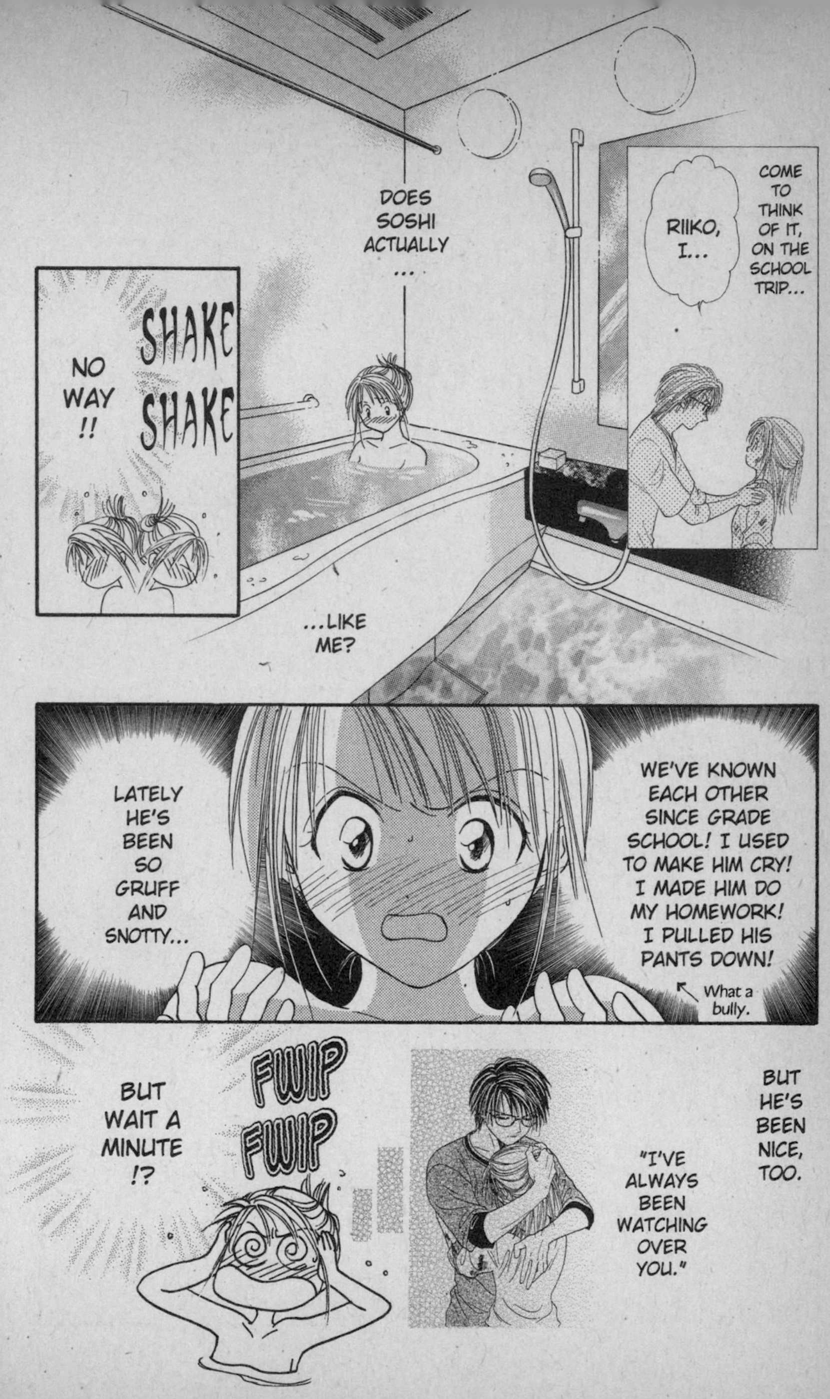
COME TO THINK OF IT, ON THE SCHOOL TRIP...
RIIKO, I...
DOES SOSHI ACTUALLY...
...LIKE ME?
SHAKE SHAKE
NO WAY!!
WE'VE KNOWN EACH OTHER SINCE GRADE SCHOOL! I USED TO MAKE HIM CRY! I MADE HIM DO MY HOMEWORK! I PULLED HIS PANTS DOWN!
What a bully.
LATELY HE'S BEEN SO GRUFF AND SNOTTY...
BUT HE'S BEEN NICE, TOO.
"I'VE ALWAYS BEEN WATCHING OVER YOU."
FWIP FWIP
BUT WAIT A MINUTE!?

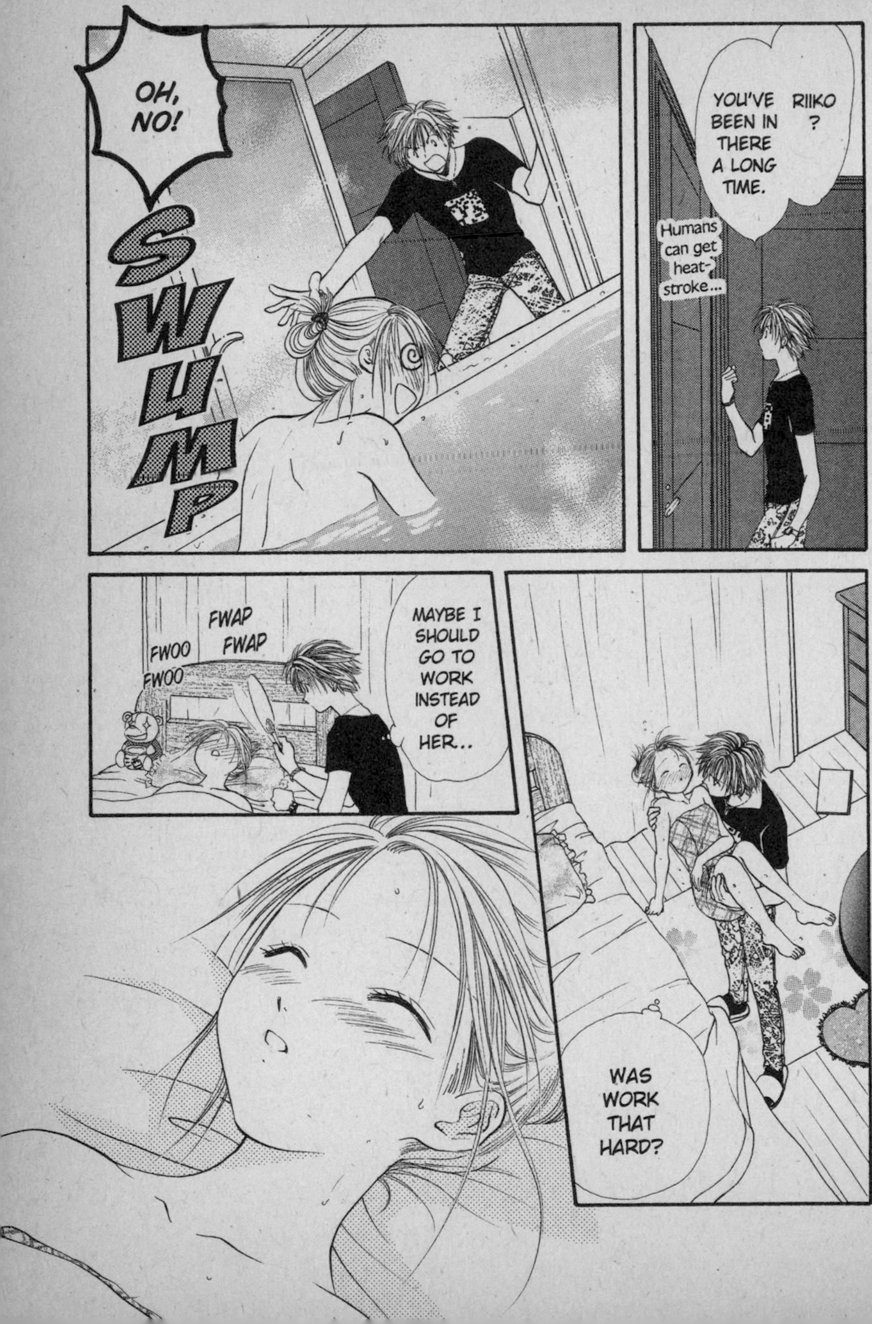
RIIKO?
YOU'VE BEEN IN THERE A LONG TIME.
Humans can get heat-stroke...
OH, NO!
SWUMP
WAS WORK THAT HARD?
FWAP FWAP
FWOO FWOO
MAYBE I SHOULD GO TO WORK INSTEAD OF HER...

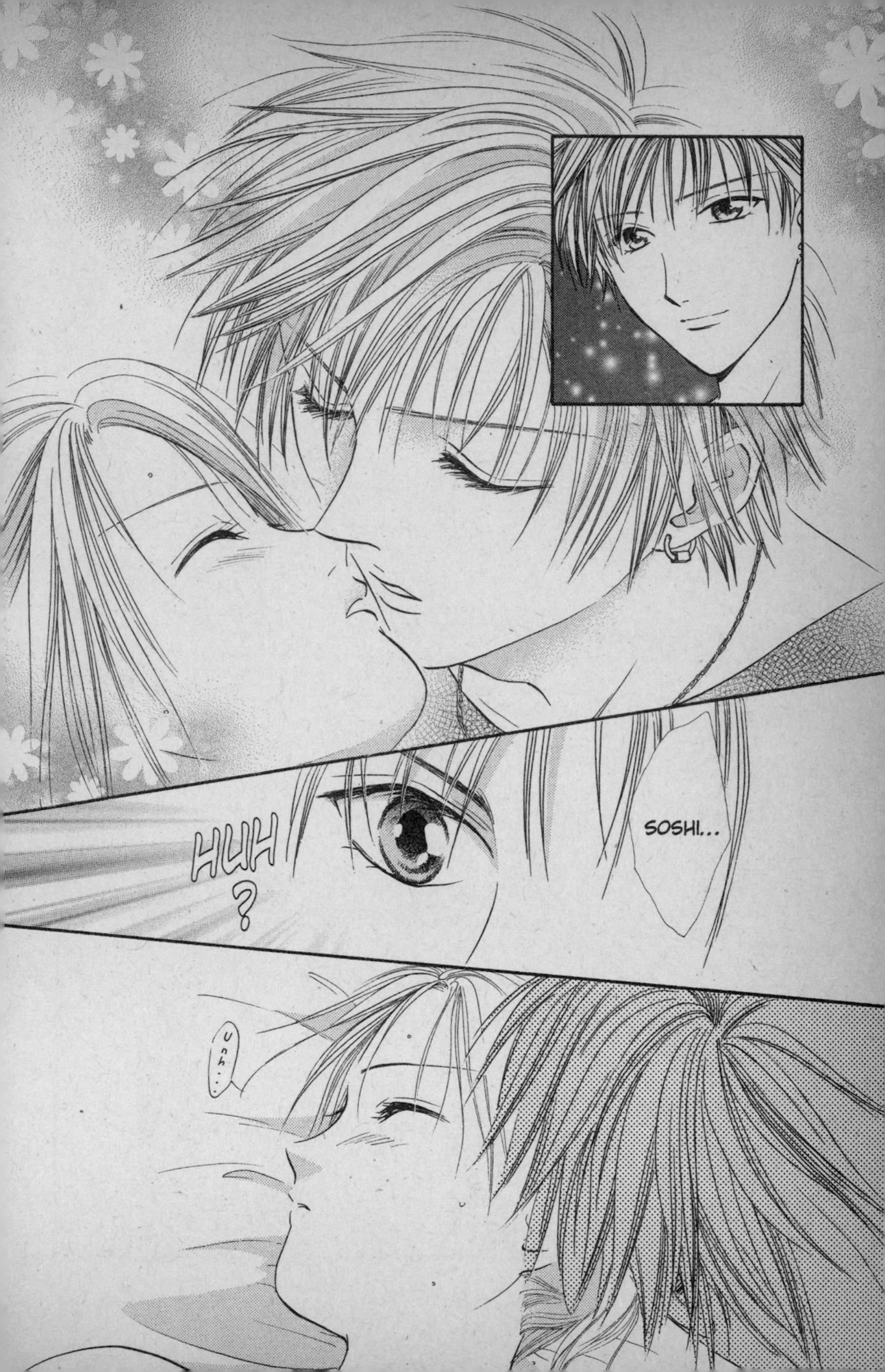
SOSHI...
HUH ?
Unh...

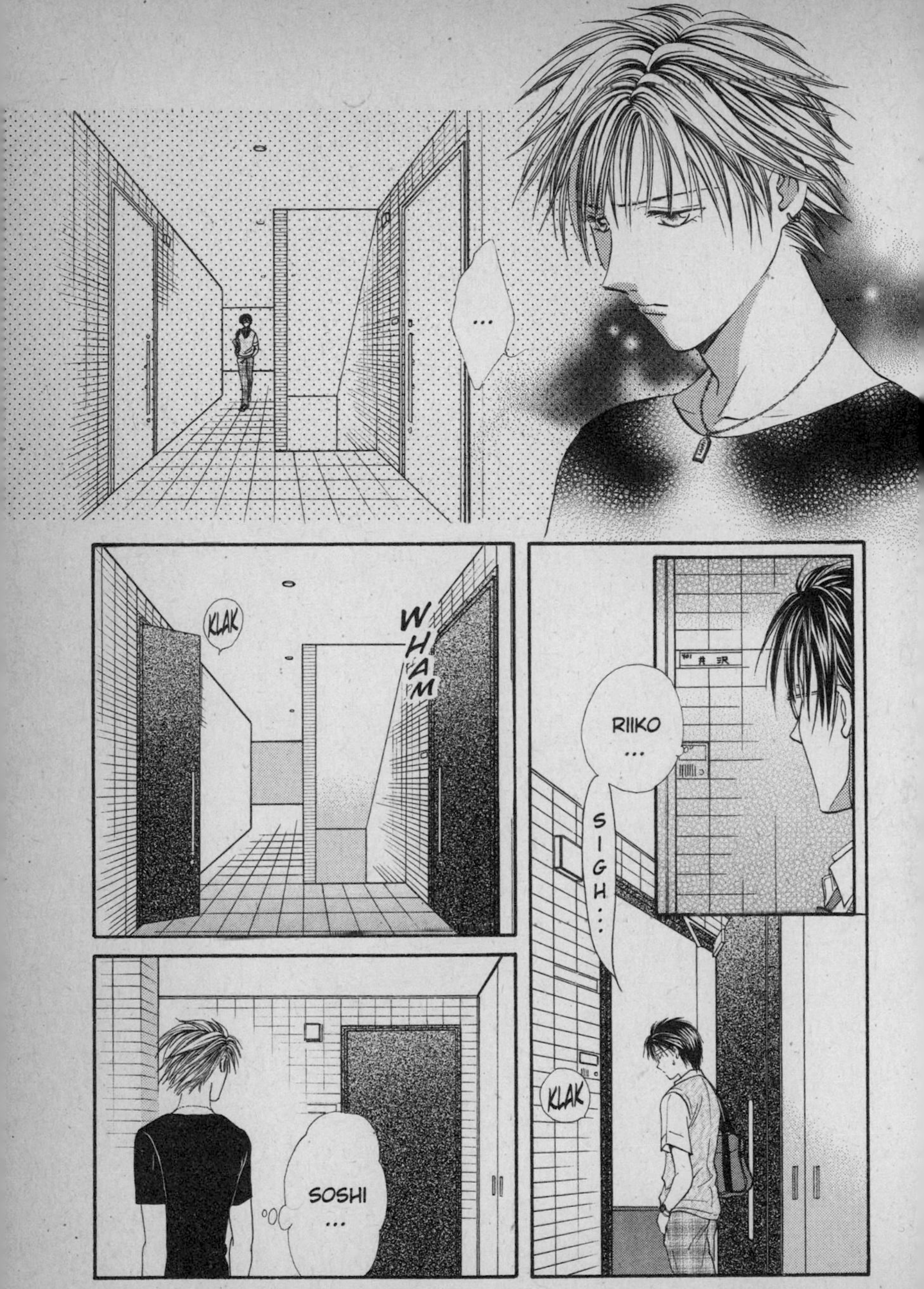
...
RIIKO ...
SIGH...
KLAK
WHAM
KLAK
SOSHI ...

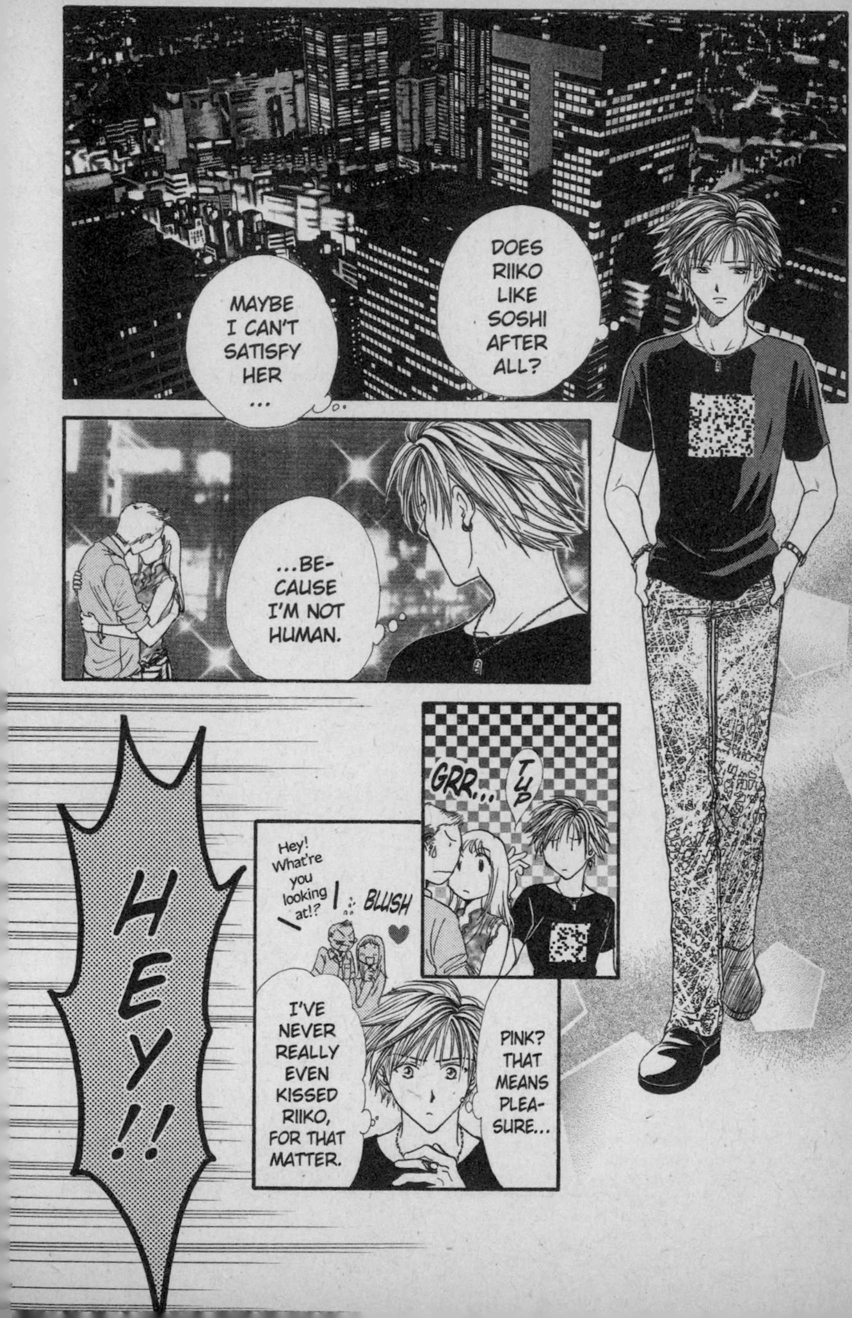
DOES RIIKO LIKE SOSHI AFTER ALL?
MAYBE I CAN'T SATISFY HER ...
...BE-CAUSE I'M NOT HUMAN.
TUP
GRR...
BLUSH
Hey! What're you looking at!?
PINK? THAT MEANS PLEA-SURE...
I'VE NEVER REALLY EVEN KISSED RIIKO, FOR THAT MATTER.
HEY!!

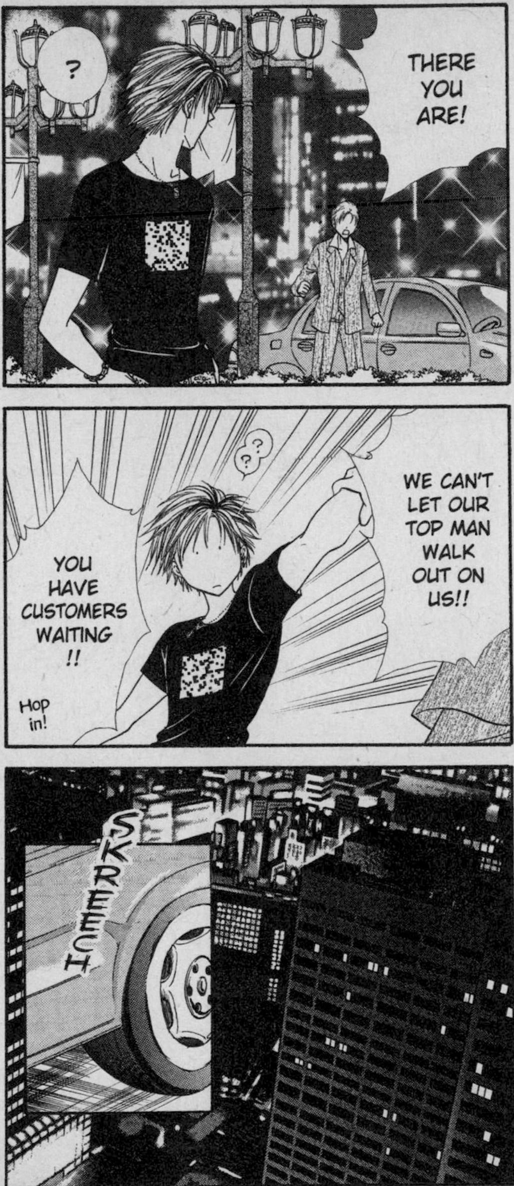
THERE YOU ARE!
?
WE CAN'T LET OUR TOP MAN WALK OUT ON US!!
? ?
YOU HAVE CUSTOMERS WAITING !!
Hop in!
SKREECH

In this volume Night gets a job as a male escort at a nightclub. These clubs sure come up a lot in shojo manga these days. Maybe that's because it's a quick and easy way to set up a reverse harem situation. I'm really not interested in that kind of thing, so I don't go for that scene. I mean, why spend all that money? Although, one time, I was meeting my editor in a hotel lounge, and the waiter went down on one knee to take my order. That was nice (smile). Well, maybe that's because I like the master-servant relationship. (Is that it!?)

Male escorts sure have a tough time, though. Really tough. But Night is a figure, so he never gets tired. I guess he's perfect for the job. Oh, a lot of people tell me they want a Night for themselves. I'm sure androids will exist by the 22nd century, though you'll be dead by then. Hey, the robot cat Doraemon came from the 22nd century! Astroboy's fictional birth was supposed to be in the year 2003.

I felt the most envious when Night said, "You're a hard worker!" ♥ Say that to me!! (smile). He does the chores without complaining, and he's always smiling (although Night does get depressed because of Riiko's feelings for Soshi). I don't care if you're not human, Night! (I must be getting tired.)

Oh, I was interviewed by a magazine when I went to Germany, and the two female interviewers said that Night is like a dream come true for women. And the only reason he costs a million dollars is because Riiko added so many options. But isn't a million dollars pretty cheap for all that? Kronos Heaven is such an unscrupulous company. What's Night made of, anyway? I'm trying not to draw anything that makes him seem robotic, like having his arm come off to reveal there's machinery inside!! That would ruin the illusion.

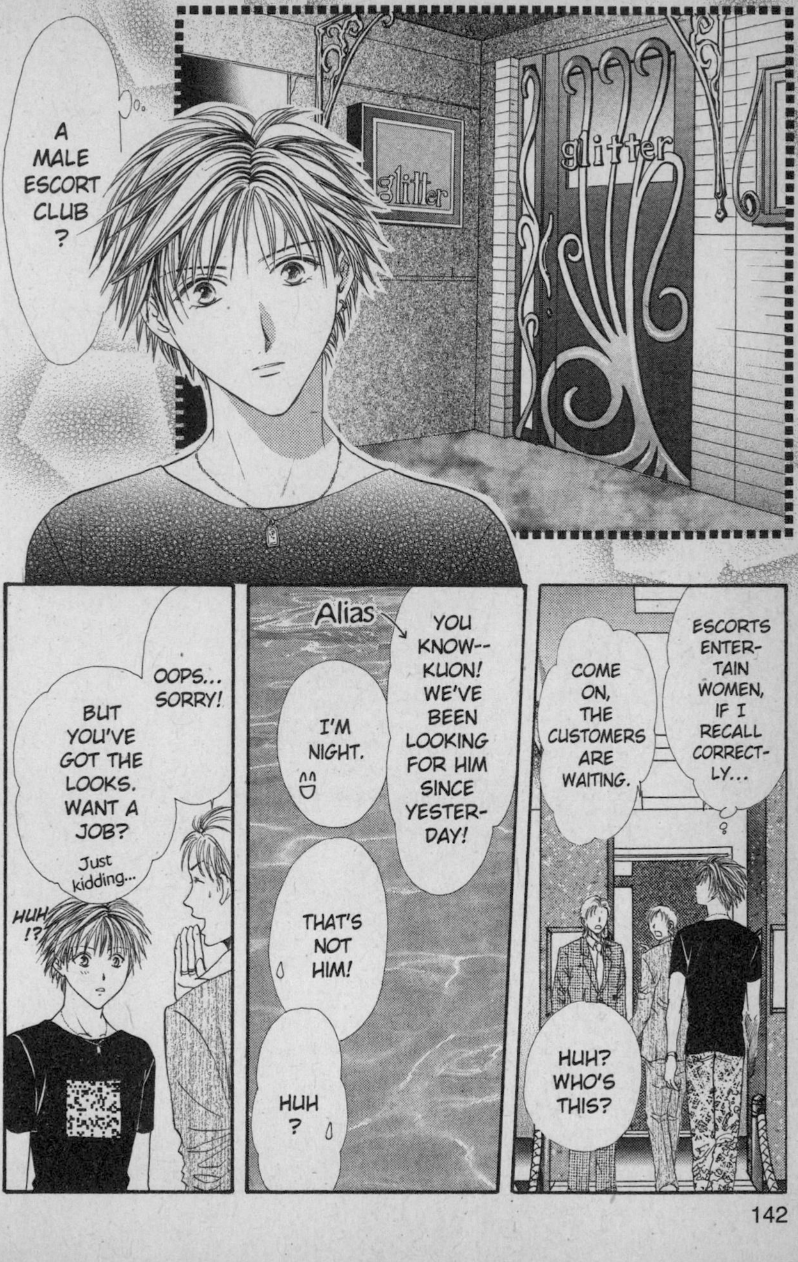
A MALE ESCORT CLUB ?
glitter
glitter
ESCORTS ENTER-TAIN WOMEN, IF I RECALL CORRECT-LY...
COME ON, THE CUSTOMERS ARE WAITING.
HUH? WHO'S THIS?
Alias
YOU KNOW-- KUON! WE'VE BEEN LOOKING FOR HIM SINCE YESTER-DAY!
I'M NIGHT.
THAT'S NOT HIM!
HUH ?
OOPS... SORRY!
BUT YOU'VE GOT THE LOOKS. WANT A JOB?
Just kidding...
HUH !?

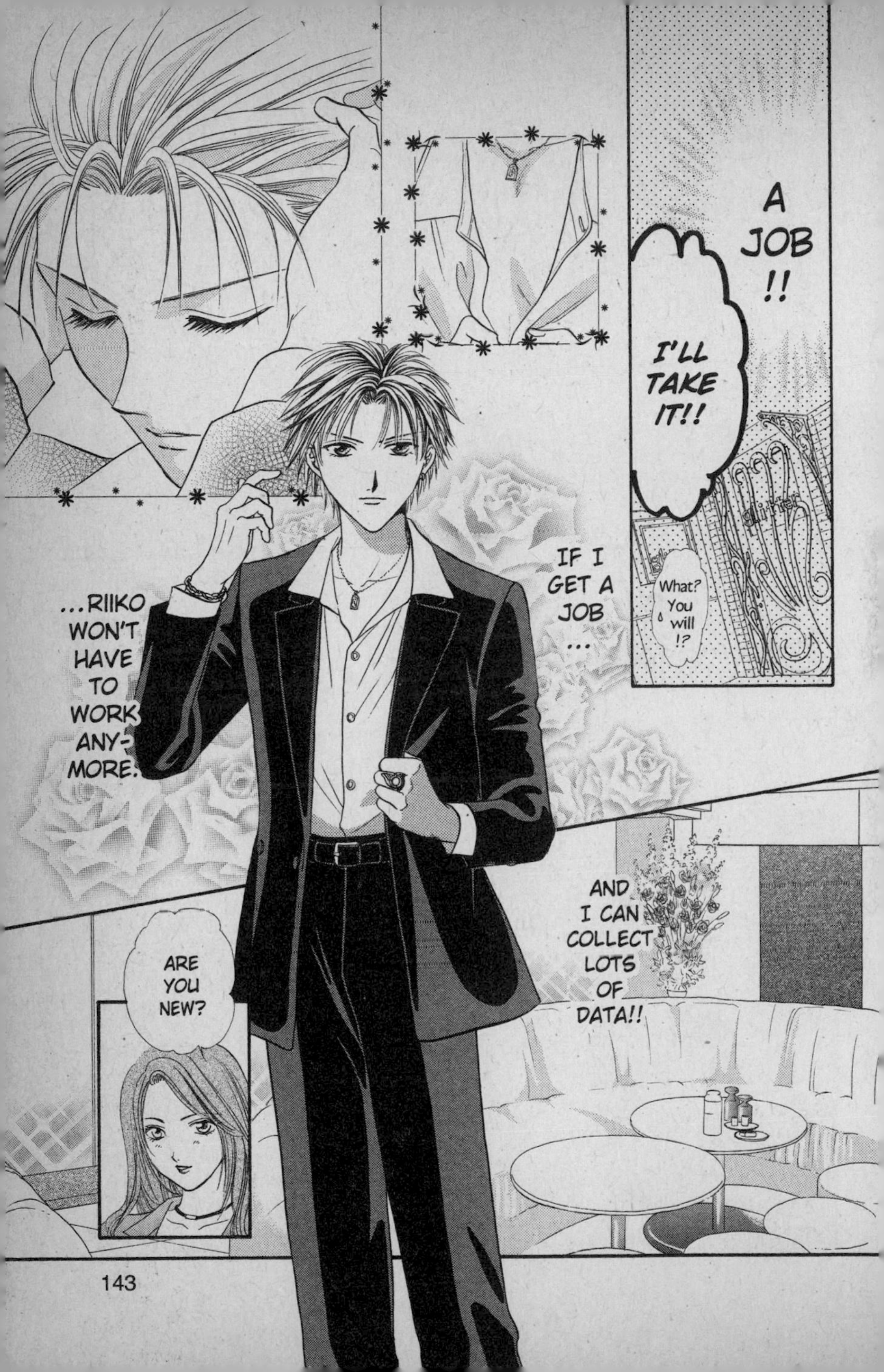

A JOB!!
I'LL TAKE IT!!
What? You will!?
IF I GET A JOB...
...RIIKO WON'T HAVE TO WORK ANYMORE.
AND I CAN COLLECT LOTS OF DATA!!
ARE YOU NEW?

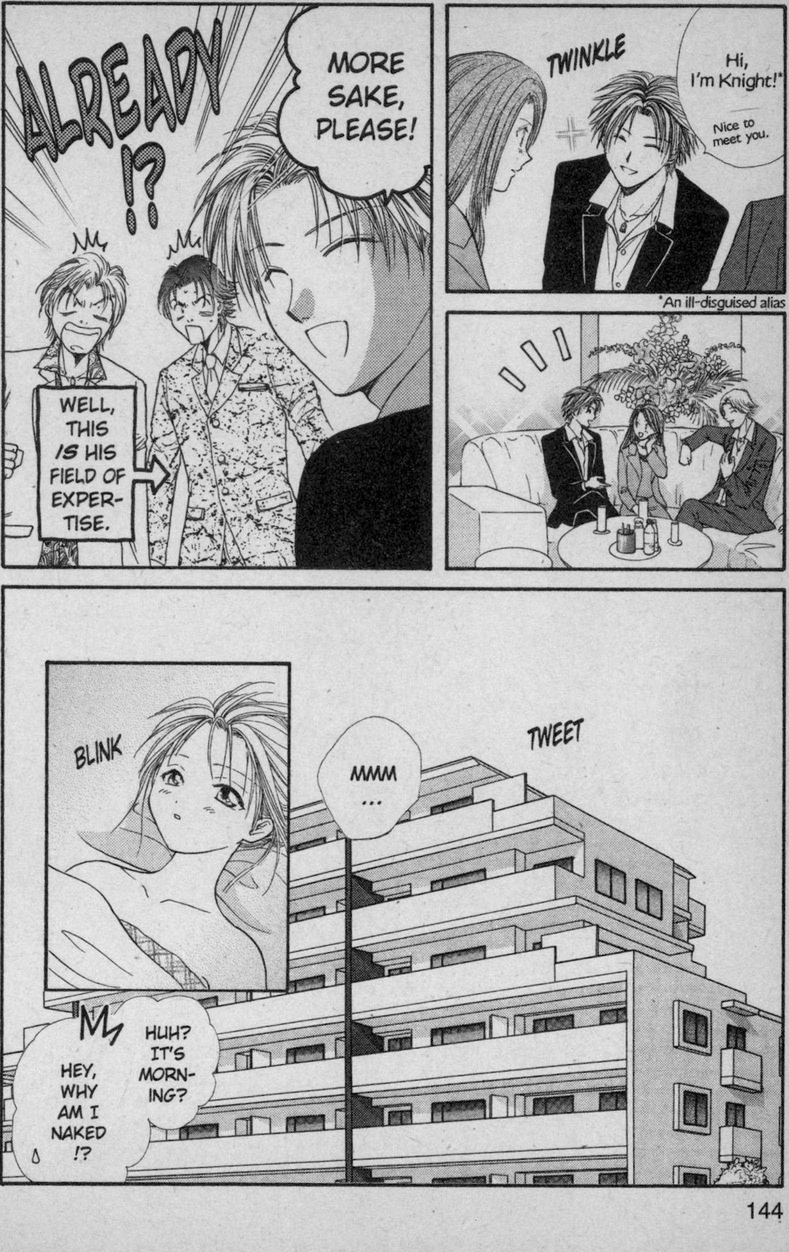
TWINKLE
Hi, I'm Knight!*
Nice to meet you.
*An ill-disguised alias
MORE SAKE, PLEASE!
ALREADY !?
WELL, THIS IS HIS FIELD OF EXPERTISE.
TWEET
MMM ...
BLINK
HUH? IT'S MORNING?
M
HEY, WHY AM I NAKED !?

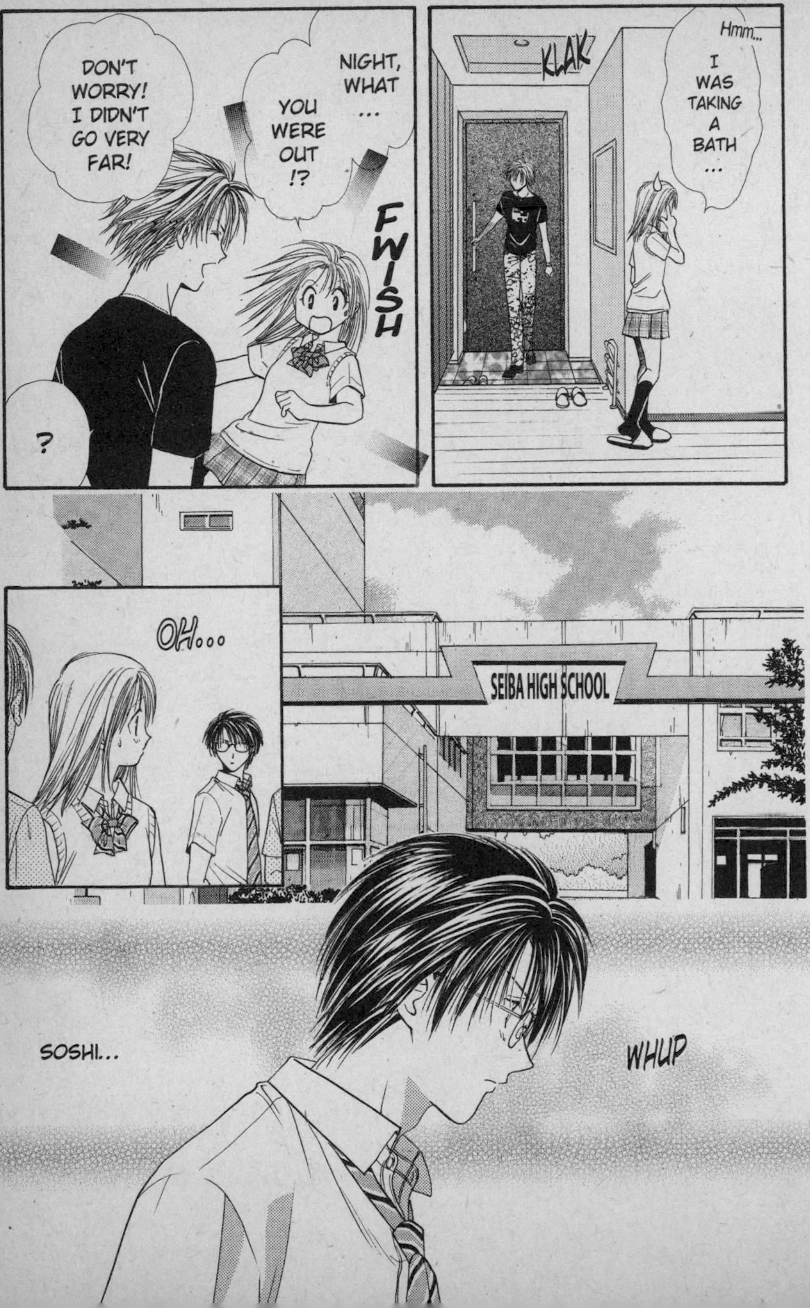
KLAK
Hmm... I WAS TAKING A BATH ...
NIGHT, WHAT ... YOU WERE OUT !?
FWISH
DON'T WORRY! I DIDN'T GO VERY FAR!
?
SEIBA HIGH SCHOOL
OH...
WHUP
SOSHI...

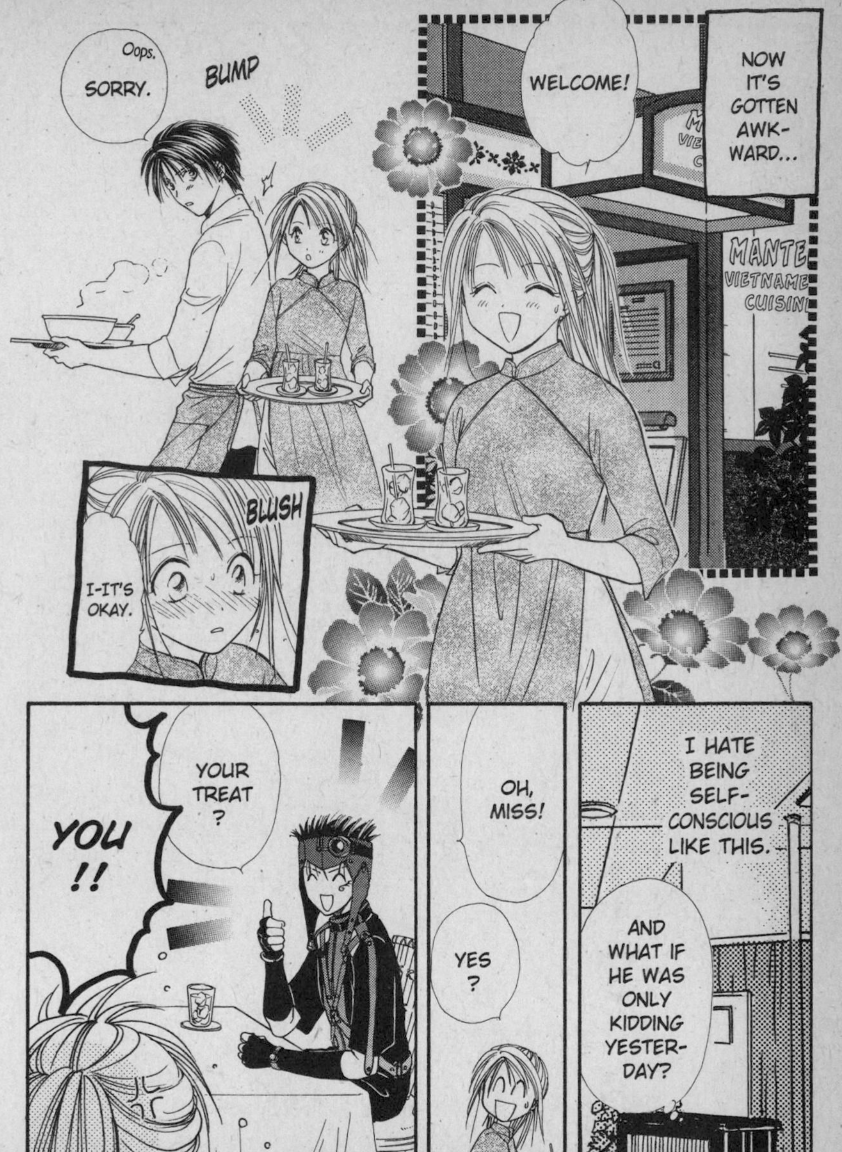

NOW IT'S GOTTEN AWK-WARD...
WELCOME!
MANTE
Oops.
SORRY.
BUMP
BLUSH
I-IT'S OKAY.
I HATE BEING SELF-CONSCIOUS LIKE THIS.
AND WHAT IF HE WAS ONLY KIDDING YESTER-DAY?
OH, MISS!
YES?
YOUR TREAT?
YOU!!

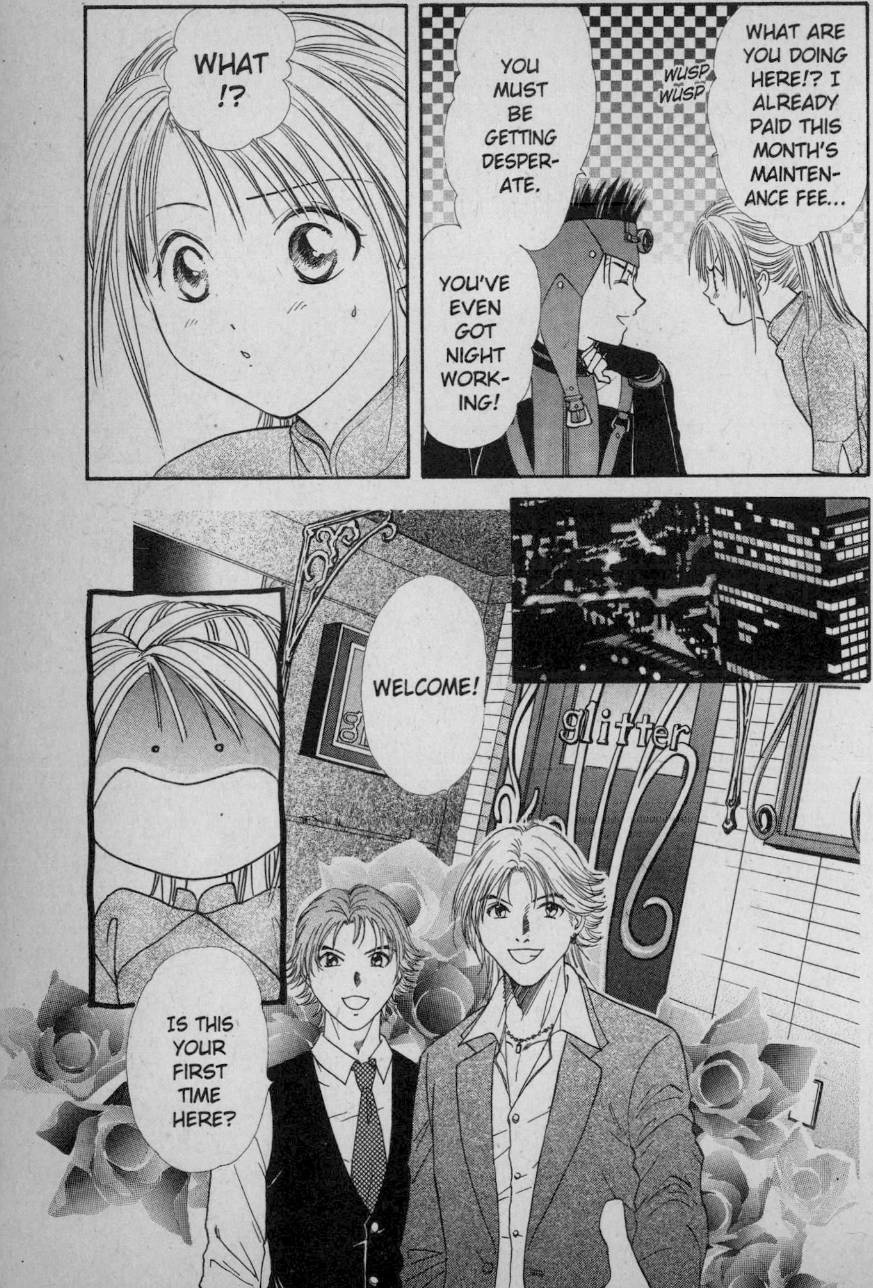
WHAT ARE YOU DOING HERE!? I ALREADY PAID THIS MONTH'S MAINTENANCE FEE...
WUSP WUSP
YOU MUST BE GETTING DESPERATE.
YOU'VE EVEN GOT NIGHT WORKING!
WHAT !?
glitter
WELCOME!
IS THIS YOUR FIRST TIME HERE?

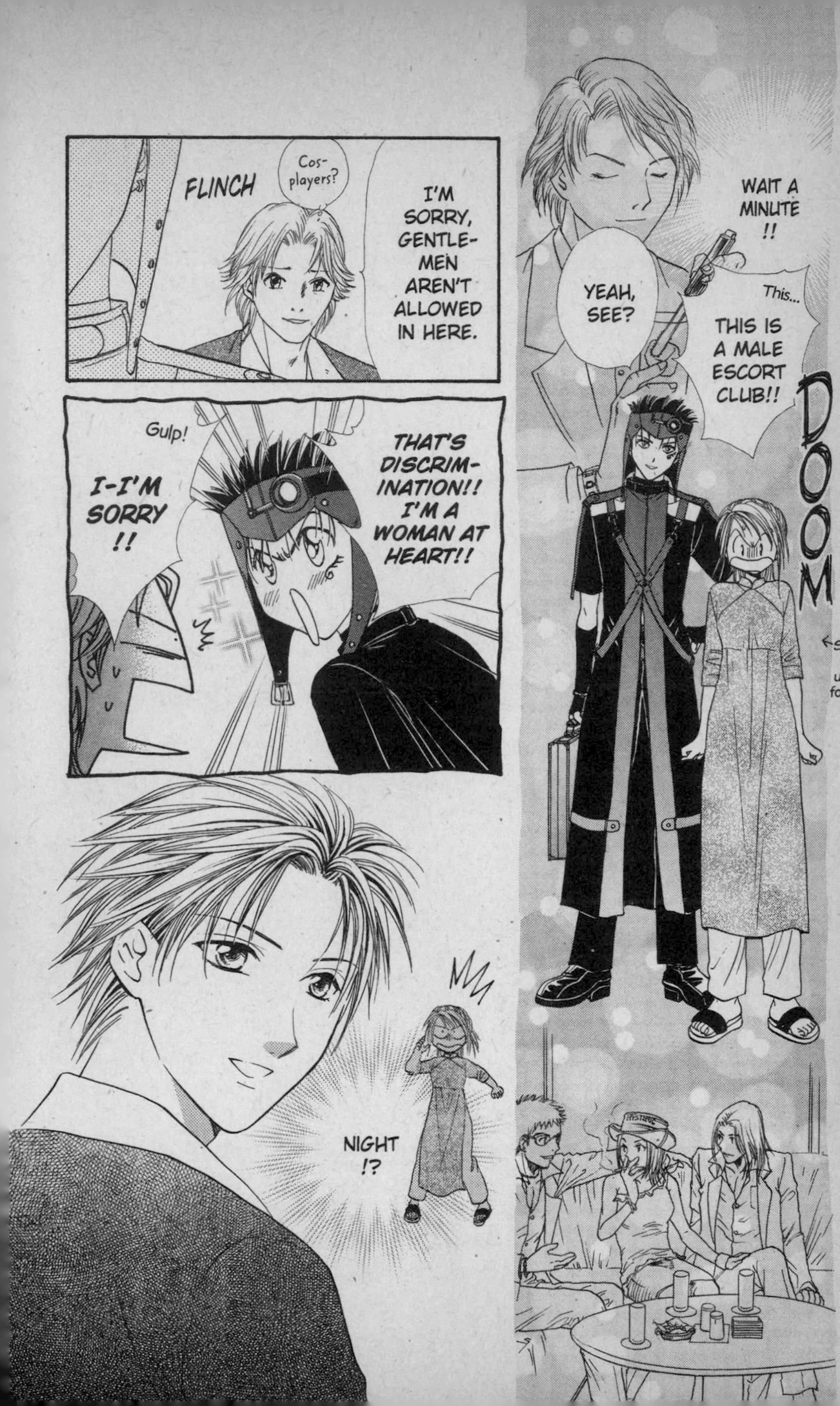
WAIT A MINUTE !!
This...
THIS IS A MALE ESCORT CLUB!!
DOOM
YEAH, SEE?
←Still in uniform.
I'M SORRY, GENTLEMEN AREN'T ALLOWED IN HERE.
Cos-players?
FLINCH
THAT'S DISCRIMINATION!! I'M A WOMAN AT HEART!!
Gulp!
I-I'M SORRY !!
NIGHT !?

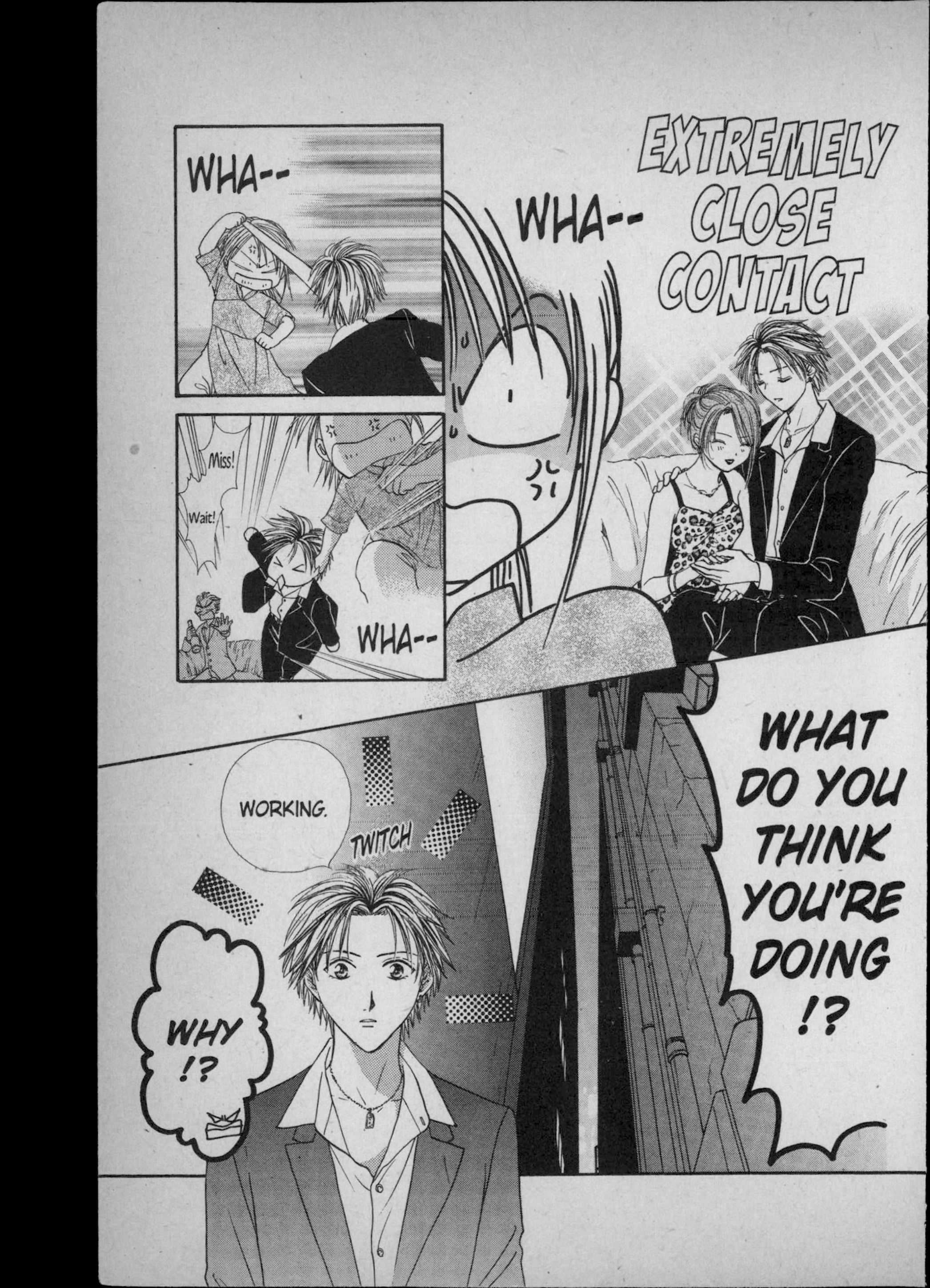
EXTREMELY CLOSE CONTACT
WHA--
WHA--
Miss!
Wait!
WHA--
WHAT DO YOU THINK YOU'RE DOING !?
WORKING.
TWITCH
WHY !?

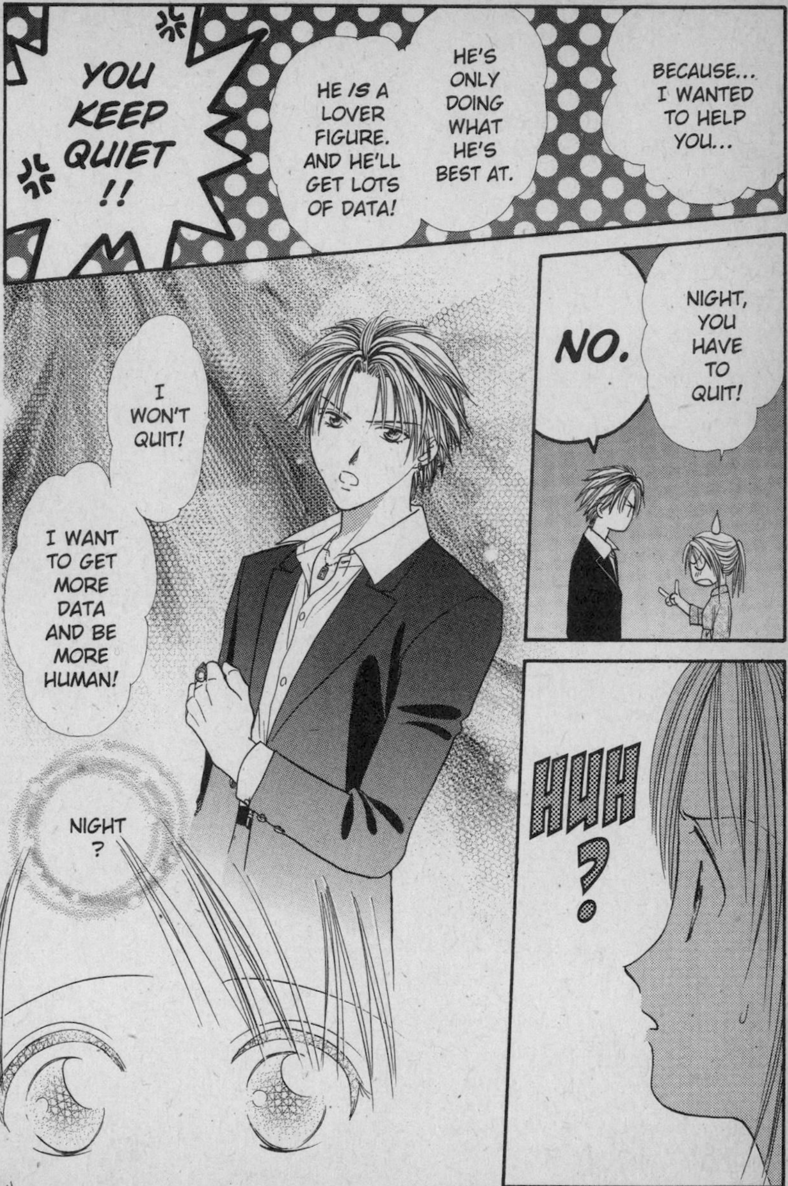
BECAUSE... I WANTED TO HELP YOU...
HE'S ONLY DOING WHAT HE'S BEST AT.
HE *IS* A LOVER FIGURE. AND HE'LL GET LOTS OF DATA!
YOU KEEP QUIET !!
NIGHT, YOU HAVE TO QUIT!
NO.
HUH ?
I WON'T QUIT!
I WANT TO GET MORE DATA AND BE MORE HUMAN!
NIGHT ?

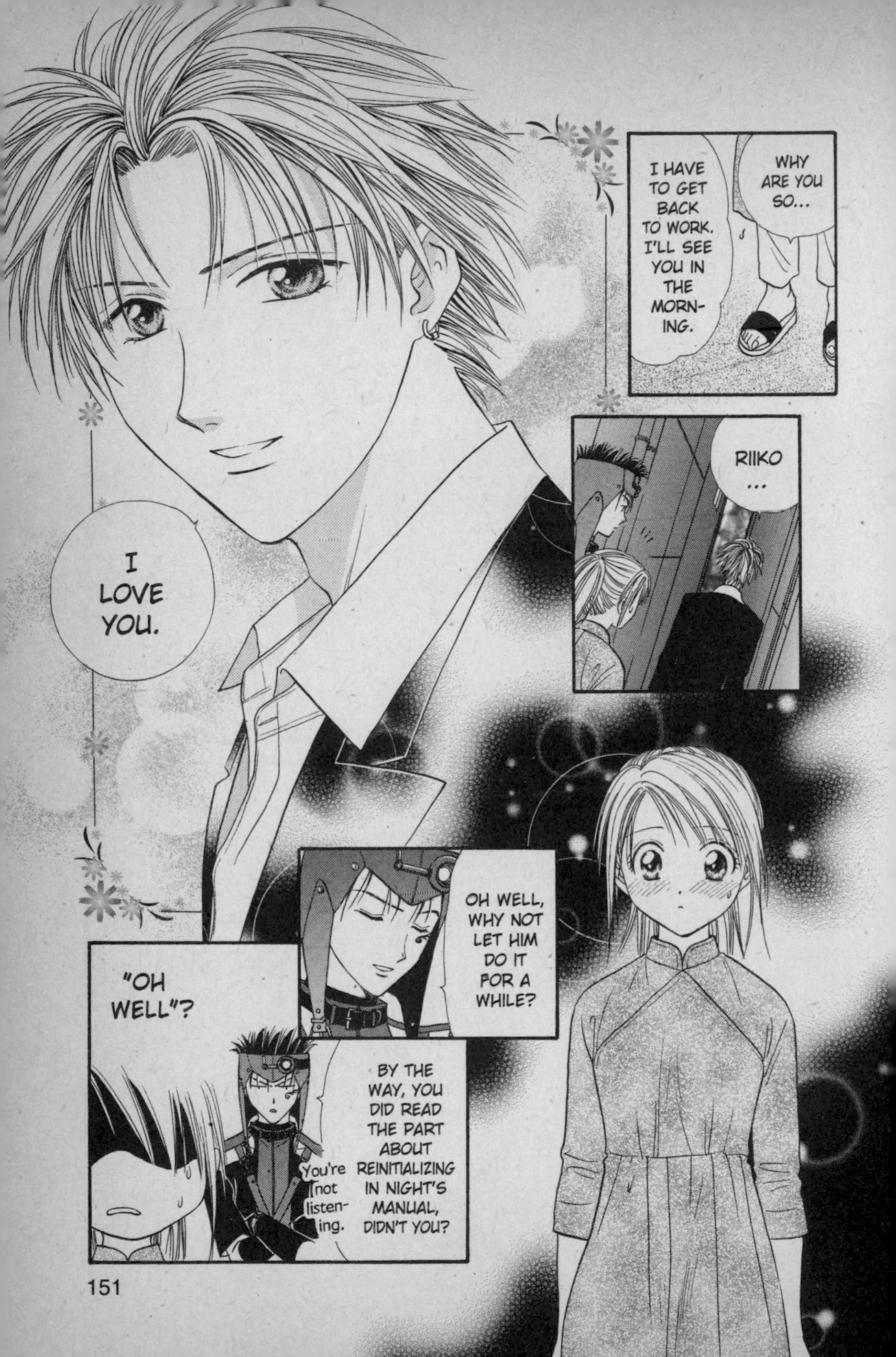
WHY ARE YOU SO...
I HAVE TO GET BACK TO WORK. I'LL SEE YOU IN THE MORNING.
RIIKO ...
I LOVE YOU.
OH WELL, WHY NOT LET HIM DO IT FOR A WHILE?
"OH WELL"?
BY THE WAY, YOU DID READ THE PART ABOUT REINITIALIZING IN NIGHT'S MANUAL, DIDN'T YOU?
You're not listening.

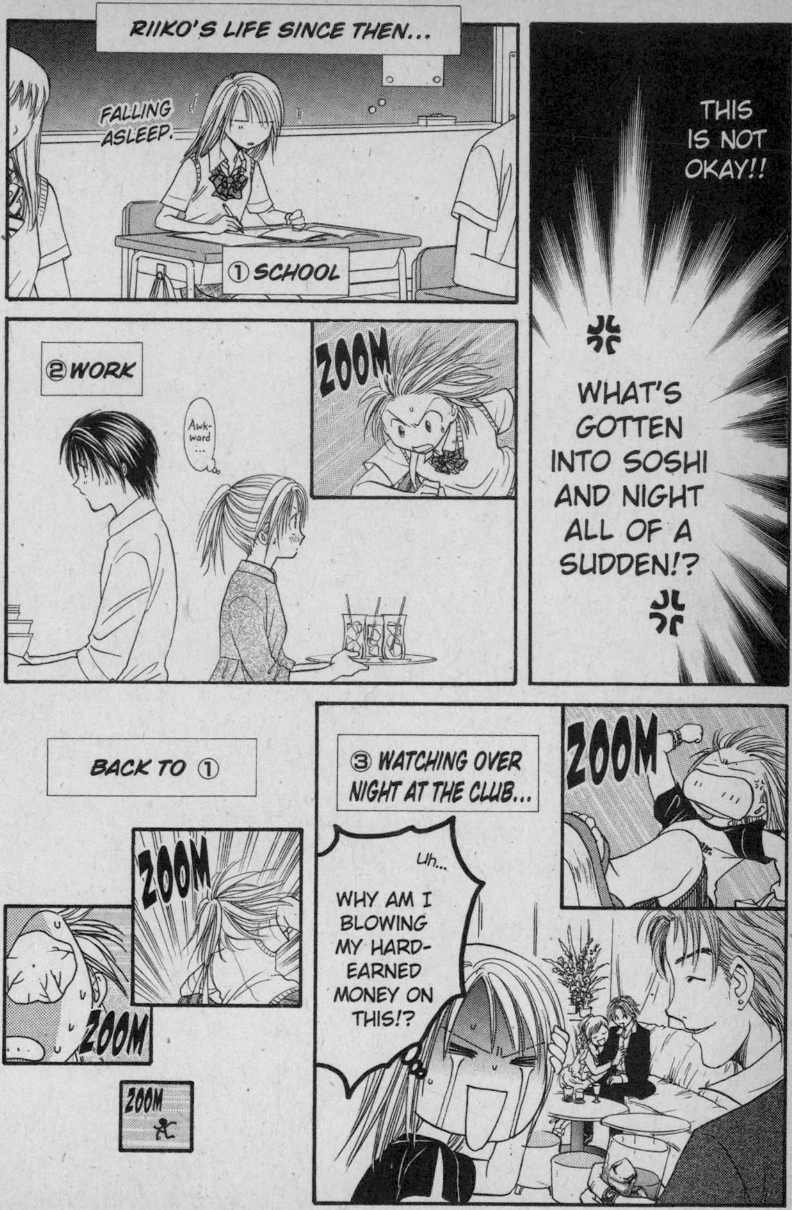
RIIKO'S LIFE SINCE THEN...
FALLING ASLEEP.
① SCHOOL
② WORK
Awk-ward...
ZOOM
THIS IS NOT OKAY!!
WHAT'S GOTTEN INTO SOSHI AND NIGHT ALL OF A SUDDEN!?
③ WATCHING OVER NIGHT AT THE CLUB...
ZOOM
Uh...
WHY AM I BLOWING MY HARD-EARNED MONEY ON THIS!?
BACK TO ①
ZOOM
ZOOM
ZOOM

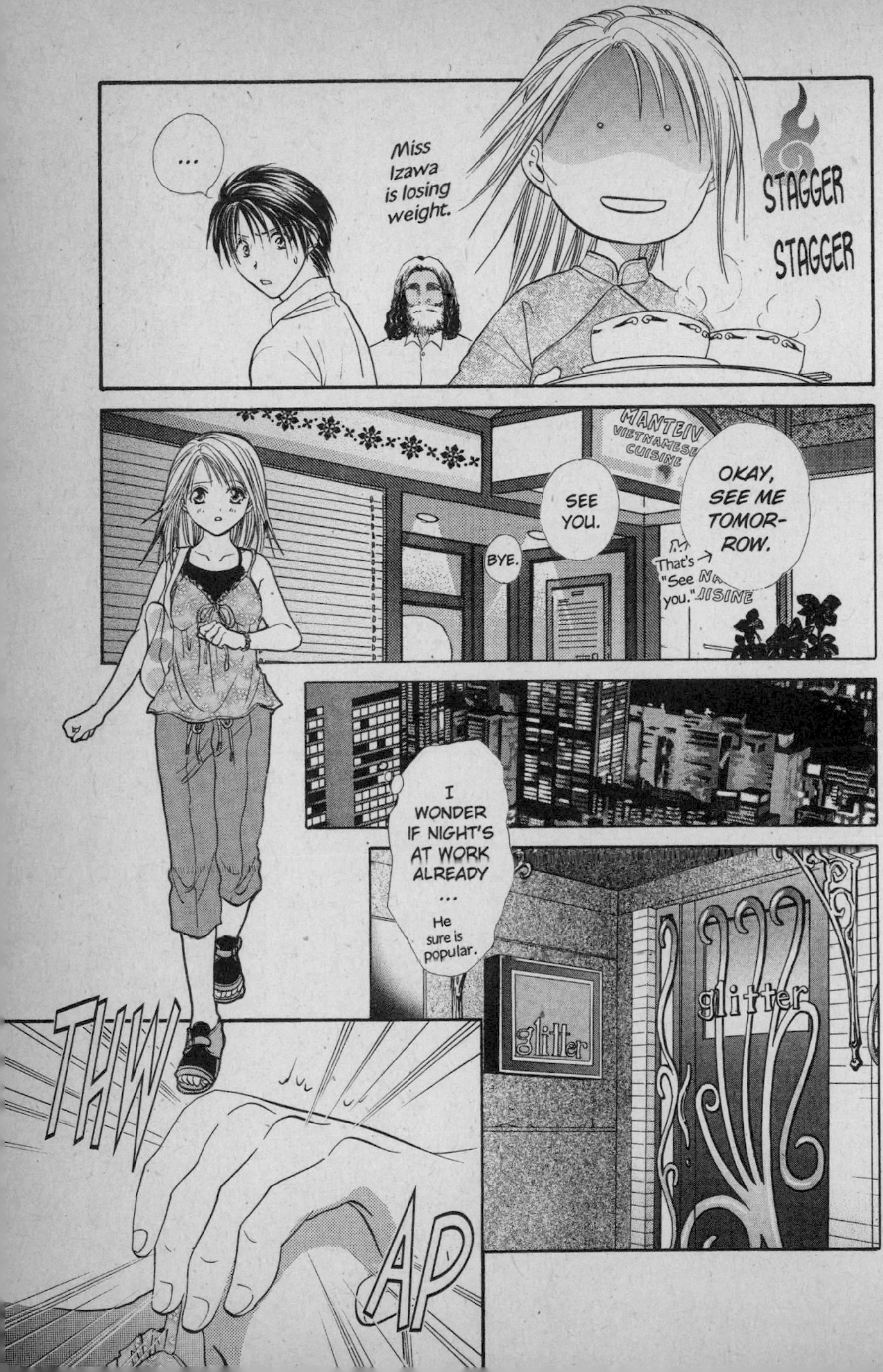
STAGGER STAGGER
Miss Izawa is losing weight.
...
MANTEIV VIETNAMESE CUISINE
OKAY, SEE ME TOMOR-ROW.
That's "See you."
SEE YOU.
BYE.
I WONDER IF NIGHT'S AT WORK ALREADY ...
He sure is popular.
glitter
glitter
THWAP

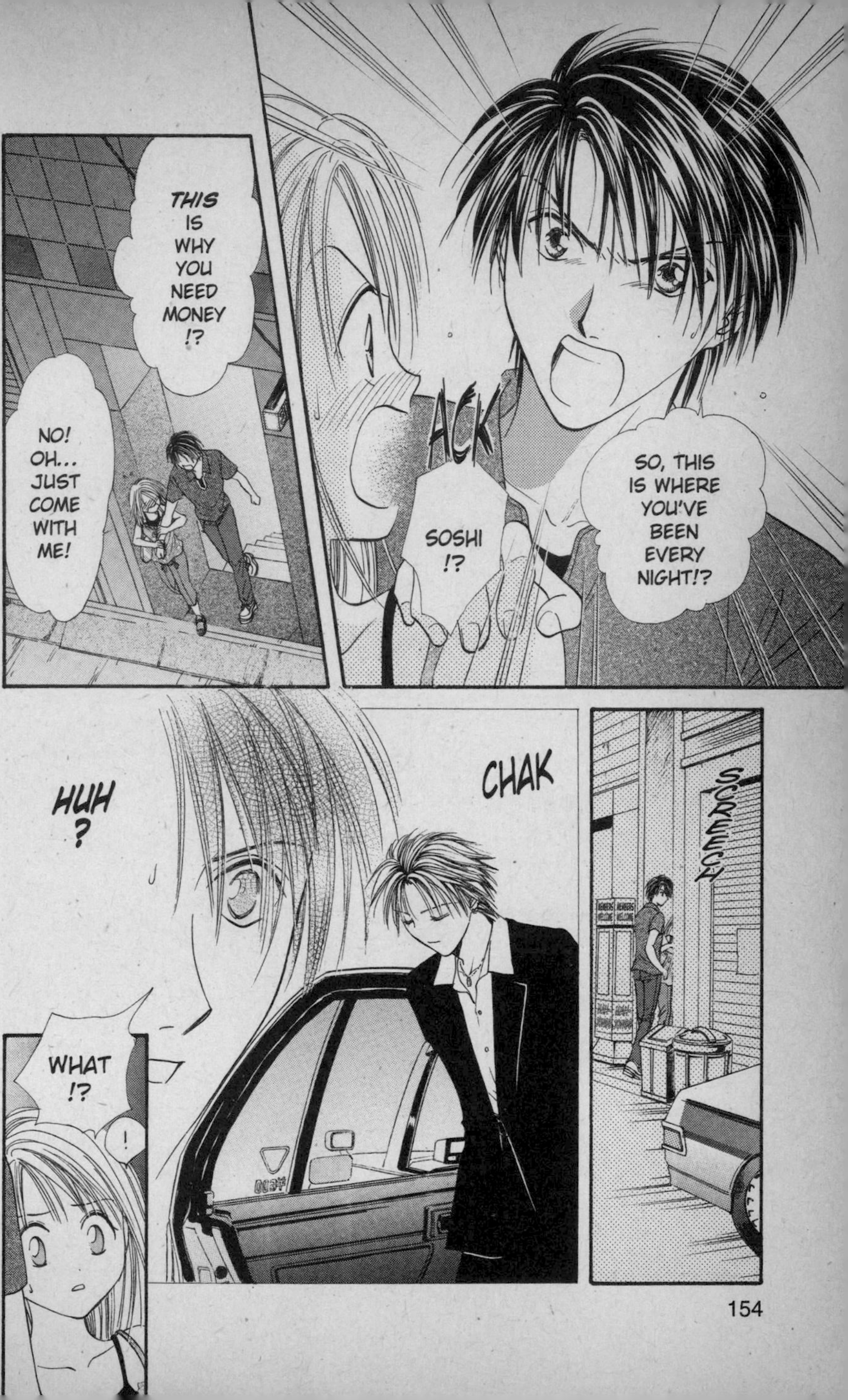

SO, THIS IS WHERE YOU'VE BEEN EVERY NIGHT!?
ACK
SOSHI !?
THIS IS WHY YOU NEED MONEY !?
NO! OH... JUST COME WITH ME!
SCREECH
CHAK
HUH ?
WHAT !?
!

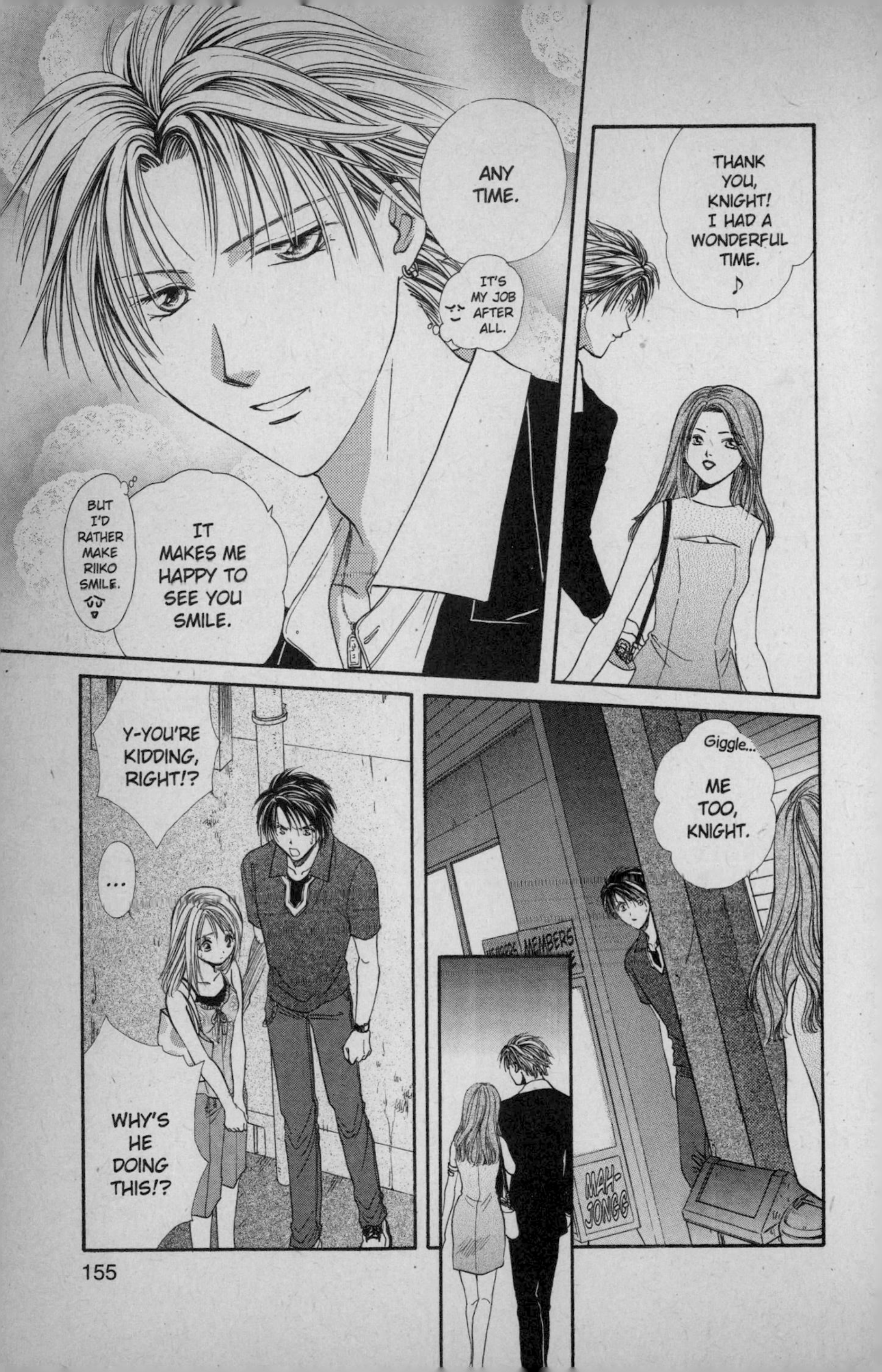
THANK YOU, KNIGHT! I HAD A WONDERFUL TIME. ♪
ANY TIME.
IT'S MY JOB AFTER ALL.
IT MAKES ME HAPPY TO SEE YOU SMILE.
BUT I'D RATHER MAKE RIIKO SMILE.
Giggle...
ME TOO, KNIGHT.
MEMBERS
MAH-JONGG
Y-YOU'RE KIDDING, RIGHT!?
...
WHY'S HE DOING THIS!?

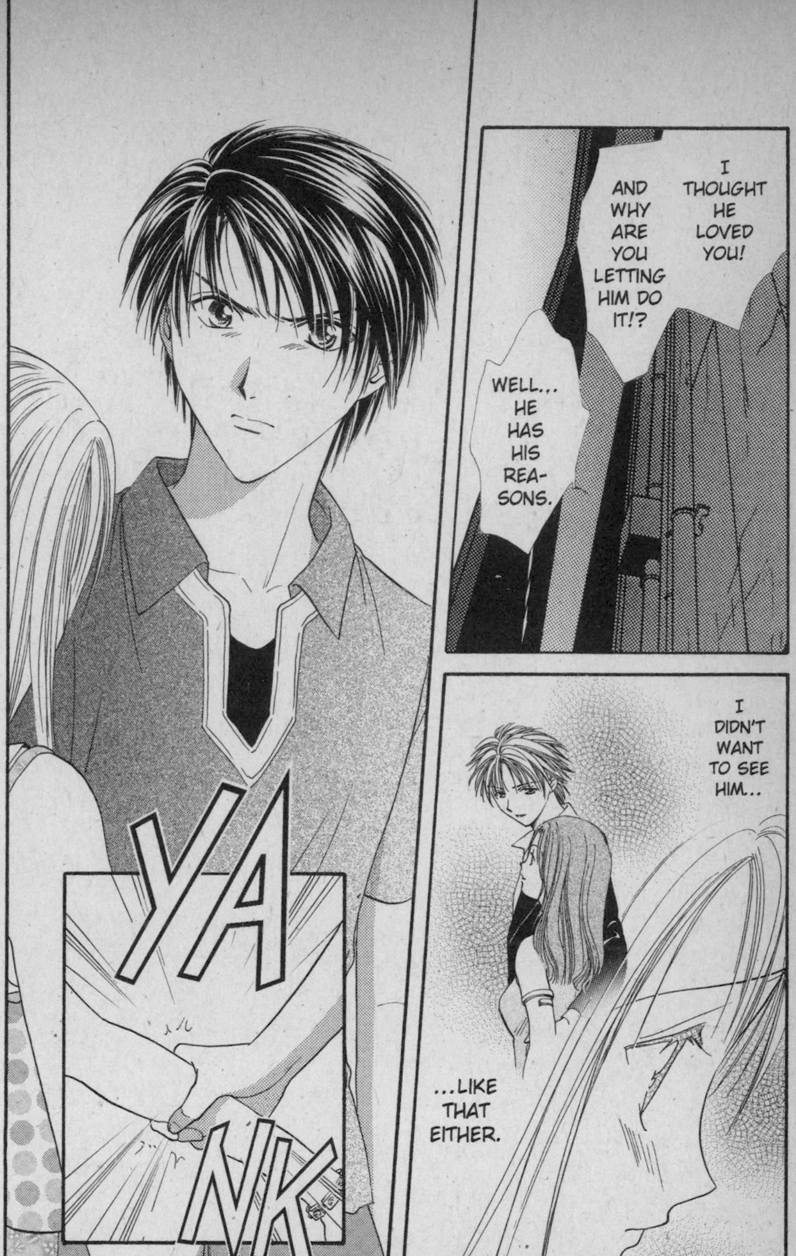
I THOUGHT HE LOVED YOU!
AND WHY ARE YOU LETTING HIM DO IT!?
WELL... HE HAS HIS REA-SONS.
I DIDN'T WANT TO SEE HIM...
...LIKE THAT EITHER.
YANK

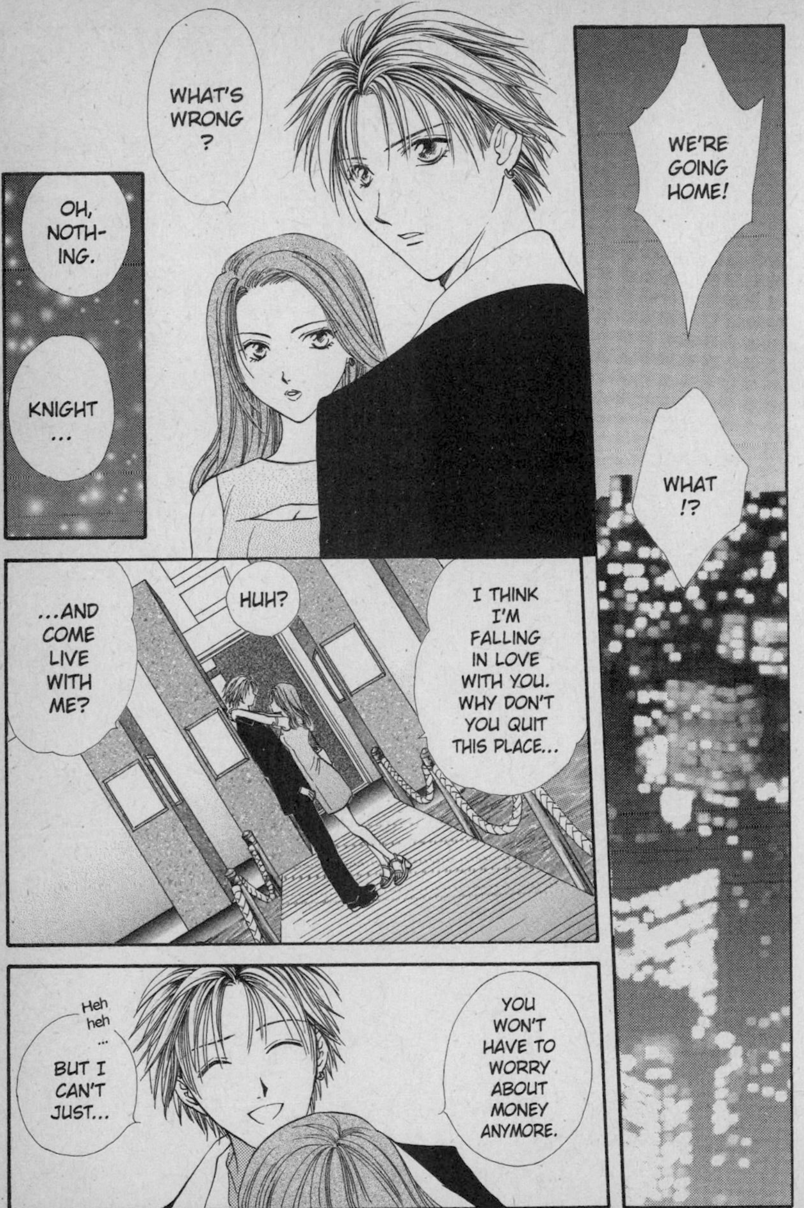
WE'RE GOING HOME!
WHAT !?
WHAT'S WRONG ?
OH, NOTHING.
KNIGHT ...
I THINK I'M FALLING IN LOVE WITH YOU. WHY DON'T YOU QUIT THIS PLACE...
HUH?
...AND COME LIVE WITH ME?
YOU WON'T HAVE TO WORRY ABOUT MONEY ANYMORE.
Heh heh ... BUT I CAN'T JUST...

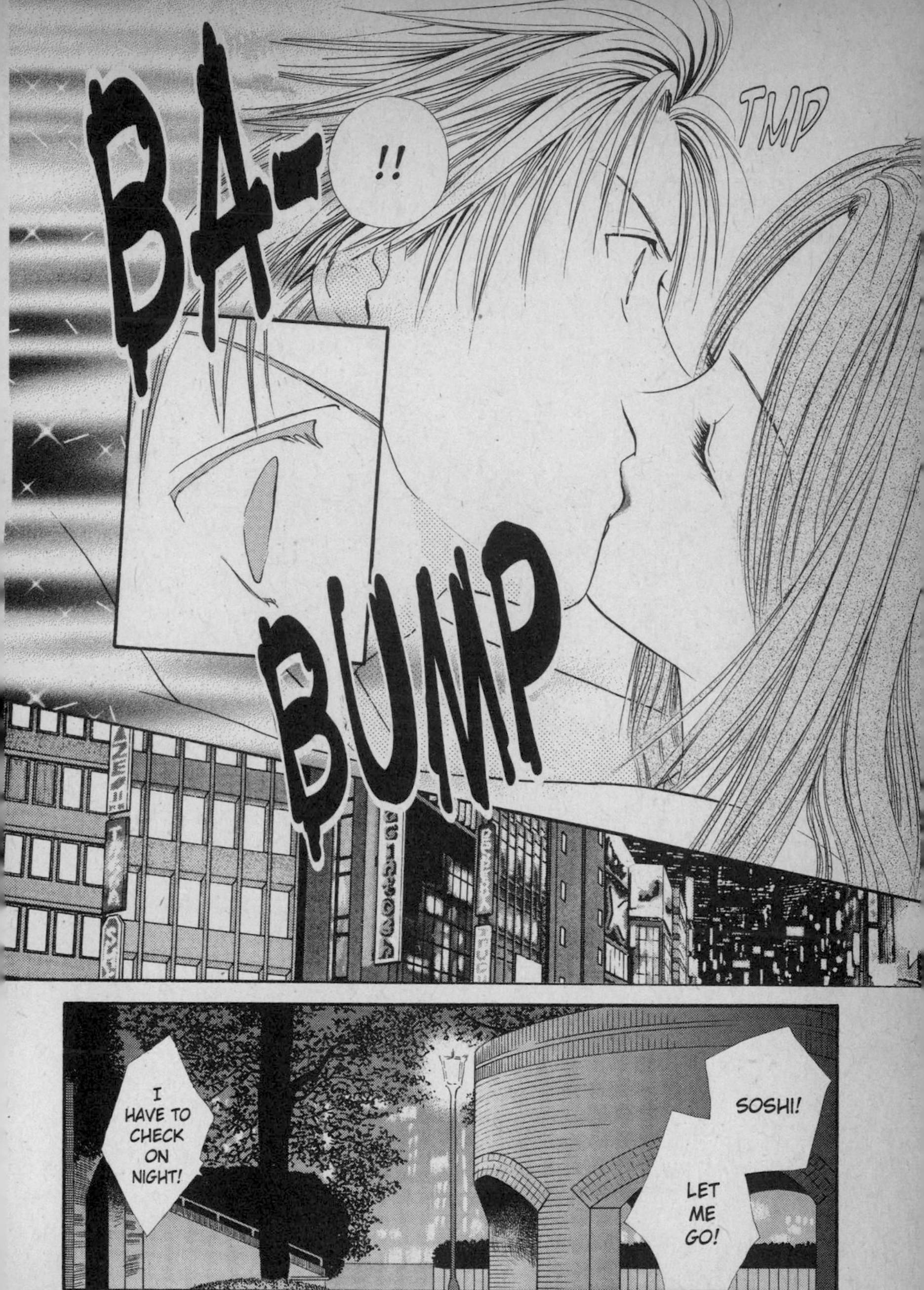
TMP
!!
BA-BUMP
SOSHI!
LET ME GO!
I HAVE TO CHECK ON NIGHT!

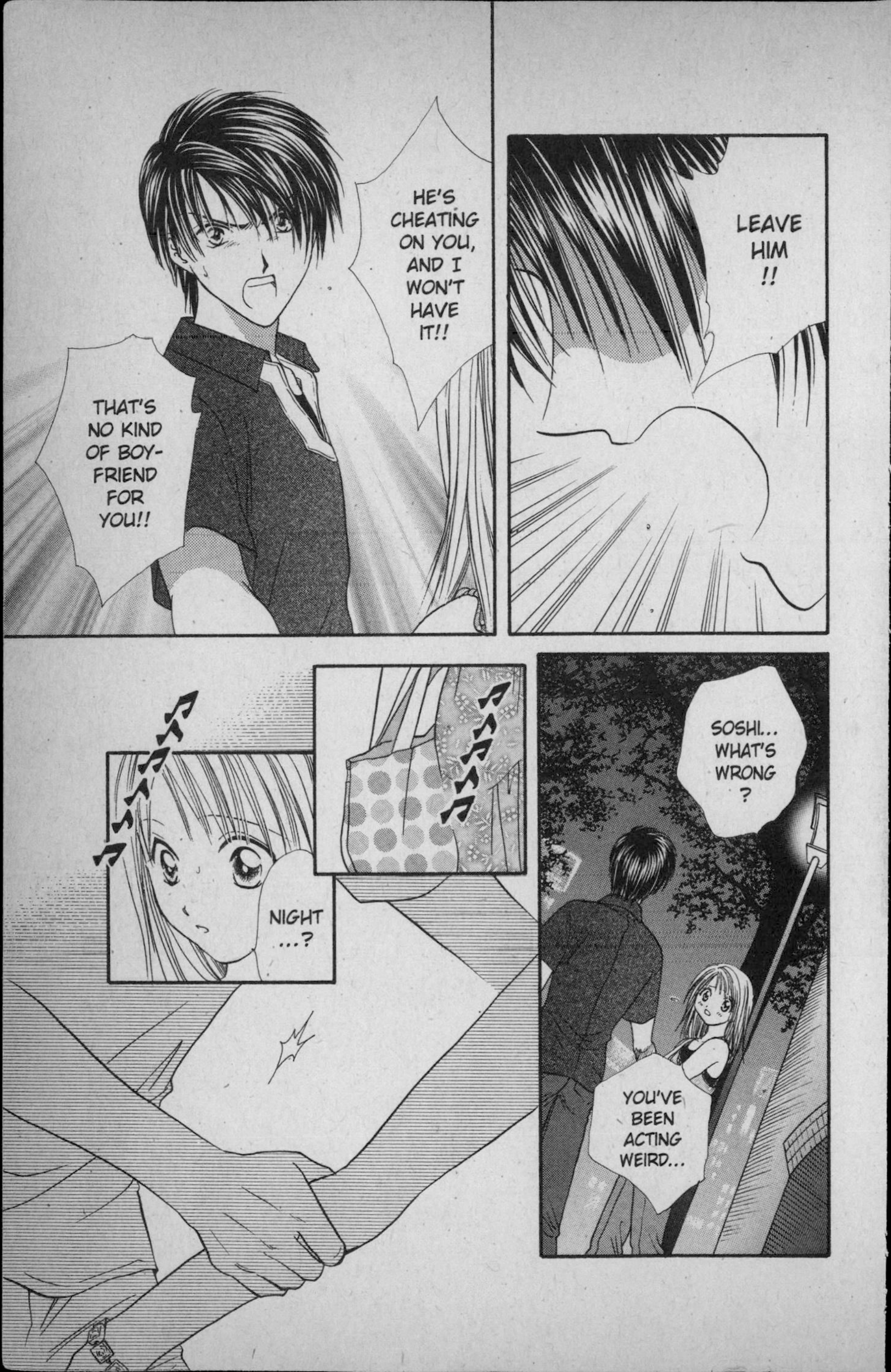
LEAVE HIM !!
HE'S CHEATING ON YOU, AND I WON'T HAVE IT!!
THAT'S NO KIND OF BOY-FRIEND FOR YOU!!
SOSHI... WHAT'S WRONG ?
YOU'VE BEEN ACTING WEIRD...
NIGHT ...?

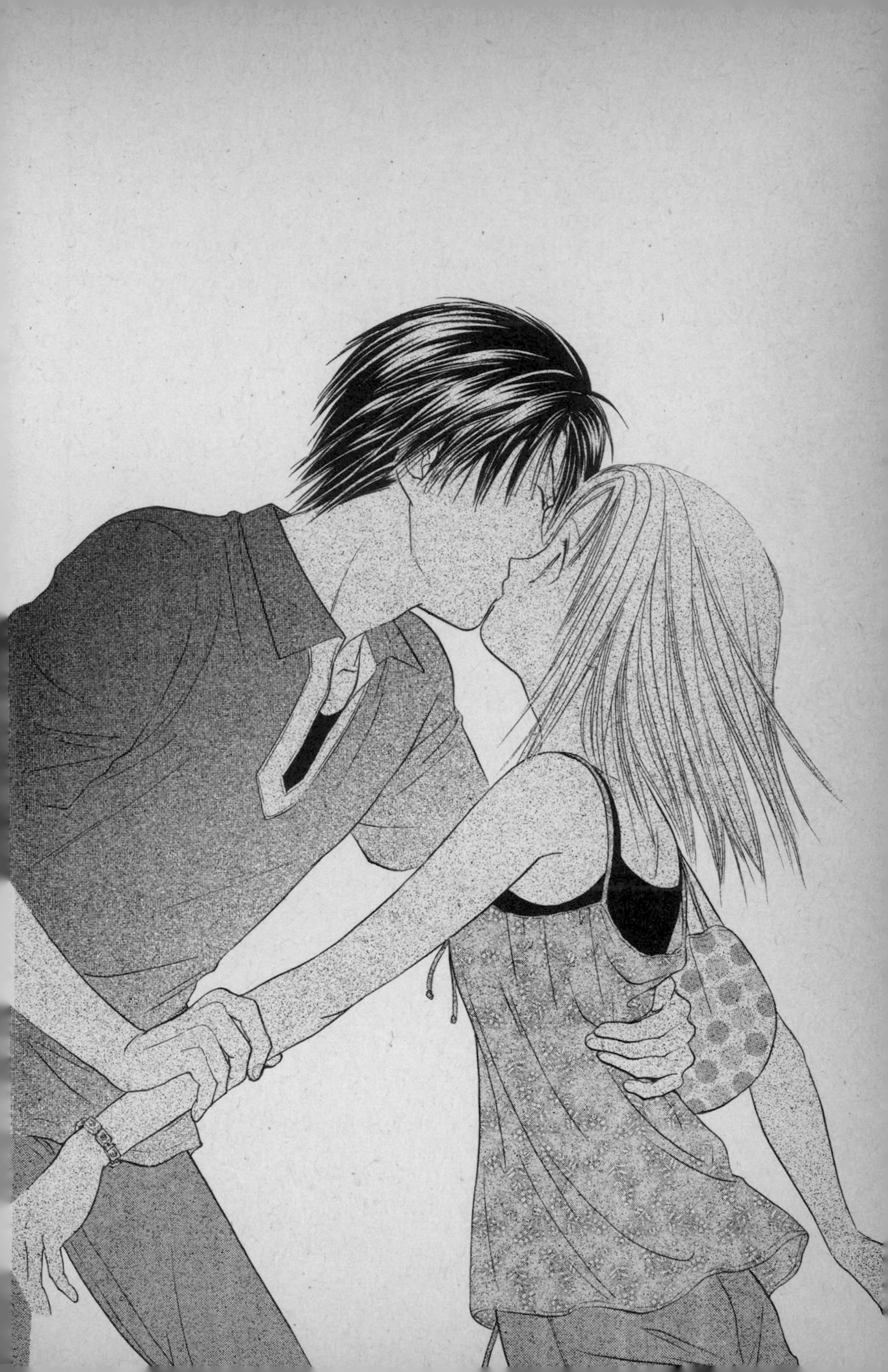

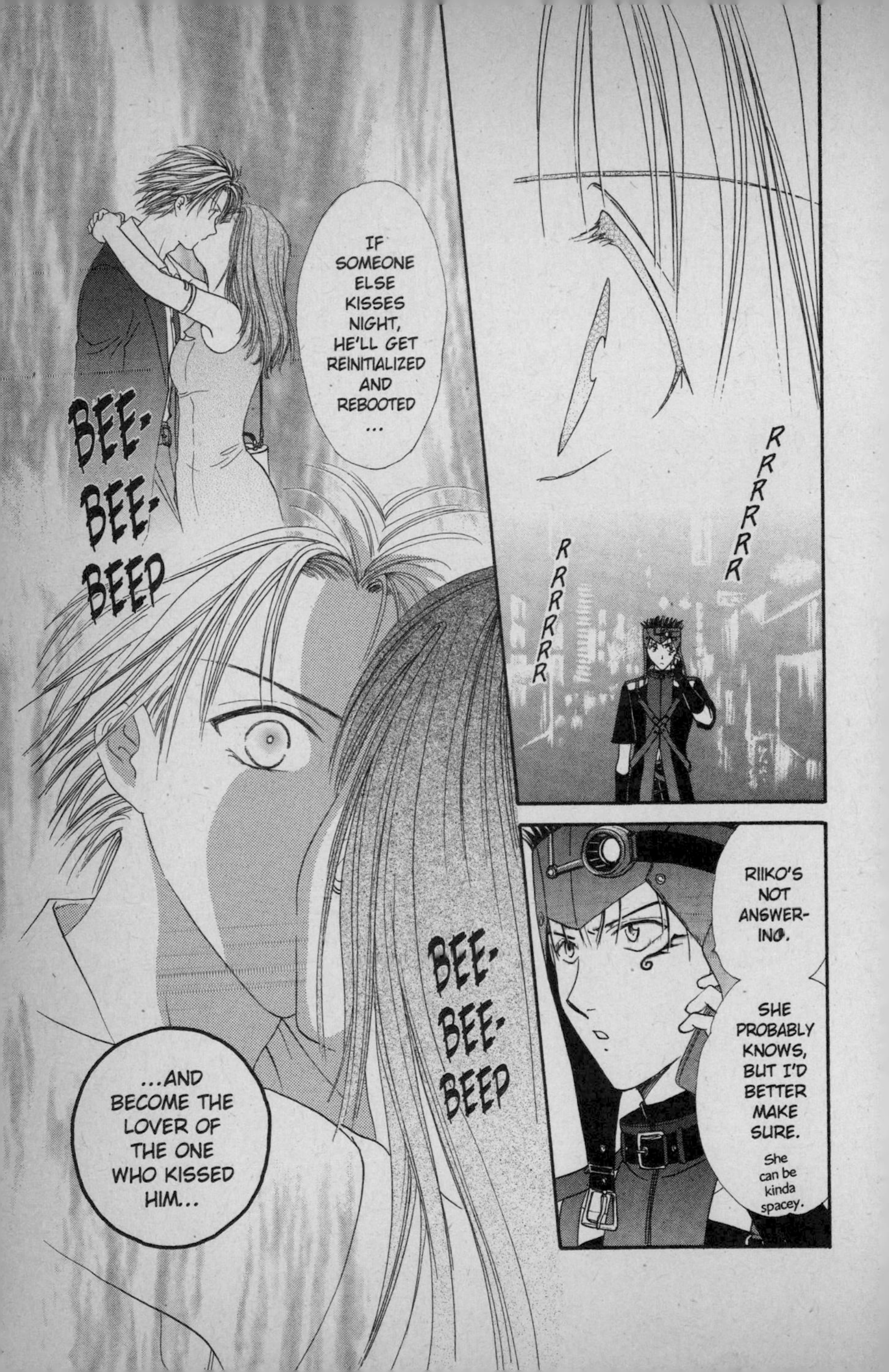
RRRRRR
RRRRRR
RIIKO'S NOT ANSWER-ING.
SHE PROBABLY KNOWS, BUT I'D BETTER MAKE SURE.
She can be kinda spacey.
BEE-BEE-BEEP
IF SOMEONE ELSE KISSES NIGHT, HE'LL GET REINITIALIZED AND REBOOTED...
BEE-BEE-BEEP
...AND BECOME THE LOVER OF THE ONE WHO KISSED HIM...

Absolute Boyfriend

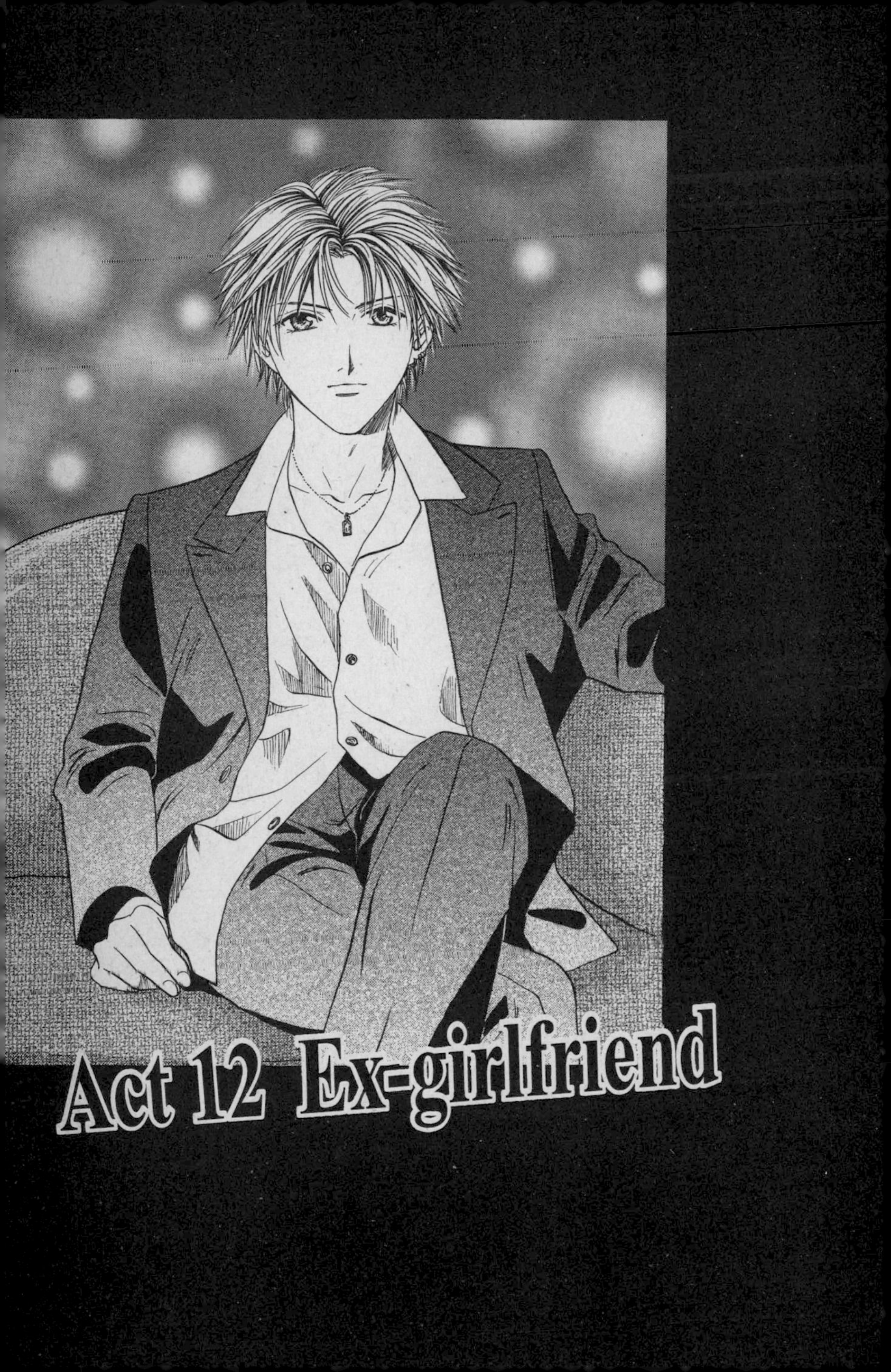

Act 12 Ex-girlfriend

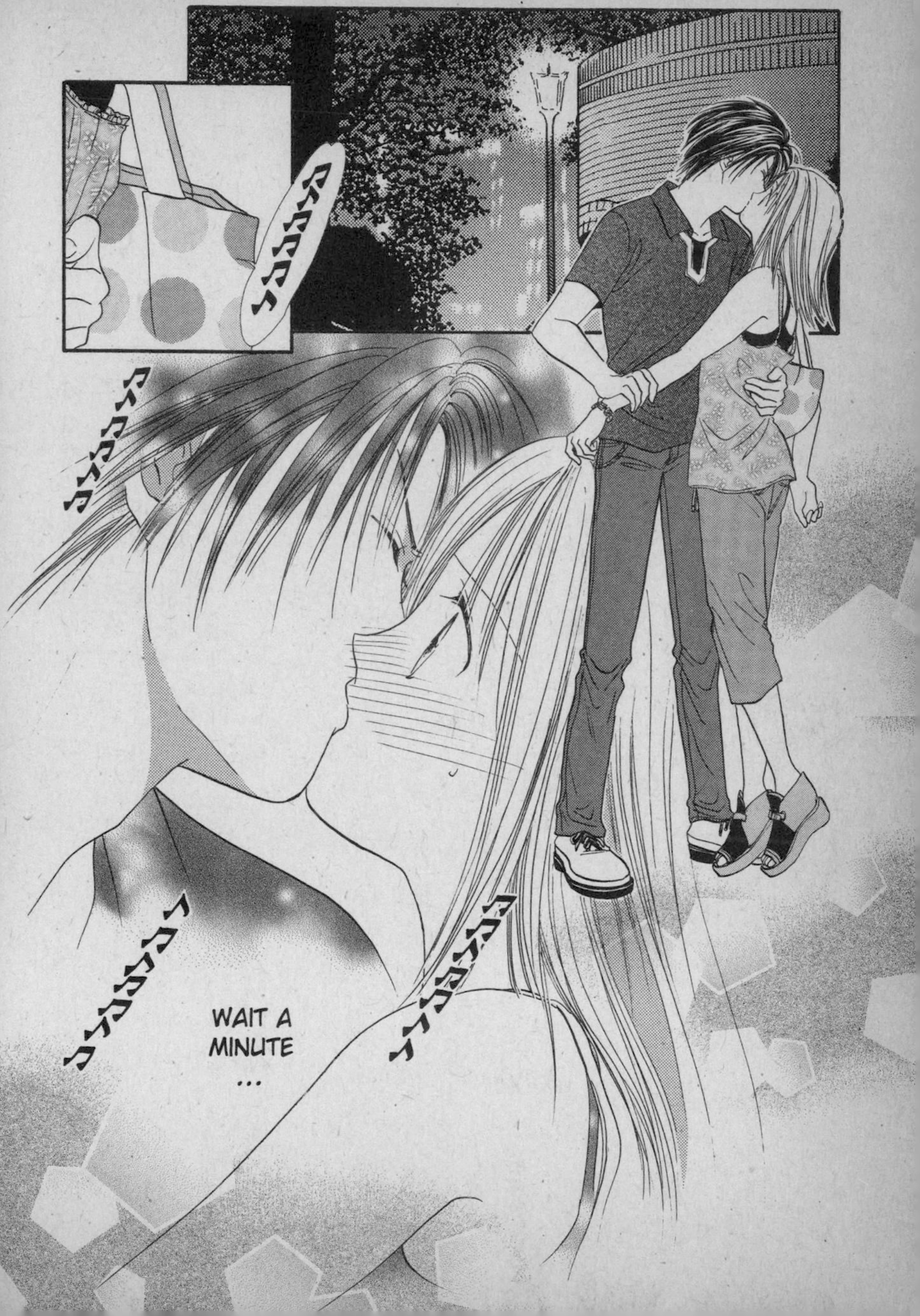
WAIT A MINUTE ...

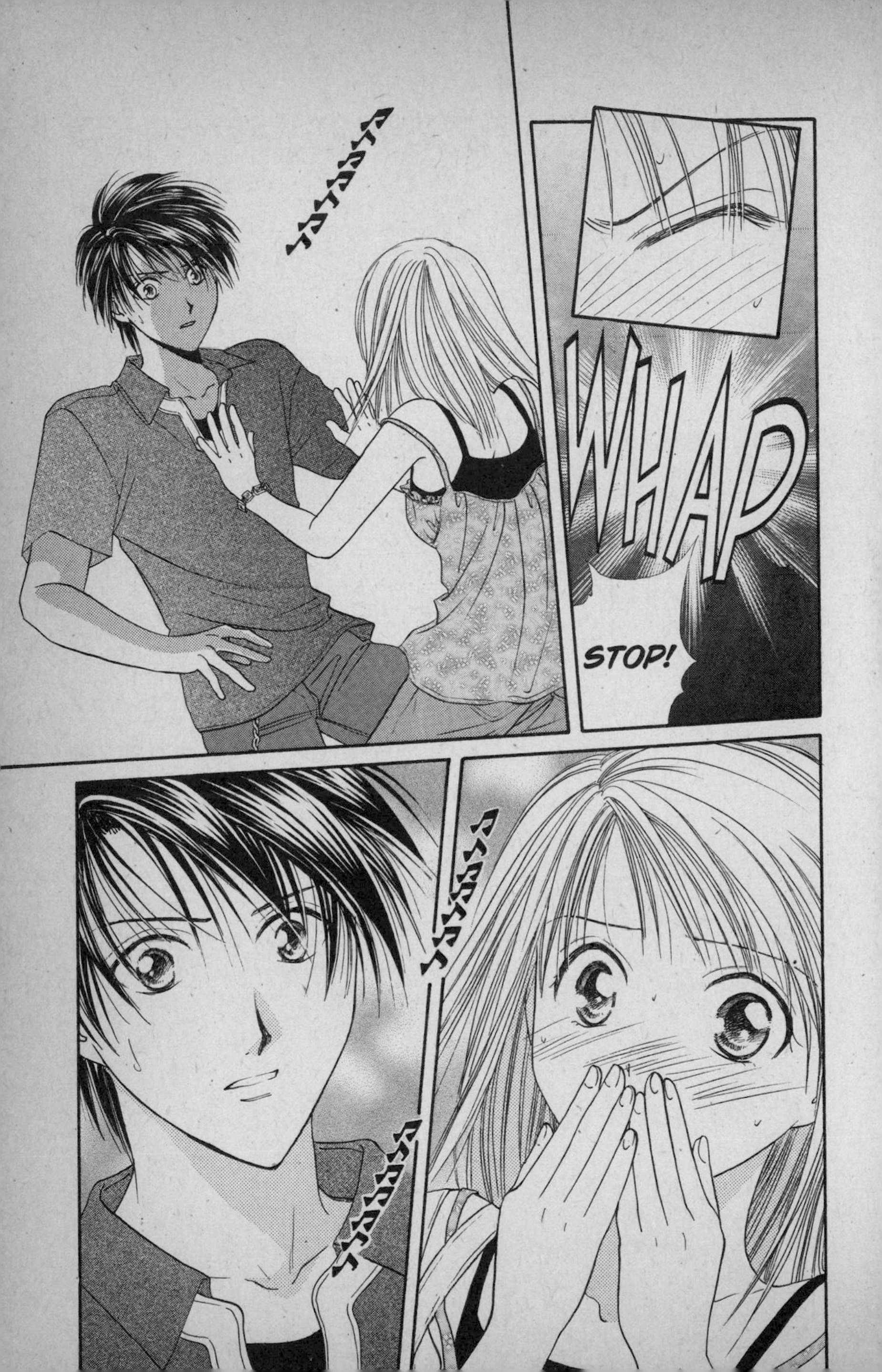
WHAP
STOP!

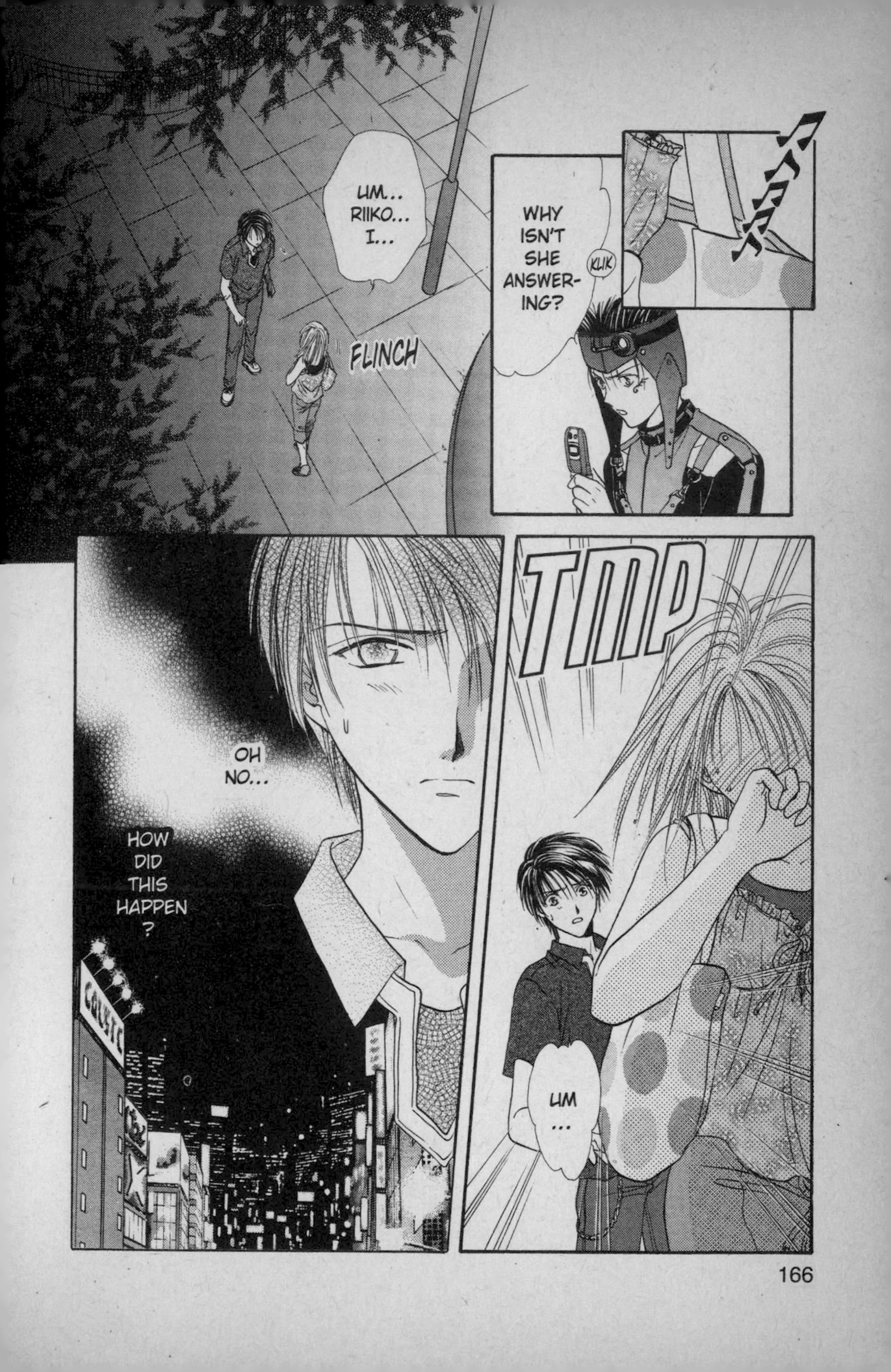
WHY ISN'T SHE ANSWER-ING?
KLIK
UM... RIIKO... I...
FLINCH
TMP
UM ...
OH NO...
HOW DID THIS HAPPEN ?

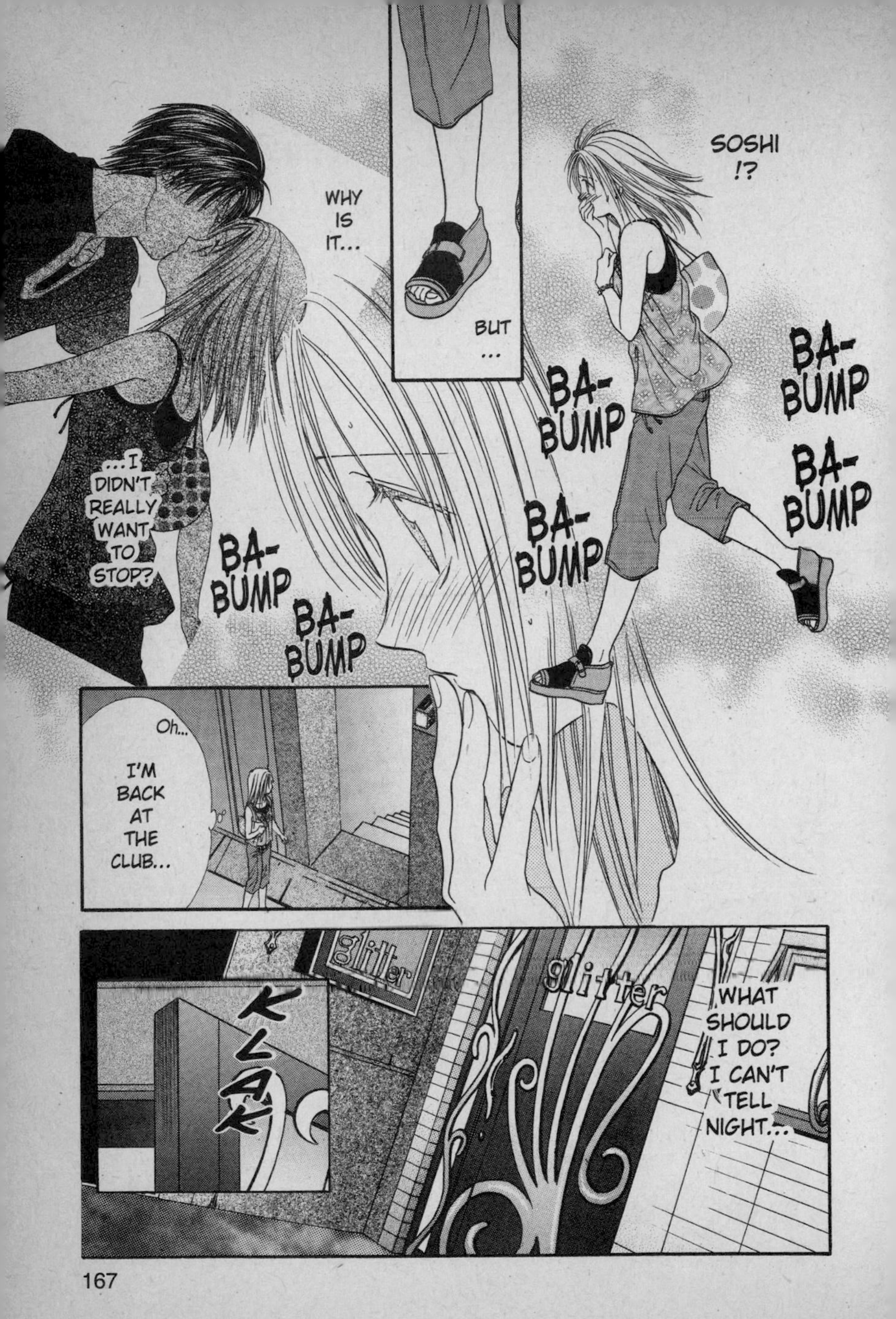
SOSHI !?
BA-BUMP
BA-BUMP
BA-BUMP
BA-BUMP
WHY IS IT...
BUT ...
...I DIDN'T REALLY WANT TO STOP?
BA-BUMP
BA-BUMP
Oh...
I'M BACK AT THE CLUB...
WHAT SHOULD I DO? I CAN'T TELL NIGHT...
glitter
glitter
KLAK

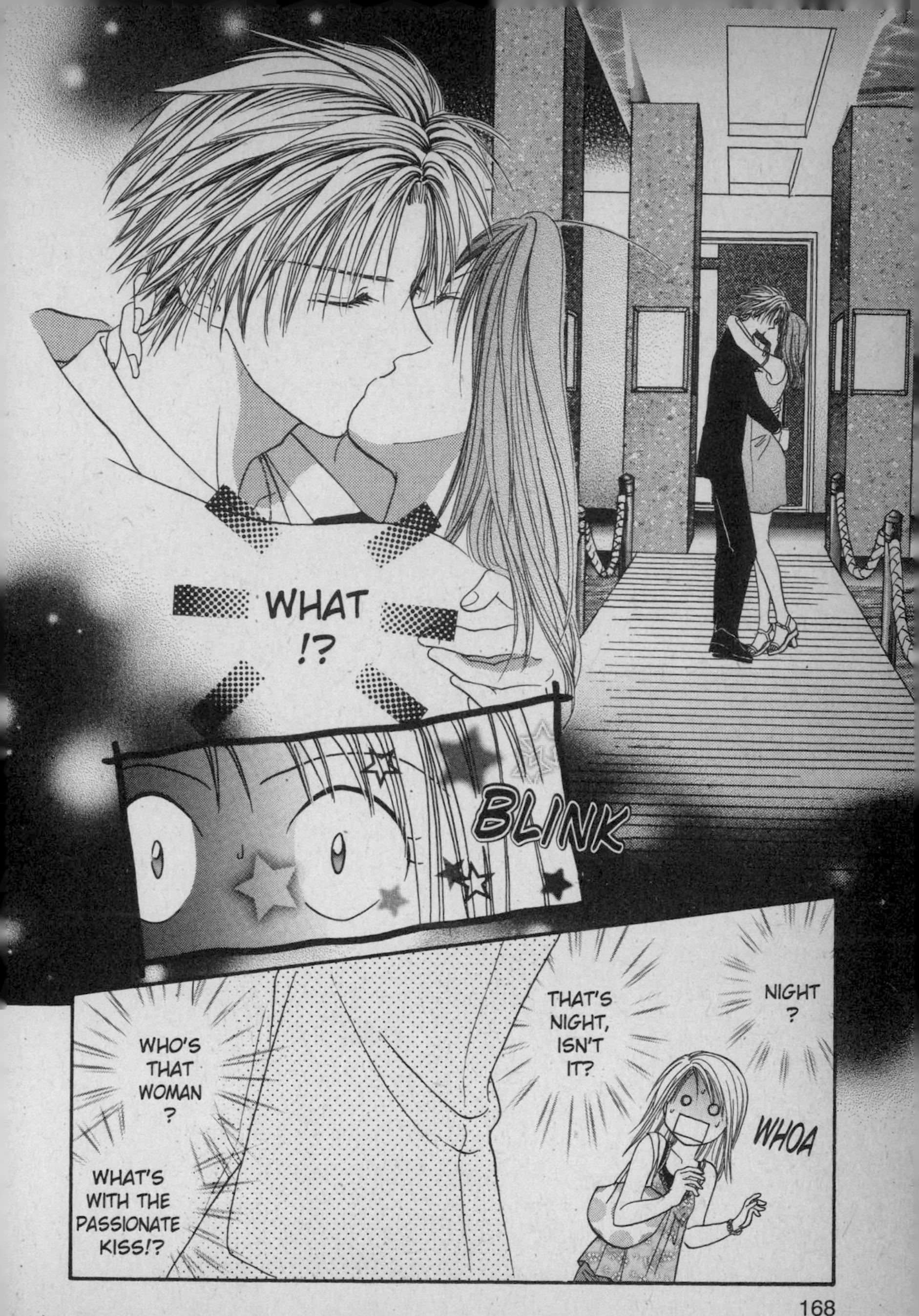
WHAT !?
BLINK
NIGHT ?
WHOA
THAT'S NIGHT, ISN'T IT?
WHO'S THAT WOMAN ?
WHAT'S WITH THE PASSIONATE KISS!?

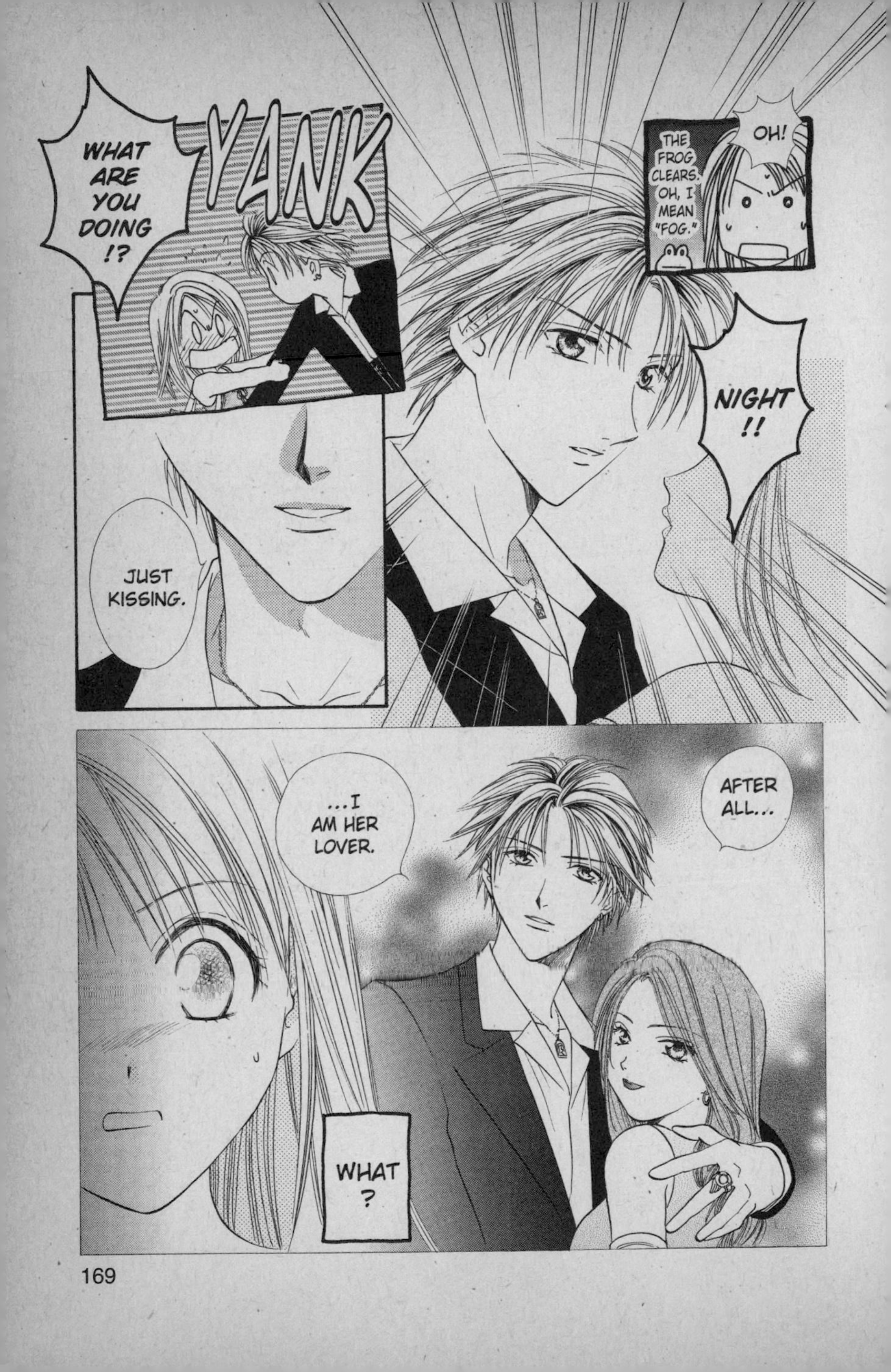
OH!
THE FROG CLEARS. OH, I MEAN "FOG."
NIGHT!!
WHAT ARE YOU DOING!?
YANK
JUST KISSING.
AFTER ALL...
...I AM HER LOVER.
WHAT?

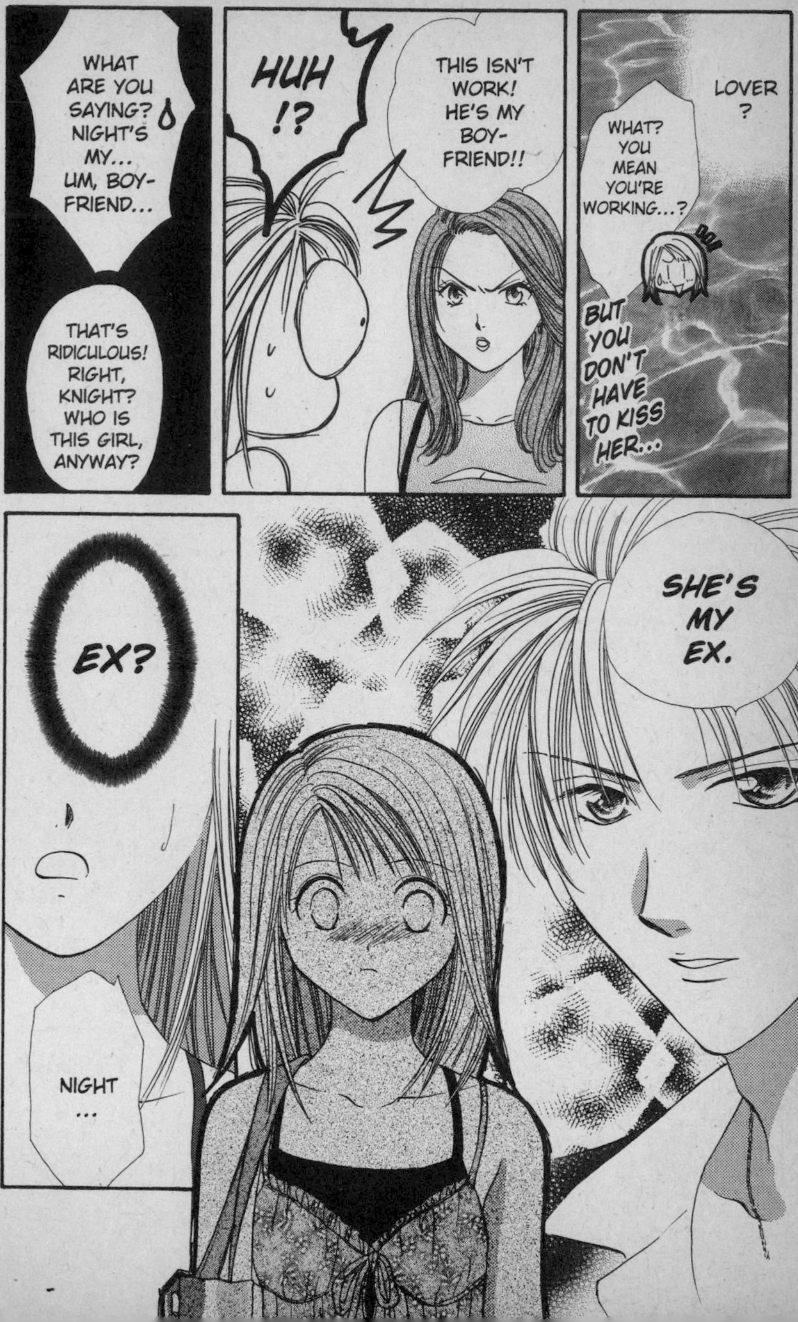

LOVER?
WHAT? YOU MEAN YOU'RE WORKING...?
BUT YOU DON'T HAVE TO KISS HER...
THIS ISN'T WORK! HE'S MY BOY-FRIEND!!
HUH!?
WHAT ARE YOU SAYING? NIGHT'S MY... UM, BOY-FRIEND...
THAT'S RIDICULOUS! RIGHT, KNIGHT? WHO IS THIS GIRL, ANYWAY?
SHE'S MY EX.
EX?
NIGHT...

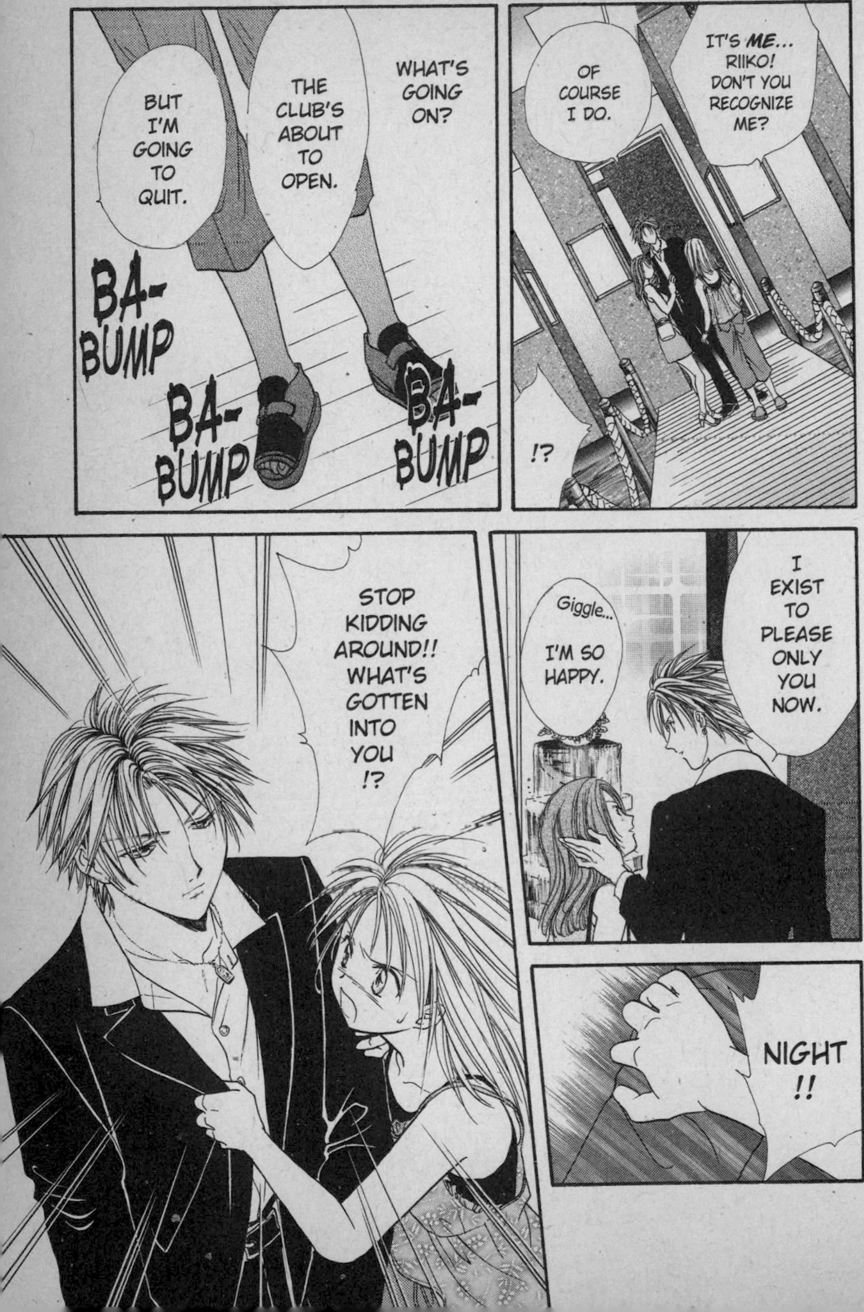
IT'S *ME*... RIIKO! DON'T YOU RECOGNIZE ME?
OF COURSE I DO.
!?
WHAT'S GOING ON?
THE CLUB'S ABOUT TO OPEN.
BUT I'M GOING TO QUIT.
BA-BUMP
BA-BUMP
BA-BUMP
I EXIST TO PLEASE ONLY YOU NOW.
Giggle...
I'M SO HAPPY.
NIGHT !!
STOP KIDDING AROUND!! WHAT'S GOTTEN INTO YOU !?

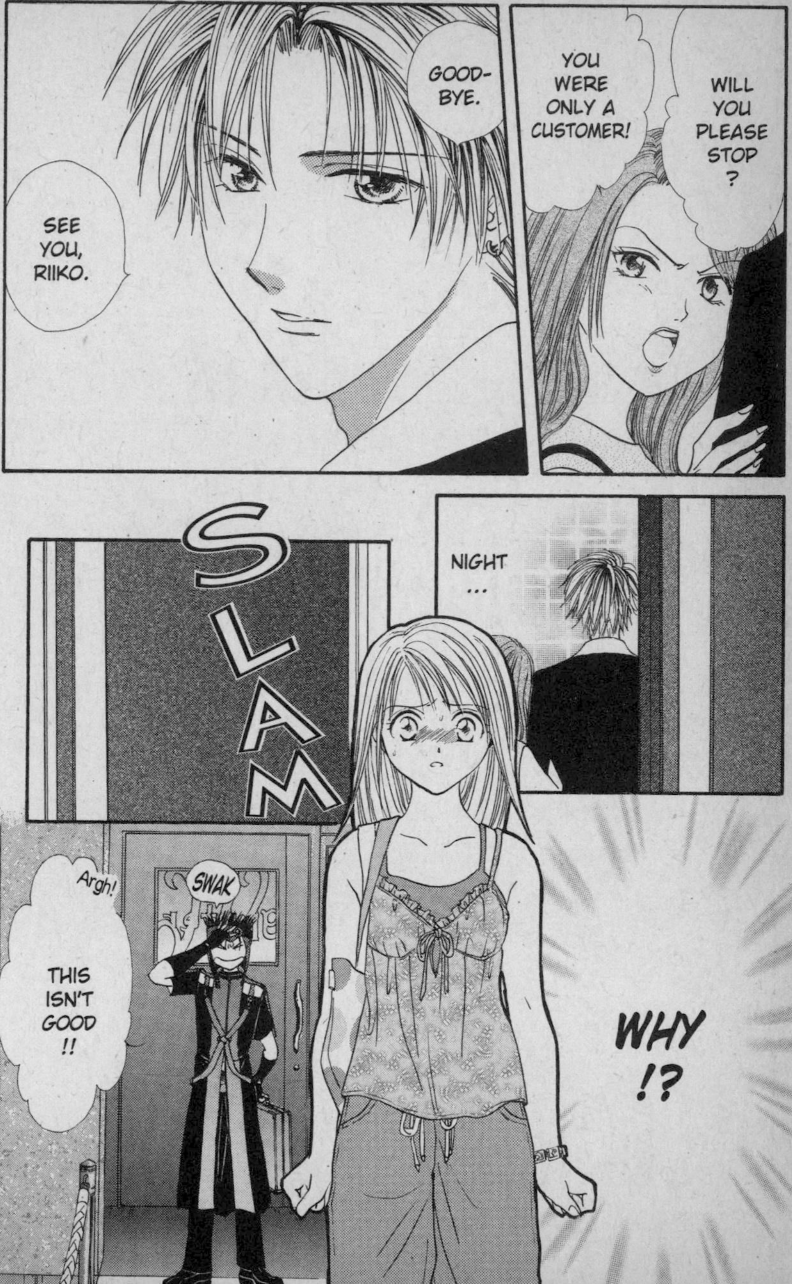
WILL YOU PLEASE STOP ?
YOU WERE ONLY A CUSTOMER!
GOOD-BYE.
SEE YOU, RIIKO.
NIGHT ...
SLAM
WHY !?
SWAK
Argh!
THIS ISN'T GOOD !!

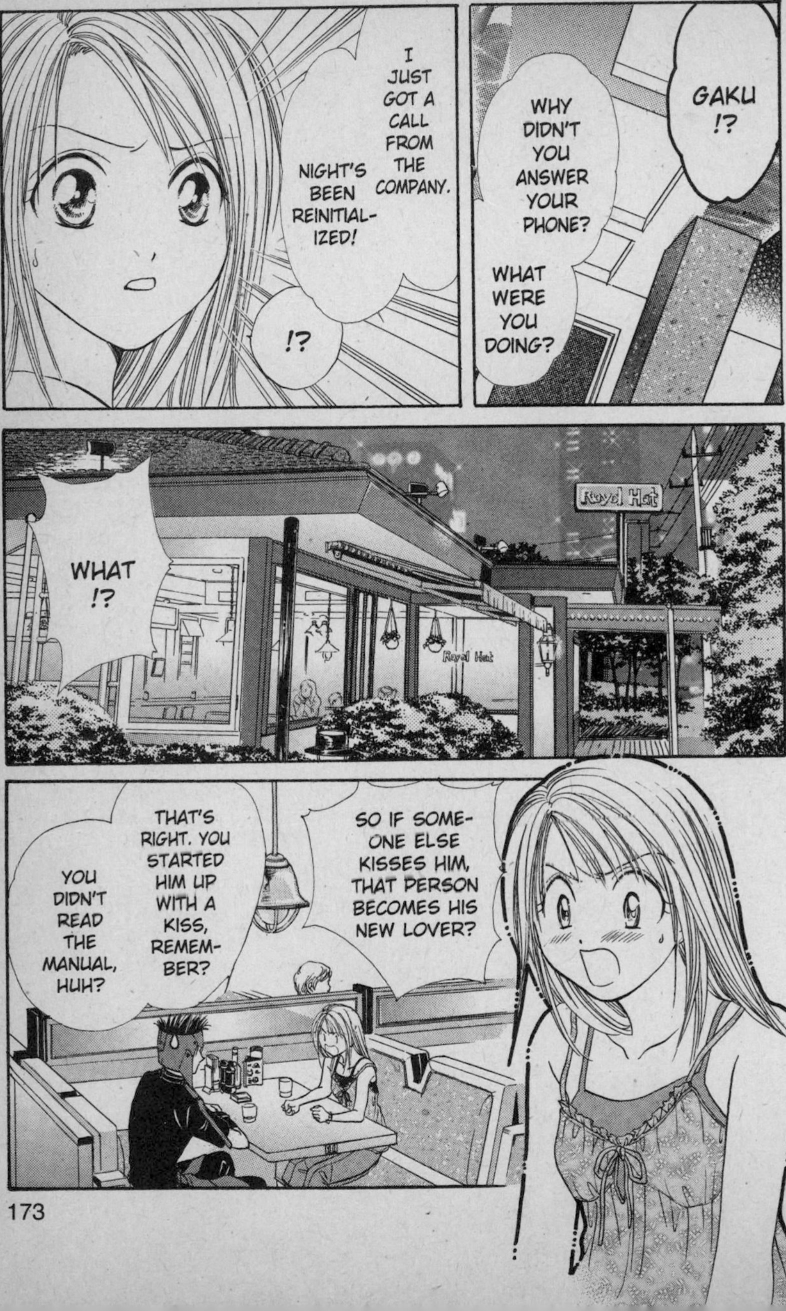
GAKU !?
WHY DIDN'T YOU ANSWER YOUR PHONE?
WHAT WERE YOU DOING?
I JUST GOT A CALL FROM THE COMPANY.
NIGHT'S BEEN REINITIAL-IZED!
!?
WHAT !?
SO IF SOME-ONE ELSE KISSES HIM, THAT PERSON BECOMES HIS NEW LOVER?
THAT'S RIGHT. YOU STARTED HIM UP WITH A KISS, REMEM-BER?
YOU DIDN'T READ THE MANUAL, HUH?

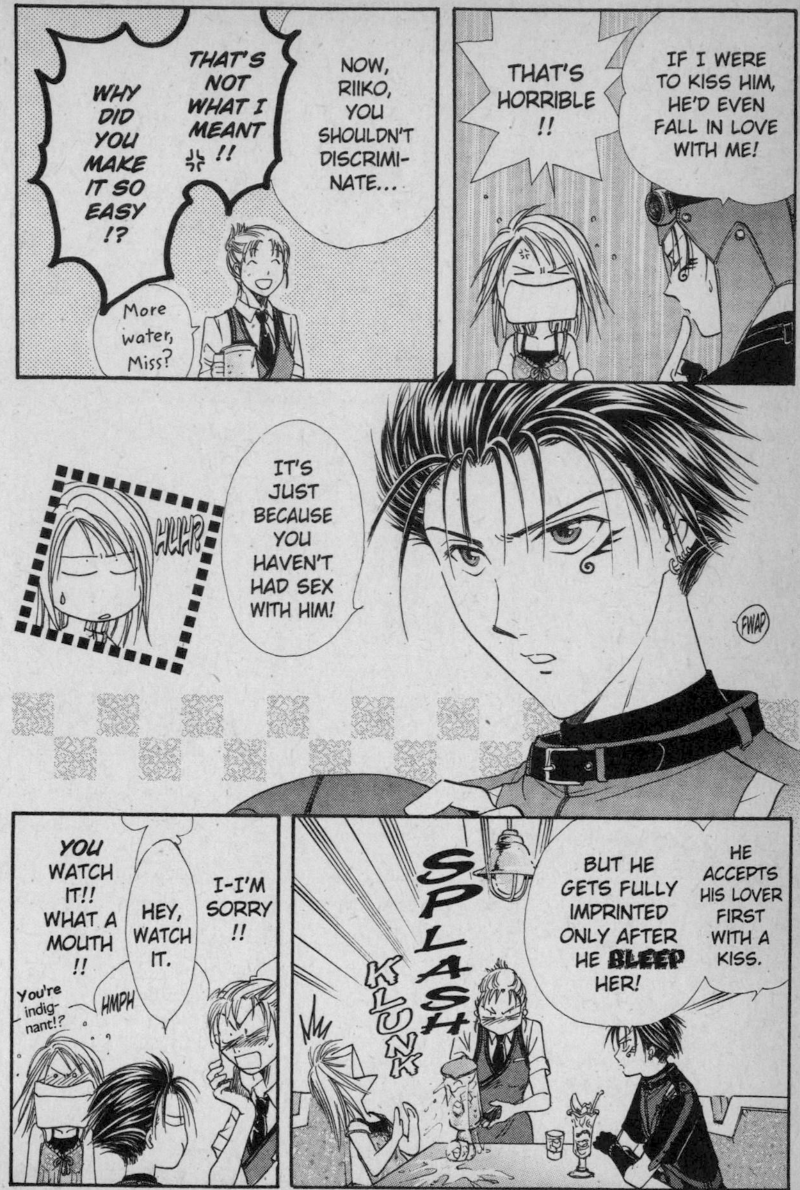
IF I WERE TO KISS HIM, HE'D EVEN FALL IN LOVE WITH ME!
THAT'S HORRIBLE!!
NOW, RIIKO, YOU SHOULDN'T DISCRIMI-NATE...
THAT'S NOT WHAT I MEANT!!
WHY DID YOU MAKE IT SO EASY!?
More water, Miss?
IT'S JUST BECAUSE YOU HAVEN'T HAD SEX WITH HIM!
FWAP
HUH?
HE ACCEPTS HIS LOVER FIRST WITH A KISS.
BUT HE GETS FULLY IMPRINTED ONLY AFTER HE BLEEP HER!
SPLASH
KLUNK
I-I'M SORRY!!
HEY, WATCH IT.
YOU WATCH IT!! WHAT A MOUTH!!
HMPH
You're indig-nant!?

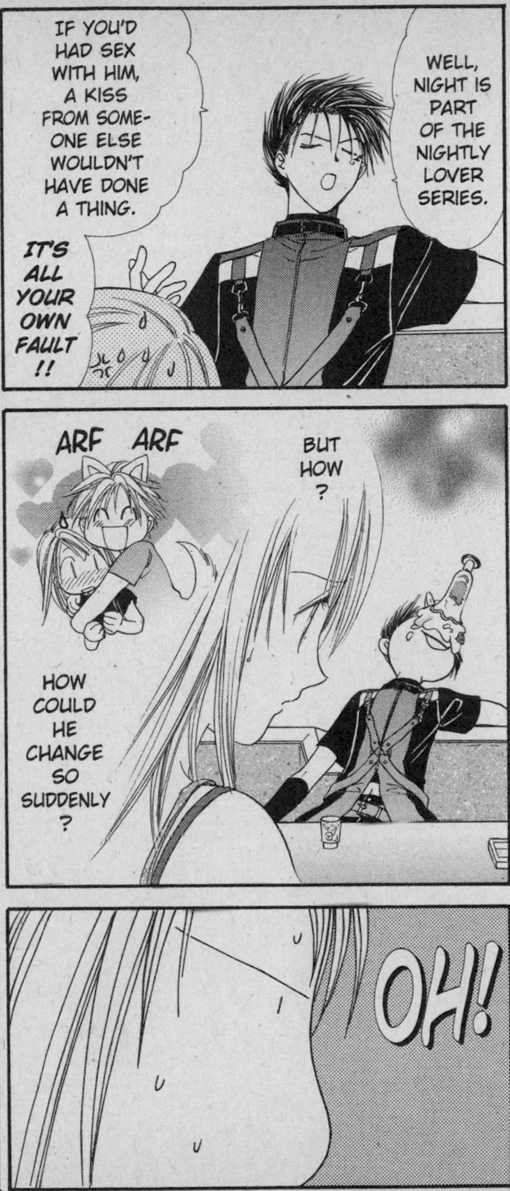
WELL, NIGHT IS PART OF THE NIGHTLY LOVER SERIES.
IF YOU'D HAD SEX WITH HIM, A KISS FROM SOME-ONE ELSE WOULDN'T HAVE DONE A THING.
IT'S ALL YOUR OWN FAULT!!
BUT HOW?
ARF ARF
HOW COULD HE CHANGE SO SUDDENLY?
OH!

Well, one of the reasons I decided to do this story is because the concept occurs so often in shonen manga. So why not adapt it to shojo?

The opinions of older women on Night: "He's cute," "He makes you want to mother him," "He makes me melt" (smile). Well, I hope everyone will enjoy fantasizing about him.

As I expected, there's a clear split between Night fans and Soshi fans. But some fans say they like Soshi best, but they want Riiko to end up with Night. (And vice versa.) So who are you rooting for, exactly (smile)? It's easy to have mixed feelings...

I'm doing a short story in issue 6 of *Shôjo Comic* this spring. That and *Absolute Boyfriend* will be like a double feature for me. And it's the first time I have a male protagonist! I'm kind of excited about it. The first manga I ever submitted had a boy as the main character. I had planned to be a shonen manga artist. I'd always wanted to be one, but I guess I couldn't pull it off... It didn't quite fit *Shôjo Comic*, anyway. But I finally got the go-ahead 16 years later. Since it's just a bonus story, the survey results don't matter as much (smile). I could do whatever I wanted. It's a fact of life when you're a professional that you can't always draw what you want. But you should be able to once in a while, or the stress can get to you... I have to remind myself of the joy of drawing manga. No, really, I do have fun (smile). I'm just greedy, so I want to draw different kinds of stuff...

Yikes, I'm out of space already! Oh, the character profiles are on the back cover, so they won't be between the chapters like they usually are (smile). The black pages between episodes with the *Absolute Boyfriend* logo remind me of the images that are inserted in anime before commercial breaks. I like them!! Volume 3 will be out in April, I think... *FY: Genbu* will be out in March... Or maybe April. Maybe not... Keep your eyes open for them! See you later! Bye!

*Yuu Watase originally wrote this in 2004. -Editor

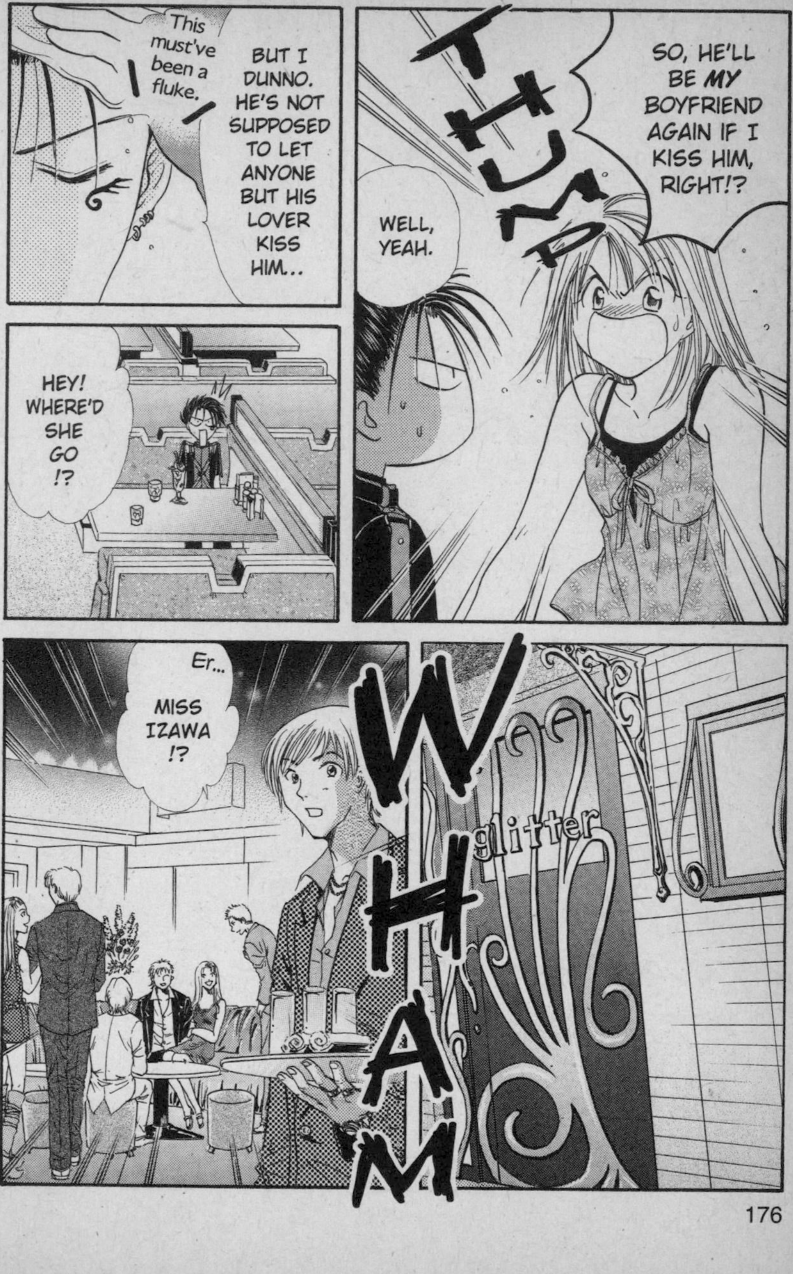
THUMP
SO, HE'LL BE MY BOYFRIEND AGAIN IF I KISS HIM, RIGHT!?
WELL, YEAH.
This must've been a fluke.
BUT I DUNNO. HE'S NOT SUPPOSED TO LET ANYONE BUT HIS LOVER KISS HIM...
HEY! WHERE'D SHE GO !?
WHAM
glitter
Er...
MISS IZAWA !?

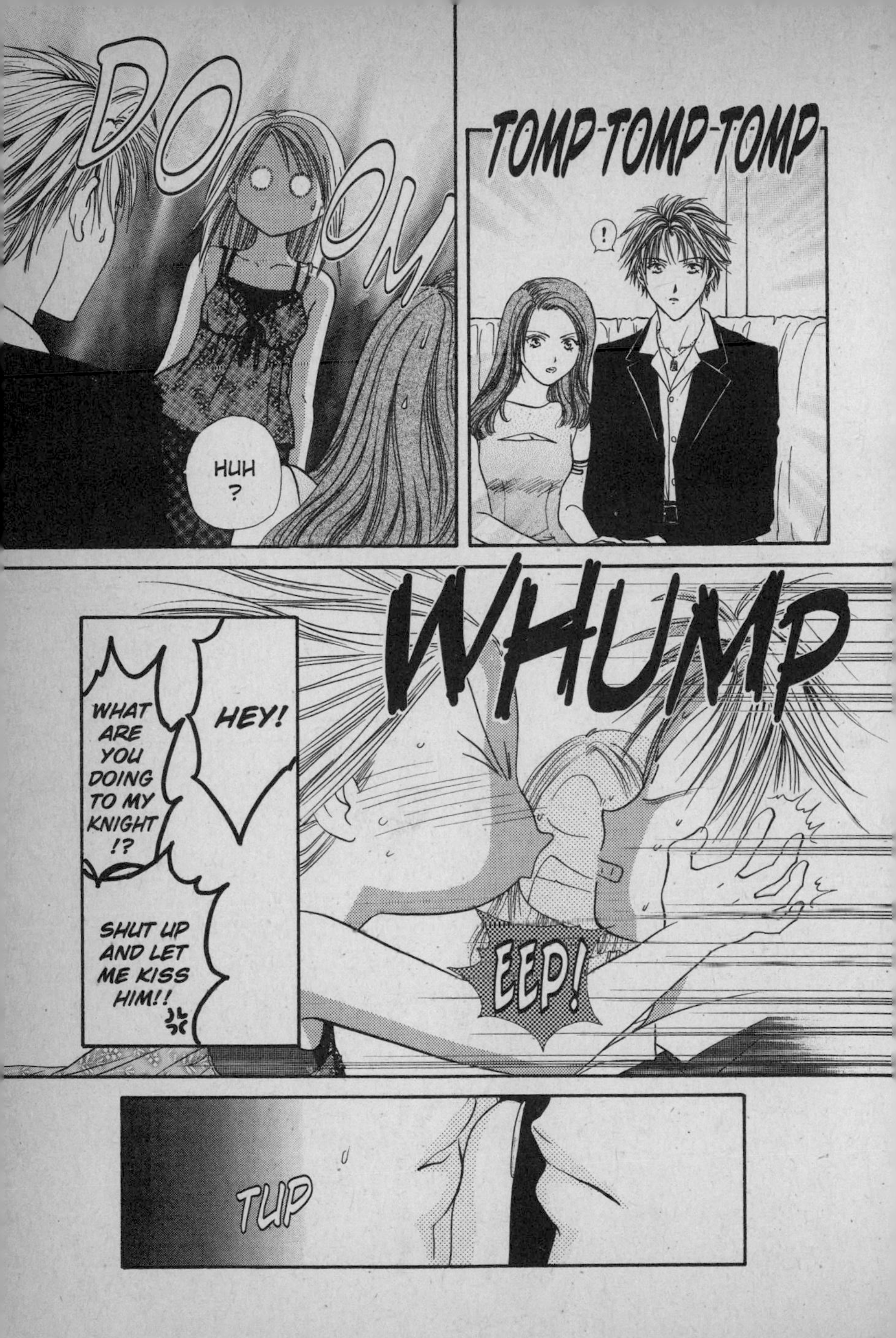
TOMP-TOMP-TOMP
!
DOOOM
HUH ?
WHUMP
HEY!
WHAT ARE YOU DOING TO MY KNIGHT !?
SHUT UP AND LET ME KISS HIM!!
EEP!
TUP

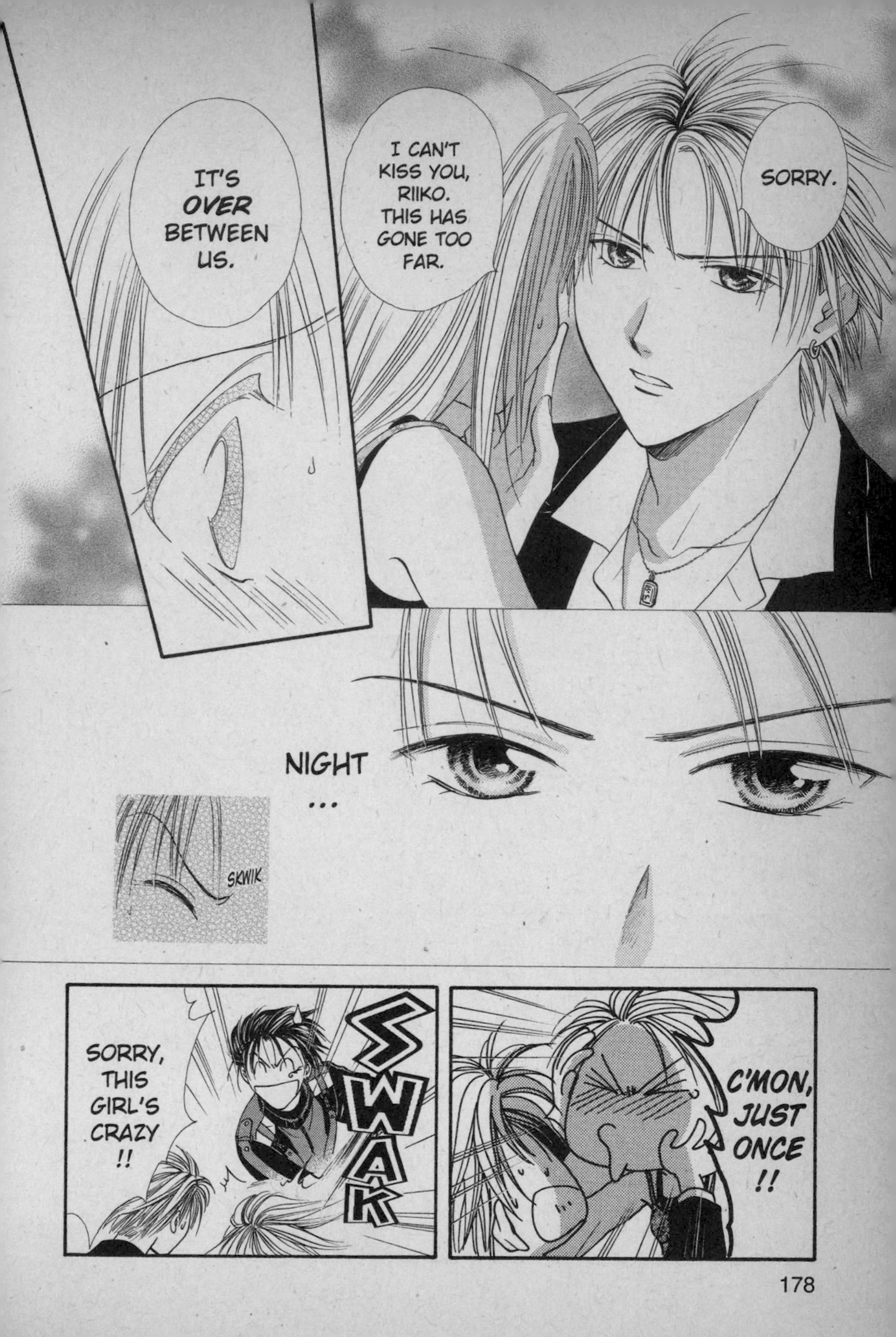
SORRY.
I CAN'T KISS YOU, RIIKO. THIS HAS GONE TOO FAR.
IT'S OVER BETWEEN US.
NIGHT ...
SKWIK
C'MON, JUST ONCE !!
SWAK
SORRY, THIS GIRL'S CRAZY !!

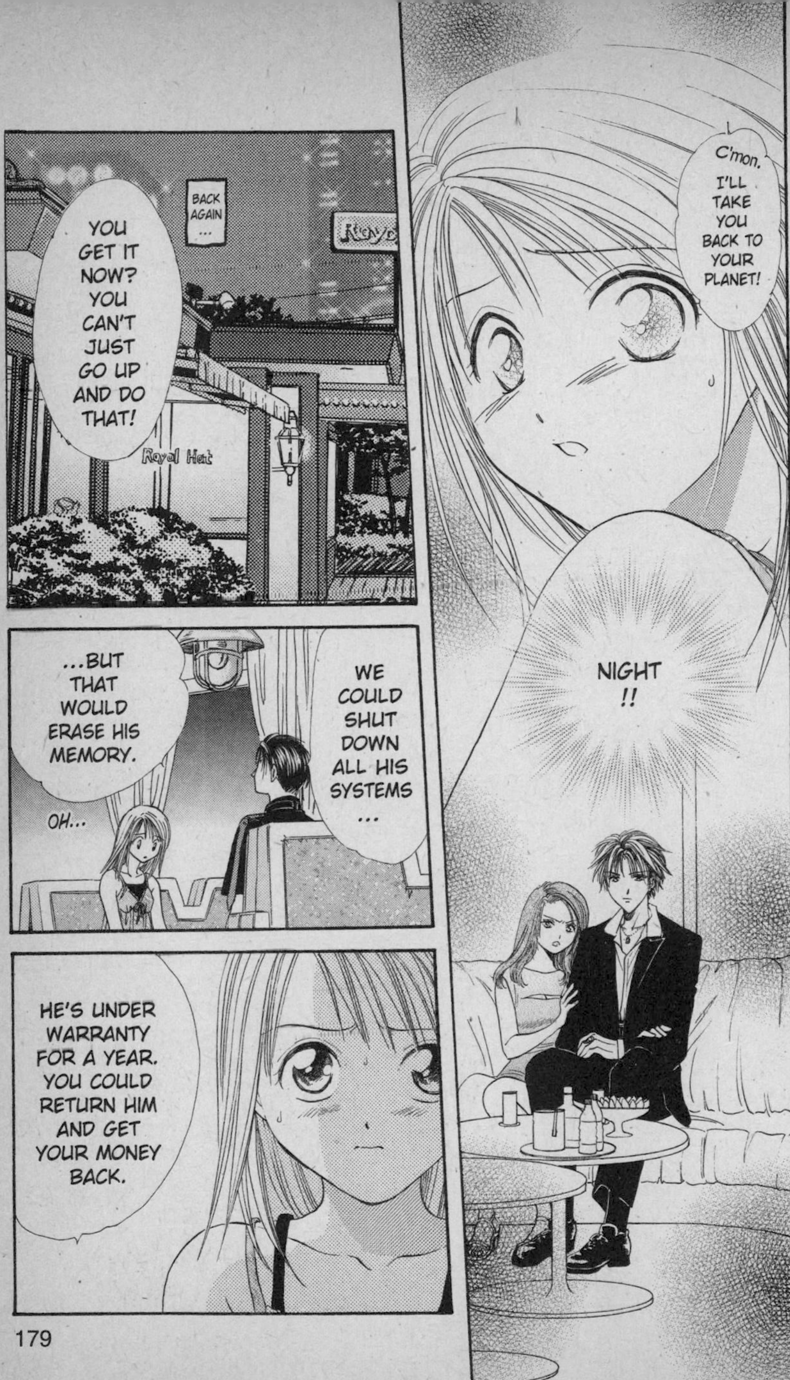
C'mon. I'LL TAKE YOU BACK TO YOUR PLANET!
NIGHT !!
BACK AGAIN ...
YOU GET IT NOW? YOU CAN'T JUST GO UP AND DO THAT!
Royal Hat
WE COULD SHUT DOWN ALL HIS SYSTEMS ...
...BUT THAT WOULD ERASE HIS MEMORY.
OH...
HE'S UNDER WARRANTY FOR A YEAR. YOU COULD RETURN HIM AND GET YOUR MONEY BACK.

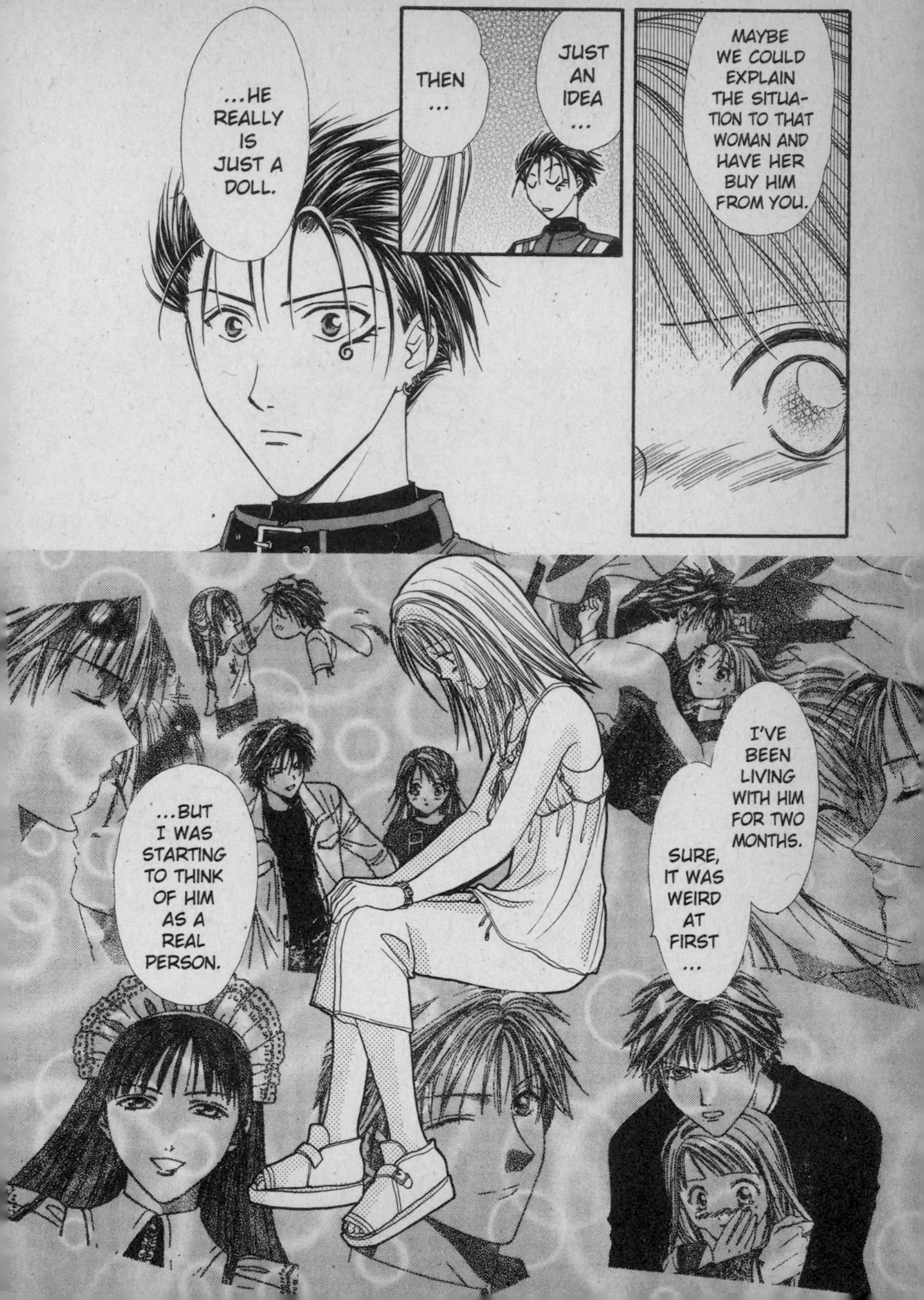
MAYBE WE COULD EXPLAIN THE SITUATION TO THAT WOMAN AND HAVE HER BUY HIM FROM YOU.
JUST AN IDEA ...
THEN ...
...HE REALLY IS JUST A DOLL.
I'VE BEEN LIVING WITH HIM FOR TWO MONTHS.
SURE, IT WAS WEIRD AT FIRST ...
...BUT I WAS STARTING TO THINK OF HIM AS A REAL PERSON.

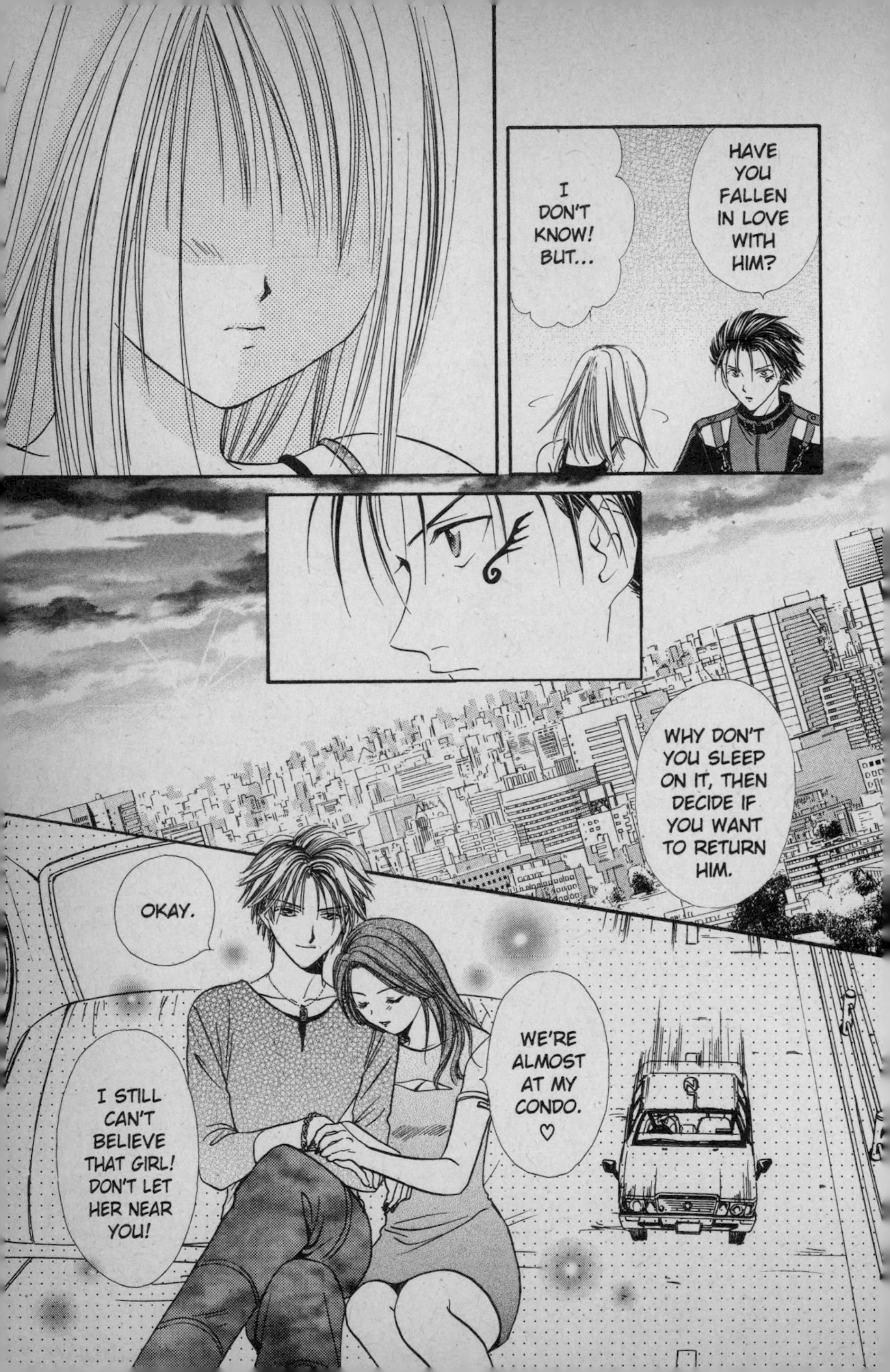
HAVE YOU FALLEN IN LOVE WITH HIM?
I DON'T KNOW! BUT...
WHY DON'T YOU SLEEP ON IT, THEN DECIDE IF YOU WANT TO RETURN HIM.
WE'RE ALMOST AT MY CONDO. ♡
I STILL CAN'T BELIEVE THAT GIRL! DON'T LET HER NEAR YOU!
OKAY.

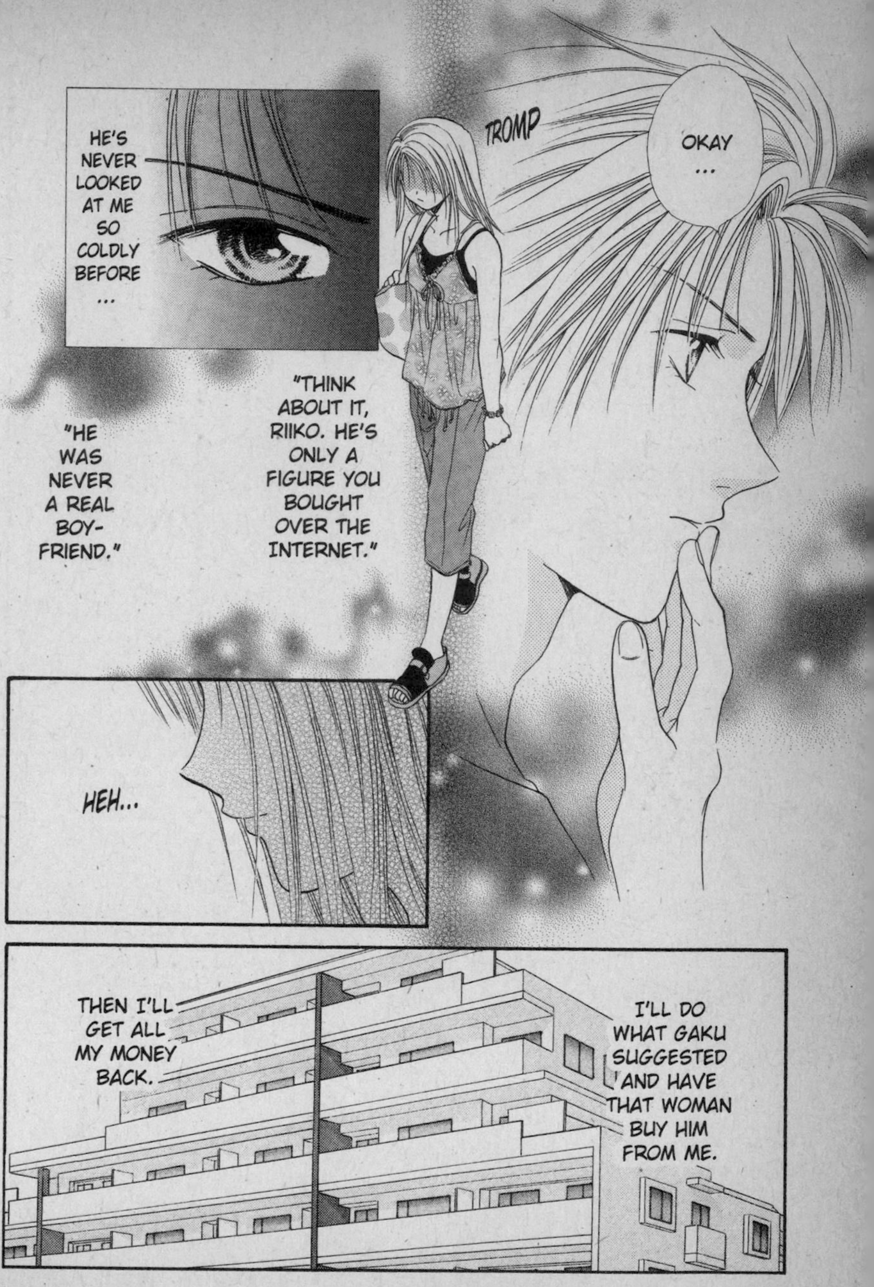
TROMP
OKAY ...
HE'S NEVER LOOKED AT ME SO COLDLY BEFORE ...
"THINK ABOUT IT, RIIKO. HE'S ONLY A FIGURE YOU BOUGHT OVER THE INTERNET."
"HE WAS NEVER A REAL BOY-FRIEND."
HEH...
I'LL DO WHAT GAKU SUGGESTED AND HAVE THAT WOMAN BUY HIM FROM ME.
THEN I'LL GET ALL MY MONEY BACK.

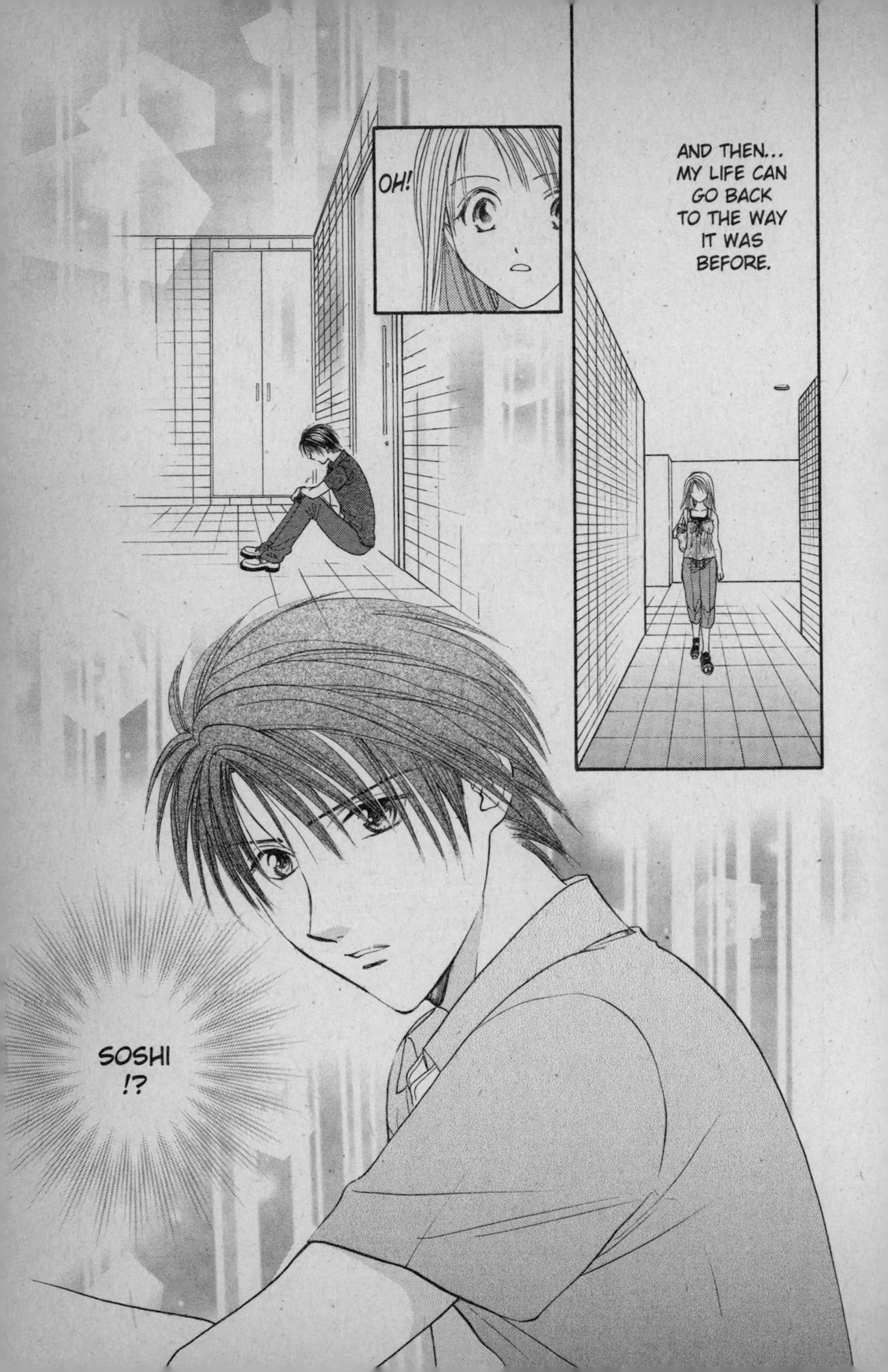
AND THEN... MY LIFE CAN GO BACK TO THE WAY IT WAS BEFORE.
OH!
SOSHI !?

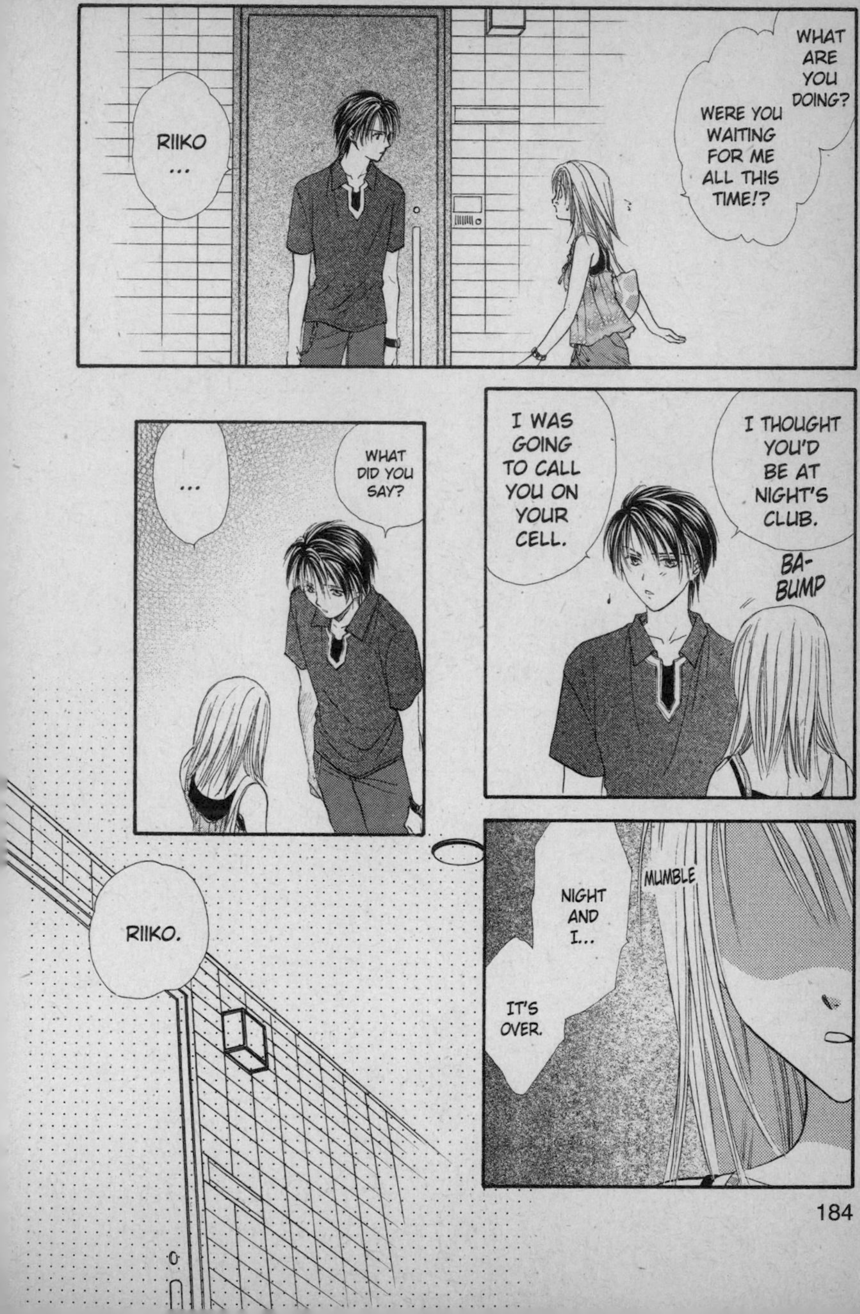
WHAT ARE YOU DOING?
WERE YOU WAITING FOR ME ALL THIS TIME!?
RIIKO ...
I THOUGHT YOU'D BE AT NIGHT'S CLUB.
BA-BUMP
I WAS GOING TO CALL YOU ON YOUR CELL.
WHAT DID YOU SAY?
...
MUMBLE
NIGHT AND I...
IT'S OVER.
RIIKO.

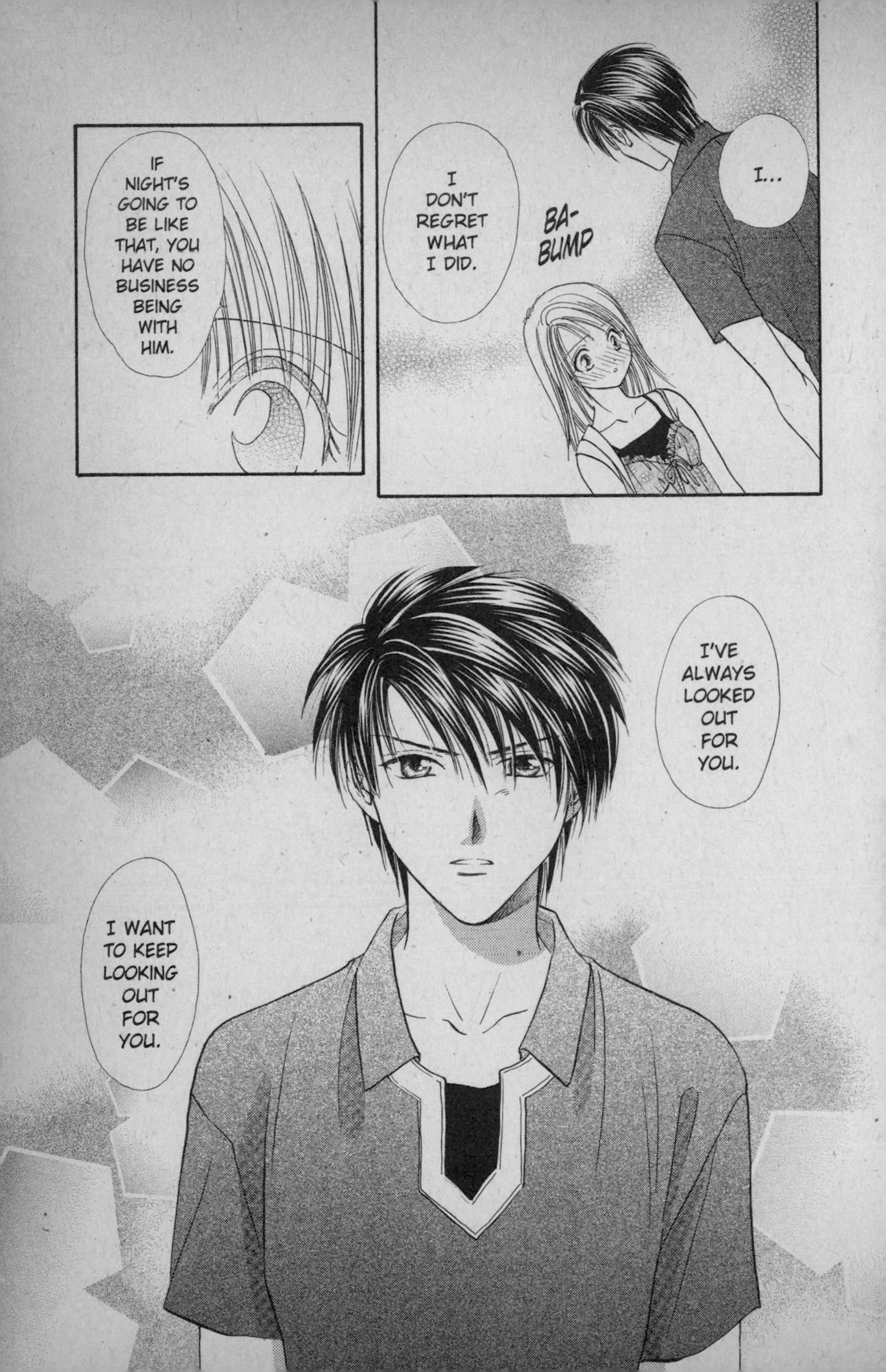
I...
BA-BUMP
I DON'T REGRET WHAT I DID.
IF NIGHT'S GOING TO BE LIKE THAT, YOU HAVE NO BUSINESS BEING WITH HIM.
I'VE ALWAYS LOOKED OUT FOR YOU.
I WANT TO KEEP LOOKING OUT FOR YOU.

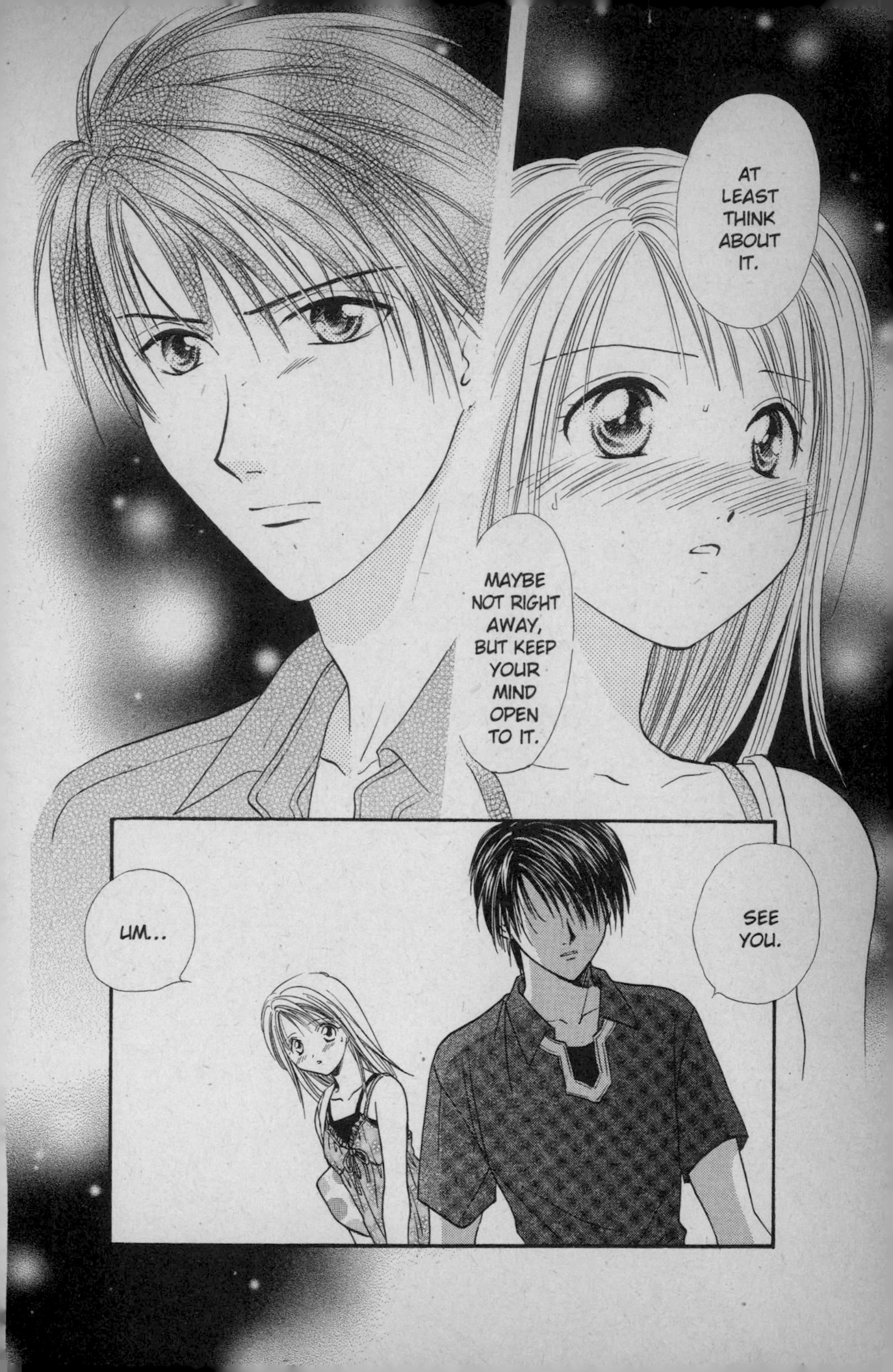
AT LEAST THINK ABOUT IT.
MAYBE NOT RIGHT AWAY, BUT KEEP YOUR MIND OPEN TO IT.
SEE YOU.
UM...

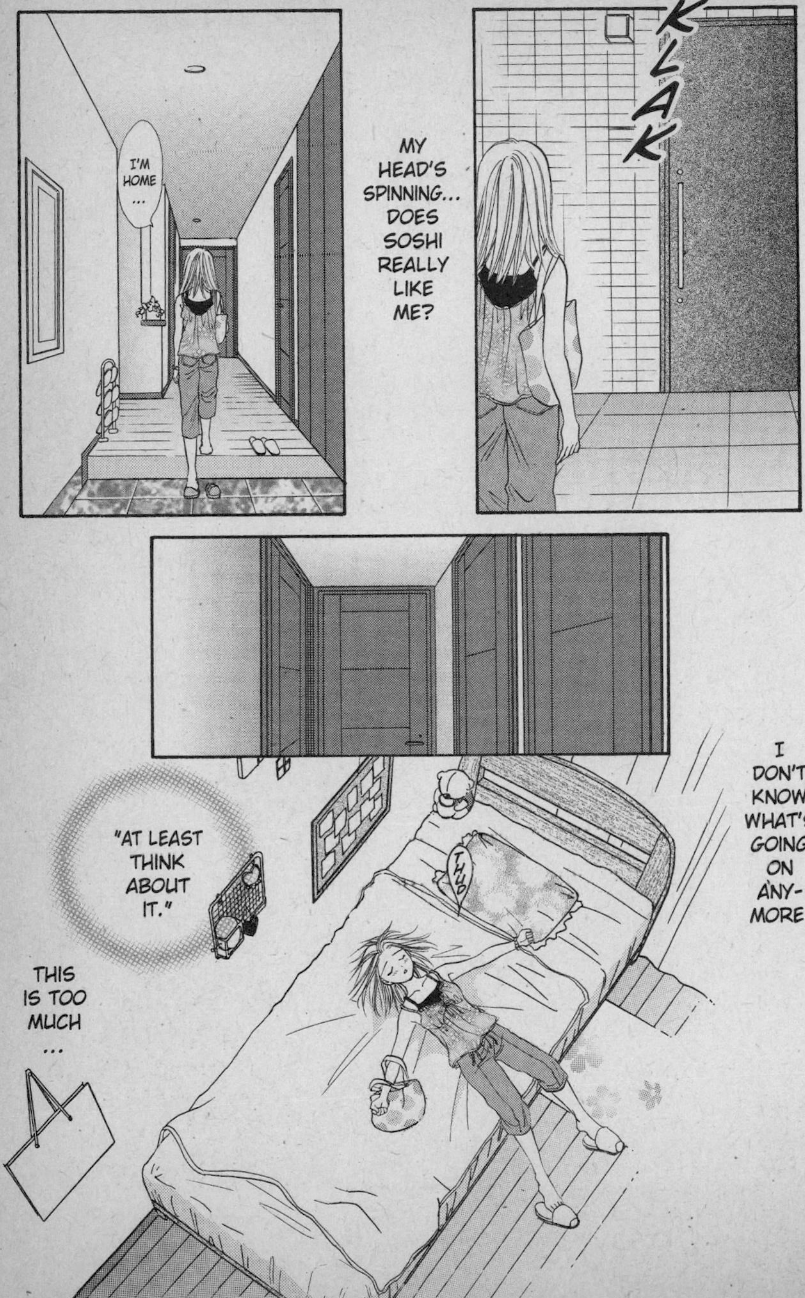
KLAK
MY HEAD'S SPINNING... DOES SOSHI REALLY LIKE ME?
I'M HOME...
I DON'T KNOW WHAT'S GOING ON ANY-MORE.
THUD
"AT LEAST THINK ABOUT IT."
THIS IS TOO MUCH...

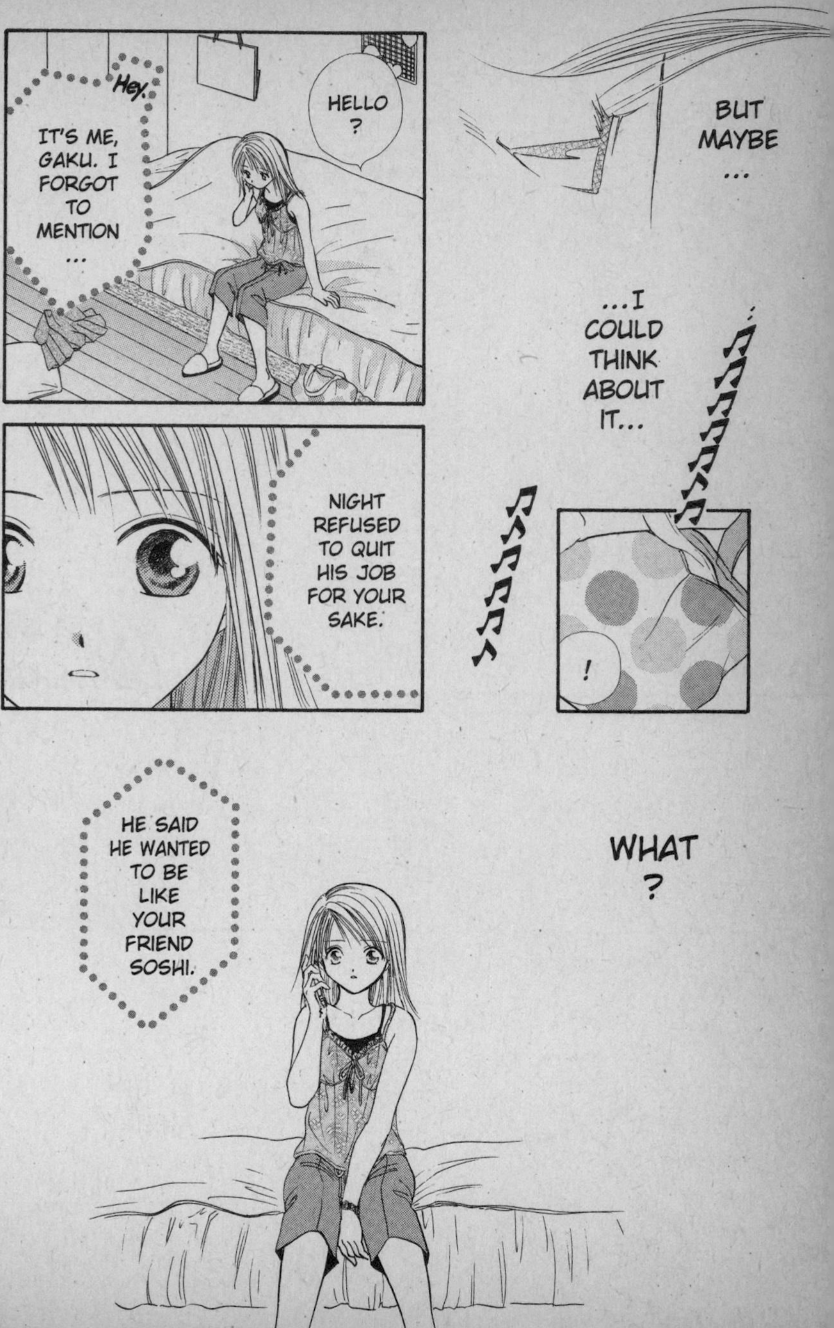
BUT MAYBE ...
...I COULD THINK ABOUT IT...
!
HELLO ?
Hey.
IT'S ME, GAKU. I FORGOT TO MENTION ...
NIGHT REFUSED TO QUIT HIS JOB FOR YOUR SAKE.
WHAT ?
HE SAID HE WANTED TO BE LIKE YOUR FRIEND SOSHI.

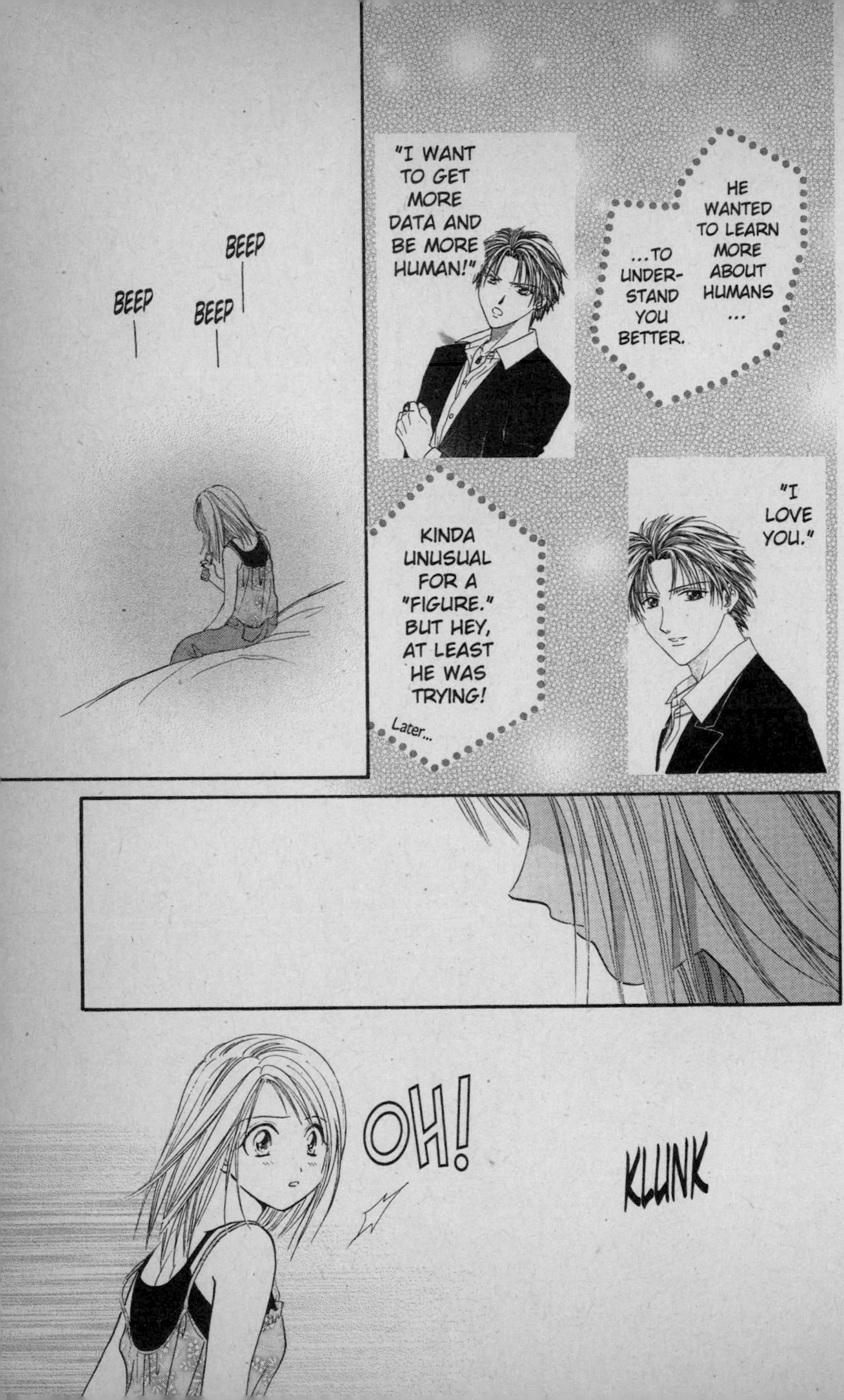
HE WANTED TO LEARN MORE ABOUT HUMANS...
...TO UNDERSTAND YOU BETTER.
"I WANT TO GET MORE DATA AND BE MORE HUMAN!"
"I LOVE YOU."
KINDA UNUSUAL FOR A "FIGURE." BUT HEY, AT LEAST HE WAS TRYING!
Later...
BEEP
BEEP
BEEP
KLUNK
OH!

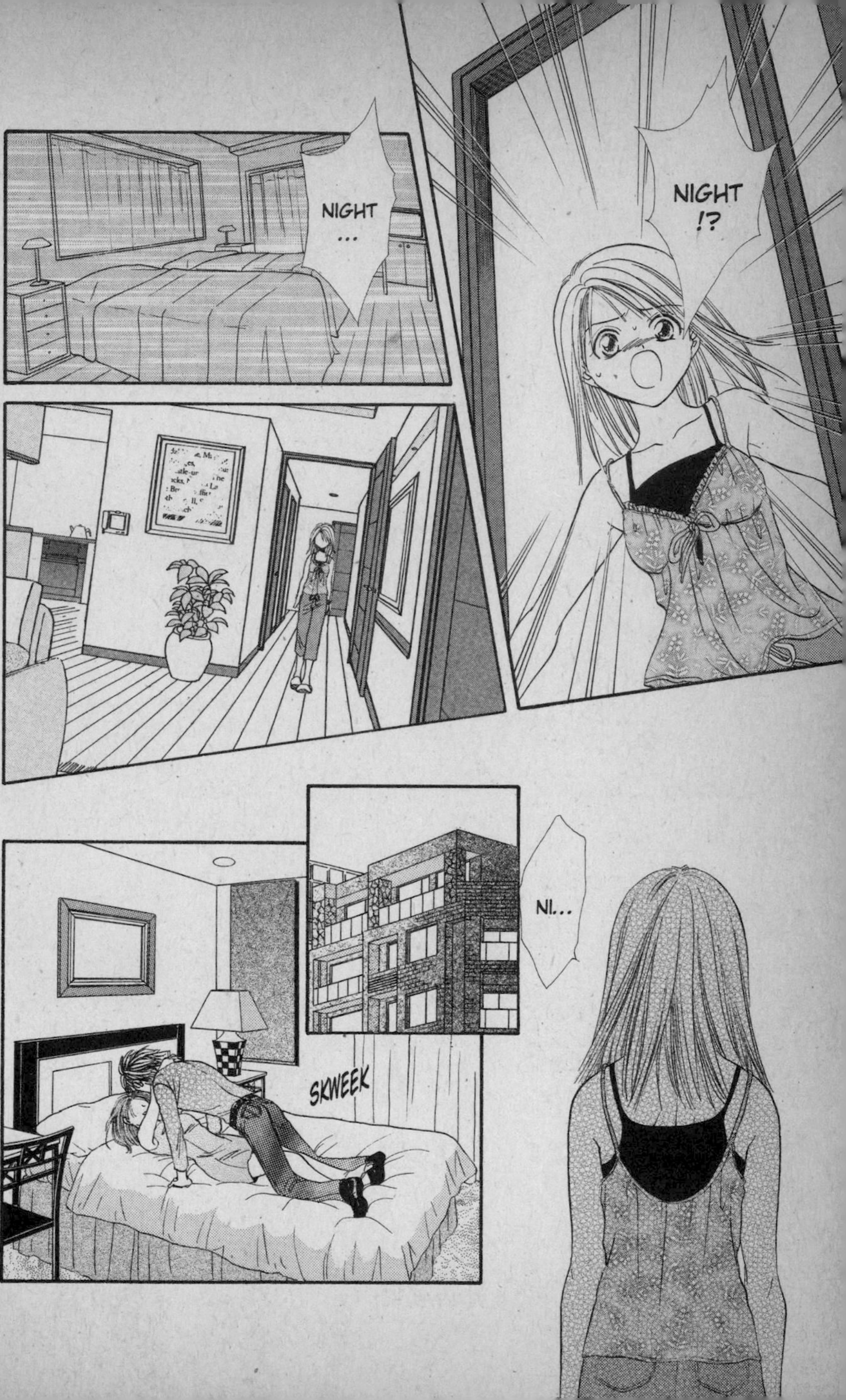
NIGHT !?
NIGHT ...
NI...
SKWEEK

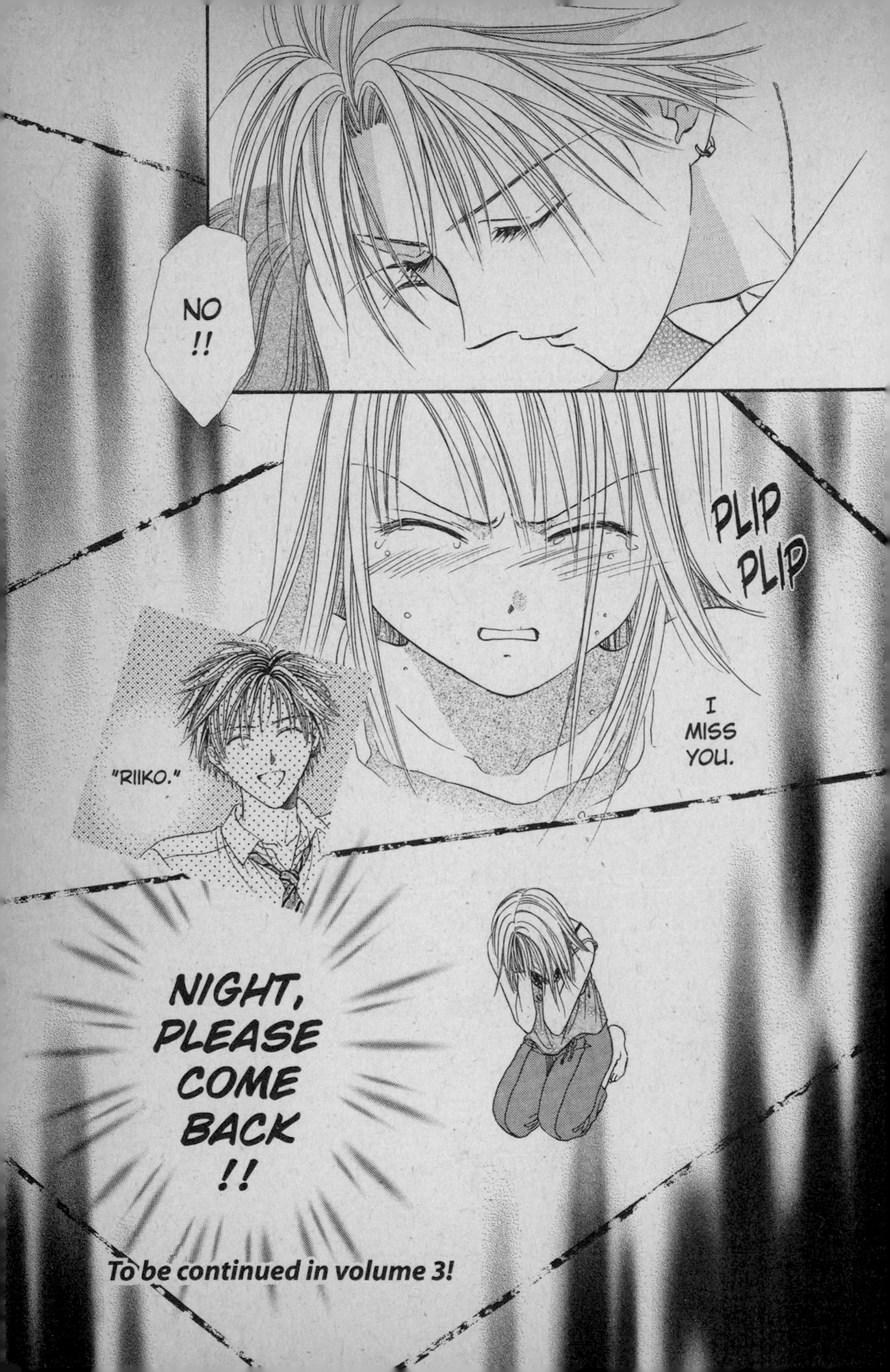
NO !!
PLIP PLIP
I MISS YOU.
"RIIKO."
NIGHT, PLEASE COME BACK !!

To be continued in volume 3!

i've messed up my stomach while on this job... And then two of my assistants got stomach problems too. What's wrong with us?! We're the gastritis sisters (ew!). i seem to have too much stomach acid, so i often have heartburn. Yes, my heart is burning with passion! One of the assistants, on the other hand, doesn't have *enough* stomach acid. i should give her some of mine. (Uh, that's not how it works.)

Yuu Watase

Birthday: March 5 (Pisces)

Blood type: B

Born and raised in Osaka.

Hobbies: listening to music, reading. Likes most music besides *enka* (traditional Japanese ballads) and heavy metal. Lately into health and wellness, like massage, mineral waters and wheat grass juice. But her job is her biggest "hobby"!

Debut title: *Pajama de Ojama* (An intrusion in Pajamas) (*Shojo Comics*, 1989, No. 3)

See her current stuff in *Shojo Beat* magazine!

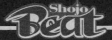

ABSOLUTE BOYFRiEND

Vol. 2

The Shojo Beat Manga Edition

This manga volume contains material that was originally published in English in *Shojo Beat* magazine, January–June 2006 issues.

STORY AND ART BY
YUU WATASE

English Adaptation/Lance Caselman
Translation/Lillian Olsen
Touch-up Art & Lettering/Freeman Wong
Design/Courtney Utt
Editor/Nancy Thistlethwaite

Managing Editor/Megan Bates
Director of Production/Noboru Watanabe
Vice President of Publishing/Alvin Lu
Vice President & Editor in Chief/Yumi Hoashi
Sr. Director of Acquisitions/Rika inouye
Vice President of Sales & Marketing/Liza Coppola
Publisher/Hyoe Narita

Printed in Canada

Published by ViZ Media, LLC
P.O. Box 77010
San Francisco, CA 94107

Shojo Beat Manga Edition
10 9 8 7 6 5 4 3 2 1
First printing, August 2006

www.viz.com

RATED T+ FOR OLDER TEEN

PARENTAL ADVISORY
ABSOLUTE BOYFRIEND is rated T+ for Older Teen and is recommended for ages 16 and up. This volume contains suggestive themes.

store.viz.com

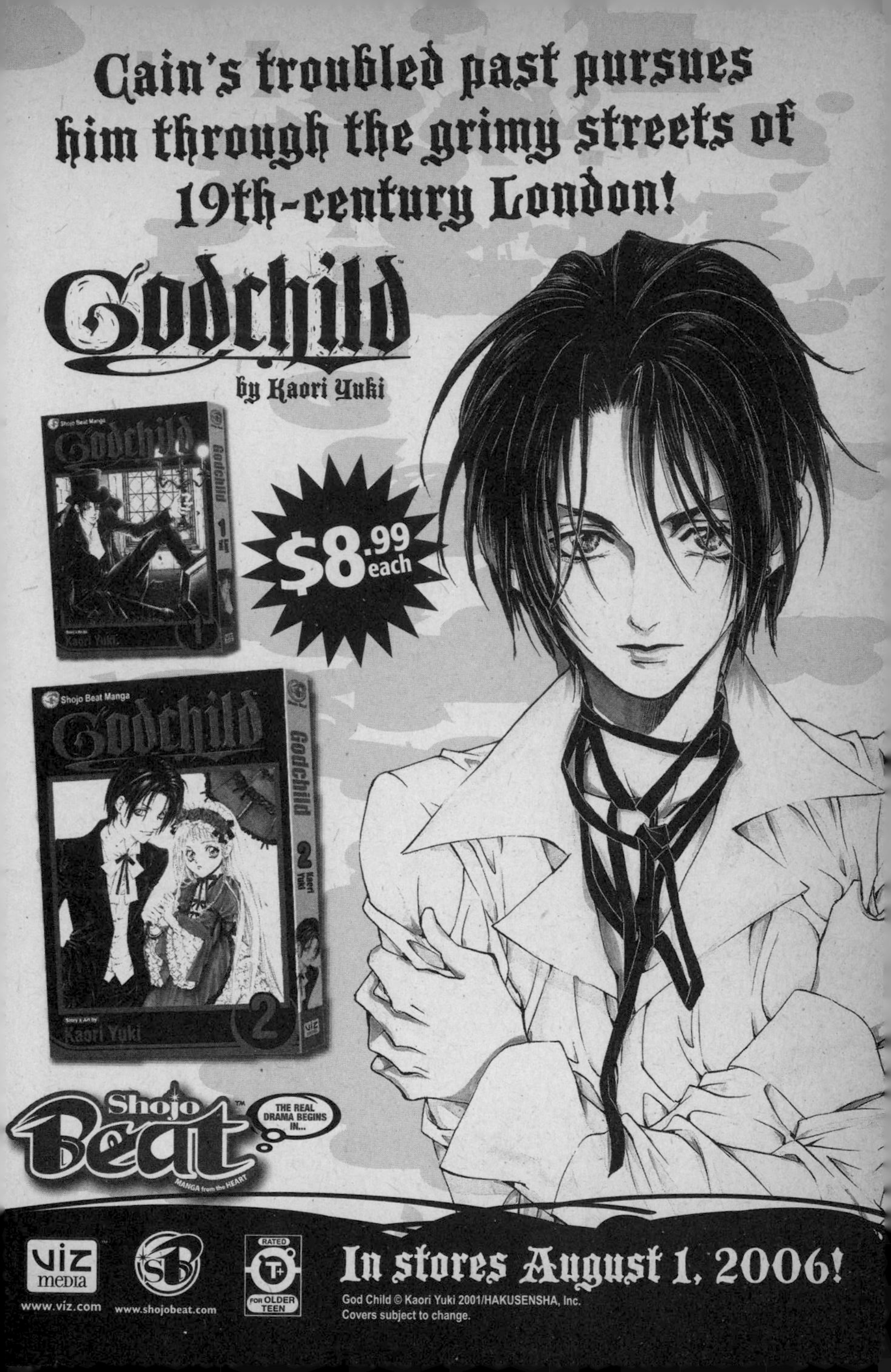

Cain's troubled past pursues him through the grimy streets of 19th-century London!
Godchild
by Kaori Yuki
Shojo Beat Manga
Godchild
1
Kaori Yuki
$8.99 each
Shojo Beat Manga
Godchild
2
Story & Art by
Kaori Yuki
Shojo Beat
THE REAL DRAMA BEGINS IN...
MANGA from the HEART
viz media
www.viz.com
www.shojobeat.com
RATED
T+
FOR OLDER TEEN
In stores August 1, 2006!
God Child © Kaori Yuki 2001/HAKUSENSHA, Inc.
Covers subject to change.

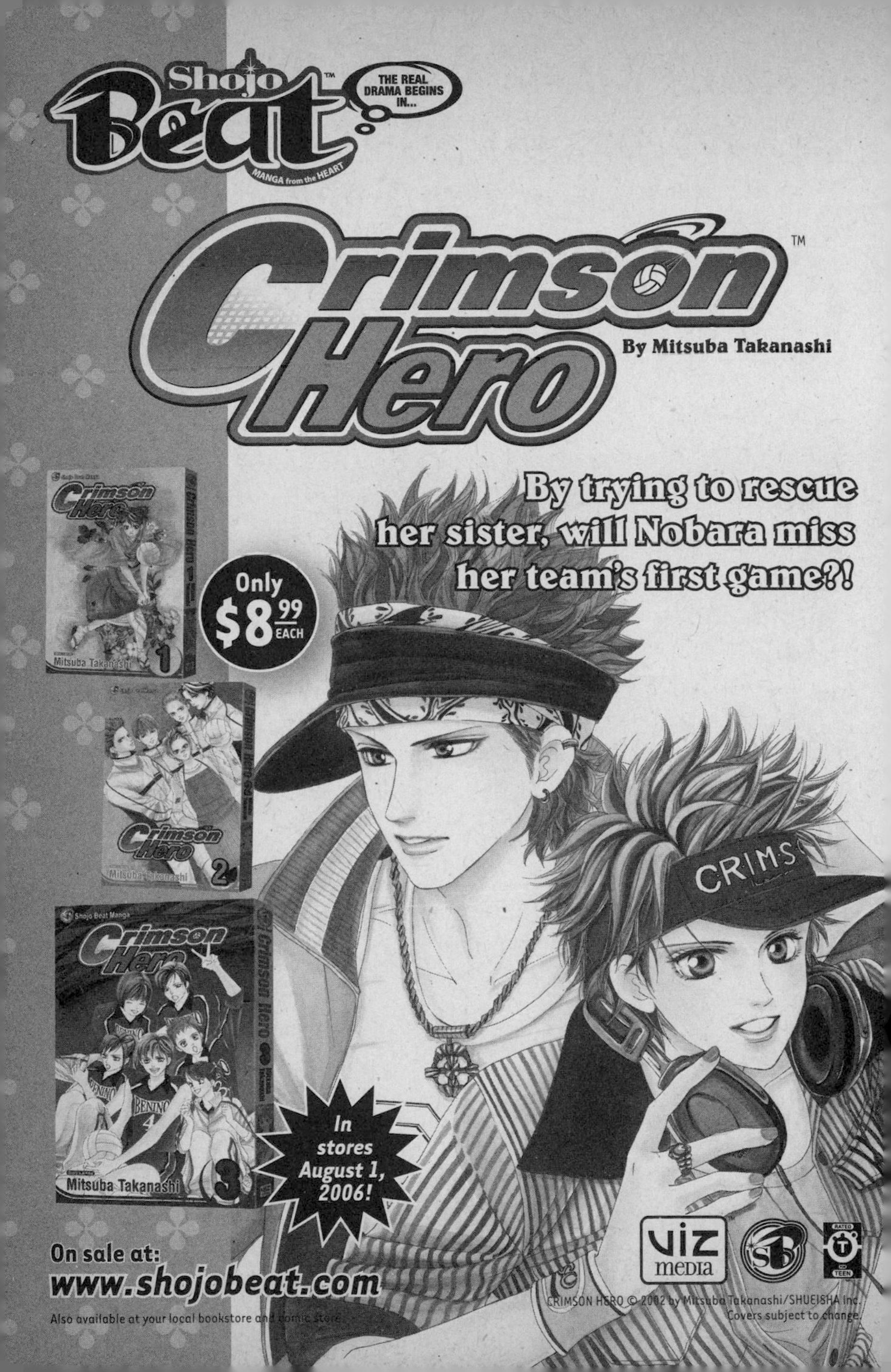
Shojo Beat
MANGA from the HEART
THE REAL DRAMA BEGINS IN...
Crimson Hero
By Mitsuba Takanashi
By trying to rescue her sister, will Nobara miss her team's first game?!
Only $8.99 EACH
In stores August 1, 2006!
On sale at:
www.shojobeat.com
Also available at your local bookstore and comic store
viz media
CRIMSON HERO © 2002 by Mitsuba Takanashi/SHUEISHA Inc.
Covers subject to change.

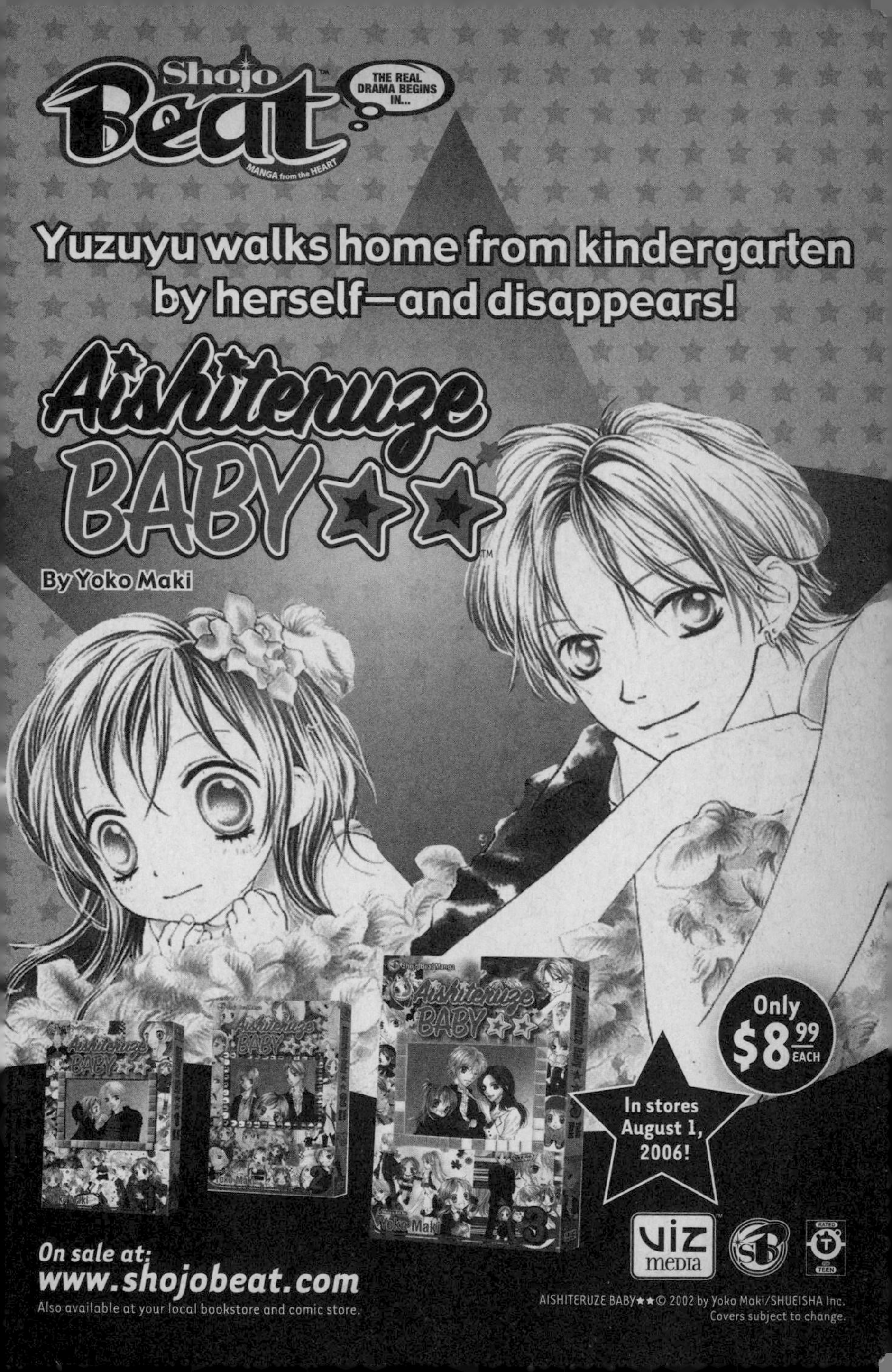

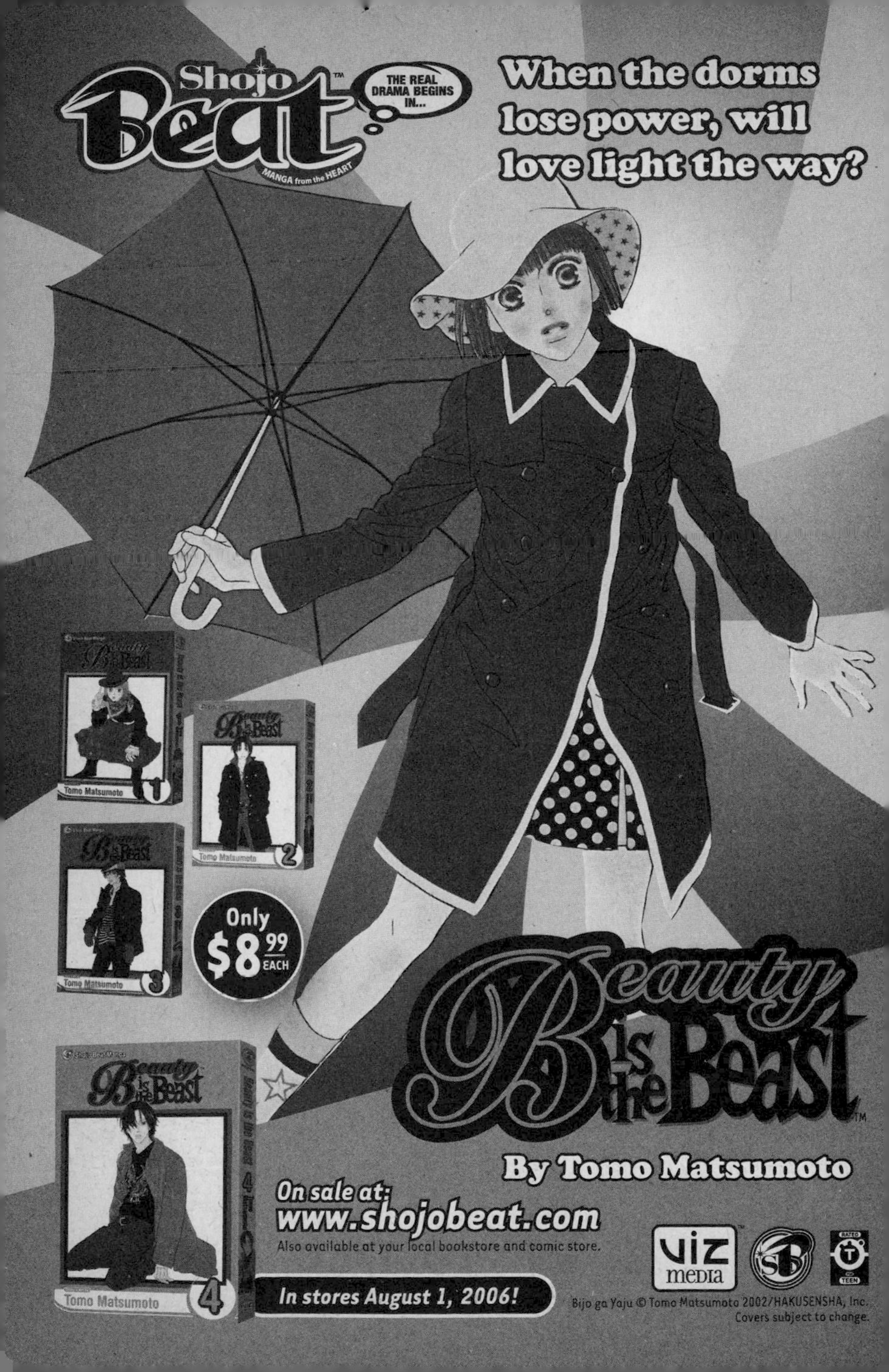
Shojo Beat™
MANGA from the HEART
THE REAL DRAMA BEGINS IN...
When the dorms lose power, will love light the way?
Only $8.99 EACH
Beauty is the Beast™
By Tomo Matsumoto
On sale at:
www.shojobeat.com
Also available at your local bookstore and comic store.
In stores August 1, 2006!
viz media
Bijo ga Yaju © Tomo Matsumoto 2002/HAKUSENSHA, Inc.
Covers subject to change.